P9-EFH-107

YALE HISTORICAL PUBLICATIONS

Leonard Woods Labaree · Editor

MISCELLANY

XXXIX

PUBLISHED UNDER THE DIRECTION OF
THE DEPARTMENT OF HISTORY

GLOUCESTERSHIRE

A STUDY IN LOCAL GOVERNMENT

1590-1640

BY

WILLIAM BRADFORD WILLCOX

Instructor in History in Williams College

NEW HAVEN · YALE UNIVERSITY PRESS

LONDON · HUMPHREY MILFORD · OXFORD UNIVERSITY PRESS

1940

Printed in the United States of America

TO

W. F. W.

WHOSE SCHOLARSHIP IS MATCHED

BY HIS WISDOM

FOREWORD

This book represents a new technique in scholarship, an attempt to examine English local government, its pattern and practice, from what is to be learned from one county. Thanks to the collecting zeal of Mr. Roland Austin, most of the letters and accounts books of John Smyth of Nibley have been brought together in the Gloucester Public Library. Those manuscripts Mr. Willcox has used and they alone would afford an excellent basis for a study of Gloucestershire. But he went beyond them; he searched all over the county, hunted up parish registers and church-wardens' accounts; he found sources in borough halls, solicitors' offices, and country houses. From Gloucester he went to London and deciphered the evidence of witnesses about Gloucestershire matters in star chamber, chancery, exchequer, and the court of requests. It is almost impossible to overestimate what we may learn from those records about local conditions and methods of government. Although Mr. Willcox has told us much less than he has learned, has indeed limited himself in this book to a discussion of local government and its working, he has nevertheless given us a new picture of late Elizabethan and early Stuart England, at least as far as Gloucestershire is concerned.

It is to be hoped that other counties will be studied in the same way. Some of those counties have collections of manuscripts comparable to those of Gloucestershire, and about a few of them, Hampshire, for example, surprisingly little has been written. There is not a county that cannot be explored from the enormous resources in the Public Record Office. If twelve or fifteen selected counties in different parts of England were to be studied in the way Mr. Willcox has studied Gloucestershire, we should be on our way toward an understanding of local government. Fortunately for us, Mr. Willcox has been able from printed materials in other counties to make many comparisons.

One cannot read this book without realizing that the Gloucester folk of the late sixteenth and early seventeenth century were still pretty rough customers. That was true in particular of the Forest of the Dean but in a less degree of the whole county. They were not awed by officials; they were willing to use passive resistance and sometimes active resistance; they liked a riot now and then and there were those in Gloucestershire and other counties who seemed to enjoy a long-drawn-out quarrel as a substitute for the private war of feudal times. There were also those along the back streets of country towns who on dark nights were handy with daggers. If the gentle folk and the more respectable families refrained in most cases from the less dignified forms of crime, they found some release in litigation. The well-to-do man had learned how to use lawyers to wear down his poor neighbor and to bring a tenant to terms.

It is worth remembering that Warwickshire was adjacent to Gloucestershire and that William Shakespeare as a young man may have found his way to the Cotswold games. The people among whom he was brought up were probably not so different from the untamed men of Gloucestershire that move through the pages of this book. Neither Warwickshire men nor Gloucestershire men were far away in time from the Wars of the Roses and the struggles and turmoils on Severn side. Smyth of Nibley as a boy had listened to old men and women whose fathers as youngsters had climbed the trees to watch the skirmish on Nibley Green in 1470. To Shakespeare the battles between the White Rose and the Red in the wide valley of the Severn must have been not merely stuff out of Holinshed but tales of his grandfathers. It is not surprising that he believed in strong royal government and in the preservation of order and degree.

We must not think ill of him for that. Upon order and degree still hung the hope for peace and orderliness in the country. So great was the prestige of the squire that the country was likely to be as well behaved as its squires. If they were on the job, each in his own community and as a body at quarter sessions, the villages were likely to be quiet. If they were men of hot blood, lords of lands who had not forgotten feudal ways, there was disorder and trouble over upland and vale.

As the squires by experience in local government and by experience as well at Westminster came at length to realize the worth of orderly processes, the country became civilized in a modern sense. No doubt the disorders of the Civil Wars that were to follow made men the more eager afterward for country quiet. When the countryside had become peaceful, then it was and not till then that royal power could be limited without loss to order, then it was that parliament could with advantage begin to take charge.

WALLACE NOTESTEIN

PREFACE

THE following pages are a study in social as much as governmental history. The government of the late Tudors and the early Stuarts was one of men rather than of laws, and the way in which the men administered the laws was determined by the way in which they and their neighbors lived. Hence institutions in this period are intelligible only in human terms, and the operation of government cannot be divorced from the life of the people. My aim is to describe government as it operated in a rural community, against the background of the life of that community in the half century before the Civil Wars.

This aim is consonant with a recent trend among students of the period. The emphasis used to be on the policies and troubles of the monarchs, or on the developments of opinion among their articulate subjects. It is becoming more and more evident that such matters were the façade of England, which can be fully understood only in relation to the interior. England, in other words, was not London, and the English were going their way with scant interest in London politics or London opinion. What was that way? How did men live, and what were their immediate concerns? Who governed them and how? To what extent were their affairs regulated by statute and privy-council order, to what extent by the discretion of neighbors who happened to be officials? Such questions as these are receiving more and more attention. Until they are settled, the outward history of the time remains unrelated to the core. Buckingham's failure before La Rochelle, to take a minor example, was the *débâcle* of a system as much as of a man, and the system can be understood only through detailed examination. The more momentous failure of the king's personal rule, in 1640, was due to the fact that the taxing power had been paralyzed by local feeling throughout the country. Great events, in short, were moulded by internal conditions.

Certain aspects of those conditions either have been or are being examined, and I am indebted to a number of such investigations. Most of them have for their focus an institution, an official, or a social class; so far as I am aware, the focus of a county has not been attempted. County records have been published in great numbers of recent years, but they do not seem to have been utilized for what I have in mind. I am not concerned with describing the theoretical structure of local government, or with detailing the duties laid down for local officials by statute and expounded in legal manuals. This has already been done. I am concerned with what the officials did, and how they did it, rather than with what they were supposed to do—with the human beings of practice rather than the institutions of theory.

The focus of a county necessitates arbitrary limitations of time and place. The period from 1590 to 1640 is the span between the heyday of the Elizabethan régime and the twilight of the Carolinian; the span is closed at both ends by national crises, which are outside the scope of a study of normal government. I have adhered strictly to the geographical limits of Gloucestershire, thereby segregating what was an administrative rather than a social unit. Bristol is omitted: it was a county in itself and is a subject in itself, which could not be included without destroying all semblance of unity.

There are two major advantages in studying the government of a single county. The first is structural. Because the field is limited, it is possible in small compass to examine each official and institution, and also to obtain an idea of their complex interaction. There are inevitable gaps, and questions which go unanswered; even the most abundant material does not throw light on all of a complicated subject. Taxation, the army, manorial law, the guilds—an author would be rash indeed if he pretended to write definitively on such disparate matters as these, or to be a specialist in all of them. I make no pretense to more than familiarity with them, and claim no more for my material than that it elucidates most of the aspects of my subject. The result suggests that a few common theories might be modified: that the sheriff, for example, was a more active and harassed official than is often supposed, that the manor was a more important unit of government, that one of the usually accepted forest courts was nonexistent. But these suggestions are incidental to my chief concern. That is with how the people were governed, and with the working relation between agencies hitherto examined for the most part as separate entities.

The other advantage of studying a county is technical. Because of the nature of the indices at the Public Record Office, it is possible to isolate almost all the cases from a given county which came before certain London courts during the period. This is to open a gold mine. The depositions in exchequer and star chamber contain some of the richest ore which the historian can find; its only drawback is that there is too much of it, so that it must be sampled in some way. For this purpose the county is ideal, and the mine yields a sample which is abundantly rewarding. If it happens to be augmented by a local collection of papers, like those of John Smyth at Gloucester, the student will not lack for material.

The editing of such material raises a controversial question. I do not believe that documents should be published with all the original obscurities which modern type can reproduce, and I see no logical mean between this extreme and that of modernization. While the latter is dangerous, the danger seems part of an editor's responsibility; I have therefore modernized both spelling and punctuation. The names of people remain as they were, unless the person is well enough known to have a standardized spelling. I have retained old grammatical forms, because to change *thorough* to *through*, or *sayeth* to *say*, would be to destroy the peculiar rhythm of seventeenth-century English.

For help in obtaining access to manuscripts, I am

indebted to more people than I can name in the space of a preface: to the staffs of the Public Record Office and the Gloucester Public Library, to various families long rooted in the county, to local solicitors and antiquaries, and most of all to the diocesan clergy, without whose uniform helpfulness my local research would have been impossible. For a grant to assist that research, I am indebted to the 1900 Fund of Williams College. For advice and criticism of the book, in whole or in part, my thanks are due to Miss Joan Wake, Messrs. G. D. Ramsay and Hartley Simpson, and Professors J. E. Neale, R. H. Tawney, Conyers Read, and Wallace Notestein. The initial form of this study was a doctoral dissertation submitted in 1936 to Yale University, from which it received in that year the John Addison Porter Prize. The dissertation was written under the direction of Professor Notestein; I have had from him, at that time and in the four years since, both valuable advice and an invaluable stimulus.

The peculiar difficulties of organizing my subject make expedient a full table of contents, from which the scheme of the book will be apparent. Chapter I sketches the geographical and social background. Chapters II, III, and IV deal with those institutions and officials whose authority was derived directly from the central government. Chapters V and VI, and the latter part of VII, show them in action. The first part of the seventh, and the three final chapters, are devoted to four subsidiary spheres of government: those of the forest, the town, the parish, and the manor. Within the compass of these ten chapters I hope to explain how men were governed in Gloucestershire, and by doing so to illuminate a corner of Stuart England.

W. B. W.

Williamstown, Mass.,
27 August, 1940.

CONTENTS

ABBREVIATIONS

Add. MS.	Additional Manuscript, British Museum.
A.P.C.	*Acts of the Privy Council of England.*
Bodl. MS.	Bodleian Manuscript, Bodleian Library, Oxford.
C.	Record of the court of chancery, Public Record Office, London.
E.	Record of the court of exchequer, Public Record Office.
Glouc. Corp. Rec.	Gloucester Corporation Record, Guildhall, Gloucester.
G.P.L. MS.	Gloucester Public Library Manuscript.
H.M.C.	*Historical Manuscripts Commission, Reports* as cited.
Harl. MS.	Harleian Manuscript, British Museum.
Lansd. MS.	Lansdowne Manuscript, British Museum.
N. & Q.	*Gloucestershire Notes and Queries.*
Req.	Record of the court of requests, Public Record Office.
S.P.	State Paper, domestic series, Public Record Office.
St. Ch.	Record of the court of star chamber, Public Record Office.
Tewkes. Corp. Rec.	Tewkesbury Corporation Record, Town Hall, Tewkesbury.
Trans.	*Transactions* of the Bristol and Gloucestershire Archaeological Society.
V.C.H.	*The Victoria History of the County of Gloucester.*

GLOUCESTERSHIRE

I

DESCRIPTIVE INTRODUCTION

A CHAUFFEUR once remarked, "Over the bridge to the west of Gloucester there's an A. A. man. He's the most important A. A. man in England. If he points with his right hand you go to South Wales, and if he points with his left hand you go to the north." This is a simple but accurate explanation of why Gloucestershire has been important since the days of the Romans. The county is the meeting place of north and west and south. A traveler from London to St. Davids, or from Plymouth to Carlisle, is likely to pass through the streets of Gloucester; in the seventeenth century he would have been sure to do so. It is said in Gloucester that there is still more traffic at the Cross, where the two main streets intersect, than at any other spot outside London.

The reason is not far to seek. Gloucester is at the head of the Bristol Channel, and at the foot of the Vale of Severn. Three centuries ago there was no bridge below the city; all land travel into Wales from the southwest, south, and southeast had to come as far north as Gloucester.[1] Above the city, the vale is the beginning of a natural highway to the north. On the west are the hills of Wales, on the east the Cotswolds. Between them is the vale, flat and fertile; at its northern end the land slopes gently down to the

1. There were two fords of the Severn below the city, at Aust and Gatcombe, but neither seems to have been much frequented. The river often rose suddenly, because of rains in the north, and might sweep away the traveler. The Gatcombe ford was safe only in summer "in a long dry time when it makes low veer, the wind above, and in the neap time if one watch that opportunity"; even then it was dangerous without a guide. (G.P.L. [Gloucester Public Library] MS. 16,528, fo. 95.) Local opinion favored making the detour by Gloucester bridge.

Irish Sea, and to the narrow coastal plain which runs between sea and mountains from Chester to Carlisle.

This highway was the route from Scotland to Wales and the southwest. It was also an obvious way of reaching London; instead of crossing the Pennines, it was longer but far easier to skirt the Irish Sea, go south through Cheshire to the Severn, and then either into the valley of the Trent, or down the vale to Tewkesbury or Gloucester, and across the bleak but level Cotswolds to the valley of the Thames. This was especially true of an army. It is not accident that the Vale of Severn has been almost the vale of English history, from the mythical time

> When Severn down to Buildwas ran
> Coloured with the death of man,

to the day when Cromwell saved London on the field of Worcester. The Severn was one of the most important rivers of England, and Gloucestershire commanded its mouth.

Its boundaries have changed little since the seventeenth century. Monmouthshire has taken a corner of the Wye by Monmouth; Worcestershire has taken a spearhead, with Broadway at its center; Warwickshire has taken Clifford Chambers, and some land to the south of it. There are fewer islands of other counties within the borders of Gloucestershire, and fewer islands of Gloucestershire in other counties. But the changes are slight. In general, the shire of today is the shire of the Tudors and Stuarts.

Nature divided it into three parts, and marked the divisions with unusual distinctness. In the center is the vale, bounded on the east by the sharp wall of the Cotswolds, and on the west by the hilly Forest of Dean. These three parts are different in almost every way, and three centuries ago the difference was even more pronounced. The vale was then a country of farms and orchards; the Cotswolds were given over to sheep-raising, and the forest to lumbering, mining, and sporadic rioting. Now the sheep have gone, and most of the forest has been turned into farms; only the vale remains as it was.

In the northern part of the county the vale is wide, for the Leadon valley, toward Herefordshire, forms a part of it. But at Gloucester it is so narrow that the town seems to be in a cup of the hills, rather than a river valley. A few miles to the south it narrows still more; at Berkeley, where the Severn begins to be the Bristol Channel, it is only seven miles from the Cotswolds to the hills of Dean.

But what the valley lacks in size, it makes up for in fertility. This is some of the richest farming country in England. "The ground throughout yieldeth plenty of corn, and bringeth forth abundance of fruits: the one through the natural goodness only of the ground, the other through diligent manuring and tillage; insomuch as it would provoke the laziest body that is, to take pains, seeing that it answereth back again with the increase of an hundred fold, that which is sown. . . . The houses in it are almost innumerable, the churches passing fair, and the towns standing very thick." [2]

The vale has always been the most populous part of the county. But though the towns stood very thick, few of them were of any size; like most farming countries, it was mostly one of villages. In the southern part there were only two towns of consequence: Thornbury, with its great unfinished castle, and Berkeley, also with its castle, the seat of the family which owned a large part of Gloucestershire. Of the two, Berkeley was the larger and more impor-

2. William of Malmesbury, quoted by William Camden, *Britain, or a Chorographical Description of the Most Flourishing Kingdomes, England, Scotland, and Ireland,* p. 357. This fertility was the subject of endless comment, and even of fable. Thomas Fuller solemnly reports that at Slimbridge in the spring, if a wand is left on the bare ground, it will be covered by new grass overnight. *The History of the Worthies of England,* I, 546; see also Michael Drayton, *Poly-Olbion: A Chorographical Description of . . . Great Britain,* pp. 229–30; John Smyth, *A Description of the Hundred of Berkeley and Its Inhabitants* (*The Berkeley Manuscripts,* III), p. 4 (cited hereafter as Smyth, *Description*).

tant; it had once been a seaport of considerable prosperity, but had never recovered from the damage done it during the Wars of the Roses.[3]

In the northern part of the vale there were also only two towns, Tewkesbury and Gloucester, both of them far larger than Berkeley. Tewkesbury was smaller than Gloucester, and until 1609 was a manorial town; in that year it was chartered as a parliamentary borough. On the northern border of the county, at the junction of the Severn and the Avon, it was "a great and fair town having three bridges to pass over, standing upon three rivers, famous for the making of woolen cloth and the best mustard, which for the quick heat that it hath, biteth most and pierceth deepest." [4] The townsmen were prosperous, and land values were high even when the cloth trade was depressed. In 1632, "two little tenements now converted into a cowhouse, . . . having no outlet or backsides to them," brought £2 5*s.* a year in rent; the whole manor (which was the old lands of the abbey) was worth £473 a year, or just under a pound an acre.[5]

Now the mustard and the cloth are gone, and Tewkesbury has become a slow market town. But age has dealt kindly with it, and in appearance it has changed less than any other town in the county. It is a beautiful place, with the great Norman abbey brooding over it. The streets are wide, and must always have been so, for they are lined with old houses. Among these there is a large amount of black and white, for Tewkesbury is on the southern edge

3. Smyth, *Description,* pp. 84–86.

4. Camden, *Britain,* p. 359. The third "river" must have been one of two small brooks which flow into the Severn near the town. The mustard was proverbial, as witness Falstaff: "His wit is as thick as Tewkesbury mustard." The simile is surprising, however, for the local mustard-balls were supposed to clear the wits rather than thicken them. "It is very wholesome for the clearing of the head, moderately taken; and I believe very few have ever surfeited thereof, because not granted time, but demanded present payment for the penalty of excess." Fuller, *Worthies,* I, 548.

5. From a survey of the manor, G.P.L. MS. RF 302.13.

of the black-and-white belt. This part of the county (and especially the peninsula to the north, jutting into Worcestershire) is also a region of brick, which farther south is rarely found. The two in combination are singularly pleasing, and a welcome change from the nondescript architecture of the southern vale.

The focus of all the county, except its southern edge, was of course the city of Gloucester. "A proper and fine city, I assure you it is, both for number of churches and for the buildings." [6] It lies to the east of an island in the Severn; three sides of the town were walled, and the fourth was open to the river and lined with quays. In the midst of them was the West Bridge, the secret of the town's importance, and from it a causeway crossed the island to another bridge at Over, where the Leadon joins the western branch of the Severn. There was a royal castle in the city, which served the citizens as a stone quarry; its walls, by the end of the period, were "tottering and molding and wasting away and falling down more and more," so that few men dared approach them.[7] The great monastery had gone the same way; its only remnants were the bishop's palace, since destroyed, and the cathedral, which dominated the town as completely as it does today. There were also eleven other churches, an abundance which aroused much admiring comment.

These monuments were only relics of past greatness. The town had been famous in the middle ages, and as amply privileged as London; but it had suffered in the Wars of the Roses, and had never recovered its earlier prosperity. The crown had recently made it a chartered port, and a county of itself. There were some who believed

6. Camden, *Britain,* p. 361.

7. "A maid or woman . . . did climb some part of the said old castle wall to gather wallflowers; and as she was upon the said wall, the stones of the place where she stood fell down, and the said maid or woman fell also down therewith. But (God be thanked!) she took not much hurt by the said fall." E. (Records of the Court of Exchequer) 134/17 Chas. I/T/1; see also Harl. (Harleian) MS. 4713, fo. 35.

that it might again become famous, and control the trade of a third of the kingdom.[8] But it was doomed, if only by the increasing size of ships, and already it was changing from a seaport to an inland town.

Five or six miles to the west and southwest of Gloucester, in sight from the city, is a line of dark hills. This is the Forest of Dean, an isolated outpost of the Welsh mountains, and "the famousest and best wooded forest in all England."[9] It rises abruptly from the vale on the east, and on the west falls even more abruptly into the valley of the Wye. The character of the country is far more Welsh than English: rolling uplands, cut by sudden ravines; hills which are gentle on one side, and on the other drop away unexpectedly into the Wye or the Severn. In the seventeenth century, when most of the forest remained, it must have been as dour a place as the Brecon Beacons.

Its isolation was not only geographical, but political and social as well. It was a royal forest, with officers and courts of its own. In tranquil times, county officials had little to do with it. But these times were rare, for the inhabitants were an unruly lot. They were mostly miners or lumbermen, and through working in the royal mines and woods they had acquired a number of time-honored privileges; their favorite one seems to have been that of flouting authority. They had little dealing with outsiders, either in the county or elsewhere, and outsiders dealt with them at their peril.

The center of the forest was the Speech House, where the forest courts met and still meet. It stands completely by itself, at a crossroad in the middle of the wood; a less cheerful spot for a courthouse is hard to imagine. The capital of the forest—the seat of such authority as there

8. See *John Taylor's Last Voyage, or Adventure* (London, 1641), reprinted in *The Works of John Taylor the Water Poet,* II, 25–30; Camden, *Britain,* pp. 361–62. For a discussion of the importance of the port at this time, see below, pp. 148–50.

9. Lansd. (Lansdowne) MS. 213, printed in *N. & Q.,* III, 366.

was—was the town of St. Briavels: a little Norman shell-keep guarding a little church, both perched on a hill-top above the Wye. The castle was the only one in the forest, and authority had to have a castle at a time when even the foresters' barns had arrow-slits instead of windows.

From near St. Briavels, there is a view which is notable even in a county of views. Below is the Severn estuary, broad and winding between its mud flats. Beyond it is Berkeley, the castle half hidden in the trees. In the far distance is Gloucester, with its spires and cathedral tower set in a green flatness of meadows, hedgerows, and orchards. The backdrop of the scene is a wall of hill, appearing in the south out of the haze by Bristol, running northeast across the entire county, and disappearing in the distance toward Broadway and Stratford.

This wall cuts the county into two almost equal parts. Beyond it is a world as different from the vale as the vale is from the forest. The Cotswolds are not hills, as they appear to be from the west. They are a plateau, which rises abruptly from the valley of the Severn, and slopes imperceptibly down to the east into the valley of the Thames. To the northeast it continues almost to Leicester; to the southwest it is cut by the steep valley of the Bristol Avon, then continues into the Mendip Hills, and drops into the plain of Somerset at Wells. The wall which bisects Gloucestershire is the edge of this plateau. In the north it is a simple slope, in the south a series of shelves; everywhere it is steep. Aside from the Avon valley, it is broken only once. This is at Stonehouse, where the Frome (the Stroudwater of the seventeenth century) has cut a narrow ravine into the heart of the plateau. Elsewhere, from Broadway to Wotton, every road to the east goes up a memorable hill.

A traveler climbing one of them finds himself in another world. Flat or gently rolling country, with occasional sharp valleys; few woods and no orchards; stone walls instead of hedgerows. There seem to be few villages, for the reason that most of them are tucked out of sight in the little valleys. Ozleworth, for example, was a village "seated in the depth of a deep valley, where the inhabitants may (if usually they do not) cut, make, and cast their billet wood and faggots in at their chimney pots, to save other carriage." [10]

These villages and towns are entirely of stone. Their architecture is too famous to need description; it may be mentioned, however, that with the exception of Chipping Campden, all the best examples are just outside the Cotswolds. The really typical Cotswold town, such as Nympsfield or Minchinhampton, has the charm of simplicity, but quite lacks the beauty of Broadway or even of Winchcomb. The architecture is austere, often to the point of dullness. There is little ornament, and what there is is simple. When it can be dated, it is found to be conservative to a degree: at Stanton, for example, two houses of 1615 and 1618 have square-headed windows with Gothic drip molds.

The men who built the houses were equally simple. "A people that carry their thoughts level with their fortunes; low spirits, but true hearts; using plain dealing, once counted a jewel, now beggary. These hills afford nothing but cottages, and nothing can we present to your Highness [Queen Elizabeth] but shepherds. The country healthy, and harmless; a fresh air, where there are no damps, and where a black sheep is a perilous beast; no monsters; we carry our hearts at our tongues' ends, being as far from dissembling as our sheep from fierceness." [11]

It was one of the great wool-raising districts of England. The sheep were long-necked and stocky, with large bodies and broad buttocks; their staple was deep and

10. Smyth, *Description,* p. 307. The village, except for the church, has now almost disappeared. Its reputation has been transferred to Inglestone, near Wickwar: if the inhabitants forget their keys, they can reach down the chimney and unlock the door from inside.

11. [Sir Egerton Brydges, ed.,] *Speeches delivered to Queen Elizabeth on her visit to Giles Brydges, Lord Chandos, at Sudeley Castle,* pp. 8–9.

thick, and even the forehead was tufted with good wool. The entire plateau was given over to raising it, and it was exported all over Europe.[12]

The excellence of the sheep was supposed to be due in good part to the Cotswold climate. It was a healthy air for beasts and men, cold in winter, and in summer "wholesome and digestive." At Symonds Hall, above Wotton, the air was so keen "that it hath created a common and constant proverb of bringing to our tables Symonds Hall sauce, meaning a good and hungry appetite to eat. . . . And we hundreders are persuaded, that if any English situation could by[13] wholesomeness of air promise eternity of days, it were here to be expected; so that the inhabitant be furnished with a great wood pile for winter."[14] Not only for winter, but for the spring and autumn as well; there is an edge to the wind as late as June, and as early as September. Hence another proverb of the countryside, "Winter never dies in her dam's belly." [15] Life in the Cotswolds was a more rigorous matter than in the abundance of the vale.

Because of the wool trade, there were a number of towns in this part of the county. The principal ones on the border of the plateau were Wotton under Edge, Dursley, Stroud, and Winchcomb; in the heart of the Cotswolds, Chipping Campden, Stow on the Wold, Northleach, Cirencester, Tetbury, and Chipping Sodbury. Their heyday had been the middle ages, and by the seventeenth century they were declining with the decline of the local wool trade. Stroud was "a mercat town sometimes better peopled with clothiers," and Winchcomb was "a poor beggarly town." [16] Dursley "heretofore hath been famous in the said county for cloth," but was now famous prin-

12. Camden, *Britain,* p. 364; Drayton, *Poly-Olbion,* p. 233; Fuller, *Worthies,* I, 547–48.

13. *bee.*

14. Smyth, *Description,* p. 323.

15. *Ibid.,* p. 33.

16. Camden, *Britain,* p. 362; S.P. (State Papers, Domestic Series) 16/448/79, quoted in *N. & Q.,* I, 412.

cipally for the numbers of its poor.[17] Neither Chipping Sodbury nor Tetbury was wealthy; the former was a "very poor and populous town," and the latter "standeth and consisteth much of poor artificers and tradesmen, as weavers and spinners, necessary for the trade and making of broad woolen cloth." [18] At Cirencester, the largest town of the Cotswolds and the only parliamentary borough, "now scarce the fourth part within the walls is inhabited; the remains beside are pasture grounds and the ruins of an abbey." [19] Chipping Campden was the only one which seems to have prospered; it was described as "well peopled and of good resort." [20]

Most of these towns were on streams or rivers, which were almost as important to the cloth trade as the sheep themselves. The streams were small, but their supply of water varied little with the seasons. They neither dried up in summer nor became flooded in winter, and hence provided a steady and reliable source of power.[21] Few of them were large enough to be used for transportation. Those which were, such as the Churn, were obstructed by fulling mills, and often choked with the branches of alders grow-

17. "Great numbers of poor daily resorted thither to be put on work by the inhabitants, clothiers of the same town, so as by continual resort of poor people thither the said town at the last was very much overcharged, and not able either to afford them work or maintenance, insomuch as the said poor people did much frequent unto gentlemen's houses thereabouts for to require their alms." C. (Records of the Court of Chancery) 2/Jas. I/D/5/64.

18. E. 134/10 Jas. I/M/16; C. 2/Jas. I/B/17/19.

19. Camden, *Britain,* p. 366.

20. *Ibid.,* p. 364. It was also the only place where there was much building during the period. Sir Baptist Hickes gave the town a market hall and an almshouse; for the latter see below, p. 262. He also built himself Campden House, which was a Cotswold landmark until its destruction in the Civil Wars; it seems to have been a monument of Jacobean pomposity, complete with five superposed orders and "pediments of a capricious taste." Ralph Bigland, *Historical . . . Collections, Relative to the County of Gloucester,* I, 279; see also H. A. Tipping, "Campden House and Chipping Campden Village, Gloucestershire," *Country Life,* XXX (1916), 602–08.

21. Smyth, *Description,* p. 4.

ing on the banks; a boat could get along them only with the help of an axe.[22]

The western edge of the Cotswolds is in general the watershed. It has been mentioned that the Avon and the Frome are the only rivers of any size which flow out of the Cotswolds into the Severn; all the others flow eastward into the Thames.

> At Bourton on the Water, south from Stow
> Upon the Wold, great veins of water flow
> To Burford, and to Witney, and along
> Till they make meadows large, and Isis strong.
> The famous river Isis hath her spring
> Near Tetbury, and down along doth bring
> (As handmaids) to attend her progress, Churn,
> Coln, Windrush, Yenload, Leech, whose windings turn,
> And meads, and pastures trims, bedecks, and dresses,
> Like an invaluable chain of ESSES.[23]

To the west of the Cotswolds, the rivers are larger. There is not only the Severn, but also a number of tributaries. The Leadon drains the northwestern part of the county. It rises in Herefordshire, to the west of the Malvern Hills, and joins the Severn at Gloucester; a long stream, but too small to have any commercial importance. The Bristol Avon, which forms part of the southern boundary of Gloucestershire, was also too small for boats until its last few miles; at Bristol it is swelled by a tributary, and from there to Avonmouth was navigable by the largest ships of the day.

22. Even the indefatigable John Taylor could not get up the Churn from Creeklade to Cirencester; in one day he made only four miles. See his *Last Voyage,* in *Works,* II, 12–14.

23. *Taylor on Thame Isis,* in *Works,* I, 9–10. The magistrates of Gloucester were interested in commerce on the Thames; they recommended to the privy council, in 1606, a project to make the river navigable as far up as Creeklade, "a work of great moment, and much to be commended and furthered." (S.P. 14/18/14.) There was a report of progress the following year (S.P. 14/28/7), but apparently little came of the project.

The third tributary was of greater importance. The River Avon rises in Rockingham Forest, between Northamptonshire and Leicestershire, flows through the counties of Warwick and Worcester, and joins the Severn at Tewkesbury. It is the longest of the tributaries, and in the seventeenth century was the only one of any commercial value. It was then the border of Gloucestershire for only a few miles to the west of Clifford Chambers, and again to the north of Tewkesbury; its navigability was therefore a matter of only minor interest in the county. But one attempt to improve it may be mentioned, because it throws light on the waterways of the time.

Shortly before 1635, one William Sandys offered to make the river navigable from near Coventry to its junction with the Severn. The work would be done at his own expense, and in return he would receive tolls levied on river shipping. The government approved, and agreed to reimburse riparian landowners whose property was injured; the scheme would be a great help to trade, now hindered by "the length and foulness of the ways." Commissioners were appointed by the crown, and reported that they found great enthusiasm for the idea in the upper Avon valley, "a deep inland country, most part of the year not passable with carts." [24]

The government, within a year, had shifted onto Sandys the burden of paying the landowners. The commissioners were told to summon before them all who refused the compensation which he offered, and to make formal inquiry into the value of their property; on this basis they were to make a fair appraisal, "having always regard to the benefit that the owners . . . shall receive by the work itself." The whole procedure soon alienated one of the commissioners, the sheriff of Worcestershire, who claimed that Sandys was betraying the country because "he goes about

24. Anonymous, *River Avon. Orders in council* [etc.] . . . *in the Year 1636, Relative to the Navigation of the River Avon,* pp. 10, 16. The project roused lively interest as far away as Bridgenorth; see *H.M.C., Tenth Report,* IV, 429.

to entitle his Majesty to men's inheritances." Sandys' agents were attacked and beaten by the sheriff's men, and their boat confiscated.[25] This was in 1637, after which there is no mention of the work; it was doubtless one of the many fine hopes which were dashed by civil war.[26]

The great artery of water traffic in Gloucestershire was of course the Severn. It looks today as if nothing more than a rowboat could have got up as far as Gloucester, but in fact the river was navigable for more than 160 miles from the sea. It was narrow and swift; its lower reaches were encumbered by sandbanks, and clogged by refuse washed in from the mines on the forest side. Yet boats of as much as thirty tons plied the river to Worcester and beyond. The explanation lies in the tide. This is higher at Bristol than at any other harbor in Europe, and every fortnight it floods up river. On these tides, twice a month, at least two hundred tons of commodities were carried from Bristol to Gloucester.[27]

As far north as Tewkesbury, the Severn was vitally important. In 1607–08, for example, the winter was a cold one, and for months the river was frozen. The result was a

25. S.P. 16/315/79 and 16/343/67.

26. John Taylor, in 1641, says that the river was navigable to within four miles of Warwick. (*Last Voyage,* in *Works,* II, 27.) But he may mean only that it was navigable for him; his ideas on the subject were extreme.

27. Smyth makes the statement that the river was not passable for ships of burden even as far as Berkeley, and that flat-bottomed barges could go beyond only at the highest tides. (*Description,* p. 343.) This is preposterous. The port of Gloucester was Gatcombe, above Berkeley and across from the present port of Sharpness; there were twenty to twenty-four feet of water there at high tide, and anchorage for ships of 150 tons and more. Ships of forty tons could ply the river above Gloucester when the tides were highest, "at the spring of the year and the fall of the leaf." (E. 134/13 Chas. I/M/30.) Smaller boats went up at least as far as Bewdley; see below, pp. 148–50. For further references to the navigability of the Severn, see Lansd. MS. 40, fo. 84; MS. A.P.C. (Acts of the Privy Council) LII, 509; Taylor, *Last Voyage,* in *Works,* II, 22–23, 28, 30; Thomas D. Fosbrooke, *Abstracts of Records and Manuscripts Respecting the County of Gloucester, Formed into a History,* I, 59; [Samuel Rudder], *A New History of Gloucestershire,* pp. 45–46.

domestic crisis in the town. "By the reason of the rivers froze, so as no wood nor coal might be brought to the town, great scarcity and extremity followed, so as no man could keep his trees and hedges from cutting and spoiling by the poorer sort. And great hindrance for malt-making and for transporting, by the river so long being frozen, insomuch as no passage could be had to Bristol at Paul's Fair but by land and horseback." [28]

Such a frost was rare. A more common hardship inflicted by the river was flood. In the early part of 1611, an unexampled flood at Tewkesbury continued for two months; but it seems to have done no more than destroy two of the town's three bridges.[29] At Gloucester, however, a number of the poorer sort lived within range of the high waters, and a flood meant real hardship. In 1636–37, the city paid for relief and rescue of some poor "whose houses were drowned with water." [30] Three years later, a surplus in the treasury was spent on two parishes which had been inundated, "by reason whereof the poor of the parish . . . are in great distress and want, and many of them sick." [31] The Severn was useful, but at times took toll for its service.

While the river was the major route of commerce, the routes of travel were largely overland. A glance at the map will show the principal roads.[32] Many of them are the

28. Tewkes. Corp. Rec. (Tewkesbury Corporation Records) 1, fo. 28.

29. *Ibid.*, fo. 29v.

30. A man and his rowboat were hired for five days, and £1 3*s.* was given in relief by the city chamberlain. Glouc. Corp. Rec. (Gloucester Corporation Records) 1501 (chamberlains' accounts), fo. 40.

31. Glouc. Corp. Rec. 1567 (city quarter sessions), Michelmas, 1640.

32. The map shows the county boundaries as given in the 1611 edition of John Speed, *The Theatre of the Empire of Great Britaine.* Speed does not show roads, and there are no maps which do until John Ogilby, *Britannia, . . . An Illustration of the Kingdom of England and Dominion of Wales: by a Geographical and Historical Description of the Principal Roads Thereof* (London, 1675). This volume shows the principal roads as a series of strips, each adorned with the points of the compass. From these strips the road-map in this book has been made; it is a safe conjecture that the main roads had not changed between 1590

Roman routes: the Fosse Way, the roads from London to South Wales and from Gloucester to the north. Most of them are also the highways of today, but to this there are three major exceptions. The road from London to St. Davids left Cirencester aside, and ventured instead into the wild valley of the upper Churn. The road from Gloucester to Coventry spurned the Vale of Evesham, and went across country from Winchcomb to Chipping Campden, and thence to Clifford Chambers. The strangest road of all was that from Bristol to Gloucester. It began normally enough, from Bristol to Iron Acton and Tortworth; then through Michaelwood Chase, and up the slopes by North Nibley. At this point it lost its head, and went straight over Stinchcombe Hill to Dursley; from there it followed the valley of the Cam, and rejoined the natural route at Cambridge. The importance of Dursley as a wool center was perhaps the reason for detouring out of the vale, and a hilly route is comprehensible in an age when wheeled vehicles were rare. But the crossing of Stinchcombe Hill is hard to explain. There is no modern road across it. While the old one remains, it is so inordinately steep that it would take a hardy packhorse to get over it.[33]

All three of these routes have been superseded. In most places the road itself remains, but it is used only by the countrymen. These three changes, however, are the excep-

and 1675. The lines are solid where the road is evident, and dotted where it is doubtful. (Ogilby was not always accurate: if a traveler had gone into the Forest of Dean, armed only with the *Britannia,* he might have spent the rest of his life in trying to get out again.) For a modern interpretation of Ogilby's maps, see the Ordnance Survey, *A Map of XVII Century England with Description, Chronological Tables, and a Map of London circa 1660* (Southampton, 1930).

33. The present route along the Severn is probably the same as the one which parliament took order for repairing in 1554 (1 Mary 3, c. 6), although the wording of the statute is inconclusive. Ogilby indicates this route as an alternative to the one through Dursley, but does not consider it important enough to map. It must have been the road for wheeled traffic, but such traffic was extremely uncommon; see Sidney and Beatrice Webb, *English Local Government from the Revolution to the Municipal Corporations Act: The Story of the King's Highway,* chapter v. For a discussion of the upkeep of these roads, see below, pp. 239–41.

tion. In general, the motorist of today goes through the same towns as the horseman of the seventeenth century. There is nothing more conservative than a road.

These narrow lanes were the arteries of county life. Down them came every sort of men and vehicle: a J.P., back from explaining his sins to the court of star chamber; a butcher, bringing his meat to market; a judge on circuit, riding with the sheriff to Gloucester assizes; a carrier, the express man of the day, with a cart full of goods from London for the gentry, and a mind full of fantastic stories for the village folk; a group of traveling players; some churchwardens and their vicar, summoned to the chancellor's court; a peddler with his packs; lawyers in search of evidence; the archdeacon on visitation; a king's messenger, riding post haste to Carmarthenshire, with a warrant to every postmaster, mayor, and loyal subject to provide him with horses and speed him on his way; merchants and burgesses; farmers with their cattle and shepherds with their sheep. Mingling with them, jostled by them, was the crowd of the migrant poor: men, women, and children, a procession of dark rags as background for the gay colors of the gentry. Six hours by the roadside on Birdlip Hill, when it was market day in Gloucester, would have given more idea of county life than can now be had from six years of research.

The procession has passed, and cannot be recalled. But it can be painted. Some of the details are lost, and the painting will therefore be unfinished. It will, however, be faithful enough to be recognized by the ghosts of the peddler and the justice.

II

THE ORGANS OF THE CENTRAL GOVERNMENT

AT FIRST GLANCE, the government of Gloucestershire seems to have been a manifestation of chaos. The county was subject to a mass of officials, ranging from the privy councilors, the high sheriff, and the lord lieutenant, to the petty constable and the tithingman; a number of courts, from the star chamber and the Council of Wales to the leet courts of the manors; a maze of jurisdictions, overlapping and undefined. Some of these jurisdictions cannot now be demarcated. This is partly because they were sometimes merged: an official might hold several offices at once, so that it is not always possible to tell in which capacity he was acting at a given time.[1] But it is primarily because men did not feel the need of exact demarcation.

The governmental system had grown in haphazard fashion. To the people it was familiar, and neighborly, and adequate. They accepted it, and did not attempt to define its parts too narrowly; it had the prescriptive authority of long usage. If one agency of government cut across the functioning of another, it did so in ways marked out by tradition. Theoretical definition, in other words, was replaced by traditional—a form which is less tangible, less precise, but just as real. The Gloucestershire squires sent men to parliament, where the bases of the constitution were being examined and remolded. But the same squires governed at home as their ancestors had done, without

1. The lord lieutenant, for example, was frequently high constable of the Forest of Dean, and sometimes lord president of the Council of Wales; his deputy lieutenants were often J.P.'s. The mayor, recorder, and aldermen of Gloucester were J.P.'s *ex officio;* hence the city quarter sessions were merely an inner group of the common council, sitting in a different capacity.

giving a thought to what seems to us confusion and inefficiency. *Quod erat, et nunc, et semper.*

Above the complex group of county officials was the authority of the central government. Its primary function was to supervise local officialdom, and to make it as effective as the men and the times permitted. In practice, this supervision extended far beyond the governmental system, into every phase of county life. It might be capricious and arbitrary; it might show itself in petty ways; it might be weak enough to be flouted with impunity. But it was always in the background, and it must be briefly considered before any detailed consideration of the system which was supervised.

This authority was legislative, executive, and judicial. But it is impossible to classify under these heads the organs through which it was exercised, because division of powers was as unfamiliar to central government as to local. Four such organs will be discussed in turn, in the order of their importance to county life. First is the court of star chamber, in which the judges were to a certain extent executives as well. Second is the privy council, and third the Council of Wales; each was primarily an administrative body, and secondarily a court. Last is parliament, which was almost entirely legislative.

Most of the London courts, both of equity and common law, had only a negligible influence on county officialdom. The sheriff had the nuisance of selecting a jury and sending it up to town, to try a local case at the common law. The J. P.'s were often busy on special commissions, principally out of the court of chancery. There was occasionally a pursuivant from one of the courts, arresting men and making trouble in the county.[2] But these are minor

2. For a discussion of special commissions, see below, pp. 62–65; for the rôle of the court of exchequer, see chapter vi. (An interesting and amusing account of the misdemeanors of an exchequer pursuivant, in Prestbury in 1611, is contained in E. 134/9 Jas. I/H/2.) Chancery was important less as an administrative body than as a means of evading suits at the common law. Lord Chandos, for example, complained that his cousin was being sued there merely because the plaintiff wished "by

matters, by comparison with the importance of star chamber.

This offshoot of the privy council had been created to curb local despotism and violence. In Gloucestershire, at least, it was still fulfilling its function by the time of James I. The number of local cases which came before it was enormous. The parties to these suits were of every class and walk of life, from noblemen to husbandmen, and the charges were equally varied. It was entirely a criminal court, dealing for the most part with the less heinous crimes. There were some cases of rape, and some of attempted poisoning; but the great majority were concerned with such matters as riot, illegal entry, slander and libel, intimidation, malfeasance in office.

The last two categories were those in which the court had the most effect on county government. If a man won his case in a local court by packing or intimidating the jury, the loser might hale him and the jurors before star chamber, and frequently did so. The same applied to officials. If a constable, for instance, feared to prosecute a powerful offender at the quarter sessions or assizes, he might instead bring suit in London. The converse was even more widely true: if an official misbehaved in office, the most effective way to bring him to book was a suit in star chamber. The court thus played an important rôle in regulating county government, and in mitigating the power of local magnates. That rôle will appear more fully through the frequent references to star chamber in subsequent pages.[3] For the present it is sufficient to point out

injunction, or some other dilatory course, to detract and hinder my cousin's trial at common law, which now at this next assizes he hopeth to have." (Harl. MS. 6995, fo. 173.) A landlord, in 1627, brought suit in chancery against his tenants, "for that it is a popular cause, wherein a country jury will incline to favor and partiality for tenants against the lord." G.P.L. MS. RZ 152.1, fo. 10.

3. The same is true of practically all governing bodies and officials described in these early chapters, from star chamber to petty constable. I have made no attempt to give, in one place, the whole picture of any one, because their activities were too widespread and their interaction too complex.

that while the court must have dispensed rough justice, it was a justice which was often sought in Gloucestershire, and which made itself felt from one end of the county to the other.[4]

The second organ of central authority was even more important. While the star chamber was an offshoot of the privy council, the council had surrendered none of its power to the court. It retained even its judicial aspect: if a man felt that justice had been denied him, he could get action more promptly and more cheaply by a petition to the council than by a suit in the court. If his petition was accepted, the council would either enjoin his enemies from proceeding further, or instruct the sheriff or lord lieutenant to intervene. Even if the case was outside its jurisdiction, pressure might be brought to bear on the offender. By legal and personal means, the council endeavored to make the way of the bully more difficult.[5]

4. Star chamber was not a court of appeal, although its punishment of those responsible for miscarriage of justice in a lower court approximated an appelate function. Juries seem to have been sensitive to this danger. There is a case of a Yorkshire yeoman, in 1624, who was fined £10 by the quarter sessions for threatening to sue a grand jury in star chamber, if they did not bring in a certain indictment. J. C. Atkinson, [North Riding] *Quarter Sessions Records,* III, 193.

Gloucestershire was one of the counties where star-chamber suits against officials were most frequent at the beginning of the century. This appears from the excellent study of the court and catalogue of cases before it, at the beginning and end of Elizabeth's reign, made by Miss Elfreda Skelton (Mrs. J. E. Neale); the study is still in typescript, and the most accessible copy is in the Institute of Historical Research in London. My generalizations are based on a survey of all the cases from the county in the period during which they are indexed, 1602–25.

5. An example of injunction is the case of the registrar of the Gloucester diocesan court. He complained to the council that the diocesan chancellor had ousted him unjustly, and would ruin him before he could get redress through the courts. The council enjoined the chancellor from proceeding with the ouster, and stigmatized his conduct as "very foul and contrary to all right and equity, and in any man not to be allowed, much less in one of his functions and calling." (*A.P.C., 1590–91,* pp. 286-87; the case was later brought into chancery, for which see C. 24/222, Blackleeche *respons. v.* Jones.) An example of persuasion is the case of a man in Gloucester, who complained that some land of his had been seized by Lord Berkeley, and that he dared not sue because of

During the reign of Elizabeth, the paternalism of the council was not confined to preventing intimidation. Debtors appealed to its high authority, and occasionally succeeded in having their creditors put off.[6] Nicholas Poyntz, tiring of a quarrel with Sir Thomas Throckmorton, asked the council to intercede with Sir Thomas to "remit and forget all matters of mislike, quarrel, and offense offered by the said Nicholas," and in future promised to behave lovingly toward Sir Thomas.[7] Sir Richard Berkeley's son ran away, intending to go abroad. The council wrote to the mayor of Southampton to apprehend him there. He was caught, brought before the council, and sent back to his father with a letter of advice. Sir Richard was told of the boy's melancholy humor, and warned to treat him mildly "for the better prevention of further mischief, otherwise (in our opinions) likely to ensue." [8] Government still had a personal, almost an intimate touch, when the lords of her Majesty's privy council could consider the troubles of a bankrupt or of a runaway boy.

This paternalism was waning by the time James came to the throne.[9] The council was reverting to what had always been its primary concern in local government, the task of keeping the government at work. The court of star

Berkeley's "quality and calling." The council wrote to Berkeley, explaining that a land case was outside its sphere, but urging him (with surprising humility) to submit the matter to arbitration. *A.P.C., 1592–93,* pp. 314–15.

6. Action was taken in only five cases during the period, and four of them were in Elizabeth's reign; the only case in the time of James was referred to the assize judges. *A.P.C., 1590,* p. 160; *1591–92,* pp. 459–60; *1592–93,* p. 81; *1600–01,* p. 113; *1616–17,* pp. 404–05.

7. *A.P.C., 1590–91,* pp. 11–12. The settlement was arranged, but was completely ineffective; see below, pp. 23–24.

8. *A.P.C., 1592,* pp. 324–25; see also p. 294. If the boy, as is probable, was the future Sir Richard Berkeley who is buried at Stoke Gifford, he was under fourteen at the time.

9. Aside from the one case of a debtor already mentioned, there is no record after 1600 of interference by the council with the private affairs of laymen in the county. There are two cases, in the 1630's, of interference on behalf of underpaid clergymen; in both the stipend was increased at the order of the council. G.P.L. MS. 16,528, fos. 67–70; MS. A.P.C., XLIX, 580; and S.P. 16/357/132.

chamber might punish an official, but it was the council which held his nose to the grindstone—reprimanding him, praising him, exhorting him, trying to get from him the best service he could give. If a sheriff was behind in his collection of ship money, or a deputy lieutenant was slow to report a riot, he was likely to receive an ominous letter from Whitehall, expressing surprise and hinting at unmentioned punishments. Such letters were frequent, and not always effective; a man often received several, in stronger and stronger language, before he could be prodded into doing what was wanted of him. Local officials were unpaid amateurs, and it was no easy matter to keep them to the mark. But the council tried, with unflagging patience; if its policy did not run counter to local opinion, patience had in time its due reward.

There was another body which had jurisdiction in Gloucestershire. The Council in the Marches of Wales was a miniature combination of star chamber and privy council. It had been created in order to transmit and amplify the authority of the central government, attenuated by the distance from London to the border. This authority was both judicial and administrative. As a court, the council had a wide but closely defined jurisdiction in civil and criminal cases, where the plaintiff was debarred from suing at the common law either by his poverty or by the local influence of his adversary. As a council, it was charged with suppressing private incontinence and public disorder, bribery and oppression by officials, perjury by witnesses or jurors—in short, to stand *in loco parentis* to the Marcher counties.[10] The president was frequently

10. The council, in 1609, consisted of seventy-three members, ranging from the lord privy seal and lord chamberlain to J.P.'s and country gentry; each member received 6*s*. 8*d*. for each day he served. The jurisdiction of the council was carefully delimited from that of the common-law courts, particularly in civil suits. If such suits involved more than £40, they might be brought before the council on only two conditions: that they did not involve land title or chattel real, and that the poverty of the plaintiff was formally certified by at least two J.P.'s. (Instructions from the crown, G.P.L. MS. JF 6.4.) For a fuller discussion of the origin and competence of the council, see C.A.J. Skeel, *The Council in*

the lord lieutenant of the four border counties (of Gloucester, Worcester, Hereford and Salop), and he and the chief members of the council were usually on the four commissions of the peace. The council was not always stationary; it sometimes moved in a body around the counties of its jurisdiction, and held court in various cities. Its members thus had an advantage which was denied to the privy councilors, for they could investigate local conditions on the spot.[11]

The judicial work of the council may best be understood by examining some Gloucestershire cases which came before it. The Poyntz-Throckmorton quarrel, already mentioned in connection with the privy council, illustrates the difficulty which the two councils had in working with each other. Poyntz's offer of peace was unsuccessful, and the squabble continued for another nine years. First Poyntz was fined £35 in the Council of Wales (of which Throckmorton was vice-president). He petitioned the privy council, which instructed the Council of Wales to appoint arbitrators from among its members. This instruction was ignored, and the privy council enjoined the collection of the fine. Next a settlement was arranged before the privy council. Throckmorton ignored this also, and continued to prosecute Poyntz in the Council of Wales, presumably to collect the fine. He was commanded either to cease, or to allow Poyntz to transfer the case into star chamber. This seems to have met an equally blank reception, and for five years nothing happened. Then the Council of Wales re-

the Marches of Wales: a Study in Local Government During the 16th and 17th Centuries, especially pp. 90–93. For its occasional use to assist the collection of taxes, see below, p. 122 note 52, and Skeel, *Council of Wales,* p. 148.

11. *Ibid.,* pp. 252 note 1, 281. The council came to Gloucester in 1592, and was received in state by the mayor and common council, in ceremonial scarlet, "and with sixty caliver shot without Ailesgate." The councilors were lodged in the bishop's palace, and met in the chapter house. They were presented with wine and sugarloaves, for which the city thriftily reimbursed itself by a tax on the guilds, and on other tradesmen who had benefited from the visit. Glouc. Corp. Rec. 1451 (minute book), fos. 136–37; uncatalogued letter book, fo. 62.

membered to send the privy council its reason for levying the fine (which by now was six years old), and the injunction was rescinded. By the end of the next year the case was still unsettled, and Whitehall was thoroughly bored with it: "a cause that hath been often heard at this board, and divers orders and letters written in the same unto you long sithence." Their lordships thought that Poyntz had had enough, and should now be released from "this chargeable and tedious trouble"—but only if there were no reasons to the contrary. There were, and the discharge was countermanded. At this moment Poyntz left for Ireland, as well he might, and there is no further record of the case.[12]

This quarrel brings out the confused relationship between the two councils. But the Council of Wales was imbued with confusion; it was no more sure of itself when acting in Gloucestershire than when arguing with Whitehall. This appears from even a casual study of the cases which came before it. By the early seventeenth century, most of them were concerned with minor crimes: incontinence; unjustifiable verdicts by juries of local courts; assault and affray, the forcible rescue of prisoners.[13] But the court would not spurn pettier matters, and tried suits even over heriot. It could be as petty in its methods as its cases. Roger Tybbott, for example, sued to recover a cow taken as heriot. His opponents thought that he was sure to win, because he was a "relator," or informer, of the court

12. The case continued for eight years. *A.P.C., 1591–92,* pp. 141, 435; *1597–98,* pp. 16–17; *1598–99,* pp. 372 (from which the quotations are taken), 596-97, 676.

13. From a book of fines, 14 Jas. I to 13 Chas. I; Harl. MS. 4220. The suppression of incontinence and adultery was one of the important functions of the council. "If this vice did as much exceed in other parts of the land as in these [four counties], it were necessary to be punished in the same sort elsewhere; but here reformation can hardly be wrought, though the spiritual courts and temporal courts both do join in punishment. And this was inserted in the instructions [of the council] many years since by a bishop vice-president, that found the church censures not sufficient to repress the excessiveness of this vice there." Cotton MS. (British Museum) Vitellius, C 1, fo. 147v.

"and hath a brother who is an attorney there; and relators, of all men, be favored there, because you know by their means their court is still upholden. Take away relators, their court can hold no pleas. . . . Tybbott shall find extraordinary favor there, in regard that he bringeth very many causes to their court." [14]

The court was extremely susceptible to outside influence, as witness the case of Ambrose Jobbins. He was haled before the council for failing to pay fines due to Lord Berkeley. He refused to appear, and ignored a series of summonses; then he went to London to enlist the aid of Lord Sidney. Sidney went with him to see Lord Zouche, the president of the council, and from him obtained letters to the court: "justice was set aside and letters took [its] place." Jobbins was commanded to stay at home, and the matter was argued by lawyers. The council referred it to arbitration, to the annoyance of Lord Berkeley's agent. "My counsel could not be suffered to speak no more, for they saw that all was in vain. I had three, . . . the which did grieve them to see how things was carried." The agent suggested appealing to the lord chief justice, the one man about whom the council was nervous. "They are afraid at the marches that the lord chief justice will take Gloucestershire out of their commission. And [they] doth search daily for the oldest records that show that Gloucestershire to be in their commission, the which records they doth send up to London to the Lord Zouche." [15]

This introduces a question which kept lawyers busy for a generation, and which was never settled: were the four border counties within the jurisdiction of the council? The

14. G.P.L. MS. RF 354.23, fo. 29. These informers were notorious. They brought cases for which they had no proof, "relying upon the defendant's examination upon a multitude of interrogatories, whereby he shall accuse himself against the liberty of the subject. And then, right or wrong, he must give bond with two sureties of £40 to abide the hearing, to avoid which trouble and charge the informer obtains his ends, *viz.*, a composition." Anonymous, *Arguments Proving, the Iurisdiction Used by the President and Counsell in the Marches of Wales . . . to Be Illegall,* p. 13.

15. G.P.L. MS. 16,530, fo. 66 (1-1v).

point had been raised as early as 1560,[16] but it did not become an issue until the reign of King James. The court of exchequer, in 1604, pronounced the four counties to be outside the authority of the council. Three years later the government countered by increasing the civil jurisdiction of the council in those counties, and in 1617 by increasing it again. This aroused great opposition. The sheriff of Gloucestershire refused to execute a process from the council; the Hereford grand jury presented the council as a nuisance; parliament petitioned against it.

Each side delivered a volley of arguments. According to its opponents, the council interfered with the common-law courts, and punished offenders who had already been dealt with by those courts. It used torture; it refused to permit settlements outside court; it interfered with copyhold lands; it transmitted only a fraction of the fines it received. Above all, it placed the four counties in an invidious position: they were subject to two jurisdictions a hundred miles apart, in London and Ludlow, and the one in Ludlow depended solely on the will of the sovereign.[17]

The defenders of the council based their case on the condition of the marches. There was more disorder in one of these border counties than in any three others combined; the people "upon every trifle fall together by the

16. *H.M.C., De L'Isle and Dudley MSS.*, I, 321 ff. The city of Gloucester was always reluctant to admit the interference of the council. In 1597, the mayor sent some men to jail, and they sued him before the council for wrongful imprisonment. When he was served in the case, he exclaimed, "They . . . served me with process from the council in the marches; I will answer the council! They shall go to the common jail, or worse prison, and shall lie there this twelvemonth. . . . What, serve the mayor of Gloucester with process!" Glouc. Corp. Rec. 1451, fo. 170; see also fo. 167 v.

In 1605, the council tried gentler tactics. An alderman had appealed to it to rescind a fine levied on him by the common council. Lord Zouche wrote to the city fathers, approving their action. But since the offender had sincerely repented, he urged them to restore him to his place and "to abate such part of his said fine as their charities might upon his lordship's letter move them unto." This politeness was successful; the fine was decreased and the man reinstated. *Ibid.*, fo. 206.

17. S.P. 14/56/10; Anon., *Arguments,* p. 11 and *passim; H.M.C., Thirteenth Report,* IV, 252–53; Skeel, *Council of Wales,* pp. 133–41.

ears, if they find not law very ready at head."[18] The gentry were especially lawless; they "go to markets and pub[lic] places so weaponed and assisted with friends, as officers dare not attempt to arrest them without assistance from the council." These gentlemen oppressed the poor, and in harvest time took their crops; the victims had not the money to recover at common law, and their one recourse was to the council.[19] The cheapness of its justice was frequently stressed, and it was said that three cases could be settled there for the cost of one at Westminster. The court was particularly severe with "wrangling companions," or barrators, and such suits were therefore rarely brought before it.[20]

While the war of words raged about it, the council continued to function. King James was adamant in refusing to abandon it.[21] But as time went on, its power was unquestionably declining.[22] It was so weak by 1639 that the court of king's bench dared to enjoin it from assessing damages for criminal offenses, and from examining delinquents by interrogatory. The members of the council complained that the injunction had placed them in an impasse, for

18. This lawlessness made it particularly difficult to apprehend recusants, "many of the gentry being so evil affected, and most of the people so ready to bear out one another, that how rich and known soever any recusant be, yet neither their persons nor goods will be found for the king." S.P. 14/31/35.

19. Cotton MS. Vitellius, C 1, fo. 148; the arguments for and against the council cover fifty-eight folios.

20. *Ibid.*, fo. 147v; see also Skeel, *Council of Wales*, pp. 136, 167–68.

21. It was a symbol, as he told the privy council, of his prerogative justice. "None do oppose themselves against the jurisdiction of the council in the marches but certain high-headed fellows, calling them by a Scottish name mounting fellows, in English swaggering fellows, . . . who because they would oppress the meaner people and bear the whole sway of their country without controlment, do oppose themselves against government and the state of the king. . . . What prerogative to me therein appertaineth, I will hold and maintain to the uttermost." Quoted by Skeel, *ibid.*, p. 145.

22. By the reign of James, according to the author of the Cotton MS. cited above, "most men of those countries have withdrawn their obedience from that jurisdiction." (Fo. 134v.) This is certainly an overstatement; the council continued to act in the four counties until 1641, and again through the reigns of Charles II and James II.

they were "by the king's writ prohibited what by his Majesty's instructions (which we are sworn to observe) we are authorized and commanded to do." [23] But their puzzlement and their office were soon ended. When the Long Parliament met, the members for the four counties were "passionately concerned to absolve themselves from the burthen of that jurisdiction." [24] In 1641 the council was abolished; it was too inefficient to endure in a changing world. Its authority was undefined, its action was fumbling and uncertain, and it conflicted with the other agencies of government as much as it coöperated with them. But with all its faults, it had its warm supporters in Gloucestershire: men who were sorry to see it go, and eager to have it back again.[25] For while its authority was questionable and its justice often slipshod, it was a nearer, cheaper, and speedier court than those at Westminster.

The fourth organ of central authority, parliament, was in theory the most important of all. Men lived according to, or in violation of, a congeries of laws for nearly every phase of life, and nearly every action of a magistrate was "according to the statute in that case provided." In this sense, parliamentary activity had a profound effect on the life of the county. But in a larger sense it had surprisingly little. Until almost the eve of the Civil Wars, political crises in London made scanty impression on the Gloucestershire farmers and burgesses. While elections sometimes caused excitement, the electors soon settled back to their normal life. They were far from London, and the actions of parliament were rarely of immediate interest or importance to them. They went their ways, and paid little attention to the thunderheads which were rising over England. It was not until the storm was on the point of breaking that the electorate became seriously aroused.

There were two knights of the shire in each parliament,

23. S.P. 16/415/5.

24. Clarendon, quoted by Skeel, *Council of Wales,* p. 160.

25. There was a Gloucestershire petition, in 1661, for the restoration of the council; see *ibid.,* p. 168.

and two burgesses from each of the three parliamentary boroughs: Tewkesbury, Cirencester, and Gloucester. The knights differed from the burgesses, both in the social group from which they were drawn and in the character of their election. They came entirely from the gentry and lesser nobility. They were Berkeleys, Throckmortons, Tracys, Duttons—families which passed down the burdens and the fruits of office from generation to generation. The members themselves, at some time in their careers, were often high sheriffs, constables of the forest, deputy lieutenants, commissioners of survey—men who were in close touch with the government of the county, and who often had had a hand in administering it.[26]

Elections were usually a smooth and simple matter, apparently prearranged by the gentry. In 1624 came the first suggestion of trouble, when the death of Sir Thomas Estcourt necessitated a bye-election.[27] Robert Poyntz and Thomas Chester, "for some private and sinister ends," decided to interfere with the voting. They were commissioners of the subsidy, and ordered the various assessors to bring in their bills of taxation on election day. The place they chose was eighteen miles from Painswick, "where the county was to be holden." Most of the assessors were freeholders, and they tried to have the day changed in order to vote. A third commissioner agreed, but Poyntz and Chester were adamant. They threatened to fine all assessors who defaulted, "their clerks also, in their hearing, telling the assessors that the subsidy service was to be preserved before the other." In this way many of the assessors were kept from the election. Others sent in their bills by proxy, and went to vote. Poyntz and Chester ful-

26. For biographies of members during this period, see William R. Williams, *The Parliamentary History of the County of Gloucester . . . , 1213–1898,* pp. 47–53.

27. Sir Thomas had been elected against his will; the election had been disputed, but upheld by the house of commons. *Ibid.,* p. 51; John Glanville, *Reports of Certain Cases, Determined and Adjudged by the Commons in Parliament, in the Twenty-First and Twenty-Second Years of the Reign of King James the First,* pp. 99–103.

filled their threat, and levied a number of stiff fines. An absentee might be excused if he could produce witnesses to swear that he was *at* the election, but not if they could only swear "that the party absent told them, the night before, that he was to go to the election, that he was ridden forth that morning thitherwards, and as they verily believed was ridden to the said election." Other assessors, who were absent for other reasons, were excused without giving proof. The fines were collected, with the greatest severity, through the high constables of the hundreds. The Poyntz machine seems to have been a strong one. Whether it was successful is another question, and one which cannot be answered.[28]

Troubled elections were more common in the towns than in the country. The borough members were a different sort, either burgesses or influential outsiders. Those for Cirencester were rarely natives; the electors had a penchant for Wiltshire men, but sometimes went as far afield as Devon or London.[29] Tewkesbury preferred people of importance: Sir Dudley Digges, Sir Baptist Hickes, a grandson of Lord Chandos, and in 1640 (at the age of nineteen) Sir Anthony Ashley Cooper.[30] These men were

28. G.P.L. MS. 16,526, fo. 40. Sir Maurice Berkeley was elected, but it is impossible to tell for which candidate Poyntz had been working. The efforts of his machine were wasted in any case, because Berkeley was not returned in time to sit in parliament before it was dissolved by the death of King James.

29. Williams, *Parliamentary History,* pp. 152–58. A disputed election in the town, in 1624, reveals the vagueness of electoral custom. Although there had been elections for half a century, no one knew who the voters should be. Two polls were held: one, in church, of the freeholders only, and one of all the inhabitants. The result was a disagreement, which was referred to the house of commons. (*Ibid.,* pp. 155–56; Glanville, *Reports,* pp. 104–11.) The same question arose at Tewkesbury, in the elections for the Long Parliament. "We had great difference about our burgesses, two being returned by one bailiff and two by another. So the election was quashed, because we admitted some freeholders to give voices, and [it was] not resolved whether the election should be by freemen only, or all the inhabitants except almsmen." Giles Geast Rent Book, *anno* 1640; see also Williams, *Parliamentary History,* pp. 237–38.

30. *Ibid.,* pp. 232–38. For an example of the sort of work which these men did for their towns, see the report of Sir Dudley Digges' speech

in strong contrast to the knights of the county. They were often strangers to the town, and quite ignorant of its interests; "unmeet men," the privy council called them, "and unacquainted with the state of the boroughs named thereto." [31]

But if such a man was a bad representative, there were compensations for the town. A great noble might ask for the election of his candidate, and offer his favor in return. One of Tewkesbury's two first members, Sir Dudley Digges, was elected at the request of Lord Salisbury, and a similar request from Lord Chandos, in 1620, met with equal success.[32] Twenty years later, however, when the Earl of Middlesex asked for the election of his eldest son, the town authorities declined "out of care for the common good." [33]

The common good was as often helped as hindered by such an election. When Tewkesbury chose Sir Dudley Digges, he soon sent the town, "by way of thankfulness," £160 with which to buy land; he later gave further benefactions, and was always "a worthy good friend." This arrangement seems to have pleased the authorities, and some years later they extended it to Sir Baptist Hickes, a man of enormous wealth. He promptly gave them a rectory in Pembrokeshire, and became one of their more lucrative investments. This seemed to surprise the clerk of the council, who remarked that Hickes's election was "the only cause on our side of his great bounty towards us." [34]

about Tewkesbury bridge, in Wallace Notestein, F. H. Relf, and Hartley Simpson, *Commons Debates, 1621,* III, 171.

31. A letter from the council to the sheriff of Gloucestershire, in 1597, instructing him to use his influence to improve the standard of men elected from the towns. Glouc. Corp. Rec. 1450, fo. 164.

32. Tewkes. Corp. Rec. 1, fo. 42, and a loose letter from Lord Chandos in the Tewkesbury town safe.

33. *H.M.C., Fourth Report,* p. 303. For examples of similar interference elsewhere, see Mary Bateson and Helen Stocks, *Records of the Borough of Leicester,* III, 336–37, 435–36.

34. Tewkes. Corp. Rec. 1, fos. 42, 48; for the legal arrangements incident to the election of Digges and Hickes in 1624, see fo. 18.

Gloucester alone was always represented by its burgesses, or at least by men closely connected with the city.[35] It was also unusually independent of outside interference. The Earl of Leicester, in 1580, asked to be allowed to appoint a member. He was refused. Four years later he made the same request, rather more haughtily.[36] The city again refused, and gave its reasons: his earlier request had caused such "variance and offense" among the burgesses, that the common council did not even dare let them know of his second one. "The number of burgesses will not be entreated to grant a burgess-room to any man not sworn to the franchises of this city; . . . besides, the sheriffs of Gloucester make some conscience in respect of their oaths to deliver any return not warranted by the writ of summons and the statute."[37] This declaration of independence was effective; there is no record of another attempt to meddle with the irascible burgesses.

Elections in the city were orderly enough, but the aftermath was sometimes hard to distinguish from a riot. When Alderman Jones was elected to the parliament of 1604, he celebrated in style. "Immediately after the said election the said John Jones, being attended upon by his said

35. Occasionally by its recorder, who was not necessarily a native of the city; usually by one of the more important aldermen. Williams, *Parliamentary History,* pp. 191–94.

36. Glouc. Corp. Rec., printed in *H.M.C., Twelfth Report,* IX, pp. 460, 457.

37. Glouc. Corp. Rec. 1450, fo. 190. The phrasing suggests how common it was to ignore the legal requirement that a member of parliament should be a freeman of the borough which he represented.

The electoral body in Gloucester seems to have been the common council, but this assumption is based on a single entry in a minute book. A Mr. Robinson, elected for the parliament of 1621, "hath in this house, for the good of the city and at the entreaty of this house, made public declaration that he is contented to resign (and doth resign as much as in him lieth) his place to Mr. Gibb." The sheriffs were instructed to return Gibb as one of the town members, and the common council agreed to protect Robinson and the sheriffs "from any penalty or danger from the same." (*Ibid.,* 1451, fo. 476v.) If the council could persuade one man to resign in favor of another, and authorize the election of the second, it seems a safe assumption that it was the council which elected in the first place.

sons, suitors, and confederates, in riotous and triumphant manner like a conqueror, did march before them unto the said booth-hall door, whither they did cause and procure to be brought two barrels of strong beer against their coming forth, at their own costs and charges (being a thing which was never known or done before in Gloucester), where they were forthwith in jollity drunk up in hats and caps, and the bells of Christ Church were caused by them and their confederates to be rung for joy." [38] Jones seems to have justified the fears of the privy council about members from the towns.

When King Charles called the Short Parliament, in 1640, the three boroughs seem to have had no trouble in selecting their members. Tewkesbury, as usual, picked men of good connections; Cirencester elected two of its customary representatives; Gloucester chose two new men, one of whom was later a Roundhead, one a Cavalier. In no case is there record of undue disturbance.

But the election of the knights of the shire was a different matter. As soon as word went abroad that the king was going to call parliament, the county politicians became active. In December of 1639, Sir Maurice Berkeley wrote to John Smyth, Lord Berkeley's steward:

Sir: I this afternoon received a letter that doth assure me, the king hath declared himself in council to hold a parliament in April next. I do most earnestly desire you, and will acknowledge it for a special expression of your love, added to those many I have ever formerly received from you, if you will be pleased to reserve yourself, unengaged to any,

38. After the election, "puffed up with a proud and arrogant conceit of his doings therein," Jones threatened revenge against those who had not voted for him. (St. Ch. [Records of the Court of Star Chamber] 8/207/25.) This was the same man who was diocesan registrar in 1590, and appealed to the privy council; see above, p. 20 note 5.

Jones did not receive his wages as a member, and twelve years later obtained a chancery writ to collect them. The city's defense was that he had not attended the parliament to which he had been elected, and therefore should not be paid. (Glouc. Corp. Rec. 1451, fo. 262-62v.) The wages of a member were sometimes, as in 1593, paid by a special assessment on all the burgesses. *Ibid.,* fo. 142.

until we know who will stand to be knights for our shire; and that then we may both join, and go one way for both voices. And this I desire again, as the expression of the continuance of that love I have ever received from you, and shall ever acknowledge in whatsoever I may express myself

Your most faithful and affectionate friend,

MAU: BERKELEY.[39]

It was difficult for Smyth to remain unengaged. At the time when he received this letter, he had already written to London to inquire whether Lord Berkeley "will, with the voices of myself and other his freeholders, give more especial assistance to one than to another of those three or four gentlemen that stand to be knights of this shire for the next parliament, none of the name of Berkeley being any one of them. And what his lordship shall direct, I will be most ready to execute with some hundreds of voices." [40] His lordship at first was noncommittal. "Sir Raphe Whitefields, one to whom my lord is much obliged, hath been an earnest suitor unto his lordship for Sir Baynham Throckmorton. He is a gentleman unknown to his lordship, and therefore [he] leaves it to the grave considerations of Sir Maurice and yourself; though I know his lordship would willingly serve Sir Raphe in anything." [41]

Soon there was stronger political pressure from another source, and Lord Berkeley took the matter out of Smyth's hands. The lord chamberlain decided that Sir Ralph Dutton would be a proper member for Gloucestershire. He said as much to Lord Berkeley, who wrote to Smyth that the chamberlain's request was a command. "Wherefore I would have you use all the means and power you have

39. G.P.L. MS. 16,525, fo. 89. John Smyth, aside from being a steward and a country gentleman, was the author of *The Berkeley MSS.* At this time he was an old man, with great local influence.

40. In another letter, a fortnight later, Smyth begs for word from London "of such occurence from court or city, touching parliament, ship money, or the like, as you hold fitting for us in the country to feed our fancies upon." G.P.L. MS. 16,533, fo. 99 (1v, 2v).

41. *Ibid.,* fo. 100v.

amongst my tenants, and all others in whom you have any interest, that I may give my lord chamberlain satisfaction, who will take it into his observation how it takes effect." [42]

In spite of whatever efforts Smyth may have made, the lord chamberlain did not have his way. The campaign began quietly enough. The gentry conferred together at the assizes, and agreed upon Sir Robert Tracy and Sir Robert Cooke as candidates. Cooke was a new man, and a Puritan; Tracy was a Royalist, who had been an intermittent member since 1620. Since the gentry were in apparent agreement, and usually controlled "the plebeians," the election was expected to be a mere matter of form. "There passed faithful promises on all sides, nor was anything else expected but mutual assistance from one to the other." When the day of voting arrived, Tracy stayed at home; he was ill, and confident of victory. "In his behalf, and that the election might not want state, credit, and countenance, divers gentlemen of their own accord presented themselves with their tenants and retinue." All was going smoothly, when suddenly a new candidate was set up in the person of a Mr. Stephens, "for opposing of this ship money, in which cause he had suffered, having been put out of the commission of the peace."

This dark horse upset the apple cart. Stephens had been a county member in 1628; he was an ardent parliamentarian and Puritan, and it was suspected that Cooke was secretly supporting him in place of Tracy. There were thus three candidates for two places. Tracy and his faction were Royalists. Cooke and Stephens were Puritans, on the verge of being Roundheads: one of Tracy's followers told Cooke that "he would never more trust any man that wore his hair shorter than his ears."

The Royalists, however, seem to have felt that Cooke was a lesser evil than Stephens, and Cooke and Tracy were their choice. They took every weapon which came to hand. Since the high sheriff was a relative of Tracy, his influence was used to have the county court moved to

42. *Ibid.*, 16,525, fo. 90.

Winchcomb, which was more convenient for Tracy's faction than for Stephens's. The upshot was that Tracy and Cooke were elected, "and yet the general cry goes altogether for Stephens." The latter disputed the election, but without success. Tracy and his friends had conquered the unexpected opposition, and for the last time the old régime carried the county.[43]

Within a few months a change appeared. It was scarcely evident in the towns, which elected to the Long Parliament almost as many Royalists as Parliamentarians.[44] But the county chose Nathaniel Stephens and John Dutton. The former, as we have seen, was an embattled supporter of the house of commons. The latter, while a Royalist, was a moderate one; he was one of the wealthiest men in England, but had gone to prison rather than pay ship money. When the county elected two recalcitrants, the old guard had indeed lost control.

The center of authority was shifting, and the house of commons was beginning to reach for the sovereignty of England. The court of star chamber and the Council of Wales were soon to fall before it; even the privy council was to lose much of its power and all of its paternalism. Hindsight can discover signs of this coming change, even in Gloucestershire. From the accession of King Charles, parliament was growing more important to the county;

43. "I have been the more punctual in these relations, because I have heard it observed by a judicious man that there is a kind of cunning, underhand canvass of this nature the greater part of this kingdom over. Which if it be true, we are like to have a brave lower house of it, when such instruments shall be chosen out that (if their hearts were known) affect nothing more than to hold the king's nose to the grindstone, and ruin the church." From a lively letter (S.P. 16/448/79), printed in *N. & Q.*, I, 410–13.

44. See Williams, *Parliamentary History,* pp. 158, 194, 238. The two members from Gloucester were assisted by a lobbyist. He was sent to London as soon as the Long Parliament met, with £20 from the treasury, and instructions from a committee of the common council on how to spend the money to further the city's interests. In the next year one of the city sheriffs was paid £7 14*s.* for a present which he had given to "Mr. Recorder, speaker of the commons house of parliament." Glouc. Corp. Rec. 1452, pp. 170–72; 1501, fo. 153.

elections were becoming less perfunctory, and at the end were acrimonious. The court of star chamber remained active, but the Council of Wales was becoming less and less important, its jurisdiction more and more questionable. The privy council had ceased to intervene for the protection of individuals, and was confining itself to supervision of officials and regulation of industry. The central government, in short, was beginning to approximate that of a modern state.

III

THE CIVIL GOVERNMENT OF THE COUNTY

THE HIERARCHY of county officials may be roughly divided into two parts, the civil and the military. At the head of the first was the high sheriff; below him were undersheriffs, bailiffs, hundred bailiffs, high constables of the hundreds, petty constables, and (in so far as they were administrative officers) justices of the peace.[1] At the head of the military organization was the lord lieutenant; below him were the deputy lieutenants and the officers of the trained bands. The primary business of the sheriff was the preservation of order, and that of the lord lieutenant was the supervision of the troops. But neither official can be so easily pigeonholed. The sheriff was sometimes concerned with pressing men for the wars, and the lord lieutenant and his deputies with the preservation of order. While it is thus impossible to draw a real line between the two divisions of government, their action and interaction will best be understood by looking at each one separately.

There were three sheriffs within the borders of Gloucestershire: one for the outshire, or county of Gloucester, and two for the inshire, or county of the city of Gloucester. The latter were little more than administrative agents of the city council. Once a year they went to London, to account to the exchequer for the farm of the city.[2] During

1. Another official must be left in obscurity. About the coroner the records are silent, except for one reference to his jury; see below, p. 56 note 54.

2. In 1589, there was an amusing scandal about this accounting. John Walkeley, one of the sheriffs, came into the cathedral in his scarlet gown, and after the sermon made a public announcement about one of his predecessors: "John Dorney . . . the last term came away out of London and left his part of the queen's farm of the city unpaid, and laid the fault on me. Let him go up in the beginning of the term and appear at the exchequer, at his peril." Walkeley was punished for his speech,

the rest of the year their major duties were collecting fines and maintaining order. The two sometimes conflicted; the attempt to collect a fine would produce disorder. An instance of this, in 1584, shows the hardships of a sheriff's life. A man had been fined for shirking jury duty. The sheriffs went to collect the fine, but received instead of money only "froward answers." They levied a distress on his property, and he resisted. An exchange of blows drew blood from one of the sheriffs, and the other "was assaulted and thrown down and had many blows given him, coming only in aid of his fellow." The offender had £10 added to his fine. His servant was fined £1, because he "gave countenance" against the sheriffs instead of aiding them.[3]

These city sheriffs were minor figures. But the sheriff of the county was a person of importance. He not only collected fines and preserved order. He impanelled juries, and enforced the decrees of local or outside courts; he collected certain taxes, and accounted for them in London; he arrested debtors and criminals, and kept the jails. Many of these tasks were deputed. But the final responsibility for their performance rested on the sheriff, and his rôle was by no means always confined to supervision. In moments of crisis he took matters into his own hands, and played an active part in government.[4]

The sheriff was drawn from the same social class as the knights of parliament, and usually came from one of a dozen county families. The position was onerous as well as honorable, and men evaded it when they could.[5] The fees

"so inadvisedly and rashly done regarding the time and place." Glouc. Corp. Rec. 1451, fo. 131v.

3. *Ibid.*, fo. 102v.

4. Subsequent pages contain numerous examples of the personal activity of the county sheriff; see especially pp. 131–32, 199–201. This activity is underemphasized in the usual accounts of the office, of which one of the fullest is in E. P. Cheyney, *A History of England, from the Defeat of the Armada to the Death of Elizabeth,* II, 342–58.

5. A man petitioned the privy council, in 1602, to be excused from the office on the ground that he was a newcomer to the county, and not yet settled on his land. (*H.M.C., Salisbury MSS.,* XII, 498.) Another man,

for entering and leaving office were far heavier than the perquisites of office, and the crown appointed only the wealthy. The appointment might jeopardize a man's fortune, even then, by committing him to the payment of money which he could not collect. Take for example the case of William Dutton.

Dutton and his undersheriff were bound by recognizances to collect some £10,000, due to the crown as fines from a large number of small offenders. They collected only a fraction of this sum during their term of office, and went on trying after they had returned to private life. The offenders were both violent and litigious. When cattle were confiscated, the pound was broken open and the animals stolen before they could be sold. Dutton and his man were "most grievously threatened, abused, and hardly entreated . . . as well by very unmeet, undecent words and speeches, but also with blows, assaults, hurts, wounds, bloodshed, rescues, and threatenings," to the danger of their lives. They had also been pestered with suits in the Council of Wales, which took up so much time and money that the queen's business was neglected. In desperation they petitioned the exchequer to enjoin the proceedings before the council, and give them a chance to redeem their commitment.[6]

A large part of the sheriff's routine work was in con-

in 1640, wrote to Secretary Nicholas to acknowledge "with much thankfulness the favor you have done to my son in keeping him from the shreevewick this year. It manifesteth you have not forgotten the old love betwixt your father and me, which argues a generous mind in you. I wish I knew how to make you requital." S.P. 16/448/4.

The social position of the sheriff in this period was unquestionably higher than that of the average J.P. It is surprising to find that by the eighteenth century their positions were apparently reversed; see S. and B. Webb, *English Local Government: The Parish and the County,* p. 375.

6. About 1592; E. 112/16/138. The converse of this case is another, in 1624, which indicates how a sheriff might reimburse himself for the expenses of his office. A debtor wrote to thank a friend for "your endeavors with the sheriff for my present peace," and begged to have them continued. "Then I shall not only endeavor to gratify him both with the £12 and the buck next week (of which I hope not to fail him of either), but with some addition of bounty towards him at the end of his term." G.P.L. MS. 16,531, fo. 97.

nection with the various courts. The county court has already been mentioned; its importance seems to have been slight, except at times of parliamentary elections.[7] Quarter sessions will be dealt with later, along with the justices of the peace. The third court was the assizes, and here the sheriff had considerable importance. It was his duty to hold prisoners and produce them for trial, to prepare the courtroom, to impanel the jury, and to execute the sentences of the court.

The care of prisoners was a minor task. But it was one which was sometimes ticklish, because of the nature of the prison. The county jail was Gloucester Castle, an island of royal jurisdiction within the county of the city, and the only place within it where the sheriff of the outshire had authority. But that authority was tenuous to a degree. It was supposedly exercised through a constable, who bought his office from the crown for the fees which were entailed, and who commonly entrusted the care of prisoners to a keeper or deputy-keeper.[8] Such elaborate delegation of responsibility might have succeeded if the castle had been in good condition. It was supposed to be: repairs were to be made, at the expense of the outshire, whenever the quarter sessions so ordered. But apparently the order was never given. The castle was a ruin, and the walls were so low that prisoners escaped unless constantly watched.[9]

7. Local records mention this court only as an electoral body. For the fullest description of it during the period, see C. H. Karraker, *The 17th-Century Sheriff. A Comparative Study of the Sheriff in England and the Chesapeake Colonies, 1607–1689* (Philadelphia, 1930), pp. 37–52.

8. The constable, in 1634, kept a brewery in Gloucester, and sold his beer to the prisoners. Every city brewer had to pay him 12*s*. a year as "castle cowl," a traditional perquisite of his office. (E. 134/10 Chas. I/M/55.) These and other fees must have been lucrative, because this constable had paid some £200 for his position; he lived in a house suitable for him "or for any other sufficient man of fashion to dwell in." After his death, his widow used the castle as a stone quarry: she hired the prisoners to dig out the stones, and sold them for roads and conduits. E. 134/17 Chas. I/T/1.

9. From the two exchequer cases just cited. Bristol Castle, throughout most of this period, was also under the jurisdiction of the Gloucestershire magistrates. Their authority was theoretical rather than real: the

Since the keeper could neither watch them all himself, nor afford to hire servants to do it, the sheriff was occasionally without a prisoner for the judges of assize.

There is an example of these difficulties at the beginning of the period. In 1590, the keeper petitioned the privy council to be allowed to lease the castle green from the constable. The sheriff had been annoyed because so many prisoners had escaped, and had deprived the keeper of the keys of the castle. The latter's defense was that the jail-breaks had been made by the castle green "where th' old keeper dwelleth, by whose furtherance (maliciously envying the suppliant) divers escapes and abuses have been committed." The next year the keeper petitioned again. This time it was because a new sheriff was demanding of him greater bonds than he could afford, for the safe delivery of prisoners for debt. The sheriff was profiting from the experience of his predecessor. He was insuring himself against the escape of prisoners, and making the keeper pay the premium.[10]

So much for the prisoners. The judges before whom they were tried usually sat in Gloucester, in the same hall used for quarter sessions.[11] The assizes were a public stage as well as a court. The meetings were social occasions, where even a witness was supposed to be properly

castle was apparently a den of thieves until 1630, when it was transferred by the crown to the corporation of Bristol. John Corry, *The History of Bristol, Civil and Ecclesiastical; Including Biographical Notices of Eminent and Distinguished Natives* (2 vols., Bristol, 1816), I, 267–70 and note.

10. *A.P.C., 1590–91,* pp. 284–85; *1591–92,* p. 253; the quotation is *1590–91,* p. 285. The council exhorted both sides to a better performance of their duty, and referred the matter to the judges of assize. For further light on the conditions of the prisoners, about 1610, see St. Ch. 8/161/27.

11. At least once, however, they were in Tewkesbury, where one judge sat in the town hall, and one in a tent nearby. (Giles Geast Rent Book, *anno* 1637.) The Gloucester hall was sometimes provided with straw in winter, to keep men's feet warm, and at other seasons strewn with rushes and decorated with flowers. Frankincense was seemingly used at all times, to disguise the reek of the crowd. All this was paid for by the city. Glouc. Corp. Rec. 1500, *passim;* 1501, fos. 13v, 42v, and *passim.*

dressed.[12] They were also the scene of public penance, a form of discipline reminiscent of the kindergarten. If an offender was convicted by star chamber, the sentence was likely to include a confession at the assizes, perhaps another at the quarter sessions, and in extreme cases even a third before the mayor and aldermen. This punishment was considered a disgrace, and in at least one instance a man petitioned to be left in prison rather than confess at the assizes.[13]

The judges were aware of their dignity, and inclined to stand upon it. They were annoyed, for example, "that the preaching courses, on the Sabbath days in the morning before them, have been preached by younger men that have supplied the course of some of the prebendaries, and not by the prebendaries themselves." [14] But they were also human, and not above receiving presents. Noblemen, gentry, and burgesses sent gifts of food, and the sheriff contributed handsomely in lieu of his old obligation to provide the whole of the judges' diet. As a result, they had to buy only the incidentals of their enormous meals.[15]

The sheriff's other responsibilities to the judges were of a more serious nature. The major one was the selection of a jury, a task which sometimes taxed his honesty and that of his subordinates. If the case was important, he was likely to choose the jurors himself, and to be "pressed for favor therein by special letters and messengers." [16] If the

12. "Paid the tailor . . . to make Hinderly a suit against he came to the trial at the jail delivery . . . 6*s.* 8*d.*" *Ibid.*, 1501, fo. 100v.

13. *H.M.C.*, *Salisbury MSS.*, XII, 45–46; see also John Hawarde, *Les Reportes del Cases in Camera Stellata, 1593–1609,* pp. 134, 373.

14. The prebendaries were ordered to preach their own sermons in future. MS. Cathedral Act Book, Gloucester, I, 44v.

15. For a detailed account of such presents at Gloucester, see W. D. Cooper, "The Expenses of the Judges of Assize Riding the Western and Oxford Circuits, . . . 1596–1601," in *The Camden Miscellany,* IV (London, 1858), 46–47. For similar entertainment provided by the sheriff of Derbyshire, see J. C. Cox, *Three Centuries of Derbyshire Annals,* II, 56–58.

16. Smyth, *Description,* p. 339. Smyth himself was not averse to using such pressure: his accounts contain an entry of 10*s.* paid "to the sheriff to return an indifferent jury." G.P.L. MS. 16,528, fo. 15.

case was unimportant, he was likely to leave the details to his bailiff. Since the bailiff was a poorer man, he was more susceptible to bribery. An example in the reign of King James shows the system at its worst.

A man was charged with rape, and "put himself upon the country." A relative of the accused, before the trial, bribed the bailiff to secure a friendly jury, and the bailiff bought the promises of a number of men "to appear of his jury and to show him favor and acquit him, whatsoever evidence should be produced against him." The bailiff brought these men into court, and presented their names to the sheriff. The sheriff innocently selected a jury from the list, and the case went to trial. The evidence against the defendant was damning, as the judges pointed out in their charge. But the jurors were squeamish, "knowing it to be a fearful thing before Almighty God unjustly to spill blood," and brought in an acquittal. The court was unimpressed by their pious scruples, and bound them over, then and there, to answer in star chamber for their "lewd misdemeanors." [17] The bailiff got his money, and the culprit his acquittal; apparently none but the jury was called to account.

The lot of jurors was often a hard one. If they were honest, they might be ignorant, and their ignorance might either be punished as dishonesty or taken advantage of by the unscrupulous.[18] Their jury service gained them nothing, and placed them under the Damoclean sword of star chamber. Many were willing to buy immunity, and the government was willing to let them—provided they paid enough. The privy council, in 1607, laid down certain conditions on which men might be excused. There must

17. St. Ch. 8/42/21.

18. In one of Lord Berkeley's lawsuits, for example, the jury decided for him. One of their number was a gentleman of learning, who favored the other side; he persuaded them to let him draw up the verdict. He twisted its meaning in the process, and thereby "abused the truth of his own conscience and of all his fellow jurors." They protested, but had no redress. John Smyth, *Lives of the Berkeleys (The Berkeley MSS.,* I–II), II, 316–17.

always be enough available jurors to serve the ends of justice, and some men of every degree; those with wisdom and experience were to be least readily discharged. There was to be a sliding scale of fines for exemption, ranging from £20 to £6 13*s.* 4*d.*, "to be increased as the values and abilities of the persons may induce you." [19] The size of these fines is the clearest index of men's aversion to jury duty.

After this digression upon the sheriff's juries, we may turn from the sheriff himself to a consideration of his deputies. At once there are difficulties. These lesser men were for the most part of humble station, and some of them appear so rarely in the records of the time that even their offices remain obscure. About others the evidence is abundant. The disparity must be accepted, and the following pages will be a summary of such material as there is.

The undersheriff was the sheriff's legal handyman. He helped him through the red tape of entering office, acted as his agent in formal dealings with the forest officials, disbursed money for the wages of J.P.'s serving at quarter sessions, and handled a large part of the routine business connected with paying the farm of the county into the exchequer.[20] He was also closely concerned with debtors. If a recognizance was forfeited to the crown, the collection of money or distraint of goods was likely to devolve on him. The same applied to private debts: creditors enlisted his aid in collecting their money from the debtor or his sureties.[21] And the debtor's desire to stave off payment bred temptation.

19. These instructions probably applied only to jurors at quarter sessions. Lansd. MS. 232, fo. 54.

20. An undersheriff, in 1635–36, spent something over £100 in a year for fees and disbursements; see his certified accounts, E. 101/560/15–16. If an undersheriff failed to pay the J.P.'s their wages, the sheriff was apparently responsible; a Yorkshire sheriff was fined £10 in quarter sessions because his deputy had refused such payment. Atkinson, *Sessions Records,* I, 194–95; for a general discussion of these minor officers, see Cheyney, *History of England,* chapters xxxix and xl.

21. For examples in point, see E. 133/1243, and C. 24/222, Clerk *v.* Poyntz.

In an age when the validity of a writ was affected by the character of the man who served it, a modicum of bribery was inevitable. The undersheriff, as one of the principal process-servers, must have been often tempted; at times he succumbed. "He hath heard of £3 more that was paid to the deputy sheriff, to procure him or his substitute to stay the sale of the cattle levied by him for three days, and hath likewise heard of £11 more." [22] "Thereupon he . . . paid him, at two several times, the sum of £4 to be discharged of the said recognizance, for which the said Thayer promised to discharge this deponent and his sureties thereof." [23] Such accusations are natural, and only their rarity is surprising.

As an officer of police, the undersheriff appears only once. He was trying to arrest one Anthony Bustard, suspected of complicity in Essex's revolt. He went to Bustard's house and demanded admittance; in his hand he carried a staff of office, not as undersheriff but as bailiff of the hundred of St. Briavels. Bustard refused to let him in, and he concluded that the house harbored traitors. He gathered a company of men to help him, and promised them £2 if the arrest were made. They started for the town cross, to proclaim Bustard a rebel. At this point the door was opened, the company swarmed into the house, and the curtain falls. Bustard was apparently cleared of suspicion, since he later brought suit for illegal entry.[24]

This undersheriff was also bailiff of a hundred. But there was no connection between the two offices, although one man might hold both. The hundred bailiff is one of the most obscure figures in local government. There is little information about him, and in consequence he has been

22. E. 134/22 Jas. I/H/25.

23. The deponent was a husbandman who had forfeited to the crown an £80 recognizance. The undersheriff distrained some cattle from him and his sureties, thereby precipitating the £4 gift. Instead of discharging the recognizance, he made a further distraint. The husbandman got his cattle back, on his promise to pay £1 more; this he failed to do until he was arrested, "whereupon this deponent paid the same." St. Ch. 5/T/6/19.

24. St. Ch. 5/B/95/35.

confused with the bailiff of a manor, the sheriff's bailiff, and even the high constable of the hundred.[25] Almost the only thing which can be said with certainty about him is that he was not the same as any of these three. He bought his office from the crown, and the grant was for life. But he might sell it as he saw fit, together with the "fees, profits, and commodities thereunto belonging." What these were is impossible to say; they were apparently large enough to make the office a form of investment. One man might be bailiff of several hundreds, and might appoint a deputy to do the actual work.[26]

This work was similar to the legal work of the under-

25. The confusion of manorial and hundred bailiff can be explained by the history of the hundred court, which survived in this period only where it was in private hands. (Webb, *English Local Government: The Manor and the Borough,* I, 50.) These private courts were in hundreds, like Berkeley, which were coterminous with a manor; they merged with the leet court of the manor, and the hundred bailiff merged with the manorial bailiff. It is for this reason that the "hundred" bailiff of Berkeley was elected in court down to 1900. (Helen M. Cam, *The Hundred and the Hundred Rolls, an Outline of Local Government in Medieval England* [London, 1930], p. 147; see pp. 145–48 for a discussion of the hundred bailiff during the middle ages.) I have found no indication that a hundred bailiff was elected in court, but it was the normal way of choosing a manorial bailiff. For another example of this combination of offices, where witnesses are evenly divided as to whether a man is bailiff of the manor or the hundred, see E. 134/22 Jas. I/E/3.

One man, similarly, was at times both hundred bailiff and sheriff's bailiff, a combination which has led a contemporary and a modern author to imply that these two offices were identical. (Henry Best, *Rural Economy in Yorkshire in 1641, Being the Farming and Account Books of Henry Best,* Surtees Society, XXXIII, 90–91; Cheyney, *History of England,* II, 389.) This could not have been true; the sheriff's bailiff was appointed by the sheriff, and only for the duration of his year of office.

J. C. Cox asserts that *high constable* and *bailiff* "were used as almost equivalent expressions for the same office, namely, the principal official or reeve of the hundred." (*Derbyshire Annals,* I, 95.) While this may have been true in the Midlands, I have no reason to think that it was true in Gloucestershire.

26. From the one local case which throws light on this official. A man was bailiff of three hundreds, and the office was sold and resold three times during his lifetime. When the last buyer was fraudulently ousted by an earlier one, he brought a chancery suit to recover his property. C. 2/Jas. I/H/20/8.

sheriff. The bailiff summoned jurors from his hundred for trials at the assizes and sessions.[27] He delivered warrants and writs, collected money due to the crown, and might be called to London "to answer the duty of his audit." [28] He had the power to distrain, and he or his deputies were as likely as the undersheriff to be bribed for not using it.[29] If he had further authority or other duties, there is no record of them.

The other official of the hundred was the high constable. Some of his functions are indistinguishable from those of the bailiff. He summoned juries, at least for trials before special commissioners. In some instances he distrained, as in the case of the assessors who were fined for voting instead of assessing. He received warrants from the sheriff for the arrest of rioters. He also played an active part in the collection of ship money, and perhaps of other taxes.[30]

27. From the deposition of the hundred bailiff of St. Briavels. The jurors whom he summoned were the freeholders "nominated upon the sheriff's book." (E. 134/16 Chas. I/M/36.) In the same hundred there was a "bailiff at large," who served for ten years; his duties were to collect herbage and pawnage money from the inhabitants for their common in the forest. (E. 134/16–17 Chas. I/H/1.) He was apparently another example of the combined hundred and manorial bailiff.

28. The hundred bailiff of Wotton in 1596; G.P.L. MS. 16,529, fo. 22. The officers of this hundred seem to have been a trial to some of their neighbors. "Now the upstart hundred of Wotton, with the officers thereof, storeth and sayeth that now they are more stronger than ever they were. So I tell them that they doth revive like unto a man that hath been long very sick, and upon a sudden his stomach is very good and doth make a very good meal, as though he should recover and live long; but within two or three days after he dieth." 1605; *ibid.,* 16,530, fo. 68.

29. For an example, where deputy bailiffs were bribed with cash and with "12*d.* in ale at an alehouse," see E. 134/11 Chas. I/E/1.

30. The high constable was in theory a general tax-collector, and had duties in connection with the trained bands. (Cheyney, *History of England,* II, 391 ff.) I have found no indication that he performed either function in Gloucestershire, but my evidence is purely negative. For the activities mentioned in the text, see above, p. 30, and below, pp. 63, 126–28, 200.

There were two high constables in each of the larger hundreds, and one in the others. I have no information about how they were chosen. In the neighboring county of Somerset, they were appointed sometimes by one parish within the hundred, and sometimes (if a manor embraced a hundred) by the manorial steward; in the kingdom as a whole, at least

In one respect he differed from the hundred bailiff. The high constable, as his name implies, was a policeman. The work of arresting men was usually deputed to the petty constable, but his superior might perform it in person if the occasion warranted. As with the undersheriff, we have only one sight of him in this rôle: the high constable of Grumboldash involved in a rough-and-tumble fight with a man and his wife and their son, during which the wife "did in struggling hit her mouth on the end or side of a staff, . . . and thereby hurt her mouth."[31] If this was typical of his police work, it was more undignified than dangerous.

The high constable was either a gentleman, or a yeoman of considerable substance.[32] The same is not true of his

by 1655, they were normally chosen by the J.P.'s, either in or out of sessions. E. H. Bates Harbin, *Quarter Sessions Records for the County of Somerset,* I, 9, 30, 342; II, 313; Michael Dalton, *The Countrey Justice, Containing the Practice of the Justices of the Peace out of Their Sessions,* p. 53.

31. St. Ch. 5/H/14/34. Another high constable appears in a different light. He was "a man of great wealth and ability," who showed his ability by staging a riot in the streets of Thornbury, and making a bonfire of the ducking stool. When the mayor collected men to put out the fire, there was a pitched battle between the rioters and the citizens. (*Ibid.,* 8/128/1.) For a similar case, in which a high constable was dismissed by the sessions for riotous conduct, see J. H. E. Bennett and J. C. Dewhurst, *Quarter Sessions Records of the County Palatine of Chester, 1559–1760,* p. 70.

32. In 1623, the report that a man has been high constable is adduced to buttress the claim that he is accounted, "in the country where he dwelleth, to be a very honorable, wealthy, and substantial man." (St. Ch. 8/208/5.) A modern author asserts that by the reign of King James, "the status of the office had steadily declined: instead of . . . the 'yeomen of the better class' spoken of by Lord Bacon, we find alehouse-keepers and petty tradesmen, hardly less ignorant than the petty constables they were supposed to instruct, undertaking the office for the sake of profit . . . without any serious intention of learning their work." (W. L. M. Lee, *A History of Police in England* [London, 1901], p. 113.) The author deepens this picture of gloom by remarking that the office was executed by paid and permanent deputies, that the constable was increasingly permitted to shirk his responsibilities and use his office for tyranny and extortion, that his moral character and that of the J. P.'s were steadily deteriorating; his conclusion is that the Civil Wars are explained by the police system of the Stuarts, which compelled men to defend their opinions with their swords. (*Ibid.,* pp. 83–86, 111, 114, 120–21, 123.) It is needless to add that these rampant generalities

immediate subordinate, who was a man of little learning and less social position. The petty constable was at the bottom of the list of civil officials, and in some ways was the most important of them all. His authority could be, and was, easily flouted. But he was close to the people, closer even than the justice, and to the ordinary villager he personified authority. The information about him is abundant, and it is revealing enough to be dealt with at some length.

He was chosen in a variety of ways. Sometimes he was appointed by the J. P.'s, sometimes by the steward of the manor; often he was elected in the manorial court. In one case the inhabitants of certain houses filled the office in succession, while those of the others went scot free.[33] In another, a parish hired the same man as constable for seventeen years; two of the local gentry paid half his wages, and the other half was divided among the parishioners.[34]

Constable and *tithingman* were usually interchangeable terms, just as *parish, township,* and *tithing* were interchangeable terms for his bailiwick. At times a large parish had both a constable and a tithingman, and the

are undocumented. Most of them are directly contrary to the evidence.

33. St. Ch. 8/235/20. This was by no means peculiar to Gloucestershire. For similar cases, in which the office went either with houses or with parcels of land, see H. H. Copnall, *Nottinghamshire County Records,* pp. 18–19; Cox, *Derbyshire Annals,* I, 108–09, 112; S. C. Ratcliff and H. C. Johnson, *Warwick County Records,* I, 184. For appointments by justices, and supervision of the constables by juries and J. P.'s in quarter sessions, see W. J. and W. L. Hardy, *Hertford County Records,* V, 87, 169, 250–51.

The clearest evidence which I have found of a constable's distaste for office is at Bibury. One Nathaniel Coxwell was elected in court, and ordered to take his oath of office before a J. P. within eight days, on pain of a £1 fine. He neglected to do so, and at the next court his fine was declared forfeit. He went on ignoring the orders of the court, and absenting himself from its meetings, for the better part of a decade, 1630–40. The fines imposed on him were sometimes as much as £2 each; there is no sign that they were collected, or that they ever induced him to submit to the direction of the court. Court roll of Bibury, no. 79 in case 6 of the Sherborne MSS.

34. He was paid 17*s.* a year. E. 134/16 Jas. I/M/19.

constable was then the superior. This was true at Wotton, where the tithingman's sole duty was to present yearly in the manorial court "a writing in paper of mill-wight and ale-wight within his tithing." The constable had no duty to the court, and never made a presentment; but if the tithingman was fined for omitting his, the constable might have to pay the fine.[35] If there was no tithingman, the constable either made the presentment himself, or brought in two men from the tithing to make it for him.[36]

These presentments usually dealt with such things as false weights and measures, waifs and strays in the parish, felons' goods which had been confiscated, and often petty crime as well. In a typical example, three men are presented for selling ale contrary to the assizes, one for encroaching on the lord's waste, one for "affray with blood" and one for simple affray, one for violating local traffic laws by driving three wains through the town.[37]

The constable had a number of other routine duties. He distrained on goods of defaulting debtors. He received a sum of money each year from the parishioners, and laid it out on various minor taxes, repairs to parish property, gifts to migrant paupers.[38] In most of these activities he resembled the churchwarden, who will be discussed later in connection with the parish. But he was alone in his most important function, which was that of police.

His principal duty was to preserve the king's peace, and

35. G.P.L. MSS. 16,529, fo. 22; 16,530, fo. 14. For a discussion of the constable as a manorial official, see Webb, *Parish and County,* pp. 26–29. The combination of a constable and several tithingmen in one parish was apparently peculiar to the western counties; see William Lambard, *The Duties of Constables, Borsholders, Tythingmen, and Such Other Lowe and Lay Ministers of the Peace,* p. 10. A synonym for tithingman, *headborough,* was not used locally, but appears in occasional royal warrants; for a discussion of these terms, see Cheyney, *History of England,* II, chapter xli. I have used *constable,* for the sake of clarity, whenever it appears that the parish had only one officer.

36. It was not always clear which he should do; see G.P.L. MS. 16,531, fo. 101.

37. *Ibid.,* 16,533, fo. 39.

38. Details are to be found in a constable's accounts, *ibid.,* RF 216.12. For the constable as a tax-collector, see below, chapter v.

to arrest those who broke it. Neither task was easy in as lawless a county as Gloucestershire, and the roll of the constable's woes is a long one. We first see him trying to keep the peace. A man by the name of Hodgkins was harvesting some wheat which he claimed was his. The constable questioned his right to it, and asked whether he meant to carry it away. Hodgkins' reply was that a question of ownership was no concern of a constable.

"It is mine, and I will have it, or I will kill or be killed."

The constable asked by what authority he would have it.

"What hath the constable to do in this matter?"

"Nothing," replied an onlooker, "but to keep the king's peace," which the constable then commanded him to keep.

"Art thou the constable? Have at thee first!" The result was a battle royal, and a suit in star chamber.[39]

Like the hundred bailiff, the constable had a black staff of office. This he carried with him when going to make an arrest. It was supposed to serve the same purpose as a modern policeman's badge, but seems to have had little effect.[40] The culprit frequently resisted, especially when he had friends to back him up.[41] Even more often he used the weapons of a rich vocabulary, and drove off the constable by threats. "Lousy knave and rascal knave!" [42] "If

39. St. Ch. 8/210/17.

40. "Thomas Bishop, . . . seeing the said Somers with a black staff, did swear that he would forthwith put on his clothes and come unto him." Instead he behaved so outrageously that the mayor had to be routed from bed to help the constable. *Ibid.*, 8/71/5.

41. This was particularly true in the Forest of Dean, and is well illustrated by the affair of Richard Carpenter. The constable and three companions went to arrest him, but first stopped at an alehouse to buttress their courage. A friend of Carpenter warned him, and then went to the alehouse to delay the constable with talk and drink. By the time they returned to the house, they were met by a crowd of some forty men, half of them armed; Carpenter had meanwhile been disguised as a woman, which apparently deceived no one. The constable and his men were roughly used, and Carpenter's brother boasted "that if the sheriff should come and bring two hundred men with him, he should not carry away his brother, Richard Carpenter, from his father's door." E. 133/1160.

42. The same man marveled that the constable dared arrest his servant "so near his nose." St. Ch. 8/119/10.

he did come again, he would beat him and let his guts about his heels." [43] These threats were not idle. If the constable did not go home, he risked a knife in his ribs. He often went home.[44]

A further duty was the supervision of watch and ward. Here also he had his troubles, of which one example is worth mention. After the discovery of the Gunpowder Plot, in 1605, the constable of Stanton was ordered to search for and arrest Thomas Percy, one of the conspirators. The constable appointed some villagers to keep watch. He made the mistake of including among them a recalcitrant yeoman, who persuaded a number of his friends to refuse to serve unless the constable provided him with "many things which the speedy execution of the said service would not permit." Otherwise the constable could keep watch by himself. To round off his refusal, the yeoman called him a "false knave, cosening knave, and bribing knave." [45]

Watch and ward were not the only way in which the constable was dependent on his neighbors. When a number of prisoners had been arrested, he often could not guard them alone. He was then forced to call in the butcher and baker as impromptu jailers, and he was lucky if they were dependable. A case in Frampton on Severn illustrates the trouble he encountered. The Justices had committed four prisoners to his custody, to keep overnight and bring be-

43. Glouc. Corp. Rec. 1567, p. 10.

44. His theoretical redress for an attack was an action of trespass. (William Lambard, *Eirenarcha, or of the Office of Iustices of Peace,* pp. 132–33.) The attacker might also be presented by the jury at quarter sessions; for an example, see Hardy, *Hertford,* I, 24. But the form of redress most commonly sought in Gloucestershire seems to have been a suit in star chamber. The plaintiff was usually either the constable or the private citizen for whom he had been acting; in one case (St. Ch. 8/119/10) the high constable sued in the name of his subordinates, the petty constable and tithingmen.

45. The constable responded with a star-chamber suit. (St. Ch. 8/178/27.) A simpler method was to prosecute in the manorial court. At Painswick, for example, a man was fined £1 in 1614 for a number of offenses, among them that of neglecting the watch, "being by the constable demanded." G.P.L. MS. R 229.45.

fore them in the morning. He took them to an inn in the village, where he lodged them for the night.[46] Since he had no intention of staying up himself, he set a guard of a butcher, a baker, a smith, and a husbandman, and then went home to bed. When he returned in the morning, he found all the prisoners but only one watchman. He drafted another jailer from the house, and went out to seek reinforcements. When he returned the second time, he found one prisoner gone, and was told that he had wandered off into another building with two of the villagers. He followed, and found the two without the prisoner. When he asked for him, "they both answered and said he was there, but he was gone they knew not whither." [47]

This is typical of the sort of scrape in which constables found themselves. It is of course true that we hear of nothing except their difficulties. When the path of duty was smooth, their work was done without leaving any record in the files of state papers or star chamber. But with due allowance for this, there is ample evidence that the constable's life was a troubled one. And no wonder. He was the lowest of officials, and hence the most easily flouted. He had no one to fall back on but his neighbors; even when they remembered their duty to help him, their help was unreliable. His office demanded a high degree of tact and courage, and there is no reason to think that he had more than his share of either. He usually had little educa-

46. This was against the letter of the law: a constable might imprison only in the stocks or the common jail. (Lambard, *Eirenarcha,* p. 133.) But his conduct would apparently have been permissible if the prisoners had been of the gentry, for whom the stocks and jail were considered too ignominious; see Dalton, *Countrey Justice,* pp. 5, 410.

47. S.P. 16/194/60, fo. 5. The constable of Painswick was involved in similar difficulties in 1614, in connection with a murder case. A man refused to help him suppress the disturbances which led to the murder; after the crime, a tithingman and another refused him their aid in taking some suspects to be examined by a justice. The delinquents were fined in the manorial court. G.P.L. MS. R 229.45.

For the constable's work in connection with the military, see below, pp. 95–96. The fullest details which I have found of his work elsewhere are in J. P. Earwaker, *The Constables' Accounts of the Manor of Manchester from the Year 1612 to the Year 1647,* I–II.

tion, as his writing testifies, and he was frequently called upon to deal with men far above his social status. It is not surprising that he was often a harassed man, one who commands more sympathy and less censure than he ever received from his superiors.

One group of these superiors remains to be considered. The justices of the peace were the backbone of county officialdom, and the range of their functions was so wide that their position is hard to define.[48] As keepers of the peace they were subordinate to the sheriff; as justices they were superior to him, and it was his duty to carry out their decisions. From the point of view of the central government, they were the instruments for almost any task. They might be used for inspecting drainage, ordering musters or pressing men for the wars, collecting taxes, supervising the clothiers. From the point of view of the people, they were policemen, judges, and general advisers to the neighborhood. Above all they were the spokesmen for the county. If the privy council was interfering too much with local interests, or the exchequer with local purses, their lordships at Whitehall were likely to receive a firm protest from the Gloucestershire J. P.'s.[49] If the government persisted in its policy, the justices were likely to be afflicted by a sudden inability to carry out orders.[50] They might be hardworked agents of the crown, but they never ceased to be local squires.

48. These functions were being increased by parliament as the period went on, and a number of them will appear incidentally in later chapters. One of the best contemporary accounts of these statutory duties is of course Lambard's *Eirenarcha;* a concise and excellent modern account is contained in the introduction to Joan Wake, *Quarter Sessions Records of the County of Northampton,* pp. xi–xlviii.

49. For examples in point, see below, pp. 101, 105, 169, 172; 208–09, 212; for similar cases in Devon, see A. H. A. Hamilton, [Devon] *Quarter Sessions from Queen Elizabeth to Queen Anne,* pp. 8, 17, 45–46.

In Elizabeth's reign, Gloucestershire justices were occasionally summoned to London to discuss local affairs. In 1596, for example, the privy council summoned a group of J. P.'s and gentry for this purpose. (*A.P.C., 1596–97,* p. 259.) Under the Stuarts, communication with the council was almost entirely by letter.

50. As with the saltpeter monopoly, and the attempts to destroy tobacco; see below, pp. 155, 160–61.

Not all the J. P.'s came from the squirarchy. Some were nobles: Henry, Lord Berkeley, for example, was a justice for most of his long life.[51] Some were burgesses: members of the corporation who were justices *ex officio*. But these were exceptions; the vast majority of the J. P.'s were drawn from the same ruling caste which supplied the knights, sheriffs, and deputy lieutenants of the county. They were influential men, by family tradition as well as by office. "We see now by common experience, if a man purchase but the ill will of a justice of peace in his country, . . . how it is requited again one time or another." [52]

Many of them were no better than they should have been, and the records of star chamber are full of their transgressions. Sir Henry Winston, J. P., struck two bailiffs who were arresting a man; he also "showed some pity to two or three small offenders." For these offenses he was prosecuted "of malice" by Sir Thomas Throckmorton, and sentenced by star chamber to a £1,000 fine, and public confession at the Gloucester assizes.[53] Sir Thomas himself seems to have been a chronic trouble-maker. He had scarcely ended his quarrel with Poyntz before he was in new difficulties. He had tried to clear his prospective son-in-law of a murder charge, in consideration of £800; he had abused his authority as a J. P. in order to profit from an unjustifiable conviction; he had imprisoned a man in his house, to force him to give evidence. For these and other crimes, at one time and another, he was fined £2,200 in star chamber and sentenced to imprisonment and public penance.[54]

51. In 2 Elizabeth, when he was still a youngster, he sent the lord keeper a New Year's gift, "which gave him the mindfulness of putting him into the commission of the peace, wherein . . . he continued all the residue of his life." Smyth, *Lives of the Berkeleys,* II, 287.

52. William Woodwall, *A Sermon . . . Wherein Are Chiefly Shewed Both the Originall & Accidental Causes of Euerie Dearth and Famine, and Especially of This Dearth in England Now, 1608 and 1609,* pp. 13–14.

53. *H.M.C., Salisbury MSS.,* XII, 45–46.

54. Hawarde, *Reportes del Cases,* pp. 134–37, 243. Hawarde reports only the decisions in these cases. The depositions in one of them contain

Sir John Stafford was a common informer. He was rebuked for bringing suit in a cause which was no concern of his. Two years later he did substantially the same thing, and "was greatly blamed by the court that being so worthy a gentleman, so honorably descended, and otherwise so well deserving in himself, that he would stoop to so base an office as to be an informer, who albeit they be necessary in every well-governed state, yet for the most part they are of the meaner and worst kind of people." [55]

These misdeeds were peccadillos by comparison with those charged to George Huntley. He first appears, as a young man, in connection with a robbery in 1595. This affair was a local *cause célèbre,* and some of its details are worth attention. Three brothers, by the name of Purnell, were attacked on Cromhall Heath and robbed of some £400. They raised the hue and cry, and the robbers were tracked to a valley within two miles of Huntley's house. When Huntley was told of this, he sent out his servants to arouse the neighboring towns, and himself stayed at home. About midnight he went out to look at the weather, and heard two men ride into his court. He mistook them for his own, and asked why they had stayed so long. One of them answered,

"Oh, be you there? I am glad I have found you, for I have ridden all night and tired my horse to come unto you."

Huntley recognized the voice; it was a man named Bridges, the last person he had expected.

"What do you here at this time of night?"

further enlightening accusations against Sir Thomas. A suspect, held on a murder charge, was offered his freedom if he would give Sir Thomas some of his sheep. He refused, and was told "that his tail should break his neck for refusing to bestow the said sheep." Sir Thomas tried to influence the coroner's jury which was investigating the murder. He sent for his bailiff, who was on the jury, and expressed his surprise that he would befriend the suspect; "I will not wish thee to hold with him." More delicate intimidation was tried on other jurors: "Let the rest of Sir Thomas Throckmorton's tenants that were of the jury use their discretion." St. Ch. 5/W/20/8.

55. Hawarde, *Reportes del Cases,* pp. 331–32; see also p. 242.

"I promised to come to you as I came from Bristol."

Huntley replied that he did not like it, and explained that "there was a robbery done that night, and the hue and cry was abroad, and that he feared he was one of them that did the robbery." Bridges denied it hotly, but kept his distance. His companion made the mistake of coming closer. Huntley seized him "and demanded of him what he was, who answered he was a good fellow. This examinate, still holding him fast, said he must know him better. And thereupon Bridges said, 'I pray you let him go! He is one that you know.' But this examinate replied he would not let him go, for he would hang for neither of them both." The prisoner submitted, after a struggle, and his companion rode away.

The second man was captured in the morning, and both were imprisoned in Huntley's house.[56] They refused to be examined by the nearest justice, Sir Thomas Throckmorton, because one of them was a runaway servant of his, and hence feared that he would receive "the more extremity and less favor." The pair stayed at Huntley's, where the Purnells came to identify them. The identification was singularly vague. One of the brothers admitted that one of the prisoners "was very like one that did rob them"; and another said "that he would neither excuse him nor accuse him." Huntley was convinced that they were both guilty. He offered them the alternatives of revealing the money, in which case he would help them in every way he could, or of keeping silence and going to the gallows. They chose the former, confessed the robbery, and succeeded in locating some £200 of the stolen money.[57]

The reason for the Purnells' vagueness now appears.

56. Huntley was in the commission of the peace, but had been commanded by the lord keeper not to take oath until some pending suits had been settled; he therefore said that he had "not intermeddled as a justice." His keeping the men in his house was thus clearly illegal; even if he had acted as a justice, it would have been against the letter of the law: a J. P., like a constable, might imprison only in the common jail. Lambard, *Eirenarcha,* p. 133.

57. S.P. 12/252/63.

Huntley was fulfilling his promise to help the prisoners. He suggested that the Purnells should take the £200, and in return let him hush up the whole affair. They agreed, "for that they were poor men, and had been undone if they should not have had their money again." [58] The prisoners were arraigned before some J. P.'s in Cirencester, who were not told that they had already confessed. They were accordingly released on bail, at which the Purnells professed to be amazed.[59] Huntley's strategem was on the verge of succeeding, when in some way it was betrayed. He and the Purnells were hailed before star chamber, convicted, imprisoned, and heavily fined.[60]

Another case, almost thirty years later, shows that Huntley's conduct did not improve with age. He had started life as "a poor, mean man," but by 1622 he had raised himself by his dark practices to a great estate. He had driven his son to suicide, and he was no better justice than parent. The star chamber had several times put him out of office for misconduct, presumably of the sort we have just seen. But he ignored the court. "He gets much money, and works his own ends, and in great contempt of the decree still executes his office." One of his favorite means of getting money was to summon a man, bind him over for the quarter sessions, take a surety for his appearance, and then for a small additional sum release him before the sessions.[61]

The case to which these charges were incidental was one of illegal arrest. He had procured from his cousin, the undersheriff's deputy, a warrant against Sir Nicholas Poyntz. Poyntz came to call on him, "owing not a penny and thinking him his friend," and was arrested in the parlor. He was imprisoned in the house all night, and not allowed to send for bail. The next day four of his captors,

58. S.P. 12/252/60. This agreement made the Purnells accessories after the fact; see Lambard, *Eirenarcha,* p. 290.

59. S.P. 12/252/97; see also S.P. 12/252/ nos. 61–62, 64, 74, 96, 98–99.

60. Hawarde, *Reportes del Cases,* pp. 23–25.

61. This was apparently a common abuse; see Lambard, *Eirenarcha,* p. 188.

who were Huntley's plowmen, put him on a horse and led him toward the common jail. On the way they passed a cousin of Huntley's who was also a J. P.; Poyntz demanded redress, but the justice would do nothing. Later they came to an alehouse, where the plowmen stopped to refresh themselves. Poyntz broke from them, locked them in, and "recovered a strong house and kept it with weapons." The plowmen went for the constable, raised a posse of some three hundred men, and laid siege to him. Some higher officials then appeared, who demanded sight of the warrant. "Seeing but a bare warrant upon a *laetitat*, . . . the officers would do nothing in it. So George Huntley came himself and tore the warrant. And so Sir Nicholas Poyntz, grievously hurt, went home." [62]

This strange behavior is seen only through the eyes of Huntley's enemy, Sir Nicholas. Much of his evidence must be discounted, but enough remains to show that a justice could be arbitrary and high-handed. It is more than likely that Sir Nicholas gave him reason. If Huntley had started as "a poor mean man," he was not born to the ruling class. Poyntz was; his family for generations had held office in the county.

Even when justices were of their class, the gentry did not stand in awe of them. Life was too informal; the community was too small; men knew each other too well to be impressed by the accident of office. A J. P. might be arrogant and quick to fight, but the shoe was as likely to be on the other foot. Arrogance was common, and violence was in the air men breathed. We have seen how a justice treated a gentleman; we shall now see in two cases how gentlemen treated a justice.

The J. P. in question was the worthy, honorably descended informer, Sir John Stafford. In the first case, he was trying to obtain justice for himself. He had lost a bullock, and heard that it was in Henry Townsend's close.

62. S.P. 14/135/65. It is impossible to be certain that this was the same George Huntley who was before star chamber in 1595, but the resemblances are almost conclusive.

He went to investigate; Townsend told him nothing but lies. Sir John said so, and threatened to make trouble for him. Townsend answered that he cared for nothing he could do. Sir John wanted to take him to an officer; he refused to go unless he were charged with a felony, and "very rudely and irefully did clap his hat on his head," which was one of the most common ways of insulting a justice. He took up his pike, and seemed on the verge of attacking Sir John, who was wholly unarmed. "In respect of all which matters, and to prevent the danger of the said Townsend's pike, he this defendant did suddenly with a very small riding wand give the said Townsend only one blow over the face, to amaze him, and withal this defendant suddenly did wheel about his horse from the said Townsend, thereby to escape all danger." Townsend then seemed to realize the danger of flouting authority, and as suddenly gave in. He agreed to go to an officer, and was given the choice of any justice in the county.[63] Later, however, the one blow struck to amaze him was made a charge against Sir John in star chamber. The judges fined him £20: "it was a great offence because he was a justice of the peace and ought to keep the peace, and thus [he was] a bad example." [64]

In the second case, Sir John was exposed to more flagrant contempt, this time in the performance of his office. A Mr. Thomas Jarvis was summoned before him, by a warrant which had no seal. Jarvis took exception to it, but was forced to appear by the constable. Sir John explained that he never used a seal on such a warrant. Jarvis replied that it was invalid, "and was not to be sent to men of his sort in such a fashion, and in such manner, and likewise said that he could direct the said Sir John Stafford in his

63. St. Ch. 5/S/70/4. Such freedom in choosing a justice seems to have been conventional. When a warrant from Sir Thomas Sackville was served upon a churchwarden of Bibury, in 1635, the latter refused to appear on the ground that Sir Thomas "had sent him word that he kept or had a book of revenge, and that he would not leave him worth a groat." Bibury MS. 146 in Sherborne MSS.

64. Hawarde, *Reportes del Cases,* p. 234.

office. Mr. Jarvis did then walk up and down before Sir John Stafford with his hat sometimes on his head, and sometimes off, and sometimes sitting, and sometimes walking, and in contemptuous manner softly whistling with his mouth and making a noise; and thereupon the said Sir John said to the said Mr. Jarvis, 'I am glad to see you so merry. . . .' By reason of the contemptuous behavior of the said Mr. Jarvis . . . Sir John Stafford called the said Mr. Jarvis knave, and Mr. Jarvis then answered that peradventure he was as good a man as ——, and so stayed his speech." [65]

Contempt, violence, and oppression are the darker side of the picture. The lighter side is the mass of work which the justices accomplished. Keeping the peace was only part of it; later chapters will show that they were active in almost every field of government. Here it will be sufficient to mention only two spheres of that activity, special commissions and quarter sessions.

A special commission was created by a writ under the great seal, to perform a specific task. This might be either public or private. Sometimes it was to collect taxes, or investigate drains; sometimes it was to survey disputed land, or to take depositions of local witnesses in a suit before one of the London courts. Any man of local prominence might be appointed a commissioner, and we even find a doctor of divinity taking testimony in a libel action.[66] But of those commissioners whose names have survived, the majority were justices. If only because of their experience, they were a natural choice. While a commissioner's work was thus not a part of the J. P.'s office as such, it was a likely addition to his burdens.

The procedure of a commission varied with its purpose. The most important one, the commission of the subsidy,

65. St. Ch. 8/246/26, fo. 16. A J. P. in Shipton Moyne, about 1620, received a terse message from one of the neighboring gentry: "Tell the justice of peace from me that he lies, that the justice is a knave, and that I will knock the justice's pate." *Ibid.*, 8/175/24.

66. G.P.L. MS. RX 354.28.

will be considered later. The others were created for equally definite ends. The sewer commissioners, for example, were to inquire into the drainage of the countryside, and to see that ditches were well scoured. They made out a list of jurors, sent it to the high constable, and ordered him to have the jury assemble before them at a given time and place, on pain of a £2 fine. The jurors were "diligently to view and survey all the defaults within their limits presentable," and to present them before the commission.[67]

These presenting juries sometimes vitiated the work of a commission. A juror was supposed to be impartial, then as now, and might be discharged if it was thought that he was under the influence of a commissioner.[68] He might also be influenced by his own interest or by public opinion to deliver an untrue verdict. A special commission from the exchequer, for instance, impanelled a jury to inquire into conditions in the Forest of Dean. The verdict was ready after three weeks. But the commissioners had reason to suspect that some of the questions they had asked were uncomfortable ones for the jurors to answer honestly. Before they received the verdict, therefore, they asked how it had been arrived at, and offered their assistance "in reconciling any such wants as haply might be found in their presentment." The jury peremptorily refused. It would explain nothing "except we would first receive their presentment, which the foreman held in his hands signed and sealed by them all (only one excepted), *de bene esse* as their absolute verdict." The commission refused with equal firmness. The presentment was left in the foreman's

67. *Ibid.*, 16,524, fo. 34. For a contemporary definition of *sewer,* and a discussion of the work of sewer commissioners, see Dalton, *Countrey Justice,* pp. 155–57.

68. When Stafford was one of the commissioners, "Henry Came was put off from the jury under color of going to tables with Sir John Stafford." (G.P.L. MS. 16.529, fo. 70.) The jury's verdict was also safeguarded, and a juror might be presented for revealing it prematurely; for an example, see Copnall, *Nottinghamshire,* p. 24.

hands, the jury was dismissed, and the exchequer was requested to issue a new commission.[69]

These particular commissioners may have been none too impartial themselves, although partiality in a public investigation exposed them to the censures of Whitehall. Their local prejudice had freer rein in a private case, particularly one between a native and an outsider. We see it at work in one of the quarrels between John Smyth and Benjamin Crokey, in which a local commission surveyed and valued the lands of Wotton School. Crokey complained of its findings to the house of lords, and asserted "that no better justice might be expected from gentlemen of this county." The house arranged what amounted to a change of venue: the land was to be revalued by a new commission of gentlemen from Wiltshire.[70]

These private cases formed a large part of the work of special commissions, but it was work which was often done with singular inefficiency. The place selected for the hearing might be inconvenient, and the commissioners selected by one side or the other might be unable to reach it.[71] Some of the commissioners might become impatient, and leave before the others arrived. In such cases the jurors and witnesses would have to be discharged, after the litigants had paid their expenses. The commission would be returned, a new one sent down from London, and the whole procedure begun over again.[72] There is no question

69. E. 178/3837.

70. G.P.L. MS. RX 354.26. For an account of a jury presentment before such a commission, see Smyth, *Description*, pp. 337–38, 346–47.

71. Such an impasse occurred in 1598, when a commission in an exchequer case met in the parish church of Upton St. Leonards. It was winter, and the commissioners considered the church "very unmeet, by reason neither convenient houseroom nor horsemeat nor man's meat was to be had for money in that place, the time being very cold and moist." The commissioners selected by the plaintiffs never appeared, pleading other business, and the defendants were forced to petition the exchequer to have the commission renewed. The commissioners fervently urged the court to set the next hearing in Gloucester, where they might keep warm. E. 134/40 Eliz./H/3.

72. John Smyth has left an amusing account of one of these footless meetings. "There met not a complete number of commissioners. Dr.

that a great deal of necessary work was accomplished by commissioners. But as was so often the case, it was not accomplished without waste effort.

This work, for the average justice, was varied and time-consuming. But it was also spasmodic, and cannot be compared in scope or importance with the work which he regularly encountered in quarter sessions. When he was on the bench, he was in much the same position for the shire as a privy councilor for the nation. The sessions were a court, with criminal jurisdiction over offenses which were too serious to be handled by one or two justices alone, and not serious enough to be held over for the assizes.[73] But the sessions were also an administrative body, with the wide responsibilities of a privy council *in parvo*. In various ways, from general decree to individual decision, the bench sought to regulate the daily life of the community.[74]

There were two courts of quarter sessions, just as there were two groups of sheriffs, one for the outshire and one for the inshire. In accordance with a special provision of the city charter, both met in Gloucester unless there was some extraordinary reason, such as plague, for meeting

Baber [D.D.] came thither betimes in the morning, and stayed until about twelve o'clock alone. And then came the high sheriff and Dr. Hill, a canon of Bristol, two other of the commissioners. About twenty of the jury returned were ready to appear, who after they had put Crokey to £5 charge in diet returned as they came. Only the three commissioners made certificate of their attendance, and the reason that they could not proceed, to my lord chancellor, to the end that a new commission may be had. . . . There were some speeches passed between the commissioners and the idiot Crokey and myself, not worth a hasty relation." (G.P.L. MS. 16,529, fo. 52.) The only result of the hearing seems to have been a chance for the litigants to insult each other.

73. For the offenses within the jurisdiction of the court, see Lambard, *Eirenarcha,* pp. 404–84. I have omitted petty sessions entirely, because the material contains only passing references to them.

74. The inshire sessions already showed signs of developing into what the Webbs describe after 1689 as "an inchoate provincial legislature." (*Parish and County,* p. 533; see also pp. 533–50.) The trend is most clearly perceptible in the enactments relating to bastardy and to alehouses, for which see below, pp. 67–69, 141–42. Whether the same was true of the outshire sessions is a matter of conjecture.

elsewhere.[75] The courtroom was in the Booth Hall, a building which was used indiscriminately for the city market, the assizes, the two quarter sessions, "and other general assemblies whatsoever." [76]

While records of the inshire sessions remain, those of the outshire sessions are almost nonexistent.[77] But at this time there was little distinction between city and country life, especially as it was reflected in the courts: the bailiff and benchers of a leet considered much the same questions as the magistrates of Gloucester. It is therefore a tenable assumption that the sessions for the city were little different from those for the county, and that a description of one would apply almost as well to the other.

The most striking aspect of the Gloucester sessions, as a criminal court, is the absence of the death sentence. Although the records are not complete, those which sur-

75. At the beginning of the period, the outshire sessions met once at Cirencester and once at Chipping Sodbury. (Harl. MS. 4131, fos. 514, 532.) In 1639, there was an attempt to move these sessions permanently to Cirencester. But the lord keeper decided that they should remain in Gloucester, "in regard the county is large, the ways in winter dirty, and Cirencester not so commodiously situated for the convenience of the whole county, and hay, wood, and other provision thought . . . more scarce and dear there." Glouc. Corp. Rec. 1451, fos. 1–2.

76. In 1613, a £200 tax was levied on the city for the repair of this hall; only £158 was collected, and it was ordered that defaulters should be summoned before the assizes. (Lansd. MS. 232, fo. 67v.) For the use of the hall as a market, see Glouc. Corp. Rec. 1451, fo. 449.

In most counties the sessions were held at an inn. A special hall was a luxury, which may have had something to do with the fact that these outshire sessions later became an unusually efficient court. (Webb, *Parish and County,* pp. 424, 429–30.) Middlesex also had a hall of its own at this period, given by Sir Baptist Hickes; for the enthusiasm which his gift aroused, see John C. Jeaffreson, *Middlesex County Records,* II, p. xxiii.

77. The only record of the outshire sessions which I have been able to find is a MS. in the British Museum. It contains ninety-three folios of jury indictments, 1595–1601, and is miscatalogued as assize records. If this fragment is any index, the criminal business of the court was indistinguishable from that of the inshire sessions. The most common offenses were petty theft, affray with violence, evading a constable, playing games during divine service, keeping an unlicensed alehouse, obstructing or not repairing the highways. There are indictments for murder, but they are extremely rare. Harl. MS. 4131.

vive contain only one such sentence, imposed on a woman for stealing cloth.[78] This does not mean that there was a lack of violence and lust, with their concomitants of murder and rape, or that other capital offenses were less common than elsewhere. It means merely that the justices were averse to trying a prisoner whose life was at stake, and passed on the task to the judges of assize.[79] Quarter sessions were concerned with less serious matters.

The most common offense was bastardy. This problem was common to every county in England, and there were as many ways of dealing with it as there were counties. The law gave considerable latitude to the justices.[80] They

78. Glouc. Corp. Rec. 1566, Trinity, 1636.

79. The jurisdiction of quarter sessions over capital offenses is a problem which I have never seen satisfactorily answered. In some counties there were few or no death sentences; at least one editor has concluded, from the nature of his sessions records, "that the crime in the county was not serious." (J. W. Willis Bund, *Worcester County Records . . . Calendar of the Quarter Sessions Papers,* p. lxiii.) Without the assize records, this conclusion is quite unwarranted. But why were capital cases handled almost exclusively by the assizes in some counties, like Worcestershire or the city of Gloucester, and in others frequently tried by quarter sessions? Lambard's explanation is inconclusive, that J. P.'s "in the trial of felons are not nowadays much occupied," because they are required by statute to certify their proceedings at the next assizes. (*Eirenarcha,* p. 553.) This deterrent would have affected all counties equally, but in fact there was a great disparity between them. For examples of capital convictions at the sessions, see S.A.H. Burne, *The Staffordshire Quarter Sessions Rolls,* III, 266–69, 304–11; Hamilton, [Devon] *Quarter Sessions,* pp. 30–31, 39; Hardy, *Hertford,* I, 16; William Hudson and J. C. Tingey, *The Records of the City of Norwich,* I, pp. cxxxii, 314. For similar cases which the sessions refused to handle, see James Tait, *Lancashire Quarter Sessions Records,* pp. 273–74, 302. In the North Riding of Yorkshire, a number of felonies seem to have been either treated as misdemeanors, or disposed of by a plea of clergy or a fine; see Atkinson, *Sessions Records,* I, 41, 147; III, 206, 226, 267.

80. By 18 Elizabeth, c. 3, a bastardy case might be handled by two justices alone, and the punishment left to their discretion. If the bastard was chargeable, imprisonment of the mother for a year and a day in the house of correction was made mandatory by 7 James I, c. 4. Neither statute provided punishment for the father. See also Dalton, *Countrey Justice,* pp. 40–42.

The discretionary power given to justices out of sessions may well explain the difference in the number of cases which came into court in different counties. These problems may have been settled by small

used it to the full, and their policy is the clearest indication of the independence of the court as an administrative body. There is no sign that they were influenced by moral considerations. They sometimes deplored bastards, in conventional terms, but their primary concern was with a potential charge to the parish.[81]

This is most clearly indicated by their attitude toward the parents of a child who had already died. In this case the mother appeared in court and proved that the child was dead. If individuals or the parish had paid for the care of the mother or child, the father was ordered to repay the money. The case was then closed, without punishment for either parent.[82]

Indictments were often brought before the child had been born, and were then automatically referred to a later session. When it was established that the child had been born and was alive, the mother was usually committed to prison for a year and a day, according to the statute. If the putative father could be found, he was punished only with a fine.[83] He was likely to have avoided this by leaving

groups of justices in counties such as Middlesex, where the sessions records scarcely mention bastardy, and by the whole bench in counties such as Somerset and the city of Gloucester.

81. My account of Gloucester policy is based on a study of the extant volumes of sessions records, Glouc. Corp. Rec. 1566 and 1567, which contain sufficient evidence to warrant generalizations. In other counties, however, the printed evidence is sometimes meager; this must be borne in mind in the subsequent comparisons.

82. In Somerset and Lancashire, the parents of a dead child were treated with similar leniency; see Bates Harbin, *Somerset,* I, 5, 11; Tait, *Lancashire, passim.* In Hertfordshire and Middlesex, on the other hand, the putative father was flogged, and imprisoned until the child's death had been proved; see Hardy, *Hertford,* V, 104, 107; Jeaffreson, *Middlesex,* III, 12.

83. The treatment of the father in other towns was similar. At Reading, he seems to have been punished only financially, and at times to have escaped even a fine if he married the mother; at Southampton, he usually paid, but in one case was offered the choice between a £5 fine and a whipping. (J.M. Guilding, *Reading Records. Diary of the Corporation,* II, 305, 449, 464; III, 148–49, 188, 282, 284, 293–94, 397; J. W. Horrocks, *The Assembly Books of Southampton* [1602–1616], I, 97; II, 70, 86, 95.) County quarter sessions had no universal policy. In one case in Somerset, the father was left to the church courts because

town in haste. There was then nothing to do but attach any assets which he had left behind him, and punish those who had helped him escape.[84] By every means in their power, the justices strove to prevent a bastard from becoming chargeable to the community.

The other common offense was petty theft. This was of every sort, from beans to silver spoons. Sometimes the matter was referred to a jury. Its verdict was usually an acquittal or an *ignoramus*, and in either case the prisoner was discharged. A number of these small crimes seem to have been settled by the magistrates themselves. The regular punishment which they meted out was burning in the hand; women were occasionally sentenced to be whipped about the town, but this was rare. Occasionally the bench would punish prisoners, and then deliver them to the

only the mother's confession implicated him; she was released from prison when he obtained a license to marry her. In another case, however, the father was imprisoned for a year, after which it was ordered that he should not be further punished unless he were found to be wealthy. (Bates Harbin, *Somerset,* II, 228; I, 158–59.) In Staffordshire, the mother and father were put in the stocks; in Worcestershire, the father was fined and imprisoned, and the mother imprisoned for only ten days. Burne, *Staffordshire,* IV, 393; Willis Bund, *Worcestershire,* p. 248.

84. An instance in point is that of a servant who ran away before his child was born. He thoughtfully left with his master and another man the large sum of £40; the justices committed the mother to prison, and made the two men trustees to maintain the child with the father's money. Glouc. Corp. Rec. 1566, Epiphany and Easter, 1634.

The quarter sessions elsewhere showed the greatest ingenuity in obtaining support for bastards. If the mother was married to a man of means, the husband was often held responsible for his illegitimate stepchild. (Atkinson, [North Riding] *Sessions Records,* II, 200; Ernest Axon, *Manchester Sessions,* pp. 90–91; Hardy, *Hertford,* V, 84, 112; Tait, *Lancashire,* pp. 126, 177, 213.) Sometimes another man was made to pay, merely because he also had lived with the mother. (Bates Harbin, *Somerset,* I, 209, 299–300.) There is one case in which the responsibility was assigned to a man who received money from the putative father's lands, and two others in which the father of the putative father was held liable, if his son had decamped or would not pay. (Atkinson, [North Riding] *Sessions Records,* I, 7; Hardy, *Hertford,* V, 150, 218.) The bench seems to have exercised a discretionary authority which had little relation to the letter of the law.

assizes to be tried again for the same offense.[85] In one case, on the other hand, the justices practically reversed a sentence of the higher court.[86] This flash of independence was unique, but it indicates the length to which their temerity might go.

The routine work of the sessions was as varied as that of the privy council. They granted hunting licenses, and punished those who hunted without one.[87] They appointed wardens to protect the fish in the Severn and its tributaries, within the limits of the inshire.[88] They suppressed illegal games, such as skittles and shuffleboard, and made sure that informers received their shares of the fines.[89] They enforced attendance at church. They regulated alehouses. They stopped the making of malt when grain was scarce. They supervised the system of apprenticeship, and

85. In 1639, for instance, two persons were held for the assizes to be tried for housebreaking and stealing goods, "for some of which goods they were now convicted and burnt for it." Glouc. Corp. Rec. 1567, p. 8.

86. "Whereas Mary Cugley . . . and Dorothy Biddle, her apprentice, were both arraigned at the jail delivery, the said Dorothy Biddle for felony and the said Mary for being accessory thereunto, the said Dorothy being found guilty of petty larceny and Mary Cugley acquitted; it appearing to this court that the said Mary Cugley did entice and compel the said Dorothy to steal by beating of her, it is now ordered that the said Dorothy Biddle shall be whipped in Bridewell and so be discharged from her apprenticeship, and that the said Mary Cugley shall continue in the house of correction for one month, and to be kept hard to labor and to have the due correction of the house." *Ibid.,* 1566, 5 July, 1638.

87. Such licenses might be granted only to those whose income was at least £100 a year. For a discussion of the statutes, see Lambard, *Eirenarcha,* pp. 446 ff.; for typical examples of their enforcement, see Glouc. Corp. Rec. 1566, 6 June, 1631, and Michaelmas, 1633.

88. Two such wardens were appointed in 1636, to search for illegal nets "and other engines and devices," and to present their users at the sessions; each of the two was to receive half of the fines collected. (*Ibid.,* Trinity, 1636.) For a similar official in the outshire, who bought his office from the crown, see below, p. 154.

89. Informers were licensed by the court to compound with men whom they had accused, and who had pleaded not guilty. The details of procedure are obscure, but it appears that such cases were dropped as soon as the informer had been bought off. For examples, see Glouc. Corp. Rec. 1566, Easter and Trinity, 1636; for another case, of a conviction and fine for playing skittles, see *ibid.,* 1567, p. 30.

at times intervened to mitigate its rigors.[90] These justices, in short, were busy men. The government valued their work at 3*s.* apiece for each meeting of the court, but this is scarcely a measure of its value to the community.[91]

The sessions were occasionally enlivened by contempt of court. John Carter was committed "for coming before the court with his hat on his head." [92] A man used "seditious words" against a justice and the mayor, and found himself saddled with a £25 fine; the J. P.'s dignity was assessed at £5, and the mayor's at £20.[93] But while the court would not countenance an affront, its procedure was by no means rigid. The magistrates could use almost the same informality on the bench as off it. In 1639, for example, a man petitioned that he had been imprisoned for wounding Nathaniel Stephens, and wished to be released. He was advised to address his petition to Stephens, "upon answer whereof this court will take the matter into their consideration." [94]

This reference of the offender to the offended is typical of the justice which the J. P.'s dispensed. Some of their

90. In one case they freed an apprentice whose master had beaten him immoderately. In another the master had died, and his wife had left the country; the boy, on his mother's petition, was apprenticed elsewhere. In a third the apprentice had run away, and the master was ordered to pay back to the runaway's father the money which he had had from him. (*Ibid.*, 1566, Michaelmas, 1638; Michaelmas, 1633; Michaelmas, 1632, and Epiphany, 1632/33.) The system of apprenticeship was commonly abused by antedating the indentures; it was therefore ordered in 1614 that every apprentice must be bound to his trade in the presence of the mayor, and his name entered in a register. (*Ibid.*, 1451, fo. 249.) This register is still among the city archives. For the regulation of alehouses and malt-making, see below, pp. 138–41.

91. The only accounts which I have found of payments to Gloucestershire justices indicate that few attended all of the quarterly meetings. See E. 101/560/6–7, and for a general discussion of justices' fees, Lambard, *Eirenarcha,* pp. 369–70, 627 ff.

92. Glouc. Corp. Rec. 1566, Trinity, 1635.

93. *Ibid.,* Epiphany, 1634/35. For similar cases elsewhere, see Copnall, *Nottinghamshire,* pp. 24–25.

94. Glouc. Corp. Rec. 1567, p. 9. For other examples of such mediation, see Bates Harbin, *Somerset,* II, 249; Burne, *Staffordshire,* IV, 255–56; Hardy, *Hertford,* V, 186–87, 191, 215; W. H. Stevenson, *Records of the Borough of Nottingham,* IV, 177 note 4.

cases were stereotyped, and were settled in cursory fashion according to the statute in that case provided. But their work for the most part was a mixture of law and common sense, and they governed as much by informal mediation as by formal statute. We have a sight of this informality out of court, in 1602, when a number of men were brought before two Winchcomb justices for attacking John Chamberlayn, J. P. One of the accused was a gentleman, who took responsibility for all the others. He begged the justices to intercede with Chamberlayn to give up his prosecution, and solemnly promised never to misuse him again. The J. P.'s believed him (which turned out to be a mistake), and persuaded Chamberlayn to drop the case.[95]

This sort of procedure was possible because the justice was close to the people. He was sometimes defied, because of this very closeness, and then he had to take time and trouble to evoke the authority which lay behind him. But more often his intimate knowledge of the community stood him in better stead than his authority. "Giles Reade . . . was much beloved of his neighbors, and might in a reasonable sort command them." [96] Such men not only administered the law, but modified it to local needs and wishes. Even the situations which came into court indicate that a great deal was done outside, in quieter ways which have left no record, by bullying and cajoling, by letters to London, by rough diplomacy over the beer glass. Few of these justices were Solons, and few were as black as Huntley was painted. To their virtues and failings they added an innate capacity for their job.

95. St. Ch. 5/C/72/14. Another instance of rough justice is that of a servant, haled before a J. P. by her employers for having stolen 16*s.* from them. Instead of holding her for trial, the justice clapped her into the stocks; she was released after three days, and the matter apparently ended there. Gloucester Diocesan Records, XCV, 12 July, 1604.

96. E. 134/16 Jas. I/M/19.

IV

THE MILITARY GOVERNMENT OF THE COUNTY

THE LORD lieutenant was the only important county official who was not chosen from the gentry. He was always a noble, and in the first part of the period he was always a native. Elizabeth kept the office in the family of the Brydges, Lords Chandos, and by 1595 the current Lord Chandos professed to believe that he had a prescriptive right to it.[1] As soon as James came to the throne, however, the claim of the other great local family was recognized. Lord Berkeley was given a joint lieutenancy with Lord Chandos, and was later appointed alone.[2] After this break with tradition there was a varied sequence of lieutenants, sometimes a nobleman from outside, sometimes the president of the Council of Wales.

The theoretical scope of the office is shown by Lord Berkeley's commission. He was empowered to gather, equip, and train all inhabitants who were able to bear arms; to lead them against an enemy within the county or without, a rebel or a foreign invader; to govern them by martial law, and if necessary to inflict the death penalty.[3] So much for theory. Since the Spaniards did not land, and the English did not rebel, only the first duty

1. He feared that the queen would appoint another lieutenant, or associate another with him, and begged Cecil's assistance in keeping the office for him alone, as his ancestors had held it before him. In this he was successful. *H.M.C., Salisbury MSS.,* V, 340, 523; Cheyney, *History of England,* II, 363.

2. This shelving of Lord Chandos caused a tempest in the social teapot; the Countess of Derby supported him vigorously. *H.M.C., Salisbury MSS.,* XV, 230–31, 371; Gladys Scott Thomson, *Lords Lieutenants in the 16th Century. A Study in Tudor Local Administration,* p. 141 note 2.

3. Rudder, *History,* p. 276 note u. Gloucestershire was exceptional among the border counties in having a lord lieutenant of its own; most of the others were included in the lieutenancy of the president of the Council of Wales. Scott Thomson, *Lords Lieutenants,* p. 56.

had practical importance. The supervision of the military was an arduous task, and the lord lieutenant was responsible for all of it. He had to see that the trained bands were trained, and that arms and equipment were supplied by the townships or by the soldiers themselves. He had to see that the pressed levies were pressed, and to superintend the collection of coat and conduct money for their march to the port of embarkation. Much of this work was deputed. But the lord lieutenant, like the sheriff, had the final responsibility for a large and cumbersome organization.

In all military matters, he was the intermediary between the central government and the people. He was usually less susceptible to local feeling than the J. P.'s or the sheriff, but he was by no means oblivious of it. In 1628, for example, complaints were rife that money spent on billeting had not been repaid by the government. The Earl of Northampton wrote twice to soothe his deputy lieutenants in Gloucester. In the first letter he assured them that the money would be repaid out of the first subsidy granted to the king "by the happy correspondency between his Majesty and his people." In the second he renewed his pledge to be "a continual solicitor for the country . . . to do that country service." [4]

This cordiality may have been motivated by uneasiness. The inshire was chronically annoyed by the cost of the military, and never suffered gladly the interference of the lord lieutenant. Chandos had discovered this, shortly after the Armada, when he was empowered by his commission to muster the city trained bands. Gloucester at once petitioned that their chartered liberties had been infringed. After a great deal of trouble and expense to the city, a new commission of lieutenancy was obtained. Chandos was required by this commission to act in the city only through

4. Glouc. Corp. Rec. 1540, pp. 151, 154. *Country* was a usual synonym for *county*. For a discussion of the Elizabethan lieutenant as a mediator between the people and the central government, see Scott Thomson, *Lords Lieutenants,* pp. 143–45.

deputies, and was specifically debarred from doing anything without the consent of at least three of them, of whom the mayor or recorder had to be one.[5] The inshire never had its own lord lieutenant, but its deputy lieutenants were as independent as the burgesses could make them.

The same was true of Tewkesbury, after its incorporation in 1609. When the lord lieutenant tried to muster the citizens in 1618, he reported to London that they met him with a complete refusal, and claimed exemption under their charter. The privy council referred the question to the attorney and solicitor general.[6] They gave an opinion that the town bailiffs were legally empowered to have complete charge of their own trained bands, to muster and train the inhabitants, and to exclude "any lieutenant or commission for musters." [7] The example of the inshire had been taken to heart.

While the authority of the lord lieutenant was being curtailed in the towns, in other ways it was growing beyond the scope of his commission. He had been created for purely military purposes. But he was an important local figure, and important figures rarely stayed in their compartments. His activities gradually spread into the field of civil government, as the privy council began to use him for a variety of purposes. There was a quarrel in the hundred of Berkeley, and a petition to the council; the lord lieutenant and J. P.'s were instructed to look into it.[8] A Bristol man had some malt stolen, and the council's pursuivant made matters worse by his misconduct;

5. Glouc. Corp. Rec., uncatalogued letter book, fo. 3. Gloucester had thus obtained the same privileged position as London, for which see Scott Thomson, *Lords Lieutenants,* pp. 57–58.

6. *A.P.C., 1617–19,* p. 252.

7. Tewkes. Corp. Rec. 1, fo. 13. I have omitted commissioners of musters, because this is the only reference to them. They were usually appointed only when there was no lord lieutenant; the Gloucestershire lieutenancy seems to have been uninterrupted throughout the period. For a discussion of these commissioners, see Cheyney, *History of England,* II, 363–64.

8. *A.P.C., 1592,* p. 91.

the lord lieutenant was told to take over the investigation.[9] There were riots in the Forest of Dean; the lord lieutenant was ordered there in person, to assist the sheriff. The king decided to raise money by a forced loan, and it was the lord lieutenant who tried to collect it.[10] This official, in modern terms, might at various times be a referee, a detective, a commander of the Territorials or National Guard, a tax collector, and a general in the regular army.

The variety of work soon necessitated a variety of agents. The most important of these, but the last to be created, were the deputy lieutenants. Gloucester had long had them, as a means of keeping the lord lieutenant outside the gates. There were none for the outshire, however, until 1601, when Lord Chandos informed the privy council that he needed assistance, and the lord keeper was instructed to appoint three men as his deputies.[11] From then on the lord lieutenant was never without them.

If the lieutenant was an outsider, and especially if he had several counties in his commission, he was likely to give his deputies a large degree of independence. But if he lived in the county, his supervision was closer. Lord Berkeley, for example, was either a strict disciplinarian, or was bullied into strictness by his masterful steward. Smyth has left a memorandum of a letter which must have brought the deputies to attention.

> That my lord . . . write to his deputy lieutenants, requiring a more speedy and careful course than hath been taken.

9. He was to get assistance from such local J. P.'s as he cared to select. (*Ibid., 1590–91,* p. 254.) Chandos once used his authority for his own purposes, when he evicted a widow from a parsonage; he was told by the council to put her back, and to explain himself. (*Ibid., 1595–96,* p. 19.) Even in this case he may have been acting as a landlord rather than an official, and there is no other sign that he or his successors used their position to increase their personal influence. They were completely different, in this respect, from such a lord lieutenant as the Earl of Huntingdon, who managed his county of Leicester with a hot-tempered paternalism which went far beyond the scope of his commission. See Bateson, *Leicester,* IV, 5–6, 61 ff., 130–31, 161, 380.

10. See below, pp. 117–19, 197.

11. *A.P.C., 1601–04,* p. 161.

That he [is] advertised of overmuch remissness and slackness, or rather a contempt in some inferior captains, than well standeth with connivance or toleration on his part. That his deputies have his authority derived to them, and copies as well of his patent as of the council's letters sent to him, and therefore cannot pretend ignorance or excuse. That he is advertised from some of his honorable friends that notice is taken of this remissness, and that if other counties were taken for precedents, that their delinquence is doubled. And that they fail not to punish such inferior constables and others as seem to neglect or contempt authority in this kind, according to the authority they already have.[12]

The deputy lieutenants, like the lord lieutenant, had a wide range of functions in local government. But since they were usually J. P.'s as well, their work in civil administration is indistinguishable from that of the justices. Their military work can best be understood by considering the whole system of which they were a part.

During the fifty years under discussion, England felt itself in constant danger of invasion. The privy council, to judge by its letters, was in a state of chronic nervousness. It was steadily harping on the necessity of preparedness, steadily bewailing the condition of the military establishment, and steadily bombarding local officials with requests and commands to improve it. That establishment was a burden to Gloucestershire. The county was far removed from the hub of national policy, and the danger of invasion was less real than the present need of spending money and effort on the military.[13]

12. G.P.L. MS. 16,071, fo. 41. It seems probable from the wording that the constables referred to were the petty constables. For their rôle as pressmasters, see below, pp. 95–96.

13. But because the county was remote, it was subject to occasional panics. The widespread fear of a Spanish invasion in 1598 is echoed in the town records of Tewkesbury; the clerk seems to have been equally perturbed by the "great rumors spread throughout the realm of the dangers and troubles then imminent," and by "the infinite charges of the realm about that fearful rumors, supposed to be in Ireland and here £300,000." (Tewkes. Corp. Rec. 1, fo. 22v.) A similar alarm,

The burden imposed on the county by the nervousness of Whitehall is most clearly illustrated by the upkeep of the beacons. There were a number of beacons in Gloucestershire, along the edge of the Cotswolds; they were supposed to be maintained and guarded day in and day out, year in and year out, ready to be fired at a moment's notice.[14] The guard was composed of men from the surrounding parishes. The petty constable chose four of the most substantial villagers who were not in the trained bands, and led them to the beacon in the afternoon. They were provided with wood and candles against the night, and had to keep watch until the next afternoon. They were then relieved by another group of four from the next parish, and so on in rotation for all the parishes around the beacon.[15]

This duty was of course neglected. In 1626 the lord lieutenant was ordered to enforce it more strictly, and nine years later the deputy lieutenants reported that they had done so.[16] Some new beacons were also built in 1635; the watch was a burden to the countryside, and in November there was a petition for relief. The council allowed the new beacons to be neglected, but insisted that the old ones should be guarded as before.[17]

twenty years later, vied in importance with a local scandal. "A huge navy of Spaniards feared, and thereupon followed great mustering, and the junior bailiff sued the elder for misbehavior in his office." Giles Geast Rent Book, *anno* 1618.

14. Each beacon consisted of a pile of logs with a covered pan on top; the pan was filled with pitch and rosin, and had a fuse of tow to light it. A carpenter and a smith were assigned to make the necessary repairs, which cost on an average between £3 and £5 a year. Lansd. MS. 232, fo. 68; Bodl. MS. Rawl. C 358, fo. 37v.

15. If a parish was more populous than its neighbors, its quota of watchmen was to be proportionally increased in units of four. Lansd. MS. 232, fo. 68–68v.

16. Glouc. Corp. Rec. 1540, pp. 79, 206.

17. *Ibid.*, p. 209. The only beacons which I have been able to locate were at Stinchcombe, King's Weston (near the mouth of the Bristol Avon), and Tolldown, south of Tormarton. (Bodl. MS. Rawl. C 358, fo. 37v.) For details of beacons in Northamptonshire, see Joan Wake, *A Copy of Papers Relating to Musters, Beacons, Subsidies, etc., in the County of Northampton, A.D. 1586–1623,* pp. lxxxviii–lxxxix, 7–8.

This watch was an extreme example of governmental fussiness. By 1635, it was forty-seven years since

Skiddaw saw the fire that burnt on Gaunt's embattled pile
And the red glare on Skiddaw woke the burghers of Carlisle.

There was small possibility of an invasion, and no conceivable reason to have beacons guarded day and night. A hilltop on the edge of the Cotswolds is bitterly cold in winter, and the villagers must have found their watch as uncomfortable as it was annoying. It is not surprising that they neglected it, but rather that they performed it at all.

The other exactions of the military authorities were more justifiable and more burdensome. They were concerned with the two types of soldiers which composed the county force: the trained bands and the pressed levies. The latter, as will soon be seen, were a nuisance and an expense. But from the viewpoint of the officials, of the taxpayers, and of the men liable for service, it was the trained bands which were the core of the system. Their precise number is impossible to estimate. At the time of the Armada they apparently contained some 3,500 men in all, but by 1608 the total had shrunk to little more than 2,000.[18] The county was divided into five divisions, which were the units for mustering the bands. Each division contributed men in rough proportion to its able-bodied population. But the diligence of local officials, or the temper of

18. A certificate from Lord Chandos, in 1587, stated that there were 308 pioneers, 200 cavalry, and 3,000 foot. The cavalry were divided into 40 lances and 160 light horse, and in every 100 foot there were 40 calivers, 20 pikes, 20 bills, 20 bows, and 10 muskets; the discrepancy of 10 is doubtless a clerical error. (S.P. 12/205/32; see also Robert Atkyns, *The Ancient and Present State of Gloucestershire,* p. 34; Rudder, *History,* p. 49.) An estimate for 1607–08 gave approximately the same numbers. (*H.M.C., Beaulieu MSS.,* p. 82.) This second estimate, however, is almost certainly an exaggeration. The most reliable figures at any time during the period are for 1608, in John Smyth, *Men and Armour for Gloucestershire in 1608. The Names and Surnames of All the Able and Sufficient Men in Body Fit for His Majesty's Service in the Wars;* he lists only 2,102 trained men in the entire county.

the people, must have varied widely from one division to another, and the relative size of the trained bands varied accordingly.[19]

The men were supposedly the cream of the county: gentry, freeholders, "good farmers or their sons that are like to be resident in the country." Residence was important. Servants were not to be taken unless necessary, because they were likely to move away; once they were taken, they might not be discharged by their masters without license from the lord lieutenant or his deputy.[20] A similar license was required for any soldier who wished to leave his town or parish. All the troops were to be "well affected in religion," and to take the oaths of supremacy and allegiance.[21]

But it was hard to maintain a high standard, for the men whom the government wished for service were the very men who had influence enough to evade it. Before Chandos was barred from Gloucester, he did his best to choose "divers and sundry of the better sort of citizens under the calling of justices of the peace. . . . Nevertheless all such as had borne office, or were persons fit for service in the city or county for the wars, were not brought in to be trained at any time, but challenged and drawn away by the diligence and endeavor of Mr. Luke Garnons, then mayor." [22] It was such diligence as this which must have

19. The range of difference between the divisions will be apparent from the following table, for 1608, which I have compiled from Smyth's *Men and Armour:*

Division	*Able-bodied men*	*Trained men*	*Percentage of trained to able-bodied*
Inshire	1,858	288	15.5
Forest	2,884	300	10.4
Kiftsgate	4,234	368	8.7
Seven Hundreds	4,713	562	11.9
Berkeley	5,054	584	11.6
Totals	18,743	2,102	11.21

20. 1628; Glouc. Corp. Rec. 1540, p. 161.
21. 1629; *ibid.,* p. 189.
22. 1588; *ibid.,* uncatalogued letter book, fo. 12.

brought grey hairs to privy councilors and lords lieutenants.

The musters were held separately for each division. The government was considerate of the soldiers, and ordered the choice of a central and convenient place, "in such sort as the men may not be driven to travel far for their assembly, nor be longer continued in the service than shall be very needful." But all the musters in the county had to be held on the same day, or the men would cheat like schoolboys. When musters were on different days, it had been found that some persons, "having been unprovided of such arms and furniture as they were charged with, have borrowed the same from some others of the county to serve for the present view, thereby to shut themselves from the charge of providing it." [23] The season of the musters was also a matter of concern. They were frequently held at "times proper for husbandry," and kept men away from their fields. King Charles, "reflecting upon the ease of his subjects," therefore ordered that the yearly muster should be held in Whitsun week, when it was thought that it would cause the least interruption to the farmers.[24]

These Whitsun musters were not the only ones, although they were those at which attendance was most strictly enforced and inspection was most careful. The trained bands

23. 1612; Lansd. MS. 232, fo. 63v. For similar conditions in Essex, see Andrew Clark, "The Essex Territorial Force in 1608," *The Essex Review,* XVII (1908), 104, 107; Andrew Clark, "The Essex Territorial Force, 1625–38," *ibid.,* XVIII (1909), 69.

24. Glouc. Corp. Rec. 1540, p. 87; for similar leniency in Elizabeth's time, see Scott Thomson, *Lords Lieutenants,* p. 89 and note 1. The city of Gloucester, in 1626, showed a flash of unusual zeal. Some of the more important members of the city trained bands, "with other gentlemen well affected unto the knowledge and practice of martial discipline," petitioned the corporation to allow them to build a practice yard at their own expense. The petition was referred to the privy council, which approved with pleasure. The corporation generously decided to pay the cost itself, and bargained with a carpenter who owned a convenient site. (*A.P.C., 1625–26,* pp. 477–78; Glouc. Corp. Rec. 1451, fo. 512.) This action may well have been inspired by a similar one at Bristol the year before, for which see John Latimer, *The Annals of Bristol in the Seventeenth Century,* p. 93.

were also drilled at other times, usually holidays, and the lord lieutenant was instructed by the crown to do all he could "to bring the country to affect the exercise of arms, and to make that the subject of their entertainments and recreations at their time of liberty." [25] The mustermasters, similarly, were told to assist the captains "at convenient times, besides the ordinary times of musters, to teach the trained soldiers their duties and postures and the right use of their arms." [26]

These captains were amateurs, chosen by the lord lieutenant from the local gentry. Each commanded a company; the men wore the captain's colors, and he was responsible for their training and equipment.[27] But in time of peace his importance was slight. The real work was done by the mustermaster, who was a professional appointed by the lord lieutenant. He had to be "a practic soldier and expert in the wars abroad," and had to have a testimonial of his foreign service. His duties were various. He supervised the drilling, saw to it that the men were able-bodied and fit for service, and inspected their armor to make sure that it was in condition, and that those who could afford to were using their own. He was obliged to remain in the county, so as to be always at the command of the lord lieutenant or his deputies.[28]

His pay was fixed only by custom. In 1629, the deputy

25. 1626; Glouc. Corp. Rec. 1540, p. 69.

26. 1629; Lansd. MS. 232, fo. 68.

27. For the wearing of colors, see below, p. 85. A captain's commission in 1630 mentions a company of one hundred men, whom he is to have ready for the king's service on any occasion; he is to be guided in his office by instructions either from the lord lieutenant or from the colonel of his regiment. (Add. MS. 28,212, fo. 76.) I have found no further reference to the colonel.

28. 1629; Lansd. MS. 232, fo. 68. In 1626, the government had distributed among the counties, as mustermasters, a number of officers from the wars in the Low Countries, to teach the trained bands a more "modern" manual of arms. (Glouc. Corp. Rec. 1540, p. 69.) Details of the old manual, and of the method of training at the beginning of the period, will be found in Surrey Record Society, *Surrey Musters,* pp. 387–89; John Harland, *The Lancashire Lieutenancy under the Tudors and Stuarts,* I, pp. xliv–xlv; see also Wake, *Copy of Papers Relating to Musters,* pp. 5–7.

lieutenants reported to the privy council that the money was furnished by voluntary contribution. Either they or the lord lieutenant "did intimate the sum desired to the country, and prevailed with more or less success as the country took notice of the pains and service of the mustermaster." [29] Sometimes the country took no notice at all, and objected to paying him anything. The inhabitants of Thornbury, in 1603, petitioned the justices to use their influence with the lord lieutenant to do away with the mustermaster and his salary, "we knowing the captains of the bands to be gentlemen of great worship, who with their officers can very well view and judge all necessaries for his Majesty's service therein without him. We generally think this charge superfluous, and do most grieve at it of all other payments." [30] When the mustermaster tried to collect his wages, he may well have grieved even more.

We have a glimpse of a captain, and incidentally of a mustermaster, at one of the rare moments when the trained bands were on the march. They were on their way to Tilbury, to meet the threatened Spanish invasion of 1588. One of the gentry had persuaded a retainer to fill his place in the company of that fiery J. P., Sir Thomas Throckmorton. The substitute had not been a soldier for years, and his arrival put Sir Thomas in a towering rage. The recruit tried to appease it by docility. "He, this deponent, did put on his armor (being a musket) and presently did go to the mustermaster and did desire him to appoint him . . . his place, which he did; and so this deponent followed

29. Lansd. MS. 232, fo. 69. There is no record of the amount which he received. In Hertfordshire, two years later, he was given £30 by the quarter sessions, and in Somerset his regular pay seems to have been £50 a year. Hardy, *Hertford,* V, 136; Bates Harbin, *Somerset,* I, 143–44, 217–18; II, 61.

30. G.P.L. MS. 16,526, fo. 30 (2). It might be expected that the privy council would have enforced this payment, but there is no record that it ever did so. An interesting letter on this subject, in which the council writes with surprising humility to the officials of Northamptonshire, is printed in Wake, *Copy of Papers Relating to Musters,* p. 125. Miss Scott Thomson asserts that the mustermaster was paid by the crown (*Lords Lieutenants,* p. 86 and note 4), but this was certainly not the case in Gloucestershire.

his direction." But as soon as the company reached Cirencester, Sir Thomas summoned the man and told him that he must discharge him unless he could buy a petronel with which to replace his musket.[31] He could not afford it; the cost, with accessories, would come to some £14. He urged Sir Thomas to spare him such great expense. "But the said Sir Thomas replied, and said that it must be so." The man then asked to be given his musket, which was apparently not his own; he hoped to sell it in part payment for his petronel. Sir Thomas refused, and the disgruntled soldier was about to seek out "the captain for the petronels" when the general discharge arrived from London.[32]

Sir Thomas was trying to convert a foot soldier into a light cavalryman. He was probably doing so for reasons of his own, but he may have been carrying out orders. The light horse was being reorganized that summer. The authorities had decided that there was no purpose in the staves which the horsemen carried, and they were therefore replaced with petronels at the owners' expense; thenceforth the cavalry was divided between lances and petronels. The equipment of a lancer consisted of corselet, headpiece, lance, sword, dagger, and pistol. The "petronel furnished," about which Sir Thomas was so insistent, included a petronel with flask and touchbox, "a cassock of the lord lieutenant's colors," a girdle and belt, and a

31. Subsequent pages refer frequently to arms and armor; it would be well at this point to define the terms. A *petronel* was a heavy horse-pistol, longer than the light pistol of the lancers and shorter than an arquebus. A *caliver* was a light gun and a *musket* a heavy one; the latter was used with a rest and the former without. A *saker* was a small cannon. The pike, halberd, and bill were all metal-tipped staves, differing in the complexity of the business end: a *pike* had a simple spear-head, a *halberd* a cutting edge and a spear-head, and a *bill* a cutting edge and two spear-heads, one at the top and one at the back of the blade. A *corselet* was the body armor: breastplate and backplate. A *morion* was a simple helmet without a visor, and a *burganet* a helmet with one; a *pauldron* was armor for the shoulder, and a *poitrel* was the breastplate for a horse. A *bandoleer* was a belt which went over the shoulder, and a *hangar* was an arrangement of straps for attaching the sword to the belt. For further details, see Wake, *Copy of Papers Relating to Musters,* pp. lix–lxii.

32. St. Ch. 5/T/24/16.

sword and dagger. The horses had saddles of moroccan leather, "with bit, headstall reins, poitrel, and crupper girths and stirrups very strong and serviceable." "And every morion, burganet, and headpiece, and every pick and halberd, armed and trimmed with the captain's colors, blue and white. And of the like colors were the strings of their flask and touchbox." [33]

If a man was "of the better sort," he was expected to provide this equipment himself. Instead of defining the better sort, the privy council left it to the discretion of the local officials.[34] Such discretion could be easily abused: equipment was expensive, especially that of the cavalry. By 1612, it cost £3 4*s.* 5*d.* for the light horse, and £4 7*s.* 4*d.* for the lancers. The costume of the footmen is harder to determine. They were of three sorts, depending on whether they were armed with muskets, calivers, or pikes. From the prices of individual articles, it would appear that the cost of a "musket furnished" was £1 9*s.* 8*d.*, of a caliver £1 4*s.* 8*d.*, and of a pike £1 5*s.* 8*d.*[35] No small investment for even a substantial farmer.

The central government tried to keep a minute check on this equipment, and to punish those who were unprovided. In 1629, for example, the privy council ordered that the muster rolls and certificates of the number of men should be sent to Whitehall, "to the end we may . . .

33. Glouc. Corp. Rec., uncatalogued letter book, fos. 3v–4v. A "pick" was a pike.

34. 1629; *ibid.*, 1540, p. 190.

35. The musket cost 16*s.*, the caliver 11*s.*, the pike 3*s.*, the mold and bullet-bag 1*s.* 4*d.*, the bandoleer 1*s.* 8*d.*, the morion 2*s.* 8*d.*, and "swords with Turkey blades, basket hilts, and with girdle and hangers" came to 8*s.* Pauldrons were still being worn, and cost 4*s.* 6*d.* the pair. (*Ibid.*, uncatalogued letter book, fo. 5–5v; these prices are confirmed by Bodl. MS. Rawl. C 358, fo. 35–35v, except that the "pike furnished" comes to only £1 3*s.*) For details of prices in Northamptonshire, see Wake, *Copy of Papers Relating to Musters,* pp. lxxxii, 32.

The caliver was still in common use at this period, but by 1618 the privy council was trying to replace it with the musket. "The modern use doth altogether exclude the caliver as unserviceable, and not to be allowed upon any musters of arms." Quoted by Clark, "Essex Territorial Force," *Essex Review,* XVII, 102.

apply fit remedies where any defects shall be found." Any man who was deficient was to give bond to appear at Oxford on a given date, with full arms and armor, there to be inspected by the king in person. Absentees would be severely punished.[36]

Some men could not afford their own equipment, and for them a supply was provided. The sources of this supply were both public and private. The public stock was kept in every town and many parishes, to be borrowed by the poorer sort and returned in good condition. The size of each arsenal varied with that of the community, and its usefulness must have varied with the initiative of local authorities.[37] The private stock was distributed among hundreds of individuals all over the county. They came from high and low: a nobleman, whose house contained a supply of pikes and muskets; a widow on the subsidy rolls, who was responsible for half a caliver; a yeoman, "unable in body," who provided two corselets for

36. Glouc. Corp. Rec. 1540, p. 191.

37. Gloucester, in 1636, had on hand 10 muskets, 14 bandoleers, 21 pikes furnished and 47 bills, 13 "guilded sakers" (*guilted sackets*), and 5 "murthering pieces"; there were also 10 barrels of gunpowder, 3 of bullets, and 2 of match. Tewkesbury had almost as much, while a small town like Northleach, in 1594, had only 2 corselets, 2 calivers, 2 swords and daggers, and 3 girdles. Glouc. Corp. Rec. 1501, fo. 32v; Tewkes. Corp. Rec. 1, fo. 5; Northleach Court Book, p. 303; for further references to local supplies, see Glouc. Corp. Rec., uncatalogued letter book, fo. 32; Tewkes. Corp. Rec. 1, fo. 95v; Bodl. MS. Rawl. C 358, fo. 37v; *A.P.C., 1617–19,* p. 367; James Bennett, *The History of Tewkesbury,* pp. 44–46.

At Tewkesbury, in 1595, the bailiffs were instructed by the lord lieutenant to turn their fifteen archers into musketeers. They did so over a period of three years, at a cost of £41. As late as 1628, however, the arsenal still contained ten bows and fifteen sheaves of arrows. The parish of Dursley, at the same period, was keeping its archery butts in repair; the inhabitants of Ablington, in 1618, were presented at the manorial court for neglecting their butts, as well as their bows and arquebuses. (Tewkes. Corp. Rec. 1, fos. 5, 21; Dursley churchwardens' accounts for 1617, 1621, etc.; court roll of Bibury, 31 March, 1618, no. 79 in case 6 of Sherborne MSS.) The free school at Chipping Campden had an arsenal of its own: the treasurer's accounts for 1639 refer to muskets, and to turning the school yard into a training ground; there is also a payment of £1 4*s*. "toward the school artillery."

the service which he could not perform himself. Most of the contributions were small, but their total was a great deal larger than the public stock.[38]

Armor was constantly being worn out or lost, and money collected from the taxpayers to replace it. At the beginning of the period, the privy council objected that these informal and sporadic taxations were "commonly laid on the meaner sort of persons, worst able to bear the same." [39] But by King Charles's time, the assessments seem to have been regularized on the basis of land.[40] This brought them into accord with the general theory of providing for the trained bands, a theory akin to the feudal: military obligation went with land, and a man's contribu-

38. The obligation of providing arms was imposed on landed proprietors, as well as on the towns, by 4/5 Philip & Mary, c. 2. The resultant private arsenals were sometimes of considerable size. Lord Chandos had one at Sudeley Castle, of which an inventory is preserved in S.P. 16/18/30. I have found no record of that at Berkeley Castle, but it was large enough so that its caretaker was paid some 20*s.* a year, in wages and for replacing worn parts of weapons. G.P.L. MSS. 16,525, fo. 32 (2); 16,071, fos. 58, 81.

The fullest information about county equipment is in Smyth's survey of 1608, *Men and Armour,* in which he purports to mention each weapon and piece of armor due from a parish or a private citizen. His records are incomplete, because he has omitted the large arsenals in towns and in country houses. It is questionable how far these omissions vitiate his figures; they certainly do not greatly affect the proportion between public and private equipment, since here they tend to balance each other. The following table, which I have compiled from his book, indicates that the public supply was much less than the private in three out of five divisions, and did not exist in a fourth.

Division	*Corselets*		*Muskets*		*Calivers*	
	Public	Private	Public	Private	Public	Private
Inshire	27	96	10	58	24	76
Forest	0	85	0	56	0	109
Kiftsgate	114	42	36	22	103	41
Seven Hundreds	65	163	29	97	88	128
Berkeley	37	197	26	214	12	138
Totals	243	583	101	447	227	492
	826		548		719	

39. *A.P.C., 1592–93,* pp. 130–31.

40. At least in parts of the county: a man at Badgeworth, in 1637, paid 1*s.* 10*d.* the yardland for the mustermaster's wages and new parish armor. G.P.L. MS. R 31.4, fo. 40.

tion depended on the size of his holding. The theory was indefinite, in that there seems to have been no attempt to fix a ratio between what a man held and what he provided. The deputy lieutenants assessed him, and apparently used their own discretion.[41] But the principle survived, at least in the mind of the government. As late as 1629, the privy council warned the lord lieutenant not to allow landowners to escape their obligation. Much land which had once contributed to horse or foot had since been divided or sold; purchasers in the future were to be warned of their obligation; and present deficiencies were to be made up "either by the owners or tenants or occupiers thereof." [42] The phrasing is singularly vague, but the underlying concept is clear.

It was intended that no one of any means should escape this contribution. A recusant was not allowed to have arms in his possession, but this did not excuse him from providing for the trained bands. He was to buy such arms as were charged to him, and to have them kept in repair by other men. At every muster, the deputy lieutenants were to appoint a man to wear this equipment, and the recusant was to pay for his proxy. After the muster, the arms were again to be sequestrated.[43]

As soon as a man was accused of recusancy, the government confiscated his armor. This happened to the notorious Earl of Castlehaven in 1625. The Bishop of Gloucester was instructed to go to Sudeley Castle (which

41. The deputy lieutenants, in 1626, complained to the lord lieutenant of a man whom they had charged with providing a horse. Although he held lands in the county worth almost £300 a year, he not only refused the horse "with unrespectful and contemptuous answer," but denied their right to demand it. "We are in this enforced to crave aid of your lordship. My lord, we hold not fit to neglect ourselves, but we chiefly regard the service. If this pass with impunity, we shall be discouraged to proceed any further." The lord lieutenant forwarded their letter to the privy council, with a request for more specific powers. S.P. 16/41/31 (I); for similar difficulties in Essex, see Clark, "Essex Territorial Force," *Essex Review,* XVII, 102–03; XVIII, 66–67.

42. Glouc. Corp. Rec. 1540, p. 190.

43. 1635; *ibid.,* p. 205.

the earl had recently bought from Lord Chandos), and seize such arms as he found. He took with him five J. P.'s, one of them a deputy lieutenant; the armor was delivered to them without resistance. There was less than the bishop expected, but the earl protested that he had no more. An investigation revealed that Lord Chandos had sold much of his arsenal before Lord Castlehaven had moved in. The latter had not replenished it, because he had his own supply in his other houses. "Here in effect he is a stranger, without any great number either of friends, tenants, servants or followers." [44]

This raid was not the bishop's only encounter with military duties. He was also responsible for the weapons of his clergy. The government was eminently fair: it excused no one who was able to pay, neither recusant nobles nor country vicars. If the clergymen could not afford substitutes to carry their arms at the musters, the proxies were sometimes furnished for them.[45] But arms they always had to have. The Archbishop of Canterbury sent instructions to the various bishops, in accordance with which the assessments were made. The Bishop of Gloucester then sent a copy of the list to the lord lieutenant or his deputies, who checked against it the arms presented at the musters. Clergymen whose arms were defective were dealt with like other defaulters.[46] "His Majesty's pleasure . . . is that in those things that tend to the enabling and fitting of men for common defense of the realm, they of the clergy

44. S.P. 16/18/30. Lord Castlehaven had been forewarned of the raid by the bishop, and had protested against it on the ground that he was not a recusant. S.P. 16/12/40; for details of similar raids in Northamptonshire, see Joan Wake, *The Montagu Musters Book, A.D. 1602–1623,* pp. xliii–xlvi, 224–31.

45. In 1590, clergymen were to be given able men, "which by reason of their smallness of house and retinue they could not provide, to wear the armor which they had in readiness for her Majesty's service." *A.P.C., 1590,* p. 84; see also Scott Thomson, *Lords Lieutenants,* p. 92 and notes 1–2.

46. 1635; Glouc. Corp. Rec. 1540, p. 205. The bishop occasionally inspected the arms and armor of the clergy; for an account of such an inspection, and of the bishop's detailed report, see *N. & Q.* V, 126–31.

are no more to be exempted nor spared than any of his Majesty's other subjects."[47]

In spite of all these contributors from various walks of life, in spite of the exactions of the government, in spite of the efforts of lieutenants and mustermasters, and the constant exhortations of the privy council—in spite of endless trouble taken, the trained bands were not a success. As early as 1612, the privy council was gloomy about them.[48] But the revelation of weakness did not come until the eve of the Civil Wars. We have a description of the Gloucestershire trained bands in 1640, by a man who knew them well. It is a summary of effort wasted. There was "a gross ignorance and supine neglect of military discipline, there being no ground for the study and exercise of arms that might keep the body of the state in health and vigor. Nor is it unlikely that extreme vassalage was the end of that long sluggish peace. . . . The trained bands, accounted the main support of the realm and bulwarks against unexpected invasions, were effeminate in courage and uncapable of discipline, because their whole course of life was alienated from warlike employment; insomuch that young and active spirits were more perfect by the experience of two days' service."[49]

47. 1626; Glouc. Corp. Rec. 1540, p. 74. I have found no reason to suppose that this obligation aroused resentment among the Gloucestershire clergy. It did cause opposition, however, among the clergy of Derbyshire and Northamptonshire. Cox, *Derbyshire Annals,* I, 239–41; Wake, *Copy of Papers Relating to Musters,* pp. lxii, 123.

48. The council wrote to the lord lieutenant that the years of peace under King James had bred the neglect which comes with security. "We cannot but very much doubt of a great decay of such arms and furniture as are requisite . . . for the continuance and support of the peace we do enjoy." Lansd. MS. 232, fo. 63.

49. John Corbet, *An Historical Relation of the Military Government of Gloucester* (London, 1645?), pp. 10–11. A commentator on county records has asserted that the slackness of the gentry in training the soldiers was a sign of restiveness, and that King Charles incurred odium by his attempts to make the system efficient. (J. E. Morris in Wake, *Copy of Papers Relating to Musters,* pp. cxiv–cxv.) I find no sign of this feeling in Gloucestershire. There was unquestionably a passive resistance to the orders of the central government—there always was,

There is a simple reason for this decadence: the trained bands were not used. They were intended for defense against domestic disturbance or foreign invasion, and could not be used in a period when neither danger materialized. They were called out when the Armada was in sight, and again when a royal army was marching upon Gloucester; in the fifty-four years between, they never came within smell of war.[50] The men were not even supposed to volunteer for active service. When instructions for a levy came from the privy council, there was always the provision, implicit or expressed, "None of them taken out of the trained bands, which you are still to keep entire." [51]

The troops which saw active service were the pressed levies. These were recruited from all the untrained and able-bodied men of the county between the ages of eighteen and sixty.[52] They were mustered from time to time, "that upon any sudden occasion such levies may be made of them as shall be required." [53] The sudden occasions were frequent, and the demands on the county exacting. In 1590, Chandos was instructed to levy the inordinate number of one thousand men.[54] During the rest of Eliza-

in any field of its control. But a simpler explanation lies in that infinite incapacity for taking pains which was common to so much of local officialdom.

50. It will be seen later that the bands of the forest division were once used to curb a riot. This is scarcely military service, but it is the only instance of their useful employment.

51. Glouc. Corp. Rec. 1540, pp. 24 and *passim.*

52. The number of these men is impossible to determine, because no two estimates agree. One made in 1587 gave a total of 11,700; another in 1607 gave only 4,560; Smyth in 1608 listed 18,743. S.P. 12/205/32; *H.M.C., Beaulieu MSS.,* p. 82; above, p. 80 note 19.

53. 1626; Glouc. Corp. Rec. 1540, p. 78. At a muster in 1590, even household servants were included; those who failed to appear were imprisoned overnight. *Ibid.,* uncatalogued letter book, fo. 54.

54. *A.P.C., 1590,* p. 287. A modern author conjectures that the reason for this extraordinary levy was a depression in the cloth trade, and a consequent abundance of unemployed; W. St. C. Baddeley, *A History of Cirencester,* p. 239 note.

beth's reign, levies were made less often than in other counties, but more men were taken; the average was two hundred.[55] Pacific King James was not so demanding, but pressing began again at the end of his reign. Four hundred were taken in 1624, and fifty in 1625, both for the Mansfeld expedition; two hundred were taken in 1627, presumably for the Isle of Rhé.[56] There was then a twelve-year interval of quiet, until the outbreak of the war against the Scots.

Men were pressed for the navy as well as the army. In 1590, the privy council ordered a census of the fishermen who had been or who might be pressed.[57] No use seems to have been made of it, and there is no record of pressing for the sea until 1635. In that year it was ordered that a muster should be taken of all the sailors, fishermen, and bargemen within the county, or on board ships belonging to any town in the county; 250 of them, aged between twenty and fifty, were to be pressed and taken to Chatham. The procedure was repeated two years later,[58] and again two years after that.

This third levy, in 1639, is of interest because it involved an official who was not usually concerned with the military. Instructions for pressing seamen were transmitted from the lord admiral, through the pressmaster, to the sheriff of Gloucestershire. "Before the letters came to my hands," the sheriff reported to Secretary Nicholas, "the substance of them was divulged; so that the greatest part of the sailors started aside and hid their heads, that I could not perform the service in that manner I desired."[59] He sent out warrants to summon all the seafaring men of the county before him and the pressmaster; they waited three days for them, but with scant result. "Many of those that were at home started aside, and some

55. *A.P.C., 1592,* p. 225; *1596–97,* pp. 242, 277; *1598–99,* p. 576.
56. Glouc. Corp. Rec. 1540, p. 28; *H.M.C., Fourth Report,* p. 2.
57. *A.P.C., 1590,* pp. 86–87.
58. Glouc. Corp. Rec. 1540, pp. 211, 224.
59. S.P. 16/448/4.

of those that were summoned by the officers would not appear; so that the appearance was very slender." [60] The sheriff, had he known it, was giving a small and unheeded warning of local opinion about the king's navy.

These levies for the navy were a small matter by comparison with those for the army. The menace of the press-master must have been real and constant to the poorer folk, and they must have been a patient lot. Year after year, they would be shipped off without adequate training, pay, or food, to sicken in the Irish bogs or be killed on the dunes of Holland or the Bridge of L'Oix. Yet they never defied the authorities, and rarely even protested. When they were pressed, they went, and they were lucky if they saw Gloucestershire again.[61]

The procedure of raising a pressed levy is well illustrated by the example of Sir Henry Winston, who was a deputy lieutenant of Lord Chandos in 1601. A large number of men from the various divisions had been ordered to assemble in Gloucester. From these Winston was instructed to choose fifty for service in Ireland; if he could not fill his quota from those assembled, he was to choose such others as he saw fit. He excused one man because he was too old, and two more who made oath that they were householders and members of the trained band, and had not given bribes to procure their discharge. He also excused two petty constables, and took two substitutes whom they had brought with them. He had still not gathered the necessary fifty, and started out to look for

60. S.P. 16/414/52. This work of the sheriff would normally have devolved upon the vice admiral. But the latter does not appear in this case, which is the only one of pressing sailors about which I have any details. He is not mentioned elsewhere in the records, and they are almost equally silent about the lord admiral.

61. Gloucester once protested to Cecil against the pressing of men in the city, but only because it was thought to be a violation of municipal privilege. The reply of the privy council was curt: "In these businesses which so greatly concern her Majesty's service, and especially in the levy of men, you do very much amiss to stand upon such points of your privilege, and to refuse to join with the whole county." *A.P.C., 1596–97,* pp. 277–78.

more. In an inn he found a man who he knew was suitable, and promptly "laid hands upon the said Redferne and said he should be pressed and sent into Ireland for a soldier, and so brought the said Redferne with him over the way to the rest of the soldiers. And then for that the said Redferne alleged that this defendant went about to press him out of malice, he this defendant did let him go and [did] meddle no further with him." [62]

Redferne was raising one of the most common charges against military officials. The system was so haphazard, and the qualifications for service so indefinite, that vast scope was given to extortion and bribery. The lord lieutenant himself was usually above such charges, because he was not intimately enough concerned with the choice of men. The actual selection seems to have been made by a variety of officials—the deputy lieutenants, the press-master, perhaps even the petty constables—and at one time or another most of them were accused of dishonesty.[63] A case in point is that of Sir Thomas Throckmorton, who seems to have been as malicious in pressing his inferiors as he was in suing his equals in star chamber.

One of his humble enemies was acquitted of murder at the assizes. Immediately after his release, Sir Thomas prevailed on the lord lieutenant to give him the fatal groat for press-money; he was told to report at Bristol three days

62. St. Ch. 5/S/70/4.

63. A case which presumably involved the deputy lieutenants came before the privy council in 1598, on the petition of a man who had been pressed for Ireland. He claimed to be a substantial subsidy man, with numerous children and infirmities. The council did not believe him, but ordered an investigation: if the petitioner was correct, the responsible J. P.'s (*i.e.*, deputy lieutenants?) were to be told "how much her Majesty doth mislike her authority and service should be abused to serve the passion of any person." (*A.P.C., 1597–98,* p. 631.) Another deputy lieutenant was the subject of a petition to parliament in 1640: he had sent out private pressing warrants, had forced the victims to release themselves by heavy bribes, and had persecuted those who did not pay enough. *H.M.C., Fourth Report,* pp. 49, 59; for similar cases elsewhere, see Burne, *Staffordshire,* III, 156, 170; H. W. Saunders, *The Official Papers of Sir Nathaniel Bacon . . . as Justice of the Peace, 1580–1620,* pp. 67–68.

later for service in Ireland. He protested to the lord lieutenant in Sir Thomas's hearing, and the latter answered,

"Hast thou wrong? I will do thee more wrong yet, such a knave as thou art!"

He had no recourse but to go to Bristol. He did so, only to find that the captain of the levies had filled his quota a fortnight earlier. He not unnaturally came home again. Sir Thomas thereupon clapped him into jail, and the assizes released him a second time.[64] By then he must have learned his lesson, that the ill will of a justice was requited again one time or another.

There is no positive evidence of corruption among the pressmasters. But praise of one who was diligent is an indication of what the rest were like. The writer is the sheriff who was pressing sailors. "The pressmaster was so careful that he would not release any one man that was likely to perform the service. If such men had been employed heretofore that had been so trusty, I am persuaded the service would have been better performed, and those that are fit to serve not to so slight the service as now they do." [65] The constables were frequently charged with pressing from malice, and with exempting for bribes. It is impossible to tell their precise rôle in the military scheme, but it would appear that the task of pressing in the small towns was frequently deputed to them by the deputy lieutenants. During Lord Berkeley's lieutenancy, he offered to discharge any man who could prove that he had been pressed because of the constable's malice.[66] In 1625, the privy council ordered the deputy lieutenants to supervise

64. St. Ch. 5/W/20/8. Sir Thomas was proverbial in the countryside. "Old Filimore of Cam, going . . . to present Sir Thomas Throckmorton of Tortworth with a sugar loaf, met by the way with his neighbor, S.M., who demanded whither and upon what business he was going, answered, 'To offer my candle to the devil.' Which coming to the ears of Sir Thomas, at the next muster he sent two of Filimore's sons soldiers into the Low Countries, where the one was slain and the other at a dear rate redeemed his return." From that time on, "he hath offered his candle to the devil" was a local proverb. Smyth, *Description,* p. 28.

65. S.P. 16/414/52.

66. Smyth, *Lives of the Berkeleys,* II, 371.

the constables more closely, and to bind over any who they thought were corrupt.[67]

The greatest corruption was among the officers of the levies. After the men were pressed, they were delivered to one or two conductors, who either led them to the port of embarkation or delivered them to their captains at some point on the way. These captains and conductors were in the habit of releasing men for bribes; to judge by the number of complaints, they released every man who could afford a pittance for his freedom. In one case, four men paid £1 10*s.* apiece for their discharges; in another the conductors freed forty men out of 150.[68] There was a constant series of complaints and exhortations from London, but everywhere there was "such remissness and neglect as that in most counties those orders are scarce heard of, and in none put in any real execution nor anything done." [69]

Another complaint was that the conductor withheld the men's pay. One such case, in 1625, was serious enough to be brought before the grand jury at the sessions. The assistant conductor testified for his superior, and painted him as a model of rectitude: when the men got to Totnes, and were handed over to their regular captain, the conductor asked them whether they were satisfied with their pay, and with his treatment of them on the march; they all answered that they were completely content, and had been well used, "and withal wished that he were to go along and have the command of them still." [70]

Leading these men was a task to try the hardiest officer. Individuals may have been docile enough about being

67. Glouc. Corp. Rec. 1540, pp. 43–45.

68. 1592; *ibid.,* uncatalogued letter book, fos. 65–67v; *A.P.C., 1592–93,* p. 81. This abuse had been rampant at the time of the Armada, when the conjecture was made in Gloucester that "divers able soldiers were (some for favors, some for money) given discharges and released back again . . . by the captain or his inferior officers. And so was it thought that a large gain was raised thereby, notwithstanding that Mr. Mayor . . . had before given to the captain's officers some rewards for their travels." Glouc. Corp. Rec., uncatalogued letter book, fo. 24v.

69. 1625; *ibid.,* 1540, fo. 51.

70. S.P. 16/10/5 (I).

pressed. But once they were gathered into troops, they were a terror to the countryside. "We commend . . . the pains that Mr. Seymore took in the appeasing of the Gloucestershire men." "Almost half of them are run away after they came to the city of Bristol." "We are lately advertised from Captain Crompton that the thirty men that were sent out of that county were the first that attempted to run away of those under his conduction, and that led the way and enticed others to do the like, being chosen of bad and loose people." [71] These are typical comments of the privy council, at the end of the sixteenth century, on the nature of the Gloucestershire levies.

The council had infinite patience. It might be grieved to see what little effect its admonitions had, but it was quite willing to repeat them year after year. In 1600, it sent Lord Chandos a long exposition of the problem and its cure. The men sent to Ireland were running away, either before they came to embark or soon after they landed; they returned to England, and wandered about without being apprehended. The fundamental mistake was the choice of wretched men, and the council carefully pointed out what bad economy this was. Such men were "the chiefest cause of decay of the army, which decay hath required and will ever require supplies, and supplies will impose this kind of charge, by which reason you see it is in the power of the country to ease and free itself in great part of the charge of these levies from henceforth." [72]

But all the logic in the world could not improve the army. Two years later, Bristol reported that the troops arriving at the city were in deplorable condition; no one had been paid, and the men had therefore mutinied.[73]

71. *A.P.C., 1599–1600,* pp. 64–65; *1600–01,* pp. 161, 183–84.

72. Glouc. Corp. Rec., uncatalogued letter book, fo. 84. Chandos had been told, the year before, that his officers were choosing the men whom the county wished to be rid of, rather than those who were fit to serve. *A.P.C., 1599–1600,* p. 161; for a similar situation in Northamptonshire at this time, see Wake, *Montagu Musters Book,* pp. xxxviii–xli; and for a general discussion of the problem of the levies, see Scott Thomson, *Lords Lieutenants,* pp. 114–15.

73. *H.M.C., Salisbury MSS.,* XII, 169–70.

Matters were no better by 1616. The council wrote to the lord lieutenant, again urging the choice of proper men. Since the last war many of the old soldiers had died, and others had grown too old for service. Good new blood must be found. But the council made it almost impossible for the lord lieutenant to find it: "We think it very requisite that those which follow the plough and country husbandry should be exempted and spared." [74]

The most flagrant example of misconduct by the levies was in 1627. In the middle of November, two hundred Gloucestershire troops arrived in Exeter. Since the billets in town were full, the men were quartered for the night in the suburbs. In the morning the mayor was informed that they were trying to enter the city. He shut one of the city gates, "and friendly intreated the said soldiers to go to the places they were appointed."

But they had no such intention. Axes appeared, and the men were soon in full riot. They cut down the stocks, demolished some houses, and then set to work on the gate itself. Their ringleader declared that he would get into the city or die in the attempt, and swore "that he would cut the said mayor in pieces, and carry his head with him, and would make garters of his guts, with other foul abuses." The town officers finally dispersed the rioters, and captured two of them. But since the captives were the king's soldiers, it was difficult to know what to do with them. They were imprisoned for breach of the peace, while the authorities clamored for action by the privy council, and a commission of martial law for the city.[75]

The difficulties of Exeter were the difficulties of all England. Billeting such soldiers as these was becoming a

74. Glouc. Corp. Rec., uncatalogued letter book, fo. 86v. This had been the policy in Gloucester since at least 1591, when "the country hinds and servants were spared, and men found and taken in the city for ease of the country." *Ibid.,* fo. 57.

75. S.P. 16/84/61. Soldiers at this time seem to have been a particular burden to Devon; see Hamilton, *Quarter Sessions,* pp. 107–110. For a similar disturbance at Dover in 1624, see F. C. Dietz, *English Public Finance, 1588–1641,* p. 221.

national grievance, and Gloucestershire felt it as keenly as any county. Even if the men behaved themselves, there was bound to be a certain amount of friction between them and their unwilling hosts. The privy council ordered that only the well-to-do should provide billets. When men were quartered on less substantial householders, "the soldiers complain on the one side for being billeted in the houses of such poor and indigent persons as are not able to provide for him according to the entertainment allowed by his Majesty. And the billeter on the other side complains of the disorders of the soldiers, in not being content with the provision made for him according to his Majesty's said pay, but that he will be his own carver of whatsoever he likes best and can lay his hands on, to the great damage and impoverishing of the country." [76]

These soldiers were not necessarily natives of the county. In 1627 and 1628 the army was moving about England, for strategic reasons which are now obscure. "His Majesty finds it requisite so to dispose of his forces, as that they be ready upon any sudden occasion"; troops were therefore concentrated at such places as Mitcheldean, in the middle of the forest—one of the least strategic points in England.[77] Soldiers kept appearing in various parts of the county, often without warning or authorization from the privy council. Three hundred descended on Cirencester in the beginning of 1628, and were quartered on the town "in a confused manner." They were bound for Gloucester, and one of the Cirencester magistrates kindly tried to divert them. He explained his method to the deputy lieutenants of the inshire. "I sent for the commander to dinner on Wednesday and made much of him, and told him as much as you could say in the behalf of your charter and jurisdiction, and in the end persuaded him and told him I would write my letters and showed him my letters,

76. Glouc. Corp. Rec. 1540, p. 135, printed in *H.M.C., Twelfth Report,* IX, 483.

77. Glouc. Corp. Rec. 1540, pp. 122, 134. For the hardships suffered at Reading from billeting such troops, see Guilding, *Reading,* II, 440–42.

which was to divert their number to another county and the commander to intimate as much by his letter." The intimation failed to relieve the county. The troops were held in Cirencester until word was received from the privy council, and were then divided among other parts of Gloucestershire. The towns on the route of march were ordered to provide them with lodging and diet, with hackney horses at 1*s.* a day, cart horses at 8*d.*, and carts to carry the armor. The council appended its ordinary hopeful formula: "The commanders are to cause the soldiers to march together, and not to spoil or do any misdemeanors or use any violence." [78]

During the Cirencester crisis there was another invasion nearby, this time of two hundred men. "They came to Tetbury upon Sunday at night, where they have put the town to a great trouble and charge through their disorder." The deputy lieutenants of the outshire were in charge of distributing them around the county. The inshire was responsible for a tenth; since it already had four men, sixteen more were foisted upon it. "We desire that according to your proportion, you will pay your part to the town of Tetbury towards the defraying of the charge they have been at in the keeping of them, till we could meet to settle them, and like order we will take with the rest of our county that they should contribute accordingly." [79]

The cost of billeting was the major aspect of the county's grievance. The government theoretically would repay, and the privy council kept assuring the lord lieu-

78. Glouc. Corp. Rec. 1540, pp. 119–23, printed in part in *H.M.C., Twelfth Report,* IX, 482–83. Cirencester, in return for its kindness, asked Gloucester to pay a tenth of the charge for keeping the soldiers, who had cost the town £7 a day. The attempt to divert the men from Gloucester was not entirely successful: thirty-one were finally quartered there. When they arrived, they were to be paid 8*d.* apiece as conduct money, and with this they would buy their own board and lodging for the night. Thereafter they were to receive the usual weekly wage of 3*s.* 6*d.* a man. Other companies passing through the city must also be billeted, if they could go no farther that day; their wages, however, were to be paid by the outshire. Glouc. Corp. Rec. 1540, p. 124.

79. *Ibid.,* p. 112.

tenant that repayment was about to be made. But the months passed, no money appeared, and the people became restive. "The inhabitants," remarked the privy council in June of 1628, "either out of some diffidence of his Majesty's royal promise, or by the example and encouragement of some persons ill affected to his Majesty's service, or out of sinister and false apprehensions of some misunderstandings between his Majesty and his parliament, have in disobedience to his Majesty's said former commands refused to billet the said soldiers any longer." The people were assured that the king and parliament were "well and happily accorded and agreed," and that the money would be forthcoming. The soldiers were to be kept until the first subsidy came in, and then paid off, "which his Majesty desires to hasten as much as themselves, the rather for that the soldiers, being generally in great want of clothes (for the providing whereof order is already given), cannot with decency and honor to the state be put upon the march before he be clothed." [80]

The county petitioned the house of lords to relieve the burden of billeting. The house could not be troubled with such small matters, and referred back the petition to the local J. P.'s and deputy lieutenants.[81] A separate petition from the J. P.'s to the council had no more effect. The answer was that Gloucestershire was charged with quartering fewer men than many other counties of equal substance. "We find that the manifest dangers which are threatened to this state from foreign enemies do overbalance all that can be said at this present." [82] When the

80. *Ibid.,* p. 149. This glimpse of ragged men is confirmed by other testimony. It is therefore surprising to discover that the troops at this time were being swelled by volunteers. The officers quartered in Gloucester informed the privy council that they were besieged by recruits every day, and that the county refused to billet them because they were in excess of the required number. The deputy lieutenants were ordered to quarter them, provided that they had warrants from one of the officers. A month later, however, the order was rescinded. *Ibid.,* pp. 135, 142.

81. *Ibid.,* p. 151.

82. MS. A.P.C. XXXVI, 265v.

haggard army came back from Rhé, in the spring of 1628, the dangers from English enemies became much more manifest than those from foreigners. But the only concession to local protests was a commission of martial law for the city of Gloucester.[83]

Billeting was an acute grievance, and a short one. It was the concomitant of Charles's and Buckingham's reckless effort to succor La Rochelle, in 1627-28; before and after those two years there is no mention of the curse of the soldiery. Billeting was only one phase of that curse, though it was naturally the one which aroused most violent opposition: the Tommy Atkins of three centuries ago was not a person one cared to have in the house.

While billeting ceased to be a grievance as soon as the crisis had passed, the crisis itself reveals the weakness of the whole military system, and reveals it as clearly in Gloucestershire as before St. Martin-de-Rhé. The trained bands were not used for war, and the pressed levies were more dangerous to their friends than to their enemies. Englishmen still could fight. But no army, organized as Charles's army was, had a sporting chance of victory. It is true that the military organization was little more cumbersome and inefficient than the civil, and that the military fiascoes were due in great part to lack of supply. Yet they were due in even greater part to the nature of the system. There were bribery and corruption in the choice of men; there was lack of training and of discipline; above all, there was an unwillingness at home to support the army. Parliament was loath to finance an expedition to France, but no more so than Gloucestershire to billet soldiers, or to pay for marches across the county. The officials did their best. Because of the men whom they pressed, and the other men who paid the bills, their efforts were never more than chronic failure.

83. Glouc. Corp. Rec. 66.

V

TAXATION

THE UPKEEP of the military establishment was an insistent burden on county finance. Mention has already been made of the sporadic assessments for new armor and for billeting; these, however, were mere drops in the bucket by comparison with coat and conduct money. This tax was the most important of those for purely military purposes, and the most often levied. Its two parts were theoretically distinct: coat money was for clothing the pressed men, and conduct money for their marches to and from the ports. But the practical distinction was slight. The two were levied at the same time, and one was rarely spoken of without the other.

The amount of coat money was uncertain; it apparently depended on the cost of the coats themselves. In 1591, Lord Chandos acted on the assumption that the charge would be 4*s.* a man. The privy council informed him that he was mistaken, and should have known better: the coats cost 14*s.* 10*d.* apiece, and Gloucestershire was expected to pay for 135 of them, plus an additional sum "for the bestowing of some liberality upon every officer and particular soldier in their purses." [1] Chandos must straightway collect the residue, "that that county under your lordship's lieutenancy may not be noted above the rest to have dealt so straightly and sparingly in these public services that concern the honor of her Majesty and the realm." [2]

1. Glouc. Corp. Rec., uncatalogued letter book, fo. 60–60v.

2. *A.P.C., 1591,* pp. 306–07. Lord Chandos took it on himself to buy the armor for these levies from London dealers. It was sent to Cirencester; he instructed the deputy lieutenants to call for it there, and to distribute it among the various divisions. The bill, including the expenses of the buyers and the charges for carriage, came to £65 5*s.* 6*d.*, for which an assessment was to be levied on the county. Lands. MS. 232, fos. 62, 65v; Bodl. MS. Rawl. C 358, fos. 35v–36.

Lord Chandos was again in trouble with coats in 1599. He decided that it would be cheaper to buy them himself than to pay the government for them; he therefore had them made in London and sent down to the county. The experiment was not a success. The council informed him that the coats were badly made of bad material, and had been sent without inspection; they must be replaced immediately by new ones from the government tailors. His own were to be returned to London for inspection. If they passed, they could be used later; if not, he could do as he pleased with them.[3]

Conduct money varied in amount, and was determined in various ways. Sometimes the men were given a flat payment before they left.[4] Sometimes they were paid by the day, and sometimes by the number of miles they marched in a day.[5] It was all one to the taxpayer, because the assessment was not likely to be exact enough to reflect such minor differences. The authorities seem to have estimated the cost of equipping and sending out the pressed men, and then to have levied the amount of their estimate. Sometimes they called it a loan. But since repayment was rare, the loan in general practice was a tax.[6]

A minor aspect of coat and conduct money was the

3. *A.P.C., 1599–1600,* pp. 20–22.

4. The city of Gloucester, in 1596, paid 5*s.* apiece to twenty-five soldiers for Ireland, and 10*s.* apiece to their officers. This was done only after the privy council had assured the city that its privileges did not exempt it from paying conduct money. *Ibid., 1595–96,* p. 328; Glouc. Corp. Rec. 1500, fo. 316.

5. At the beginning of the period, the usual pay for soldiers leaving Gloucester was 8*d.* a day, or a halfpenny a mile; it was expected that the troops would cover twelve (or later fifteen) miles a day. (*Ibid.,* uncatalogued letter book, fo. 58.) The rate by the mile was therefore slightly to the soldier's disadvantage, but it seems to have been the more usual one; see Wake, *Copy of Papers Relating to Musters,* p. 33.

6. Miss Thomson distinguishes two kinds of coat and conduct money in the sixteenth century: the government was supposed to repay money spent on levies for foreign service, not on levies for domestic. (Scott Thomson, *Lords Lieutenants,* pp. 95 note 1, 109.) I have found no local evidence of this distinction. Whatever the theory may have been, the practice justifies the conclusion in the text.

assessment for light horse. This is mentioned only once, in 1600, when horses were needed for Ireland. Gloucestershire was £180 in arrears, and Chandos was taken to task. "For the space of almost six months you have not sent up hither that small sum of money. . . . If the like want of care had been used by other lieutenants, the service had been quite disappointed." [7]

In the lean years of 1626-28, even billeting was no greater burden than coat and conduct money. In the summer of 1626, the privy council had offered to repay the sums collected. It not only failed to do so, but added a quarter of the Bristol assessment to the Gloucestershire quota. The outshire J. P.'s protested: the men of Bristol were "flourishing and abounding in wealth, well known unto us, who see the fair proportions of our county daily purchased by them, and their readiness for more upon the first occasion that may be offered; whereas the decay of our country is the ordinary discourse amongst us, and too well known unto us all. . . . Our services in drawing the country to the disbursement of coat and conduct money for the soldiers lately sent hence to his Highness's service, upon your lordships' letters we delayed not. It was no small sum. It is yet unpaid, but we trust upon your lordships when you shall see convenient. The proportion of the trained forces of this shire, and the charges incident, are much above those of most of the others of this kingdom, which yet, and notwithstanding our fall in ability, we endeavor to make up. We have stretched to the uttermost, and our country is not well able to do more." [8]

Conditions had not improved by midwinter. There was another petition to the council, this time from the deputy lieutenants. The county was poor, and weighed down with the expenses of the trained bands. Of late it had been further burdened by equipping 1,250 pressed soldiers "wholly at our charges, of which we have made certificate

7. *A.P.C., 1599–1600,* pp. 552–53. The principal defaulters owed sums ranging from £1 10*s*. to £6 10*s*.; *ibid., 1600–01,* pp. 3–5.
8. S.P. 16/35/43.

but have not yet received a part thereof, as formerly hath been repaid to us for our country's use." The privy council gave them cold comfort: the danger to the state outweighed every other consideration.[9]

While coat and conduct money was the major military tax, there was also a minor one for the relief of maimed soldiers and sailors. The justices in quarter sessions assessed each parish in the county, chose treasurers to administer the fund so raised, and granted pensions from it to the individual applicants.[10] The amount of relief given to each man was supposed to be proportioned to "the condition and quality of the places wherein he hath served." [11] If he felt that justice was denied him, he might appeal from the sessions to the privy council. The council,

9. S.P. 16/90/35; Glouc. Corp. Rec. 1540, printed in *H.M.C., Twelfth Report,* IX, 480–81. Northampton informed Conway, a year later, that the county had a larger proportion of horse and foot than its neighbors. "Gloucestershire is a little troubled, with the billeting, mustering, paying, and the decay of many who have gone out of their estates, coming into the hands of strangers not there inhabiting." S.P. 16/94/36.

Local references to coat and conduct money give no indication of this discontent. In 1627, Chipping Campden gave a man 10*s.* "to bring him again to his colors," and North Nibley gave its petty constable £1 for coat and conduct money for four soldiers, whom the deputy lieutenants had called out by warrant; such assessments then disappear until 1639, when Dursley paid its constable 2*s.* 6*d.*, "a levy for the church land for conduct money and setting forth two soldiers," presumably for the Bishops' War. Churchwardens' accounts of Chipping Campden, 1627; of North Nibley, 26 August, 1627 (in Gloucester County Council MSS.); of Dursley, 1639.

10. The parochial assessments were to be made either by the parishioners, by the churchwardens and constable, or by the resident J. P.'s; the collections were to be given to the high constable ten days before each quarter sessions. No parish was to pay more than £2 3*s.* 4*d.* a year, or less than 8*s.* 8*d.* (43 Elizabeth, c. 3.) As much as five years before this statute, small annual payments for maimed soldiers and sailors were being made by the two Gloucester parishes of St. Michael and St. Aldgate. St. Michael's MSS., loose receipts.

The collections for the maimed were commonly lumped with those for the relief of prisoners in the king's bench and Marshalsea prisons. The latter tax had been authorized by 39 Elizabeth, c. 3, and was gathered in the same way. The large country parish of Berkeley, for example, paid for almost thirty years the annual sum of £3 9*s.* 4*d.* for the maimed and the prisoners together. G.P.L. MS. 16,070, fo. 9.

11. MS. A.P.C., XXXIX, 785.

once it was convinced that he had been pressed in the county and was now in real need, would use its influence on the local court.[12]

The council also supervised certain special taxes, levied by the crown for special occasions. It sometimes called them gifts, to make them more palatable, but they had all the earmarks of a tax. In 1620, the country was asked to contribute for the recovery of the Palatinate. The city of Gloucester assessed itself; an alderman paid £2 if he had held no other office in the city, and less if he had.[13] The tax was still being collected two years later, and the county was one of nine in arrears. The council blamed the J. P.'s, "it being observed that where the justices of peace have by their example been forward to advance the service there, it hath taken answerable effects." [14]

The country was again taxed in 1633, this time for the repair of St. Paul's. That ornament of the city of London was in decay; laymen had secured most of its land, and the remainder yielded too little to keep up the fabric. Scarcely the fault of the nation, but it was the nation which paid.[15] Special commissioners were appointed, and the long work of collection began; to spur on the laggards, King Charles himself agreed to restore the west front. The commissioners were to use their "best persuasions," and to certify the names of delinquents. In Gloucester they called before them such men as they thought most able to

12. *A.P.C., 1617–19,* p. 433; MS. A.P.C., XXXVI, 26v; XXXVIII, 58, 132. The fullest material on this aspect of the work of quarter sessions is in Bennet and Dewhurst, *Quarter Sessions Records of the County of Chester.*

13. The scale of assessment was "40*s.* an alderman, 20*s.* once sheriff or upwards, 13*s.* 4*d.* twice steward, and 10*s.* once steward." Glouc. Corp. Rec. 1451, fo. 476; for a description of this unsuccessful tax, see Dietz, *English Public Finance,* p. 186.

14. *A.P.C., 1621–23,* pp. 302–03.

15. See S. R. Gardiner, *History of England from the Accession of James I to the Outbreak of the Civil War, 1603–1643,* VII, 245–46. The first local records of this imposition are in 1633, when the churchwardens of North Nibley collected £1 8*s.* 6½*d.* for the purpose. North Nibley accounts, 15 September, 1633; the notification to the city of Gloucester, in the same year, is preserved as Glouc. Corp. Rec. 67.

contribute, "and dealt with them particularly man by man, and such as did not appear at the first or second summons we made forth new warrants for until they did appear." The council wished pledges of an annual contribution, but in this the commissioners completely failed. Their best persuasions extracted only the amount of a subsidy in the city, and a half subsidy in the rest of the county, or a total of £129 2*s.*[16]

There were also a number of local taxes for special occasions. These occasions might affect the village, the parish, the county, even a group of counties. There was no conception of a general tax for the various expenses of local government; each new public need was met by a new levy on the locality concerned. The burden fell on the individual taxpayer as a series of sporadic assessments, sandwiched between those of the central government. Typical payments in a gentleman's account book are for the mustermaster's wages, the repair of the village pound, the king's and queen's provision, the house of correction, a rate laid out by the constable for catching a prisoner, a contribution toward making Tetbury a staple town.[17] Something happened to the church at Badgeworth, and landowners of the little parish paid the heavy rate of 20*s.* the yardland; the Over Bridge at Gloucester needed repair, and the inshire was assessed at 1*s.* 8*d.* the yardland.[18]

This matter of repairing bridges was a difficult aspect of local finance. A bridge was expensive, and there was no rule for determining who should bear the expense. The result was often disagreement. Sometimes a town was at loggerheads with the county, sometimes one county with another; if the dispute could not be settled by local arbi-

16. *Ibid.*, 1540, pp. 199–200; see also pp. 195–96; 1452, p. 25; Guilding, *Reading*, III, 168. The procedure of collecting this loan is similar to that employed in Elizabeth's time for collecting loans by privy seal, for which see Scott Thomson, *Lords Lieutenants*, pp. 120–25.

17. Bodl. MS. Eng. Misc. E. 6 (John Smyth's account book), *passim.* The king's and queen's provision was purveyance, for which see below, p. 110.

18. G.P.L. MS. R 31.4 (Hinson account book), fo. 40.

tration, it was carried to parliament.[19] An example in point is that of Chepstow Bridge. The first arrangement (18 Elizabeth, c. 18) was that the responsibility should rest on the two counties of Monmouth and Gloucester. The money for repairs was raised in various ways: from tolls, from the income of lands set aside for the purpose, from assessments made by the justices in the two counties. The arrangement worked for almost thirty years, and then the bridge collapsed. At once there were recriminations. The Welshmen protested that the justices had neglected their assessments.[20] The division of Berkeley complained that Gloucestershire had done its part, and that the fault lay entirely with their neighbors: the Monmouthshire half of the bridge had collapsed from neglect, and carried with it the half on which Gloucestershire had lavished money and care.[21] More than three years after the bridge had fallen, parliament set up a new mechanism for rebuilding and maintaining it. By this statute (3 James I, c. 23) the justices were still to assess, but special collectors of the tax were created in each hundred, and two surveyors in each county to receive and spend the money collected. From that time on, the repair of Chepstow Bridge was a regular county tax.

These local assessments were a piecemeal system. The money, whether for bridges or churches or coats, was levied as each need arose, and was proportioned to the need. The important national taxes, on the other hand, were intended

19. The flooding Severn, in 1611, carried away the three bridges at Tewkesbury. Two of them were repaired, at a cost of some £50, but the town could not afford to repair the third. Ten years later, it was proposed to rebuild the third bridge at the cost of the county, and the proposal was argued in the house of commons. Tewkes. Corp. Rec. 1, fo. 29v; Notestein, *Commons Debates, 1621,* III, 171–72; IV, 307. For bridge repair in Warwickshire, see Ratcliff and Johnson, *Warwick,* I, 156, 232–33.

20. From G.P.L. MS. 16,524, fo. 30, and the Welsh petition incorporated in 3 James I, c. 23.

21. From a petition to the quarter sessions in 1603. The petitioners requested that an assessment for rebuilding the bridge should be postponed until a new act had been put through parliament. G.P.L. MS. 16,524, fo. 30.

as general blanket collections, to cover the various expenses of national government. The rate of each tax was supposedly fixed, and the yield from one year to another supposedly the same. In both respects the national system was nearer than the local to modern ideas of taxation.

The least important of these national taxes was purveyance, the old obligation to supply the royal household with provisions. A number of counties were still doing so in kind, but Gloucestershire had commuted its payment in the summer of 1590. The lord lieutenant, with the consent of the inshire and the outshire, "compounded with the queen's purveyors for the sum of £220 or thereabout, to have both counties discharged of beefs, muttons, and certain other provisions; whereupon divers meetings and conferences were at Gloucester between certain of the best calling of the shire, and Mr. Brown, mayor, and others of the best calling within the county of the city, for dividing of the said charge." [22] This sum presumably became a semiannual payment, since the total in 1639 was £440 a year.[23] The money was collected from the individual taxpayer by the petty constable; the rate was based on the holding of land, and was apparently constant from year to year.[24]

The other old tax was the Tenth and Fifteenth. These rates "at the first were only raised and levied upon corn, goods, and beasts, but now in most places are raised upon

22. Glouc. Corp. Rec., uncatalogued letter book, fo. 53. Such a composition, in money rather than kind, seems to have been exceptional at such an early date; see Dietz, *English Public Finance,* pp. 420–23.

23. Smyth, *Description,* p. 9.

24. When the location of some land near Tewkesbury was in dispute, a witness argued that it lay in the tithing of Southwick, because "the payments generally charged upon the said grounds for the king's provision, setting forth of soldiers, and other services for the king, have been usually collected by the constable or tithingman of Southwick, and not by any other officer. . . . Mr. Mathewes . . . would often set down in a book the rates which himself and every occupier of the said grounds held, who thereby would much ease himself and overcharge the rest of the said occupiers." (E. 134/14 Jas. I/H/12.) In 1636, the sheriff instructed the high constables to levy ship money according to the normal rate for the king's provision. G.P.L. MS. 16,527, fo. 72.

land."[25] In the cities, the Tenth seems to have been gathered in each parish by the churchwardens.[26] In the country, the Fifteenth was gathered by the petty constables, under the supervision of special collectors. These collectors might be husbandmen, yeomen, or gentry.[27] They were appointed by the lord keeper, presumably at the nomination of some local magnate; their business was to make sure that the constables performed their duty, and to bring the money to London. To judge from a single letter, their work was anything but congenial. Mr. Maurice Berkeley, in 1592, sent £20 to a Mr. Michael Hicks in London, and with it an explanatory note.

Good Mr. Hicks:

With my hearty commendations, and as many thanks as there is farthings in twenty pound, which I have sent you by this bearer; and I pray you be twice as bold with me in anything that I can pleasure you withal. My lord keeper hath preferred me to a great office in the country, that is to be a collector of the Fifteen, which if my lord had known me very well, what for my years and my unableness to travel, I have no doubt but that he would have pardoned me. But now there is no remedy; I must needs follow my collections, which will make me to visit you this next term. And therefore I pray you, if I chance to be behindhand, I will require your friendship to be a mean to my lord to give me some day till I can get it up. I have no good thing presently to pleasure you withal. But at my coming up if I do know of any good thing in the country, you shall be sure, if it lie in me to get it you, to have it.[28]

25. Smyth, *Description,* p. 43. It was this conversion of the tax which had led to the development of the subsidy, as a means of taxing personal property as well as land; see Dietz, *English Public Finance,* p. 382.

26. This was true at least in the parishes of St. Michael and St. Aldgate, Gloucester; see the churchwardens' accounts in the St. Michael's MSS.

27. For examples of each, see respectively E. 134/40 Eliz./H/3; E. 112/16/149; Lansd. MS. 72, no. 72, fo. 195.

28. *Ibid. Day,* in debtor's parlance, was a synonym for *delay.* A yeoman was "nominated and appointed" a collector by Sir Thomas Throck-

The most important tax, in the reigns of Elizabeth and James, was of course the subsidy. As soon as one had been granted by parliament, the machinery of collection was put in motion as fast as a money-starved government could put it. Each county was composed of divisions, of which there were four in Gloucestershire. Commissioners were appointed for each, and they summoned before them two or more inhabitants of each parish.[29] These men were appointed assessors for their parishes, and were given a specified time—a week or ten days—in which to compile and bring in their assessments. When their books had been approved and signed by the commissioners, the task of collection was turned over to the constable and other officers.[30] The rate at which the taxpayer was assessed was nominally 2*s.* 8*d.* in the pound on goods, and 4*s.* on land. But both goods and land were rated at a traditional valuation, which was only a fraction of the real one. The government accepted this slipshod system, and concentrated its efforts on making each county yield as much in one subsidy as it had in the last.

The success of the government, as usual, depended on the coöperation of local authorities. Like so many of them, the commissioners of the subsidy were not above using their power to serve their own ends. We have already seen how one commissioner tried to influence a parliamentary election.[31] But this was exceptional. The most usual abuse was tax-evasion: the commissioners assessed themselves, and were responsible for their own rates only to the privy

morton, when the latter was a knight of the shire at the parliament of 31 Elizabeth; the yeoman's subsequent troubles in collecting the quota of a recalcitrant parish are described in E. 112/16/149.

29. These assessors, according to Best, were selected by the petty constables. *Rural Economy,* p. 91; see also pp. 86–92 for a full description of the method of collecting a subsidy in Yorkshire.

30. The assessors, at least in Yorkshire, were paid for their work out of the money which they took in. (*Ibid.,* pp. 88–89.) The collectors in Gloucestershire had to post a bond to ensure payment of what they collected; see St. Ch. 5/S/70/4, a case which contains valuable details of procedure in collecting the tax.

31. See above, pp. 29–30.

council. In 1593 the council intimated, politely and sarcastically, that some commissioners were defrauding the government. "As we have cause to think that some of you are reasonably well taxed in respect of the lower rates of former times, so also to our own knowledges some others of you of the greatest likelihood and best ability might very well have strained higher, to the better example of others that no doubt do specially note your doings herein, and accordingly conform themselves." [32]

One of the commissioners so rebuked was Sir Thomas Throckmorton. He held a number of offices in his time, and seems to have been in hot water in all of them. But the government, undeterred, put him on the commission again a few years later, this time in company with Sir John Stafford, Sir John Poyntz, and two others. They were to receive the assessors' books at Wickwar, and Stafford went there to meet the other commissioners. Throckmorton did not seem glad to see him, and Stafford asked,

" 'Sir Thomas, is there any matter of gain unto you that I must not be acquainted with this commission, fearing that I should look into your doings?'

"Whereunto he answered nothing, but looked upon this defendant with a furious and angry countenance, in show as though he would have stroken him."

After some more threatenings between the two men and their followers, the commission broke up. Sir Thomas sent the book of assessments to Sir John Poyntz; Sir John saw Sir Thomas's signature and seal, assumed that the book was in order, and signed it himself, "not looking thereinto or considering thereof." It was then discovered that a name had been altered in the book, without the consent of Poyntz or Stafford. It is uncertain what happened next, but it seems that Poyntz and Stafford, on their own initia-

32. *A.P.C., 1592–93,* p. 474. For similar reprimands to the Norfolk commissioners, see Saunders, *Official Papers of Sir Nathaniel Bacon,* pp. 78–84; for a general discussion of the difficulties in collecting Elizabethan subsidies, see Dietz, *English Public Finance,* pp. 385–88.

tive, made out another book with different rates, by which the collection was made.[33]

Stafford doubtless implied by his question that Sir Thomas had used his influence to falsify the assessment lists. This was a common charge. After the assessors had made their book, the commissioners might change the amount of any man's tax. They usually did so by returning the book to be revised by the assessors. A man of Mitcheldean, for instance, was supposedly worth £500 in money and goods; the assessors valued his goods at only £3, "so low a rate as that the meanest in the parish was set as high." The commissioners, who had just been prodded by a sharp letter from Whitehall, sent back the book to have his rate changed. The assessors raised it to £6, which seems to have been considered adequate.[34]

A similar case, two years before, throws further light on assessors and commissioners. The assessors of the parish of Newent met in the chancel of the church to agree upon their assessments. One of the parishioners, caught by a shower, took refuge in the church. As he was walking in the nave, some of the assessors asked him to join them. He did so, "and at this defendant's thither coming, the said assessors told this defendant that they differed in opinion concerning the assessing of him this defendant; which when this defendant perceived, he this defendant did will them to have a regard to the service they were about, and to deal in the same without malice or partiality, willing them to raise him this defendant at as high a rate as they would, so that they would raise themselves accordingly to that proportion, or words to that effect; saying further that if they did not, then he this defendant would complain in another place." [35]

They finally taxed him at £3 in goods, which he apparently thought was fair. But Sir Edward Winter, one of the commissioners, raised the amount to £6 without con-

33. About 1601; St. Ch. 5/3/70/4.
34. 1604; *ibid.,* 8/310/25.
35. *Ibid.,* 5/W/77/13.

sulting any one. The victim was furious, and not shy about saying so.

"Hath Sir Edward Winter hoisted me up to £6 in goods in the subsidy book, that never was 'sessed at anything before! Well, he hath done very maliciously therein, and showed his evil nature and disposition in it. But it is no matter, I care not for him nor his malice—and never knight or gentleman dealt so scurvily with me as he hath done!"

He went on to say "that such dealing did stink or savor before the face of God and men, adding further that if he this defendant had worn one of the complainant's pied cloaks, the said complainant had not dealt so badly with this defendant as he had done." [36]

In the maze of charges and countercharges which are the records of star chamber, truth cannot be distinguished from lies. Defendants and complainants pictured themselves as models of persecuted virtue. The judges, reading the evidence, could not have decided easily; the modern reader cannot decide at all. But from the cases just considered, certain conclusions are apparent. A subsidy was not collected without friction, nor without dishonesty. The assessors, like the constable, were involved in trouble with their neighbors. The commissioners, who were usually J. P.'s as well, showed the same failings in one rôle as the other. There must have been many who were virtuous; they did their work and left no record. There were many more who were not, and their record is writ large. These black sheep were partial to themselves, their friends, and their followers, and arrogant and spiteful to their enemies. There was no power in the county to restrain them from

36. *Ibid.*, 5/W/11/34. Both this and the previous case resulted from the collection of the subsidies voted in 1601. An unsuccessful attempt had been made at that time to establish exemptions of £4 in lands and £6 in goods; £3 in goods seems to have been exempt. (See Dietz, *English Public Finance,* p. 383.) The question at issue in these instances seems to have been whether the men should be entered on the subsidy rolls. Once they were so entered, they would be liable for every future subsidy.

misusing their authority, and they had nothing to fear but the slow and distant anger of the privy council. When such men were in charge of the subsidy, the county was not apt to be justly assessed, or the government to receive its due.[37]

The most interesting series of taxes has not yet been mentioned. Subsidies were dependent on an accord between king and parliament. In 1626–29 there was little accord, and in 1629–40 there was no parliament. The king therefore embarked on a series of fiscal experiments. They failed, and their failure is a measure of the limitation imposed upon the crown by the nature of local government.

The first experiment was the free gift. The J. P.'s, in 1626, were instructed to gather together the inhabitants of the several divisions, and discuss with them what sums they were willing to give to the king. The Gloucestershire justices did not follow their instructions to the letter, but tried some method of their own. The privy council ordered them to do as they were told, for "we conceive that your proceeding would prove as unexpected to his Majesty as the success itself, if the matter should rest there." [38] They

37. The amounts received from a subsidy varied, and the rates were occasionally readjusted. Statistics for nineteen townships in the southern part of the county, for the end of Elizabeth's reign and the whole of Charles's, may be found in G.P.L. MSS. 16,057, fos. 1–16, 18–31; 16,061; statistics for Tewkesbury, 1620–29, are in Tewkes. Corp. Rec. 1, fos. 8–33. Both sets of figures show the expected decrease in the yield after about 1622. The Gloucester MSS., however, indicate that the yield at the end of James's reign was substantially larger than that at the end of Elizabeth's. This is contrary to the general downward trend throughout the country, for which see Dietz, *English Public Finance,* pp. 391–93.

The information about clerical subsidies is slight. At the beginning of the period, Bishop Bullingham was so badly defrauded by his taxcollectors that a large part of his property was seized by the crown; he claimed that he was consequently "constrained to give over all hospitality, and to live in far meaner estate than his calling doth require." (E. 112/15/115.) Bishop Goldsborough, his successor, had much the same trouble: £900 was due from the diocese, of which he contributed £100; some of the remaining £800 was paid to him in kind, in the form of forty quarters of wheat, but even these his collector failed to gather. E. 134/11 Jas. I/E/25; for a general discussion of these clerical subsidies, see Dietz, *English Public Finance,* pp. 394–96.

38. MS. A.P.C. XXXIV, 59v.

obeyed, and had no better success. The reply of the county was ominous: the men who appeared "made in every particular division this one unanimous answer, that they humbly submitted themselves and their estates to be disposed of by his Majesty by way of parliament, and were and ever would be ready to supply his Majesty in that course to the uttermost of their abilities." [39]

The tax was a significant failure, but the government ignored its significance. War with France was approaching, the exchequer was almost empty, and a new expedient had to be tried at once. Though it was called the forced loan, it was the free gift again with little change.[40] The change had come in public opinion. Opposition had stiffened to the point where even the commissioners of the loan refused to pay it. The tax was entrusted to the lord lieutenant, and he was soon out of his depth in trouble. On 17 February, 1627, he wrote to the privy council that Salop and Herefordshire were paying dutifully.

Yesterday . . . I met with the commissioners for this county of Gloucester, being in number twenty-five, . . . of which twelve denied both payment and subscription. . . . Pardon me to advertise your lordships that these knights and gentlemen that thus refused, did [so] in the fewest words and arguments that could be imagined. And when they were moved to enter into bond, they did it as willingly and did submit themselves as dutifully to his Majesty's and your lordships' pleasures (the premises excepted) as can be expressed. The city and the county of the city have consented, and four other hundreds of the outshire thereunto adjoining; so that we are in good hope of the rest. The next hundreds I am to go to (for I intend, out of the duty and affection I have to perfect the service, to visit the whole shire)[41] are such as the

39. S.P. 16/33/59. For a closely similar resolution by the corporation of Reading, see Guilding, *Reading,* II, 305–06.

40. The forced loan was not a novelty. Such loans had been levied intermittently throughout the period, and had at times aroused opposition; see Dietz, *English Public Finance,* pp. 81, 115, etc. I have found no record of such opposition in Gloucestershire before 1627.

41. Which he had not done for the other counties of his commission.

chiefest of those gentlemen which refused to subscribe do dwell in. We urging them that their denial might be a great hindrance to the service in respect of their neighbors, they answered that they would by no means hinder it either by persuasions or other ways. And pressing them to assist the commission (the neglect whereof I thought would be very ill taken by his Majesty and your lordships), their answers were that it was not fit for them to persuade others to do that which they in conscience had refused to do." [42]

On 2 March, things were still going well in the city and badly outside.

Though at that place [Gloucester] we had indifferent success with the inferior sort, scarce any denying but such as we then informed your lordships of, yet in other parts of that shire we found many that did refuse. I cannot say that the example of the first refusers occasioned the denial of others, for we could not discover any combination or plot. But the numbers were great; and the most eminent of them we have bound to appear before your lordships, and the poorer sort we have charged upon their allegiance to be ready to appear whensoever they shall be called. . . . Since that time we find the refusers not only to multiply in numbers, but to be far more refractory than the former, insomuch as they refuse to subscribe, lend, or to be bound to appear before the council to answer their contempts. . . . Whether the denial of the gentlemen at first, or their impunity hitherto, have more occasioned the obstinacy of so many, and emboldened the inferior rank to make such peremptory refusals, I must remit to your lordships' judgments.[43]

On the same day he wrote to Secretary Conway:

It is true that you and I do affect Gloucestershire and the gentry there as much as of any other place, and therefore are

42. S.P. 16/54/28.

43. S.P. 16/56/8. The procedure of the commissioners was governed by general instructions, for which see Gardiner, *History of England,* VI, 144. It is clear that these instructions, at least in Gloucestershire, could not be carried out.

far from pressing the disgrace or punishment of those gentlemen of worth. Yet it may be very fit and expedient (I open my heart to your lordship) that the country might see that those that refused to lend, or absented themselves from attending the service, might not pass so freely away. For it may embolden others to the like, and make us suffer largely who have been most industrious in his Majesty's service, and be laughed at for our pains. And to tell your lordship truly, some whom your lordship affects very well have been very sensible in this particular, and have been instant with me to that effect, in regard they must remain there, and every day subject to censure or contempt for doing his Majesty's service.[44]

This wave of popular feeling, like the wave which runs up the Severn, was the sign of a rising tide. It is worth noting the names of the few men who were not allowed to "pass so freely away," for most of them were leaders of the county. Thirteen of those who refused to be commissioners had to give bonds of £40 to appear before the council. Seven of the thirteen never appeared, among them Sir Richard Berkeley and Nathaniel Stephens. Sir Robert Poyntz, Thomas Nicholas (the high sheriff), Maurice Berkeley, Henry Poole, Nathaniel Coxwell, and John Dutton appeared and were imprisoned.[45] Among the lesser men, some could not be found, some gave bond to go to London, some refused bond but took oath to go, and some would neither lend, be bound, nor take oath. The commissioners, when they were finally selected, "endeavored again and again to win our country by persuasion of the necessity of the service, and offered the reasons given by his Majesty's instructions, and used the order prescribed. And [we] have examined divers upon oath, and have set before them our example and the example of others, and out of our particular acquaintance have wrought many

44. S.P. 16/56/12. For a similar situation in Nottingham, see Stevenson, *Nottingham,* V, 125–28.

45. S.P. 16/54/28; 16/56/70. Poyntz, Dutton, and Poole were released the next January. MS. A.P.C. XXXVI, 34, 249.

to assist." [46] But their "particular acquaintance" was not enough. They were helpless with any one who refused obedience, for they had no force behind them. With the temper of Gloucestershire as it was, a forced loan without force could not be an effective loan.

There was one kind of force which the government did use: the pressgang. Conway, from shame or caution, was at first unwilling to use this weapon openly; he ordered that those who refused the loan should be pressed, but without parading the reason.[47] The king, however, had no such scruples. Shortly afterward he wrote the lord lieutenant that those who had refused the loan were patently "insensible of the danger which threatens them and us, . . . thereby discovering their disaffection to their prince and country, and exposing them as much as in them lies to the foreign enemy. We . . . do by the advice of our privy council think fit that such as thus neglect us and themselves, shall serve in person for defense of our kingdoms." A hundred and fifty recalcitrants in Gloucestershire were accordingly to be pressed, "to serve on foot in our wars." [48]

This coercion was as unfair as it was brutal. In practice it affected only the poorer men, and did not touch the men whose example had inspired them. The gentry, as a

46. S.P. 16/58/1.

47. A pressing warrant was returned to London to be altered, "in regard that it mentioned the pressing of disaffected persons. His lordship would have had it absolute for the pressing of 150 men out of the county, without mentioning any such persons; and the pressing of such, and yet the sparing of the clothiers . . . , to be expressed in private instructions sent with the letter." (S.P. 16/56/100.) The same hesitance was more apparent in the treatment of men in Essex who had been pressed for refusing the loan: when they also refused the press-money, the privy council rescinded their impressment. Gardiner, *History of England,* VI, 156–57.

48. S.P. 16/89/4. Queen Elizabeth's government had handled this sort of problem more suavely. When men in Norfolk would not pay the equivalent of a forced loan, they were told that their property would be assessed at its actual value in future subsidies. The same method was used to collect Elizabethan ship money in Suffolk and Dorset. Saunders, *Official Papers of Sir Nathaniel Bacon,* pp. xxvi, 95–97; Ada H. Lewis, *A Study of Elizabethan Ship Money, 1588–1603* (Philadelphia, 1928), p. 48.

class, were too powerful to be touched. Some were fined, and a few imprisoned; but most of them could and did disobey with impunity. The government tacitly accepted what it could not remedy, and cast about for a better method of opening a gentleman's purse.

The result was the bizarre experiment known as distraint of knighthood. Few of the gentry, especially from distant counties like Gloucestershire, had attended King Charles's coronation. If they had, according to the government's argument, they would have been knighted and paid the requisite fees. Since they had not, they would have to pay for their slight to the crown. Six years after the coronation, commissioners were sent into the country to exact payment in the form of fines. They were to ferret out every man of substance. "To that end you shall send for the undersheriff, escheator, and feodary of the county,[49] for the high constables, bailiffs, petty constables, and such other as in your judgments ye think fittest to give you true information therein." They were to examine the subsidy rolls, the muster rolls, and the parish books of collections for the poor. Once they got a man into their clutches, they were not to let him go for less than £10, or £25 if he were a justice of the peace.[50]

49. The escheator and the feodary are officials about whom I have almost no information. The feodary's accounts are extant for a short period, 1590–1602, but they are not enlightening. (Bodl. MS. Rawl. B 324.) The escheator of the inshire was usually the mayor of Gloucester, but apparently not *ex officio*. The escheator of the outshire, in 1603, was the same as the feodary of 1598–1602, and presumably held both offices; see *H.M.C., Salisbury MSS.*, XV, 47–48.

50. "All baronets who were not knighted at our coronation or before, all knights who have received that order since that time, all who have lands or rents to £40 yearly value, although held in socage or though held of common persons or of us by a mesne tenure, all who have but an estate of freehold for life only, are liable to this fine, his Majesty reserving to himself the composition with all the nobility that are liable to the same." If a man had not had £40 worth of land at the time of the coronation, he was excused; many escaped in this way. The subsidy rolls were the principal basis of assessment, and the rate was in general three and a half times that of the subsidy. The payments which were actually made in the county varied from £2 to £15, and averaged between £4 and £5. E. 178/5310.

Their summons were ignored by a number of men, and in due course the defaulters heard from London. "His Majesty doth much marvel, considering that you cannot be ignorant how legal this demand is, and consequently how much the said commission is in your favor, that nevertheless you should refuse to accept of his Majesty's grace therein." This grace included an unwillingness to begin expensive legal proceedings against "those that, peradventure, more out of mistaking or ill example of others, than out of their own wilful oppositions to his service, have been herein misled." The delinquents were therefore summoned to Whitehall, "to th' end that in pursuance of his Majesty's pleasure, we may treat with you concerning the said composition before any further or more compulsory proceeding be against you." [51]

Government could not be financed by such petty expedients. Gifts and loans had raised more resentment than revenue, and the crown was in desperate need of funds. In 1634, the last experiment was tried. It was the most durable of the lot, the most remunerative, and the most disastrous. Discontent with unparliamentary taxes had been apparent in 1626, and glaring in 1627. The king was blind to it, as he was to the other factors which were turning opponents into rebels. From 1634 to 1640, he aided the process by the imposition of ship money.

This tax was no novelty in Gloucestershire. It had long been levied upon "certain havens and inland towns," and Gloucester and Tewkesbury had been among them. In 1588, the two between them had paid the cost of a vessel to serve against the Armada.[52] In 1596, Gloucester was

51. G.P.L. MS. 16,528, fo. 26. One actual bill for knighthood at this time, in fees, etc., came to £44 17*s.* (Add. Ms. 34,739, fo. 172.) The tax was therefore much cheaper than the title.

52. The ship was a bark of eighty tons, provisioned for three months. The lord admiral was to send an agent to Gloucester and Tewkesbury, "who shall particularly declare unto you all the charges laid forth in preparing and setting the said ship to the sea." The whole tone of this letter from the privy council suggests that the government was nervous about how the tax would be received, even at that moment of obvious danger. Glouc. Corp. Rec. 1451, fos. 111v–112.

assessed at £200 for ship money, of which £40 was later assigned to Tewkesbury.[53] Thus by the end of the sixteenth century the levy was an embryonic tax, imposed sporadically on the two towns to meet the cost of a specific ship.

When King Charles revived ship money in 1634, it was received much more quietly in Gloucestershire than the free gift or forced loan. This was doubtless because it was familiar, and because the people did not realize how rapidly it would be extended. The first assessment was orthodox, for it was confined to the towns. The corporation of Gloucester heard the warrant without recorded excitement, and appointed its agent to confer with those of the other ports "for the treating upon and expediting of this his Majesty's service so specially given in charge."[54] These agents could not agree on the assessment of their towns, and the privy council referred the matter to the sheriffs of Gloucestershire and Somerset.[55] They added a substantial sum to the Bristol quota, "either of themselves out of an uncharitable disposition, or encouraged by others of a misconceived opinion of the great wealth of this city."[56] The sheriffs believed that the combined levy

The nervousness was justified. There was great difficulty in collecting the money; some two hundred recalcitrants met at Painswick, and sent a delegation to London to lay their complaints before the privy council. The authorities of both towns countered by sending agents of their own, and also by complaining to the Council of Wales that the delinquents were heretics or recusants. The Council of Wales responded with alacrity, and the offenders were badgered by processes until they paid their tax. *Ibid.*, fo. 114; uncatalogued letter book, fo. 16–16v.

53. *A.P.C., 1595–96,* pp. 225–26, 461–62. Gloucestershire was to have been included in the levy of 1603, which was never made; see Lewis, *Elizabethan Ship Money,* pp. 32–36.

54. Glouc. Corp. Rec. 1452, p. 36. By the irony of fate, there is a very different entry in the same year. "The wall between the Southgate and the Barbican, . . . that hath been so long in question, shall be amended forthwith by the chamber of this city." (*Ibid.*, p. 39.) Nine years later, this wall was manned against the king and his army.

55. MS. A.P.C. XLIV, 265–66.

56. *H.M.C., Twelfth Report,* II, 74. A similar quarrel between Gloucestershire, Somerset, and Bristol had occurred in 1626, when King Charles made his first experiment with ship money in the maritime counties; see Dietz, *English Public Finance,* pp. 231–32.

on the towns, of £6,500, was more than was needed to build the proposed ship. They submitted a lower estimate, which was accepted on condition that they would furnish bonds for building the ship at their price. The privy council was convinced that it could not be done, and warned the sheriffs sharply that the service was not to be dallied with. The council was apparently right; a few weeks later it thanked the sheriffs for making a further collection.[57]

In the city of Gloucester all went smoothly. The tax was laid on every one who could afford to pay, and even the clergy were not exempt; their assessments varied from 2*s.* 6*d.* for the vicar of a small city church, to £4 for the bishop.[58] Apparently every one did pay. A surplus had been collected at the end of 1635, and was kept for 1636; in that year there was also a surplus, which was returned to the inhabitants.[59]

It was in the outshire that trouble started. By the middle of 1635, the tax had been extended to the entire county. The undersheriff reported that "all men for

57. MS. A.P.C. XLIV, 322–23, 377, 388, 442. This incident shows that the original levy was in terms of the cost of a specific ship. This was still true in London as late as 1636, when the citizens were providing the ships more cheaply than the government could do it. But the idea of converting the demand for a ship into the demand for money was evident in the Elizabethan period, and was essential to Noy's conception of the tax in 1634. See Lewis, *Elizabethan Ship Money,* pp. 62–63, 100–01; M. D. Gordon, "The Collection of Ship-Money in the Reign of Charles I," *Transactions* of the Royal Historical Society, third series, IV, 153; Dietz, *English Public Finance,* p. 267.

58. S.P. 16/313/67. The attempt to tax the clergy was one of the great novelties of ship money; see Dietz, *English Public Finance,* p. 396; and below, p. 126 note 68.

59. MS. A.P.C. XLV, 173–74; XLVII, 16–17. The surplus at the end of 1636 is surprising in the light of other evidence. There had been a dispute between the city and the rest of the inshire about the amount which each should pay, and the privy council had referred the question to the Bishop of Gloucester. At the beginning of August he reported that the city was £15 behind in its quota, and that he was endeavoring to have the rest of the inshire take over the deficit. "Our neighbors of Worcester did much spare their city, in regard of the decay of trading there, and the same reason may be alleged for Gloucester." S.P. 16/330/94; see also Gordon, "The Collection of Ship-Money," p. 151.

ought he perceives are very willing to pay." [60] But the sheriff had a different story to tell. In December "divers men give dilatory answers that they have not money, and others stand mute and say nothing." [61] By January of 1636, £3,400 had been collected out of £5,500 assessed; the sheriff certified the names of defaulters. In February, many of the chief men of the county had still not paid, although the money had often been called for.[62] There was trouble in the division of Kiftsgate; the constables and tithingmen had not returned their assessments, and eleven were cited. There was trouble in the hundred of Slaughter, where the constable of Sherborne was £21 in arrears, and Mr. Slaughter himself refused to make an £8 assessment on the inhabitants of Slaughter.[63] By November, however, the £2,100 deficit had been reduced to £324. The ex-sheriff believed that this collection had been due to his diligence; he had even used his own household servants when necessary. His efforts had exhausted him, and he begged to have the collection of the remaining arrears turned over to his successor.[64] But the privy council merely ordered him "cheerfully to proceed accordingly." [65]

His successor, in the spring of 1636, wrote to the council to inquire about his instructions, and received a gruff

60. S.P. 16/302/54.

61. S.P. 16/304/73. The rôle of the sheriff is interesting. It was the lord lieutenant who collected this tax under Elizabeth, and it was the lord lieutenant who tried to collect the forced loan. (Lewis, *Elizabethan Ship Money, passim;* above, pp. 148–50.) Yet I have found no mention of the lord lieutenant in the six years of King Charles's experiment with ship money; the sheriff seems to have been in sole command.

62. S.P. 16/302/54.

63. S.P. 16/311/78.

64. Out of the total of £5,500, £500 had been assessed on Gloucester, £60 on Tewkesbury, £20 on Chipping Campden, and the remainder on the rest of the outshire. Chipping Campden paid nothing: it had long been visited with the plague, and neighboring towns were paying it £30 a week on command of the J. P.'s. S.P. 16/335/37.

65. He might obtain warrants from the new sheriff, but not assistance in collecting the money. (MS. A.P.C. XLVI, 462.) From 1635 on, Gloucestershire was one of the five counties in which the proportion of assessments collected was the smallest. Gordon, "The Collection of Ship-Money," pp. 142, 156–62.

response. His letter had been read, "wherein, however, most of the questions and doubts by you made . . . are such and so frivolous as no other sheriff hath made besides yourself, and therefore might give us cause to suspect your backwardness in the service." His questions were duly answered, but only to deprive him of all excuse for backwardness.[66]

In the collection of ship money, the whole organization of civil government was called into play. The sheriff was at its head, but the petty constable was as much concerned. The functioning of the organization, and the difficulties of its officials, are well illustrated by a series of letters preserved among the papers of John Smyth. The scene was the hundred of Berkeley, the year 1636.

The sheriff issued a warrant to the two high constables of the hundred. They in turn issued warrants to the constables and tithingmen of the various townships. Those of North Nibley were summoned to Wotton under Edge, to consider how the assessment of £15 6*s.* "may be distributed and divided upon the inhabitants of your township with most equality and indifferency." [67] From Slimbridge £10 4*s.* was to be collected; the list of assessments was to be brought to the high constables at Tetbury. The petty constables were especially to note "how much your clergyman is rated for his mere ecclesiastical possessions, and what for his temporal and personal estate." The individual assessments were to be levied on land, unless there was "any man of ability, who by reason of gainful trade, or great stocks of money or other personal estate, have or occupy little or no land"; such a man was to be taxed at his actual worth. Large families, and those in debt, were to be treated leniently.[68]

66. He was ordered to distrain, when necessary, on goods which would be useful for the navy. (MS. A.P.C. XLVI, 154.) Sheriffs throughout the country were receiving similar brusque treatment from the privy council; see Gardiner, *History of England,* VIII, 102–03.

67. G.P.L. MS. 16,527, fo. 69.

68. *Ibid.,* fo. 71. The language of these warrants repeated the general instructions of the privy council, which were designed to secure equi-

The high constables then reported to the sheriff that they had summoned the men as directed. Constables and tithingmen appeared for the most part, and with them several of the leading citizens. "But none of them would proceed with us to the rating of the several inhabitants in their townships, . . . without first acquainting their neighbors therewith, pretending their ignorance of other men's estates and abilities." The high constables accordingly asked for further instructions, "especially if they neglect what of them is required, whereof we have some doubt out of their general unwillingness thereunto, as was observed amongst them." [69] The sheriff replied that they should carry out their warrants, and return the names of defaulters at the next Gloucester sessions, together with those from whom they had required but not received assistance in collecting.[70]

The high constables answered that they had issued new warrants to towns which had neglected the first ones, and had appointed a new meeting place. "But after we had from nine in the morning till four in the afternoon attended according to our said warrant, there came only to us [*blank in MS.*], all the rest making default not only in their personal appearance, but of bringing or sending to us any rate or assessment at all." [71] They thereupon sent

table taxation throughout the country. The attempt to tax "money or other personal estate" apparently broke down in England as a whole, as it had so often done before, and ship money became primarily a tax on land. (Gordon, "The Collection of Ship-Money," pp. 146–51; Dietz, *English Public Finance,* p. 397.) Gloucestershire seems to have been no exception. The local basis of taxation on land, however, cannot be determined from the scanty material. At Bourton on the Hill, in 1638, some woods "have of late time been taxed to pay answerable with two yardlands for the ship money," which implies that the yardland was the unit. (E. 134/13 Chas. I/M/38.) At Rodmarton, however, the tax fell most heavily on the two owners of tithable land in the parish, and on the vicar (to his intense annoyance); he does not explain how the assessments were arrived at, but implies that they were in some way connected with the tithe. From his entries in the Rodmarton Register, 1635–36.

69. G.P.L. MS. 16,527, fo. 70.

70. *Ibid.,* fo. 72.

71. *Ibid.,* fo. 73.

a third warrant to North Nibley. The old instructions were repeated, and the petty constable was commanded to come to Berkeley with three or four of his discreetest men. "We will proceed to the rating of you ourselves if again you make default of performing the same." [72] Nibley did not believe them, and a fourth and fifth warrant were issued. The threat in the fifth was peremptory. "Forasmuch as you have neglected to bring to us your assessment of £18 6*s*., . . . these are to give you to understand that unless you bring to us, before Monday night next, the said rate under your hands fair written, we ourselves will proceed to the rating of your tithing, wherein if through ignorance of the states and abilities of the inhabitants thereof, such our rate chance to be more unequal than we desire, the fault thereof is to be ascribed to yourselves." There is a note at the bottom of this letter: "Hereupon the rate was delivered." [73]

The example of North Nibley shows the sort of passive resistance with which the authorities had to contend. But while little men were using the armor of passivity, bigger men felt strong enough for defiance. Six justices refused point blank to pay the tax, or to help in any way with its collection. Two of the six had already refused the forced loan: Nathaniel Stephens and Henry Poole. The name of a third was significant: Walter Nurse, an influential alderman of Gloucester.[74] Even the patient burgesses were becoming restive.

Larger fish were also refusing the net, and the sheriff found himself involved with one of the most prominent defaulters in England. Lord Saye and Sele had lands at Norton, between Gloucester and Tewkesbury. These lands were heavily taxed, so heavily that the sheriff was nervous about collecting. "I am sorry I am to levy the whole sums

72. *Ibid.,* fo. 74.
73. *Ibid.,* fo. 76.
74. S.P. 16/345/66. The opposition to ship money in Gloucester never seems to have been so strong as in the outshire. The same was true, apparently, of Bristol, although resentment there increased as time went on. See Latimer, *Annals of Bristol,* pp. 132–34.

assessed upon my Lord Saye, inasmuch as I understand the 'sessors have dealt abusively in assessing my lord at two parts and themselves at one, whereas they are accustomed in all other payments to pay double as much as my lord. I touch upon this that I may not receive blame hereafter, if my Lord Saye should complain to the honorable board for unjustice in the assessment." [75] But he need not have worried. Lord Saye refused to pay the tax on any basis, and his assessment was converted into a fine.

The collection of this fine involved a nice question: how far were tenants liable for their landlord? In May, the sheriff was told by the council that when the landlord was assessed, and his lands were in the possession of tenants, either a distress was to be levied on the landlord's personal estate, or his body was to be attached; failing both, his name was to be certified to the council.[76] By this ruling, Lord Saye's tenants were exempt. In September, however, the decision was reversed by the personal intervention of the king. "His Majesty (being this day present in council) did order that in case the sum shall not be forthwith paid, that you levy the same by distress upon the lands so assessed, notwithstanding any former directions. And if the said Lord Saye and his tenants so distrained shall not accord between themselves touching the payment of the said money, whereby the said tenants shall have cause to find themselves grieved, they are to seek their relief in some of his Majesty's courts of equity, where they may be well assured to have such justice as they shall not receive prejudice through the default of their landlord." [77]

With this authority, the ex-sheriff levied a distress on the tenants of Norton. Twenty-five pounds had been owed since his term, and for it he distrained some cattle and sheep. The cattle belonged to a small tenant, who redeemed them for £5. "As for the sheep, neither Lord Saye, nor his tenants who were the owners, would redeem them."

75. S.P. 16/332/6.
76. MS. A.P.C. XLVI, 153.
77. *Ibid.,* pp. 345–46.

The ex-sheriff therefore kept them for three weeks, at his own expense, until he was able to sell them for a sum which exactly covered the arrears.[78] It is unlikely that the tenants sought relief in the courts, because of the cost of litigation. It seems that Lord Saye made a splendid gesture, and that at least in Gloucestershire his tenants paid for it.

There were other examples of individual resistance.[79] But for the most part, the tax seems to have been collected for at least four years without arousing violent opposition. The inhabitants of Mickleton complained of being overtaxed, and "of the favor and ear given to others of great estates and abilities." [80] There was similar trouble at Cirencester and Lechlade: the country gentry assessed the towns at such a high rate that the sheriff hesitated to carry out the collection.[81] But the objection in these cases was to the practice of the tax, not the principle.

By 1638 there were signs of more serious opposition among all classes. We have one glimpse of it among the common people. A woman and her son were talking with their hired hand about ship money. She said "that what for that, and the many other payments that came daily on, one upon another, she thought she should not be able to

78. S.P. 16/335/57.

79. One instance, in 1636, figured in the later impeachment of Sir Humphrey Davenport, the lord chief baron of the exchequer. See T. D. Fosbrooke, *An Original History of the City of Gloucester,* pp. 53–54.

80. The privy council urged the sheriff to give the inhabitants relief. April, 1636; MS. A.P.C. XLVI, 98.

81. The gentry met at the sheriff's summons, and agreed to impose on Cirencester £53 0*s.* 6*d.*, or a quarter of the hundred quota. "They were very earnest with the sheriff to send forth his warrant immediately for the raising of the money." This he refused to do until he had sent to London to get the advice of Sir Thomas Thynne. The latter was a power in Cirencester; if he had been there, "it is probably conceived that . . . they would not have prevailed so far as now they have done. Mr. Bathurst [*Batturst*] of Lechlade was not there, but it seems they had his hand consenting to whatsoever they should agree upon, and so they have obtained their desire against Lechlade as well as against this." (A letter to Sir Thomas Thynne, 1637; Add. MS. 32,093, fo. 181.) The little town of Northleach, at this time, was paying its agents 5*s.* and 10*s.* a trip "to go to see the sheriff about the shipping money." Northleach Court Book, pp. 479, 482.

live." The hired man answered "that howsoever payments went and her ability was, the king must be served." At this point the son spoke up.

"If it be so, that the king must have all, I would the king were dead!"[82]

Two years later, when money was desperately needed for the war against the Scots, none was forthcoming from Gloucestershire. The Short Parliament had been dissolved, and the king was struggling through his last five months of absolutism. His war chest was empty, the Scots were in Northumberland, and ship money had to be collected to pay them off. But collection, at least in Gloucestershire, was an impossibility.

The sheriff was still relying on his constables and petty officers. They reported that they could neither get an assessor to assess nor a collector to collect; when the sheriff ordered them to distrain, they utterly refused. The escheator of Gloucester told the sheriff "that to trust upon them for this service was not the way as before, but nominate bailiffs of his own, and make warrants speedily to them for the levying of the money, which he hath promised shall be done." First, however, the sheriff called two more meetings of the constables at Winchcomb and Tewkesbury. Nothing came of them; August was almost gone, and the total collection from the county amounted to £10.[83]

82. This was the hired man's story, but the son gave him the lie. "The said Wood told his mother that he must go to the justices for some more relief, to which his mother answered that then she saw more trouble and money must be; and he, this examinate, added that God's will must be done. Other than those, or ought of shipping money, or any word at all concerning the king, he denieth to have used then or at any other time whatsoever." (S.P. 16/387/64.) The privy council did not believe him, and ordered him held for the assizes. MS. A.P.C. XLIX, 135.

In the next year, 1639, a man in Gloucester was summoned before the city sessions for abusing a collector of ship money. The lenience of the court is a suggestive contrast to the sternness of the council: the accused and the collector were referred to an alderman "to end the difference between them, and to make them friends." Glouc. Corp. Rec. 1567, p. 17.

83. The escheator to the lord treasurer, 21 August, 1640; S.P. 16/464/64. Ninety pounds was subsequently collected, a total of less

A few weeks later, the sheriff was resorting to imprisonment. He committed some high constables and petty officers who refused to distrain, and sent warrants to arrest others who "neglected the service and will not wait on him to give an account of their doings therein." Still, however, he refused to use his own bailiffs as collectors; his reason was that "he dare not trust the bailiffs with the money because they are beggarly." [84] A month later, just before the opening of the Long Parliament, he was still trying to use the constables. "Mr. Sheriff hath been very earnest in the service, both in punishing the neglect of the officers, and in taking pains himself in traveling about the country for the speeding of the said service." His earnestness and pains were small comfort to the government; the letter was endorsed on the back by Secretary Nicholas, "The escheator of Gloucester justifieth the sheriff's diligence, albeit the sheriff has done nothing to any purpose." [85]

"Nothing to any purpose" is the last word of ship money in Gloucestershire. It epitomizes the collapse of the final experiment, and with it of a pillar of royal absolutism. Exactions for the military the county would pay. There was no resistance to them beyond grumbling petitions, and even ship money was not questioned as long as it retained its military character. Such taxes had the authority of tradition, and were outside the sphere of the house of commons. Parliamentary taxes were also paid. Their collection was laborious, haphazard, and sometimes fraudulent, but there is no trace of hostility to them. Taxes for civil government, on the other hand, when they were unsanctioned by parliament, the county would not pay and could not be forced to pay. The first attempt, in 1626–27, was too short to provoke rebellion. The second,

than 2 per cent of the £5,500 assessed on the county in 1639. See Gordon, "The Collection of Ship Money," p. 158.

84. The escheator to the lord treasurer, 7 September, 1640; S.P. 16/466/80.

85. The same to the same, 5 October, 1640; S.P. 16/469/41.

in 1634–40, aroused the people more slowly because of the peculiar nature of the tax. But it did arouse them in the end. Their anger over ship money, by 1643, was a forgotten part of a greater anger. Yet it was one of the underlying reasons why the guns of Gloucester were turned on the king and his army.

VI

ECONOMIC REGULATION

THE FINANCIAL DIFFICULTIES of the central government might have been expected to limit the scope of its activities; poverty is a reasonable motive for a policy of laissez faire. But such a policy had not yet been dreamt of in Whitehall or in the county. The paternalism of the Tudors was still alive in the Stuarts, and still permeated the agencies of government. It was assumed that the prosperity of the nation (and with it the income of government) could be maintained only by the most careful control of trade and industry. Subsidizing them was out of the question: funds were not available for pump-priming, and could not be created by the wizardry of a national debt. But regulating them was another matter. This could be done, almost without cost, by statute and proclamation, implemented by the labors of central and local authorities. It was done, after a fashion, and the fashion is the subject of this chapter.

The privy council endeavored, more hopefully than effectively, to enforce a body of restrictions which would stagger the most ardent supporter of the New Deal. Enforcement was sometimes deputed to private citizens, sometimes to special agents, and sometimes to municipal authorities, but the privy council was usually the moving force. Control was exercised, in one way or another, over the market for grain, the consumption of beer, the privileges of guildsmen, commerce on the Severn, timber in the Forest of Dean, the growing of tobacco, the manufacture and sale of cloth. These topics form the subject matter of the present chapter. They will be dealt with in sequence, but not in detail; the purpose of the chapter is to describe the relationship between government and the economic activities of the county, rather than to describe those activities in themselves.

The fundamental concern of government was the preservation of order. This concern underlay a large part of its economic policy, but appeared most clearly in its care for the food supply. Famine was always a possibility, and famine bred rioting. The transportation of grain was so slow that there might be a dangerous local shortage even when there was abundance in other parts of England. The government therefore tried to control not only the consumption of grain, but also its shipment from county to county. The ramifications of this control can best be understood by watching it at work in various crises of the period.

In 1586–87 there was an acute dearth of grain in Gloucestershire. The poor "weep and cry for corn openly in the markets, not able to buy above a peck or half a peck at once." [1] But this was only a foretaste of hardship; a longer and more serious shortage began in 1594. The inshire quarter sessions, in that year, were granting licenses to transport grain out of the county. This angered the justices of the outshire, and they petitioned the council to protect their food supply. The council replied by "charging the officers [of Gloucester], in her Majesty's name, in no case to suffer any corn or grain to pass or be laden from hence until the same should become better cheap." [2] This

1. S.P. 12/188/18. A corn barge at the banks of the Severn was attacked and rifled by a starving crowd. Two of the ringleaders, when arrested, explained that "they were driven to feed their children with cats, dogs, and the roots of nettles." (S.P. 12/188/47; see also *H.M.C., Twelfth Report,* IX, 459.) A similar attempt was planned during the depression of 1622, but not carried out; see R. H. Clutterbuck, "State Papers Relating to the Cloth Trade, 1622," *Trans. (Transactions of the Bristol and Gloucestershire Archaeological Society),* V (1880–81), 160.

The privy council, in 1587, instructed the authorities of Gloucester to examine by jury the quantities of corn in the hands of the several dealers. Licensed dealers were to give bond to serve the market, and unlicensed dealers were to be suppressed; no one was to buy or sell except in open market. These instructions were diligently observed, but prices in the city went on rising. Glouc. Corp. Rec. 1450, fo. 60.

2. Lansd. MS. 76, no. 47, fo. 103; for petitions from Norfolk to the same effect, see Saunders, *Official Papers of Sir Nathaniel Bacon,* pp. 130 ff. The Gloucester magistrates canceled the licenses which they

may have satisfied the petitioners, but it did not affect the price of grain. By autumn the price was still rising, and there was such disorder in the markets that many farmers refused to bring in their corn.[3]

This scarcity was nationwide, and lasted for another three years. By the beginning of 1597, however, the council believed that Gloucestershire was in less immediate danger than its neighbor to the northeast. Warwickshire was in acute distress, and the justices there were told to confer with their fellows in adjacent counties about obtaining supplies of grain. The council instructed the Gloucestershire J. P.'s in the application of the golden rule: the greatest possible assistance should be given to their neighbors, "as you again would wish the like to be done to your county in like case." [4]

But the local authorities were hard put to it to keep their own poor from starving. Rains had ruined the crops; prices were exceedingly high, and likely to go higher before the next harvest. It was feared that all England did not have grain enough for her needs, and the provident began importing. Sometimes this was done by a private merchant, in hopes that men of wealth in the county would buy the grain for distribution to the poor.[5] Some-

had issued, and wrote to the council to justify themselves. They particularly stressed their diligence in cutting down the amount of barley converted into malt. Glouc. Corp. Rec. 1451, fo. 152v.

3. *A.P.C., 1595–96,* pp. 180-81. Bristol was especially hard hit, because it had to stock ships for the navy. The privy council therefore ordered that agents of the city should be allowed to purchase Gloucestershire grain, even after the ships were victualed, since the city was too populous to be supplied from its own environs. *Ibid.,* pp. 158–59; see also *1596–97,* pp. 339–40.

4. *Ibid., 1597–98,* p. 316; see also pp. 314–17.

5. An example in point is that of a Bisley clothier, who contracted at this time to import a large quantity of rye from Danzig. "It would be pleasing unto almighty God, and a charitable act, to make provision of corn . . . to supply the wants of your poor and dutiful subjects, who were very likely (without some such provision made) to perish with want." When he had made his contract, he advertised it to such of the local gentry as he thought "to be most careful for the relieving of the poorer sort of people." Req. (Records of the Court of Requests) 2/130/38.

times also it was done by municipal authorities. London and Bristol imported rye, during the summer of 1597, from Poland and Holland, and Gloucester followed their example by contracting for five hundred quarters "to serve for the relief and use of the poorer sort of the inhabitants." The privy council cordially approved, and sent orders to expedite the shipment.[6]

There were intermittent bad harvests during the years which followed, particularly in 1609.[7] But it is not until 1630 that there is any further light on the activities of government. For several years before that, the inshire had been exporting grain to the neighboring counties of Wales. In 1630, however, the situation was reversed. There was dearth in Gloucester, and one of the inhabitants petitioned the privy council for license to import grain out of Wales. He offered to give security that it would not be reshipped abroad, but was told that he must also have a certificate that there was abundance in Wales. The certificate was obtained, and the license was granted. At once there was protest. The Welsh J. P.'s complained that the price of grain was rising in their counties, and urged that the license should be revoked at once. Bristol clamored against unfair discrimination: its own supply of grain had been practically shut off by governmental restraints, and why should Gloucester be favored above Bristol? [8]

The privy council apparently paid no attention. Its interest had been shifted for the moment from the inshire to the outshire. A report had been received that the clothiers near Tetbury were using an immoderate amount of oatmeal for thickening and dressing their cloth, and

6. *A.P.C., 1597,* p. 119. The contract price was 5*s.* 9*d.* a bushel. The market price of rye at the time was 8*s.* 6*d.;* barley was 6*s.* 8*d.,* and wheat 10*s.* (or 12*s.* 6*d.* in Tewkesbury). The enormity of these prices can be understood by contrast with 1620, a year of abundance, when the best wheat at Tewkesbury was 3*s.,* and barley was 1*s.* 4*d.* Glouc. Corp. Rec. 1451, fo. 165v; Rudder, *History,* p. 737; Giles Geast Rent Book, *anno* 1620.

7. Woodwall, *A Sermon Wherein Are Shewed the Causes of This Dearth Now, 1608 and 1609,* pp. 16–18, 52; *N. & Q.,* I, 200–04.

8. S.P. 16/175/66; 16/185/19; MS. A.P.C., XL, 181–82, 185.

were thereby taking food from the poor. The justices were told to investigate this rumor; if it were true, they were to stop the waste until oats were again abundant. They summoned the clothiers, who unanimously denied the charge. It had been said that one of them was using as much as fifty quarters a week, but none admitted to using even a full peck. The justices believed them, and the council believed the justices, and the matter was dropped.[9]

A far more serious diversion of grain has not yet been mentioned, because it is a subject in itself. Food and drink were almost inseparable, and for most men drink meant ale and beer. Since both are made from malt, and malt from barley, the consumption of drink had a direct bearing on the food supply. While the government deplored drunkenness on moral grounds, and even more as a threat to public order, its most immediate concern with the matter was economic, an aspect of its concern with food. This aspect is best seen in the restraints put upon maltsters, and to a less extent in the restraints put upon the sellers and consumers of drink.

Whenever there was a scarcity of food, one of the first acts of central and local authorities was to curtail the making of malt. This was particularly true during the dearth of 1594–97. In the spring of 1595, the magistrates of the inshire and outshire prohibited all malt-making for the space of five months.[10] In the autumn of the following year, the privy council was complaining that its orders to the same effect were not obeyed. It therefore reiterated them: all maltsters who had other means of livelihood must be suppressed, and the output of those remaining must be limited to the minimum needed for local consumption. For

9. *Ibid.,* p. 158; S.P. 16/177/53; W. St. C. Baddeley, *A Cotteswold Manor, Being the History of Painswick,* p. 182.

10. Glouc. Corp. Rec. 1451, fo. 155. The Gloucestershire magistrates, in this case, seem to have anticipated their statutory authority. They were empowered to prohibit malt-making by 39 Elizabeth, c. 16; but even by this act they might not prevent a man's converting barley which he had grown himself, or received as tithe. For a discussion of the statutes on this subject which were in force in 1614, see Lambard, *Eirenarcha,* p. 451.

once the justices responded with alacrity, but their zeal outran their discretion. They cut off the supply of barley to Gloucester, and thereby produced an acute shortage not only in the city, but in all the country districts which it supplied. The council instructed them to undo their work, and open the market again.[11]

The reason for this attack on the Gloucester market is not far to seek. The Severn drained away the food supply. Malt was shipped down river, either to other parts of England or abroad, and the county was thereby deprived of barley without even the compensation of a superfluity of beer. The Gloucester authorities were alive to this abuse, and provided a forthright remedy: whenever too much malt was being exported, the Severn was closed with a padlock and chain. The corporation boasted to the privy council of this device, but the brewers of Bristol were soon complaining that it cut off their malt. The council finally intervened, and seems to have succeeded in having the chain removed.[12]

Local authorities were also interested in regulating the consumption of drink. Their motives were partly economic and partly social: the desire to protect the grain supply, and the need to preserve public order. Their methods also were twofold. On the one hand there were constant attempts to enforce the statutory restrictions on wine taverns and alehouses, and to amplify them by local ordinance. On the other there were attempts to regulate the

11. The lord lieutenant and others reported that some of the justices were themselves the worst offenders, in that they converted immoderate quantities of barley into malt. (See *A.P.C., 1596–97,* pp. 152–53, 226–27, 335–36.) This abuse by maltster-justices must have been widespread throughout the country, because the restraining act (39 Elizabeth, c. 16) specifically debarred traders in barley from taking any part in the execution of the statute.

12. The chain was in place by 1593. It was used in 1594, again in 1596, and a third time in 1598; on the last occasion the Bristol brewers complained. The privy council referred the matter to the assize judges, who ordered the barrier removed. Gloucester ignored the order, the council reinforced it, and there is no further mention of the chain. Glouc. Corp. Rec. 1500, fo. 296v; 1451, fos. 152v, 157v; *A.P.C., 1597–98,* pp. 488–89.

brewers, and to prevent a brewery from becoming an informal alehouse. These two methods of control will be dealt with in turn.

The first tightening of licensing laws was done by the assize judges in 1612. They ordered that there should thenceforth be only one alehouse to a village, and two to a market town; all in excess of this quota were to be suppressed. Only "persons of good conversation" were to be given a license; once it was canceled for just cause, its holder might never again be licensed in the county. Since the current statute (7 James I, c. 10) provided only a three-year suspension, it is apparent that the judges were more stringent than the legislators. Such stringency gave great power to the J. P.'s who issued licenses; the power was abused, and four years later the judges ordered that a license could be granted only by four J. P.'s together, or by the sessions.[13]

13. Lansd. MS. 232, fo. 56–56v; Bodl. MS. Rawl. C 358, fo. 30–30v. For similar orders elsewhere, see Bates Harbin, *Somerset,* II, 144; Bennett and Dewhurst, *Quarter Sessions Records of the County of Chester,* pp. 62–65; Mary S. Gretton, *Oxfordshire Justices of the Peace in the Seventeenth Century,* pp. xxix–xxxi. A detailed account of the abuse of the licensing power may be found in a catalogue of Sir Thomas Throckmorton's misdemeanors, in St. Ch. 5/W/20/8. For a general discussion of the statutes on the subject, and the justice's rôle in enforcing them, see Lambard, *Eirenarcha,* pp. 459–60; the difficulties in enforcing the original statute (5/6 Edward VI, c. 25) are set forth in the preamble to 3 Charles I, c. 24.

The licensing of wine taverns is an obscure subject. These taverns were limited to cities and towns by 7 Edward VI, c. 5: with certain specified exceptions, no town was to have more than two; the licenses in corporate towns were to be granted by the town authorities, and in others by the justices. This act was prolonged by 1 James I, c. 25, and I have been unable to find any amending act before 12 Charles II, c. 25, which authorized the creation by the crown of two patentees to supervise the granting of licenses.

That the Edwardian system was still in effect is apparent from the case of Oxford, where licenses were granted by the town authorities. (H. E. Salter, *Oxford Council Acts, 1583–1626,* pp. 57, 68, 74, 295–96.) But the system of the Restoration also seems to have been operative as early as 1619, to judge by a chancery case in that year. A Cirencester innkeeper had borrowed money on the collateral, among other things, of his two wine licenses. The creditor was finally left with the licenses, which he wished to sell; he therefore applied to the commissioners for

In dealing with the problem of the alehouse, local authorities were sometimes strict and sometimes surprisingly lax. A man in Gloucester was forbidden to sell ale, merely because there had been quarreling in his house on the same day that a murder had been committed. At almost the same time laggard justice caught another man long after it should have done so. He had been indicted time after time for selling ale without license, and keeping an unruly house, but had never appeared to answer the indictments. The constables, after years of this futility, were given a warrant to pull down his sign.[14]

It might be assumed that the authorities wished to suppress as many alehouses as possible, and that the public wished to maintain them. But the assumption is unsound, both in Gloucestershire and elsewhere. One instance will illustrate why. Three parishes in the hundred of Berkeley, in 1621, petitioned the sessions to have a number of alehouses shut. The petition was successful, apparently through the influence of Lady Berkeley. The petitioners wrote to thank her, and to ask that the good work should be continued. One of the Berkeley inns had fallen on evil days, and needed a better proprietor. "Our desire is that the king's liege people in their travel might have entertain ment, which at that place as it now standeth they cannot have." The parishioners urged that the present inn be suppressed, and its license assigned to their candidate. "He desireth nothing but only the sign, and authority to use the same, and careth nothing at all for the house." [15]

wine licenses, to have his surrendered and regranted "in other men's names, a matter usual and of course done and permitted." These commissioners appear to have been royal patentees. C. 3/314/39; the end of the MS. is missing.

14. Glouc. Corp. Rec. 1566, Trinity, 1636; Easter, 1633. The sign was important; "it makes show to strangers that the same is an inn," and losing it was a serious blow. An inn in Gloucester was also supposed to have a tennis court. The city authorities, at the beginning of the period, restrained the proprietor of the New Inn from using his court, and ordered that his sign should be pulled down. St. Ch. 8/4/8.

15. G.P.L. MS. 16,524, fo. 35. One parish was not quit of the problem at this time; the churchwardens, years later, paid "for a warrant to put

Local magistrates were as much interested in the number as in the quality of inns. The little town of Northleach, for example, had elaborate zoning laws. No inns were allowed in specified streets and sections, or in the part of town toward Cheltenham, "other the Antelope only." There were also curfew restrictions. No one was allowed in another's house after nine in the evening, or in an inn after ten; if an offender was caught, he spent the night in the stocks. No one, except a child or servant of the house, might enter or leave an inn by anything but the front door. No innkeeper or victualer, on pain of losing his license, might lodge a guest until he had notified the town authorities.[16]

The fourth commandment was applied with especial force to the dispensers of drink. Tewkesbury innkeepers had to keep their street doors shut during the time of divine service, and might not allow drinking or gaming indoors. The brewers of Gloucester were not allowed to send ale or beer out of their houses on Sunday, and no one might come and get it, on pain of a £5 fine.[17]

These Gloucester brewers were a thorn in the side of

down our alehouses." North Nibley accounts, *anno* 1629; for similar petitions elsewhere to suppress alehouses, see Bates Harbin, *Somerset,* I, pp. xlvi–xlvii, 248; II, 42–43, 140, 248–49; Willis Bund, *Worcestershire,* p. 527; Burne, *Staffordshire,* II, 51–52, 69–70; Copnall, *Nottinghamshire,* p. 49; Hardy, *Hertford,* I, 18, 35, 68; V, 296; F. J.C. and D.M. Hearnshaw, *Court Leet Records* [of Southampton], *A.D. 1550–1624,* I, 354, 371; II, 379, 422, etc.; Ratcliff and Johnson, *Warwick,* I, 17–18, 22, 94, 139; II, 46; Saunders, *Official Papers of Sir Nathaniel Bacon,* pp. 51–53.

16. Northleach Court Book, pp. 213–14, 219, 333. The best description which I have found of an unlicensed alehouse is at Bibury, where one Robert Bennett sold "the smaller sort of drink" for 3*d.* a gallon, and a stronger brew for whatever price he could get. "Company have departed late at night . . . so drunk that the said Robert Bennett did follow after them, for fear some of them should fall in the river or into some other danger." 1635; Bibury MS. 148 in Sherborne MSS.

17. Glouc. Corp. Rec. 1451, fo. 147v; Tewkes. Corp. Rec. 2, *circa* 1608. Tewkesbury shopkeepers were allowed to have one window open "until the little bell shall be ringed unto divine service." *(Ibid.)* This is a contrast with Leicester, where no shopkeeper might do business at any time on Sunday; see Bateson and Stocks, *Leicester,* IV, 26, 36–37.

authority. Drunkenness was on the increase, and by 1628 the magistrates were gravely worried. It was becoming more and more common for brewers to sell their beer direct to the consumers, with lamentable consequences. If the practice continued, "then shall all the commonalty of the said city be thereby compelled either to buy and fetch ale and beer by the pot out of doors, or else brew in their own houses, to the great loss and unquietness of all the commons of this city, rich and poor. . . . And so should the commons be unserved and unprovided for, the people brought in use of bibbing and bolling of big crock ale, and the city thereby brought to decay and ruin as other towns hath been. . . .

"Many poor craftsmen and journeymen, resorting and sitting all day at this crock ale, not regarding their poor wife and children at home, but oftentimes being drunk, do fight and brawl and take occasion thereby to play at dice, cards, and other unlawful games, consuming their time in vain. . . ." Things have come to a parlous state, "every one at his pleasure taking on him to be a common brewer, the same brewers now selling by retail, and the alehouse-keepers and victualers brewing the drink to utter, and making it heady and unwholesome for men's bodies, to draw the more custom to their houses; whereby the odious sin of drunkenness doth more and more abound."

After the city fathers had contemplated this vision of debauchery, they passed a set of regulations. A brewer might not manufacture malt, but must buy it from licensed maltsters. He might sell his beer only in the orthodox measures, and only to "alewives, tipplers, retailers," and the other contemporary variants of a publican. These retailers, in turn, were to be controlled with equal strictness. They might sell only in standard measures, and at prices set by the mayor and aldermen. Above all, they were forbidden to brew ale and beer themselves.[18]

18. Another regulation is at odds with these, and indicates the limits of the official desire for temperance: so long as a retailer had four gallons left in his house, he might not refuse to serve a customer.

Four years later, the authorities apparently felt that these regulations were not being enforced. The brewers were therefore incorporated into a "body politic," and the quarter sessions ordered that all beer and ale must thenceforth be bought from some member of the guild. This regulation, according to the justices, had the usual twofold purpose: it was designed to control "such disorders and abuses which daily increase by brewing of strong drink above the assizes, to the increase of drunkenness and many other vices, and the unnecessary consumption and waste of grain." [19]

In this attempt to regulate drinking by organizing the brewers, the justices were employing an age-old method of economic control. The city officials of the seventeenth century, like those of the middle ages, had a double rôle: they were agents of government, and they were also tradesmen. They therefore had a double interest in the economic life of the town, and were intent upon controlling it. This they did, or tried to do, through subsidiary organizations under the supervision of the common council. Thus town government, in its economic aspect, was inextricably tangled with the archaism of the guilds.

The old guild merchant had practically ceased to exist. There were attempts to revive it, as an independent entity, at Cirencester in 1582 and 1595, and at Gloucester

(Glouc. Corp. Rec. 1451, fos. 529–31.) The situation at Cirencester, by 1618, seems to have been like that at Gloucester a decade later. The beadle of the beggars was ordered to report all alehouse-keepers who "entertain in their houses such poor as in their drunkenness spend their earnings without all care of wife and children at home, to th' end they may be made known to the justices, and no longer to be licensed to keep victualing." Cirencester Vestry Book, fo. 45v.

19. Glouc. Corp. Rec. 1566, Epiphany, 1631/32. Southampton attempted to regulate the brewers by controlling the price, quality, and kinds of beer; see Horrocks, *Assembly Books of Southampton,* I, 40, 100–01. The maltsters of each county, at the end of the period, were to be organized into a guild on the instructions of the privy council; there is no sign that these instructions bore fruit in Gloucestershire. Glouc. Corp. Rec. 1540, pp. 220–21; for the restraint of maltsters elsewhere by the sessions, see Copnall, *Nottinghamshire,* p. 52; Ratcliff and Johnson, *Warwick,* I, 33.

as late as 1646.[20] But nothing came of these efforts, and the guild merchant may therefore be ignored. The craft guilds, on the contrary, were still active. Two signs of this activity may be singled out for attention. The structure of a new guild is illustrated by the incorporation of the Gloucester metalworkers in 1607, and the working of an old one by the ordinances passed in 1614 by the Gloucester butchers' guild.

There were eight different groups of metalworkers in the city, ranging from goldsmiths to plumbers. All had had much dealing with each other, but their trades had decayed (or so it was thought) for want of formal regulation. Twenty-one men were therefore incorporated into a company, to which were added all who had served their apprenticeship with any of the twenty-one. The officers were the master and two wardens, one chosen by the company and one by the master. There was also an elected beadle, to assemble meetings and gather fines. Any one refusing office was to be fined, and ejected if he did not pay. For serious offenses a forfeiture might be levied on the offender's goods; if he did not pay, the master and wardens might either sue or distrain. Half the fines collected belonged to the sheriff, half to the company. The master and wardens were arbitrators in any dispute between members; if they failed to settle it, appeal was to the mayor and aldermen, and from them to the law. If a member objected to any of the ordinances, he could take his protest either to the mayor or to the judges of assize.

The master and warden were responsible for preventing fraud and enforcing guild rules. No one might instruct his son or servant for more than six months without presenting him to them, to be bound apprentice. No son or servant of a member might be employed by another member on less than a three-month warning, without the consent either of the first employer or of the master and wardens.

20. Baddeley, *History of Cirencester,* pp. 236–38; John Dorney, *Certain Speeches Made upon the Day of the Yearly Election of Officers in the City of Gloucester,* p. 21.

If a servant left town without license, no one was to employ him on his return until he had paid his fine. No non-member was allowed to buy or sell at wholesale, except to a member, any wares pertaining to the trades of the company.[21] All these regulations might as well have been made centuries before. The old economic order, by 1607, was giving place to new, but there was no sign of it among the Gloucester metalworkers.

The change is no more apparent among the butchers. There was the same prohibition on dealing with non-members, either in purchase or sale; no one was to sell in the weekly open market, or be the partner of an outsider. No one was to keep more than one shop, or to send any one but his apprentice or servant into the country to buy. There were elaborate regulations for the days of slaughtering, and for preventing purchase or sale of meat on Sundays. There was also a prohibition which makes one mourn the passing of the guild: "None of the said company shall kill any sheep and dress it like lamb, to sell it instead or by the name of lamb." [22]

Most of the other rules were concerned with the formal conduct of the members. If a man were fined by the officers, no one was to try to have the fine reduced. Every one was to take his proper place at meeting, and to keep it until the meeting ended or he was excused by the master. All were to attend the induction of a new mayor, and stay until he went home. On the king's holidays, and whenever else the mayor commanded, the whole guild was to attend him at the Tolsey in their best apparel, and go with him to church.[23]

21. Glouc. Corp. Rec. 1472, printed in *H.M.C., Twelfth Report,* IX, 427–30.

22. I have been unable to find that this offense was contrary to statute, but there was an indictment for it at the Middlesex quarter sessions in 7 James I. See Jeaffreson, *Middlesex,* II, 56.

23. G.P.L. MS. 11,664. The ceremonial induction of a new warden is illustrated by the weavers' guild in Gloucester: the members escorted him home through the streets with music, carrying before them "a great cake, consisting of a bushel of wheaten meal, decked with flowers, garlands, silk ribbons, and other ornaments." E. 134/11 Chas. I/M/45; for

The converse of guild restrictions was a curb on outside competition. This curb was in the hands of the town authorities, and seems to have been enforced only sporadically. The butchers were troubled by "foreigners" as late as 1640. In that year the sheriffs of Gloucester were instructed not to let any stands to outsiders, "except they will conform themselves to the old custom, *viz.*, to stay from eight in the morning to one of the clock in the afternoon, and then to pack up." [24]

But it was not only foreigners who bothered the guildsmen. Native non-members were often more effective competitors, because they were likely to be treated more sympathetically by local officialdom. In 1581, for example, the shoemakers' guild petitioned the Gloucester council against men who were openly practicing the cobbler's trade. Most of these interlopers were youths who had never served their apprenticeship. Many of them cobbled only during the winter, and in summer became day-laborers and husbandmen; they were "able and strong persons of body, very apt unto husbandry and other occupations." None of them made a living by cobbling alone, and the petitioners implied that they all would be better off in other work. The aged shoemaker, on the contrary, had only his trade to protect him from poverty; if he were ruined by these young competitors, the city would have to support him.[25] The tone of this petition strongly suggests that the authorities were loath to enforce the guild monopoly, at least against local competition. They seem to have been more interested in the orderly conduct of business than

a description of the Bristol guilds at this period, see Latimer, *Annals of Bristol,* especially pp. 25–26.

24. Glouc. Corp. Rec. 1452, p. 162.

25. *Ibid.,* 1451, fos. 77v–78. It is possible that these young shoemakers were an informal journeyman's guild. Such a guild was in existence among the weavers by the end of the sixteenth century, and was formally organized by the city magistrates in 1602; see *ibid.,* 1262, quoted in *H.M.C., Twelfth Report,* IX, 416–18. A similar situation in Southampton, in 1616, was solved by reorganizing the shoemakers' guild and bringing it under closer control of the town authorities; see Horrocks, *Assembly Books of Southampton,* IV, 68–72.

in vested privilege, and to have incorporated a group of tradesmen primarily because a guild was easier to control than individuals.

Another aspect of the city's economic life was independent of the guilds, and to a large extent independent of the city government. This was commerce. Gloucester was not only a manufacturing town and market center; it was also a port of considerable consequence, and many of its citizens made their living from the river trade. The principal export of the county was malt, and to a less extent fruit and other agricultural produce. In return there were large imports of wine from Gascony and Spain, herring from Ireland, and lead and tin from Cornwall. But these commodities were only a fraction of the commerce on the Severn. The widest variety of wares went past the quays of Gloucester at every tide. Much of it came down river from northern cities, in small boats of fifteen to thirty tons, to be transshipped at Bristol for export abroad. Wheat from Tewkesbury, bound for France; cloth and wool from Manchester; brass pots from Derby; hemp, hops, upholsterer's and haberdasher's ware, wax, thread, and (after 1624) "Shrewsbury cottons," "Kidderminster stuff," and Yorkshire kerseys—almost every kind of produce and manufacture, some of it for Bristol, some for France, some for Italy. In return there were cargoes from Bristol, Wales, Cornwall, Ireland, France and Spain, bound for towns up river or for the midland counties.[26] The Severn was the artery of commerce in western England, and Gloucester was one of the places where the finger of government was on its pulse.

The city had long had the right to levy a tax on goods landed at the quays, and had long claimed the further right to tax cargoes passing by. The receipts were supposed to cover the expense of repairing the Over Bridge, which served the city as a toll-gate. The money was collected by the water bailiff, either as a tax on separate

26. From the Gloucester port books, E. 190/1243–48; see also E. 122/54/26.

cargoes or as a yearly payment, and turned over to the corporation. Since the cost of repairs varied widely from year to year, there was an element of gambling in this aspect of city finance.[27]

The central government, as well, had a financial interest in the commerce of the town. Gloucester had been chartered as a port in 1580, over the vehement protests of Bristol.[28] The protests were ignored. A port was a source of royal revenue from customs receipts, and revenue was more important to the crown than arguments. While the yield from Gloucester was never large, it was not incon-

27. This minor *octroi* illustrates the vagueness of most customary taxes. The first recognition of the city's right to tax seems to have been a star-chamber decree in 1505, which authorized a levy of 3*d.* on every ton of merchandise landed at the quays, 4*d.* for every boat-load of timber passing the bridge (or 2*s.* for firewood), 3*d.* a ton for all other goods passing up river. Cargoes bound for Tewkesbury were excepted, because the town was privileged. This decree was copied in 1614, and was presumably still in force; Glouc. Corp. Rec. 1450, fos. 185v–186.

In 1626–27, the crown granted the city the right to tax all merchandise passing in either direction, unless destined for privileged towns. (*V.C.H.* [*The Victoria History of the County of Gloucester*] II, 164.) Two years later, however, the matter came up in court, and a number of witnesses denied that any tax was customarily paid unless the goods were landed. The water bailiff, on the contrary, testified that for years he had collected a duty of 3*d.* a ton on cargoes passing down river, and had compounded with a number of bargemen for an annual payment of 20*s.* E. 134/4 Chas. I/E/3.

28. "Gloucester is no place for trade or merchandise, because they have no lawful wares meet to be transported, nor ships serviceable or defensible to transport and return merchandise if they had any." Their ships are suitable only for smuggling, since they "slip away, come and go at every mean tide, and so may deceive as much as they will." The trade of Bristol is being ruined: its imports can no longer be sold up the Severn, because Gloucester is importing directly. Its food supply is menaced: Gloucester is exporting grain, and in three years Bristol has been able to buy less than ten quarters there. This upstart port is impoverishing Bristol, depleting the customs revenue, and creating a food shortage in the kingdom. (Harl. MS. 368, fos. 106v–107v, inaccurately quoted in Fosbrooke, *History of the City of Gloucester,* pp. 50–52.) Gloucester, in reply, emphasized its harbor facilities, and asserted that "the greater part of all corn transported into Devonshire, Cornwall, Wales and Ireland are laden at Gloucester and Tewkesbury, or cometh under Gloucester bridge." Lansd. MS. 40, fo. 84.

siderable; in one year the customs on wine alone came to £50.[29]

The office of customs collector was farmed to a private citizen, who commonly leased it to a deputy. The latter pocketed the fees of office, and forwarded the taxes to the exchequer. Taxes for the most part seem to have been paid willingly enough. But the fees, at least in Elizabeth's reign, made the Gloucester customs house a constant irritation to the boatmen on the Severn. It is impossible to say how far this irritation was due to the system, and how far to the character of the deputy customs collector. The only information about the office is about one man who held it, and that man was as stormy a petrel in the commercial world as Sir Thomas Throckmorton among the gentry. But with due allowance for his shortcomings, the troubles of the official throw light on the nature of the office.

Shortly before the period opens, one Edward Barston bought the office of deputy collector from the previous incumbent.[30] Barston was a corn-merchant, "one of the most greatest dealers in lading and carriage of commodities upon Severn." It was suspected that he was himself a smuggler, and that under the cloak of his office "he hath passed away prohibited wares, for himself and his partners, without answering the queen's majesty's custom." [31]

29. 1624; E. 190/1247. Gloucester had been included, ten years before, in circular letters from the privy council to the major ports of the kingdom; its relative importance among them is indeterminable, but scarcely germane. *A.P.C., 1613–14*, pp. 226–28, 403–04; see also *H.M.C., Salisbury MSS.*, V, 393; Camden, *Britain*, p. 362; Taylor, *Last Voyage*, in *Works*, II, 25.

30. Barston and his brother gave a £100 bond to the old incumbent, presumably for payment of the purchase money; Barston and his searcher also entered into recognizances with the crown for the performance of their duties. Barston's recognizance was eventually forfeited, and his lands and those of his sureties were seized by the crown. E. 134/12 Jas. I/E/24.

Barston originally held office under Sir Francis Walsingham, who was farmer of the customs until his death in 1590. The customs were then in the hands of surveyors until 1605, when the great farm of the customs was inaugurated. See Dietz, *English Public Finance*, pp. 322 ff.

31. E. 134/36–37 Eliz./M/14.

His business kept him out of the city most of the time; he therefore farmed his office to a subdeputy, for £16 a year, and the latter entrusted most of the work to his young son. This was in flagrant violation of the law. Barston admitted as much in court, but the admission did not break his hold on the office.[32]

At this time, in 1594, the corporation of Gloucester tried to have Barston removed, in hopes of installing an amenable burgess in his place. The Tewkesbury authorities protested to Cecil, and put forward a candidate of their own. They complained that Gloucester was trying to monopolize the river trade, and was using the customer for this end. The office had been "for the ease of the whole country erected, which the city of Gloucester would surmise to be done only for their advancement." [33]

The upshot was that nothing happened; Barston kept the customs house. His staff consisted of himself, a subordinate known as a controller, and a searcher, or customs inspector. With certain debatable exceptions, all goods had to have a cocket, or certificate of clearance from the customs house, and all cockets involved fees for the officers. The customary rate was 2*s.* for the deputy, 1*s.* for the comptroller, and either 4*d.* or 8*d.* for the searcher.[34] But

32. There is, however, no further reference to his deputy. No man might sell, or depute for money, any office connected with the collection of royal revenue; the penalty for the seller was forfeiture of his office (5/6 Edward VI, c. 16). Barston's own office was illegal under this statute, unless he had received some form of royal dispensation.

Barston also confessed other charges. As a merchant, he had dealt in illegal commodities; as an officer, he had taken bribes. Perhaps in return for these, he had neglected to take bonds from the owners that they would return him certificates of delivery, when the cargoes were worth more than £10. E. 112/16/146, in which the accusations against Barston were made by the corporation of Gloucester.

33. S.P. 12/247/24. The Tewkesbury assumption was presumably that a Gloucester burgess would take smaller fees from his fellow citizens than from outsiders.

34. E. 134/36–37 Eliz./M/14. According to one witness, these fees were somewhat higher than those at Bristol, because the Gloucester officers received no salary from the crown. According to another, however, Barston and his searcher received £6 13*s.* 4*d.* a year "to th' intent they should not enhance any fees in their said offices." E. 134/42–43 Eliz./M/11.

Barston and his subordinates reduced custom to a farce.

The goods of each merchant received a separate cocket, in theory, and the owner obtained it in person at the customs house. These requirements, when put into practice, gave the officers a leeway which they used to the full. A single boat often contained the goods of a number of men. A corresponding number of cockets should have been issued, but the officers sometimes contented themselves with a single cocket at double fees. At other times the owners were unable to appear in person. They could then obtain their cockets by proxy, but only at the exorbitant fee of eight to ten shillings. Private bargains were frequent, but risky. A boatman, for example, secured Barston's promise to pass his calfskins at 2*d.* a dozen, regardless of who obtained the cocket; Barston broke his promise, and the boatmen paid more in fees than he received for the freight.

The searcher was no better. It was his duty to inspect the goods, and then endorse the cocket. In one case he contrived to be out when a man came to his house with a cocket, and his wife endorsed it in his name, and on his instructions, for a fee of 2*s.* The searcher then raided the boat, confiscated the entire cargo, and haled the boatman before the assizes for having an illegal warrant. In another case he raided a trow and demanded sight of the cocket. The trowman answered that it was locked in the purser's chest, and hurried off to find the key. Before he returned, the searcher and his men, "drawing their rapiers, threatening to throw the people of the trow overboard, did take away the said packs and cloths, with other goods from the said trow, by force, and brought the same goods to his own house." In this case he apparently did not follow his usual procedure, which was to release the confiscated goods on receipt of a sufficient bribe.[35]

There may have been another side to his story. The Severn was a smuggler's paradise, and the searcher's job was not always a safe one. A favorite trick of the game was to clear at the customs house, and then put in at Kings-

35. *Ibid.*

rode to take on undeclared goods, brought in small trows from Gloucester or Wales. These goods were loaded onto the ship at night, in such a way that they could be discovered only by displacing all the legitimate cargo. If a searcher visited the boat, he was likely to be discouraged by a crew of "desperate hired cutters out of Wales, which will use most dishonest speeches; so that no officer shall enter aboard them but such as they are sure of." [36]

Another difficulty for the customs officials was the question of what articles were dutiable. Neither law nor practice was specific on this point, and the result of vagueness was confusion. The list of debatable articles was a long one, but they fell under three general headings: one form or another of coal, timber, and fruit. All three were important, particularly to the men of Dean, and all three had been commonly carried from "the forest side" to all parts of England, without receiving any cocket or paying any fees. "This deponent hath heard ancient men affirm that they and their fathers before them used and accustomed so to do, without the let or denial of any of her Majesty's officers." [37] Barston hoped to remove this prescriptive immunity by appealing to the judges of exchequer, and in the last decade of Elizabeth he brought a

36. Lansd. MS. 55, no. 25, fo. 79; see also *ibid.*, 110, no. 27, fo. 82. When smuggled grain was confiscated, it was usual to sell it to the poor; examples of such confiscation and sale by the authorities of Gloucester may be found in E. 134/36–37 Eliz./M/14, and in Glouc. Corp. Rec. 1451, fo. 225. According to the acts granting tonnage and poundage (1 Elizabeth, c. 20; 1 James I, c. 33), half the value of such cargoes was forfeit to the crown, and half to the informer. There is no record, however, that the city paid anything for either of these windfalls.

37. E. 134/36–37 Eliz./M/14. Barston's last suit of this nature was in 1599, against some men who refused to pay duty on cargoes of apples and pears. They claimed, in their defense, that fruit was "a commodity very casual, and so suddenly perishing as that by the laws and customs of this realm it hath never, in any man's memory, been taken or deemed such kind of merchandise that for transporting thereof custom hath been due or payable." If the whole cargo was dutiable, the merchant would be impoverished. "The nature and kind of apples and pears will not so long last or endure, but rather in the carriage will corrupt, and great part thereof be rotten before arrival unto the place appointed." E. 112/16/206.

number of suits against recalcitrant merchants. Whatever success he may have had was transient. Subsequent customers apparently gave up the effort, and the later port books scarcely mention the debatable commodities.

The disadvantages of renting what we should consider a public office to a private citizen are sufficiently illustrated by the example of Edward Barston. Although the usual agents of government might be lazy, inefficient, ignorant of the law, and disposed to exploit their office to their best advantage, their exploitation had to be less direct than that of a tax-farmer, and there was more possibility that the central government might in time control it. A farmer, on the other hand, was a power unto himself. He could be checked only by such a cumbersome instrument as the court of exchequer, and meanwhile could work annoyance and injury to men too poor to go to law.

The customer was by no means the only man who bought authority from the government. With the exception of the ulnager, who will be mentioned later, he was the one who played the most important rôle in county life. But there was a school of smaller fry, interfering by royal warrant with one or another occupation of the people. There was Humphrey Michel of Old Windsor, who as water bailiff of Severn held a court of his own to protect "the spawn and brood of trouts, salmons, and other fishes," and who could compel the coöperation of neighboring justices and constables.[38] There was Sir Jerome Bowes, who had an early monopoly of the manufacture of drinking glasses, and who invoked the aid of the county authorities in suppressing his competitors.[39] There was John Gifford, in

38. *A.P.C., 1591,* pp. 123–24. For further information on this official and his courts, see E. 112/16/139; for the rôle of the J. P. in enforcing the fishing laws, see Lambard, *Eirenarcha,* p. 454.

39. *A.P.C., 1598–99,* pp. 101–02. The principal local offender was a Frenchman, one John de Howe or Hoe. He was shipping glass to Bristol and Bridgwater, and had bargained with the customer, for 10*s.* a year, to have as many cockets as he could use. E. 134/36-37 Eliz./M/14; for further references to glass-making in the county, see Lansd. MS. 885, fo. 107; *N. & Q.,* V, 357; W. St. C. Baddeley, "A Glass House at Nailsworth (16th and 17th Centuries)," *Trans.,* XLII (1920), 89–95.

King Charles's reign, who had the important business of supplying the crown with saltpeter from the southwestern counties. His men called on the constables to provide them with carts, and half the constables ignored them. An appeal for help to the justices was met either by refusal or by open threats; Gifford and his crew were a nuisance, which the county met by its usual method of passive resistance.[40]

Another type of farmer was a more serious danger. From the viewpoint of Whitehall, the most important natural resource of the county was the timber in the Forest of Dean. The oaks of the forest had been famous for generations as the raw material of the British navy, and their preservation was a matter of national concern. But the forest was also a center of iron manufacture, and the smelting mills were devouring the timber. "These iron mills will destroy all, and ruin that part of the kingdom, if they be not instantly banished to Ireland, Newfoundland, etc. These iron mills, the lords of them have already destroyed all the common woods, their demesne woods, their tenants' woods, and all the woods they can buy of others; and the four ports in that part of the land, in Severn and Wye, left without wood for any ship to go to sea with." [41]

The privy council took cognizance of this danger in 1618, and peremptorily forbad the farmers of the ironworks to cut any wood in the forest until further notice. Since the farmers had relied on the wood when they bar-

40. S.P. 16/121/10; for the conditions attached to this monopoly, see Lansd. MS. 232, fo. 54v. The nuisance which the saltpeter men occasioned is illustrated by their visit to John Smyth at Nibley. They dug up the floor of his pigeonhouse, and undermined its foundations; Smyth ejected them twice, and appealed to the mayor of Berkeley to certify the damage. (G.P.L. MS. 16,533, fo. 128.) A saltpeter man at Mickleton was paid 11*s*. "at the agreement," which was presumably his agreement to stop work in the parish. (Mickleton churchwardens' accounts, 1639.) After these examples, it is not surprising to find that the saltpeter men in Hertfordshire were presented at the quarter sessions. Hardy, *Hertford,* V, 258.

41. Written about 1610; Harl. MS. 7009, fo. 82.

gained for their leases, this prohibition threatened to ruin them.[42] There is no record that it did so, and it may be assumed that they evaded it. Eight years later, the complaint was made that trees marked for the navy were still disappearing into the charcoal-furnaces, and that men were enclosing the forest merely "for the lucre of the wood." [43]

But the iron magnates were by no means the only offenders. Other men, high and low, were responsible for much of the loss, and the government could not stop them. As early as 1617, the Earl of Pembroke was abusing his office of chief constable, and authorizing his men to cut trees to which he was not entitled. Royal commissioners had been sent into the forest to mark trees for the king's use. They had done their work sloppily, if not dishonestly, and the earl's men disregarded the little they had done. Some of his woodcutters, when asked how they dared cut trees marked for the king, answered "that they had done nothing but that which, if it were to be done again, they would do it. . . . John Snaype, a woodcutter to the said earl, being cutting down another marked tree, was demanded how he durst so do. Whereunto he answered that for two pots of ale he would cut down that tree, or any other so marked." [44] When such a constable was served by such men, the efforts of government were foredoomed.

It was even less possible to cope with the inroads of lesser folk. As early as 1610, the forest sheltered "such a multitude of poor creatures, as it is lamentable to think so many inhabitants shall live upon so bare provision as upon spoil of the forest woods." [45] Swarms of these men were being constantly attracted to the forest by the iron industry; there was not enough employment to go around, and they lived in large part by stealing timber. The more

42. G.P.L. MS. LF 6.3.

43. S.P. 16/44/45.

44. Sound oaks were supposed to be marked for the king, and only decayed oaks given to the farmers. E. 178/3837; for further details about the commissioners, see E. 134/22 Jas. I/M/42.

45. Lansd. MS. 166, fo. 354.

respectable inhabitants petitioned against their depredations in 1626, but apparently failed to stir the government to action.[46] It may be questioned whether effective action was possible. In 1631, the privy council issued a solemn injunction against touching any trees in woods within three miles of the Wye or ten miles of the Severn, "it being the usual care of the state, and of this board in particular, to respect the preservation of timber for the upholding of navigation." [47] Two years later, navigation was being upheld in a different sense: the council was informed that a ship of seventy tons had been built of timber stolen from the king, and that another of eighty tons was building. The council ordered the seizure of the ships and the arrest of the offenders, but there is no reason to believe that the wholesale thieving was stopped.[48]

At the same time that the privy council was trying to preserve Gloucestershire timber, it was trying to destroy another product of the county. These two activities of government form an interesting parallel. Both were matters of national policy; both were pursued in the teeth of local opposition, and for this reason neither one succeeded.

46. The petition painted these unemployed as "people of very lewd lives and conversations, leaving their own and other countries, and taking this place for a shelter and a cloak to their villainies"; there was no hope of their earning a legitimate livelihood. (S.P. 16/44/45.) Their numbers grew, until by 1640 it was feared that "the poor people there would impoverish the richer sort." (E. 134/16–17 Chas. I/H/1.) They became even more of a problem during the Civil Wars, to judge by a report of the regarders in 1646. "We are not able to suppress them. They resist us, and have often beaten and abused most of us. We have no power in our commission to require the aid or assistance of any officer or soldier whatsoever. If there be not some speedy course taken for the pulling down of the cabins, and for the punishment of these beggarly persons that are common spoilers of the timber, there will be every day more and more spoils made and committed." E. 101/141/6.

47. MS. A.P.C., XLI, 207.

48. S.P. 16/250/80; 16/228/96. These depredations had not ruined the forest; a survey of 1633 contains the statement that "an old experienced ship-timber man . . . did assure me that there is in the forest ship-timber sufficient to furnish this kingdom with shipping." The timber was valued at more than £177,000; the land was worth 10*s*. an acre for wood, and not ten groats for anything else. S.P. 16/245/19.

Earlier chapters have already shown the inability of the central government to overbear local opposition. A further illustration, in the field of economic control, is the story of Gloucestershire tobacco.

As early as 1618, Virginia tobacco was an active commodity on the London market. It was selling at wholesale between 3*s.* 9*d.* and 4*s.* 9*d.* a pound, and at retail for almost twice as much.[49] An enterprising Londoner, by the name of John Stratford, had the idea of competing with the Virginia Company by raising domestic tobacco, and selected Winchcomb for his experiment. His first crop was gathered about 1622, and was a great success. Within a few years he had made a fortune estimated at £20,000, and many others were following his example.[50] By 1627 the native industry had increased by leaps and bounds. Tobacco was being raised in a number of towns in Worcestershire, and one in Wiltshire; but the principal center was northeastern Gloucestershire.[51] The smoking habit spread through the county like wildfire. It was said that the children carried pipes to school with them, and were instructed by their teachers how to smoke. "At this era people even went to bed with pipes in their mouths, and got up in the night to light them." [52]

49. The market was unstable. A buyer contracted for 11,000 pounds from the Virginia Company, at 8*s.* a pound, but then "bemoaned himself" about his bargain. "Because the same was Virginia tobacco, he could not put it off, neither would any man buy the same because it was out of request"; he therefore gave the company £100 to be quit of his bargain. C. 24/478/74.

50. The only documentary evidence about Stratford is a quotation in Baddeley, *A Cotteswold Shrine,* p. 147; for further references to local tobacco-growing, see Atkyns, *Ancient and Present State,* p. 434; Fuller, *Worthies,* I, 546; Samuel Y. Griffith, *Griffith's History of Cheltenham and Its Vicinity,* p. 62; Rudder, *History,* p. 824.

51. The productive area in the county was bordered approximately by a line from Tewkesbury to Cheltenham, and thence to Northleach and Great Barrington. This is based on a list of thirty-nine towns, in which the J. P.'s were later ordered to have the crop destroyed; MS. A.P.C., XXXVI, 54.

52. Quoted by Fosbrooke, *History of the City of Gloucester,* p. 301. Raising tobacco was supposed to benefit the poor. One grower boasted that "he did betake himself into the county of Gloucester, where poor

The growers and smokers, however, reckoned without the government. The trade of the Virginia Company was menaced by this native competition, and the privy council intervened.[53] A special messenger was sent into the county in 1627, to seize all the tobacco he could lay his hands upon, and to bind over the owners to appear before the council. He was later told to destroy the growing plant, and the justices were ordered to help him. At once there was opposition, particularly in Winchcomb: the town authorities refused to obey the messenger, and tore up the council's warrants. A sergeant-at-arms was sent to bring them to London; aside from this gesture, the council seems to have dropped the matter for the next four years.[54]

The campaign was revived at the beginning of 1631. A royal proclamation forbad the growing of domestic tobacco, and a peremptory order for its destruction was sent to the sheriff. Since this had no effect, a special messenger was again sent down from London. He soon petitioned the council for further powers. He had met with numerous insults, and the chief offenders were being prosecuted in star chamber; but this was not enough. "Forasmuch as the said offenders, with divers others, have gath-

people do much abound, and there in one year planted so much tobacco as the poor had from the work of that year's crop £1,500 and upwards." (S.P. 14/180/79.) As late as 1655, a fictional hangman was made to protest that "the very planting of tobacco hath proved the decay of my trade," because it prevented idleness and therefore crime. Quoted in *N. & Q.*, IV, 162.

53. The growing of English tobacco had been prohibited by proclamation in 1619, and the prohibition was intermittently renewed until 1639. (Robert Steele, *Tudor and Stuart Proclamations, 1485–1714* [nos. 1268, 1505, 1516, 1629, 1677, 1769, 1798], I, 150, 177, 179, 192, 200, 213, 218; see also Dietz, *English Public Finance,* p. 351.) I have found no record of attempts to enforce the proclamation in Gloucestershire before 1627. On the contrary, a man as closely connected with the Virginia Company as John Smyth was growing domestic tobacco in 1621, and selling it in Virginia. He sent a particular request to a man in the colony, in 1619, to send him some good Virginian tobacco seed; two years later, four hogsheads of his "tobacco English" were sold in Virginia, at great trouble and at a disappointing price. New York Public Library MS. Smyth 3, nos. 8, 39.

54. MS. A.P.C., XXXV, 225v; XXXVI, 54, 146.

ered their said tobacco and daily bring it to London by secret ways, and do usually sell it for Virginia and Bermudas tobacco, your petitioner doth humbly entreat [for a warrant] . . . to search and make stay of all such English tobacco, and to detain it in safe custody until your lordships shall give further direction therein." [55]

Their lordships presumably gave him his warrant, but their main attention was devoted to the local authorities. The justices were displaying that lethargy which was their usual substitute for unpopular action. The council was amazed and indignant. "We could not have believed that after so many commands by his Majesty, and his royal father of blessed memory, . . . any man would have presumed to have planted or maintained any English tobacco (which hath been found so full of inconvenience), until we have been lately informed that in divers parts of this kingdom, especially in that county of Gloucester, there is yet great quantity of English tobacco planted and continued, contrary to these strict prohibitions." The justices were therefore told to summon before them the constables of the parishes concerned, and to order them to destroy the tobacco in person.[56]

Three years later the council was informed that large quantities of tobacco were still being grown, by men "who by reason of their poverty think to be excused." Their crop must be destroyed at once, and any one resisting the officers must be haled before the council.[57] A good idea, but a futile one. In the next year there were still great stores of tobacco in the county, and the council's messenger was still meeting with threats and violence in his attempt to destroy the plant at Winchcomb and Cheltenham. The council issued its usual order for assistance from the justices, and in the following spring repeated it almost

55. S.P. 16/205/53; see also Latimer, *Annals of Bristol,* p. 116; David Royce, "The Northleach Court-Book," *Trans.,* VII (1882–83), 105 and note.

56. MS. A.P.C. XLI, 121–22.

57. *Ibid.,* XLIV, 109–10.

verbatim. But the order was not worth the paper on which it was written. In February of 1637, large quantities of tobacco were being smuggled to London, and more was expected. In June of 1638, attempts at destruction were producing riots in the county; the justices were told to punish the rioters in such exemplary fashion as to discourage all future outbreaks. They obviously failed to do so, for the same situation existed in the summer of 1639.[58] By that time the council was distracted by opposition of a far graver sort, and there is no further record of the campaign against tobacco.

The main reason for these difficulties was economic. The countryman felt entitled to his crop, regardless of its legality, and he was not inclined to stand by and see it uprooted by a "foreigner" from London. The justices and constables doubtless sympathized with this point of view, and they were notably unimpressed by letters and warrants from the council. London and the menace of star chamber were remote.

Another reason affected all smokers, whether justices or farmers. Local tobacco was cheaper than Virginian, and many preferred its taste. We have one glimpse of this feeling, at the height of the council's campaign. The agent of the patentee, by the name of Crump, heard that there was a thriving trade in local tobacco at Tewkesbury. He bought a penny package as evidence, and appealed to the town authorities. The bailiffs ordered the constable to arrest three of the dealers, which he did; at least one was released merely on her promise not to offend again. Another dealer, named Thornbury, was left unmolested to carry on an active business. His tobacco sold for 3*s.* 4*d.* a pound, as contrasted with 4*s.* 6*d.* or even 5*s.* for the "outlandish tobacco." Among his customers was the constable, who bought for himself and his friends. "Those that requested this deponent to buy the same tobacco told this deponent . . . that they did not like the office tobacco

58. *Ibid.,* XLV, 27–28; XLVI, 266; XLVII, 185; XLIX, 308.

(meaning the patentee's tobacco). And thereupon the said Thornbury requested this deponent further that he would help him to custom for tobacco, and saying that he would serve better tobacco than the said Crump had."[59] The interests of the consumer, in other words, as well as of the producer, were contrary to the policy of the government. That policy therefore failed, and was practically rescinded by act of parliament in 1653.[60] Tobacco eventually died out in Gloucestershire, but it could not be rooted out by King Charles's messengers.

Timber and tobacco were relatively unimportant in the county. Even agriculture and commerce were subordinate to the one great local industry, the heart and soul of Gloucestershire economy, which was the manufacture of woolen cloth. On this prosperity depended, and in this the central government was most acutely concerned.

The clothiers were a vested interest, whose wishes commanded attention even from the privy council. But what is more important, their employees were always a potential menace to social order. A decline in the sale of cloth, with its concomitant increase of unemployment, was a quick and serious threat to public peace. There was therefore an obvious connection between the government's insistence on the quality of cloth and the government's concern with preserving that peace. The more reliable the cloth, the less likelihood that the market would fall; the better the market, the less danger of depression and famine and riots. Factors other than quality of course affected the market, and we shall soon see what happened in Gloucestershire when these factors produced a depression. But since qual-

59. Shortly before 1637; E. 178/5315. Latimer states that tobacco sold for a shilling an ounce in 1638. (*Annals of Bristol,* pp. 141–42.) This is unlikely; quite aside from the prices given in the text, 16*s*. a pound would have been prohibitive at any time during the period.

60. *An Act Concerning the Planters of Tobacco* (London, 1653). This permitted the use of domestic tobacco on payment of a tax of 3*d*. a pound; the wording of the statute indicates that Gloucestershire was still the center of tobacco-growing. The prohibition was renewed by 12 Charles II, c. 34, and twice repeated in the ensuing decade.

ity was the steady objective of government, the means of ensuring it merit attention first.

The statutes affecting the clothier were almost numberless at the beginning of the period, and during it they were revised and increased. Aside from the underlying concern for public order, their purpose was twofold: to ensure revenue for the exchequer, and to promote the health of the industry. Each of these aims was entrusted to a separate official.

The agent of the exchequer was the ulnager. At the time when the office was created, in the thirteenth century, the ulnager was in sole charge of enforcing the statutes. But by the end of the sixteenth century he had become primarily a tax-collector, with little or no interest in the quality of the cloth he taxed. The ulnage of various districts was farmed by the crown to private citizens, who at least in Gloucestershire seem to have worked entirely through deputies. It was their duty to place the royal seal on each piece of cloth at the time of its manufacture; for this they collected from the clothier a fee of a halfpenny, and a tax of fourpence on a whole white cloth, or sixpence on scarlet.[61]

By the end of the sixteenth century, many new types of cloth were beginning to appear. Legislation could not keep up with them, and there were therefore a number of new varieties which the ulnagers had only a questionable

61. For a discussion of the origin and duties of the ulnager, see Herbert Heaton, *The Yorkshire Woollen and Worsted Industries* (Oxford Historical and Literary Studies, X; Oxford, 1920), pp. 126 ff. The author states that in Yorkshire, by the end of the sixteenth century, "the ulnager or his representative did not trouble about the dimensions or quality of the cloth" (p. 178); this is reinforced by an opinion of the attorney general in 1591, that so long as the cloth had its "subsidy seal," it was unnecessary for the ulnager to specify its contents (*A.P.C., 1591,* p. 98). Five years later, however, Gloucestershire witnesses testified that it was the function of the local ulnager to examine and measure the cloth before sealing it, in order to protect purchasers from fabric "unduly made." (E. 112/16/169.) Since there is no record that such examinations were made, it may be assumed that the ulnager was a mere tax collector in Gloucestershire as well as Yorkshire.

right to tax. Their resultant difficulties were much like Edward Barston's. The makers of the "new draperies" were scattered all over the county, even in the Forest of Dean. They defied the ulnager's deputy when he tried to tax them, and forced him to sue in exchequer.[62] During the next year, 1597, the ulnagers went a step further. Their authority was extended to the new draperies by letters patent, and they decided that they were empowered to seal cloths in the hands of retail mercers.

The retailers objected. They believed that seals were not required by law, once the cloth had left the hands of the manufacturer. If they were wrong, they professed to be willing to have seals put on in their shops. But at least in the city of Gloucester, which was the center of the dispute, the ulnagers came to town so rarely that waiting for them would have cost the mercers all their trade. A number of shopkeepers therefore sold their stock unsealed. When the ulnagers finally did appear, they made no attempt to seal or confiscate the remaining cloths; they asked instead to be given an annual bribe. The mercers refused, and as a result were sued in exchequer.[63]

The other special agent for controlling the wool trade was the searcher. The office was an old one, which was enlarged and defined by statute in 1601.[64] The searcher in towns was appointed by the municipal authorities, and in rural districts by the J. P.'s; his duty was to enforce all

62. *Ibid.*

63. The mercers made the additional defense that their cloths already had "the usual seals" when they bought them in London. A Tewkesbury retailer gave similar testimony, but added to it. When a cloth had been sealed, "if afterwards either the seal be pulled off or fall off, or that that part of the cloth whereupon the seal was fixed be sold away before the rest of the cloth (as sometimes it happeneth), the deputies of the said complainants will enforce poor men to compound with them again for the sealing, searching, and subsidies thereof." E. 112/16/178.

64. Searchers had been created for all corporate towns by 5/6 Edward VI, c. 6, and their responsibilities had been increased soon after by an attempt to confine the industry to urban centers (4/5 Philip & Mary, c. 5); searchers for county districts north of Trent were created by 39 Elizabeth, c. 20, and for all England by 43 Elizabeth, c. 10.

the statutes concerned with clothing, and to report delinquents at the sessions. His work required a certain amount of intelligence, and at least a casual acquaintance with the laws which he was supposed to enforce. He was often inadequately equipped in both respects, and the conduct of the clothiers was in no more need of inspection than the conduct of the inspectors. Supervision might have been supplied by the local justices. But many of them were clothiers themselves, and all of them tended to sympathize more with local industry than with the agents of governmental control. A case in point is that of Nathaniel Stephens, which best illustrates the difficulties of making such control effective.

In 1630, at the request of the Merchant Adventurers, the privy council appointed two commissioners to examine and reform abuses in the industry. One of the commissioners, Anthony Wither, spent his first year in Gloucestershire. He found clothiers, especially on Stroudwater, who were openly defying the statutes, and warned them that they must be ready for stricter inspection. But his greatest trouble was with dishonest and ignorant searchers, and he tried to mitigate their stupidity by leaving with each a resumé of the most important statutes.

He reported to the council that both clothiers and searchers were being encouraged in their laxity by the attitude of Mr. Stephens, J. P., and by the searcher's oath which he was administering. The details of this oath are not explained; it was based on his own "curious and subtle interpretation" of an irrelevant statute, and apparently minimized the duties of the searcher. Wither was in despair, because he was "fain to accept such oath and recognizance as he would frame, not being able to persuade him nor dispute with him (he is so learned and subtle), although it be apparent that his interpretation of the laws maketh the same useless and ineffectual." [65]

65. His oath was based on 39 Elizabeth, c. 20, which was applicable only north of Trent; he ignored changes affecting the searcher's office

The privy council took the matter in hand. The assize judges were instructed to summon Stephens before them, and to charge him "to leave this humor of singularity . . . and to follow the example of other justices, that he may rather be commended for his forwardness in so good a work, than be called to an account for failing in the performance of his duty." [66] Their exhortation had no effect on him. The Merchant Adventurers petitioned that he should be compelled to administer a stricter oath; his obstinacy was infecting other justices, and the cloth trade in consequence was falling into a parlous state.[67] Four months later the privy council returned to the attack, and summoned Stephens in person. His defense was that he believed that the oath required of him was unwarranted by statute; he was willing to administer any oath which the judges thought legal. The matter was referred to one of them, who upheld the new oath. Stephens was then discharged, on condition that he would administer it.[68] There is no record of whether the searchers in his locality increased their diligence after this episode, but there is every reason to doubt it.

The Stephens case was the beginning of a burst of governmental activity. In April, 1633, the work of the commissioners and the privy council bore fruit in a royal proclamation. The clothier was forbidden to use more than a single trademark on all his cloths, of whatever

made in the three subsequent acts: 43 Elizabeth, c. 10; 4 James I, c. 2; 21 James I, c. 18. (S.P. 16/215/56.) According to Wither, Stephens was also preventing the appointment of efficient searchers; see K. E. Barford, "The West of England Cloth Industry: a Seventeenth Century Experiment in State Control," *Wiltshire Archaeological and Natural History Magazine,* XLII (1922–24), 539. For a similar case of passive resistance by Yorkshire justices, see Heaton, *Yorkshire Woollen and Worsted Industries,* pp. 141–43. Nathaniel Stephens was the man who later figured in the elections to the Short Parliament; see above, pp. 35–36.

66. "This his scrupulous curiosity doth hinder the course of a service [of] which both his Majesty and this board have an especial care, in regard of the importance thereof." MS. A.P.C., XLII, 133.

67. S.P. 16/225/86.

68. MS. A.P.C., XLII, 293–94, 301.

grade. The searcher was instructed to affix two seals, one giving the length and breadth of the cloth when wet, the other its weight when dried. The old restrictions on tenter-frames, for drying and stretching the cloth, were revived by prohibiting the use of a lower bar. All these decrees aroused opposition.[69] But it was nothing to the storm caused by another part of the proclamation, which revived the ban on gigmills. This episode throws considerable light on the relationship between Whitehall and the clothiers, and is worth detailed consideration.

The gigmill was a machine used after fulling, for raising the nap of the cloth by brushing it with wire teeth fixed on cards. The teeth were said to ruin the fabric, "by reason the heart of the thread is fretted and almost dissolved by the gigmill, which maketh the cloth wear ill and quickly wear out." The use of the mill was peculiar to Gloucestershire, and even there most of the clothiers were said to be opposed to it.[70]

69. The proclamation is summarized as no. 1657 in Steele, *Tudor and Stuart Proclamations,* I, 197. The Gloucestershire weavers of white broadcloth petitioned against the three regulations. The use of a single trademark would hurt their foreign market, "for they having received their trade from their ancestors, who making divers sorts of cloth, some coarse, some fine, did make several marks on them by which the said cloths were distinguished, the cloths made in those ma[rks] are unto this day known beyond the seas and in good credit there. Wherefore to alter the said marks would be to the clothier great disadvantage." The use of two seals would hinder trade: measuring the cloth when wet would mean either rewetting it when the searcher appeared, or taking it to the mill only during one of his visits; either alternative would be a hardship for the clothier, partly "by reason of the remote dwellings of many of them from the places where their cloths are milled (*viz.,* some of them six, some ten miles), and partly by reason of their continual travel to buy their commodities to make their cloth, and also to London to sell the same." The prohibition of a lower bar on the tenter-frame went beyond the most recent statute (21 James I, c. 18), which merely limited its use; the bar did no harm, according to the clothiers, and the lack of it would mean that the cloth could not be made to the statutory dimensions "by reason of the wind and sun's working upon it in the drying." S.P. 16/244/1 (V).

70. It was argued that weak places in the cloth needed to be dressed by hand. The mill "giveth work alike to the weakest place as to the strongest," and thereby produced faulty cloth. "No nation useth any gigmills but England, and in England no county but Gloucestershire,

These mills had long been prohibited by statute (5/6 Edward VI, c. 22). But the makers of red cloth on Stroudwater used a slightly different machine, which they called a mozing mill, and this was not molested by the authorities until the spring of 1633. Then the royal proclamation announced that all such mills must be abandoned by midsummer. The clothiers protested vociferously. Some of them conceded that gigmills were injurious, at least for white cloth; but their mozing mills were quite different things, "ours being used only with small teasels, for the gentle raising of the wool of the said cloth, . . . which must after be perfected by our handiwork." Abolishing their mills would mean halving their output of cloth, which in turn would mean discharging half their spinners and weavers. They petitioned the privy council that either they might be allowed to go on in their old ways, or that they might not be blamed for dismissing half their workers.[71]

Petitions from other clothiers rained upon the council during the spring and summer. Some said that they would have to find another livelihood for themselves and their employees, and could not do it in the few months allowed by the proclamation.[72] Others, at Leonard and Kings Stanley, said that they could not do it at all. In those two parishes alone there were eight hundred people employed in spinning, weaving, and fulling, "whereby we were able, in some poor measure and at a very low rate, to maintain ourselves and families, so that hitherto they have not suffered any extreme want." The only trade they knew

and in that shire not above eight or ten clothiers that stand up for them. All others, both clothiers and cloth-workers, cry them down, and hath complained of them at the [?] last 'sizes in Gloucester, . . . and desire they may be suppressed." (S.P. 16/243/73.) There were nine mills in the parish of Stroud, two in Painswick, and one in Rodborough; MS. A.P.C., XLIII, 373.

71. Dressing by hand could not be quickly substituted for dressing by machine, because the "king teasels" necessary for hand work took two years to grow. S.P. 16/244/1 (IV).

72. S.P. 16/241/36.

would now be ruined, and they saw no chance of other employment. They begged to be delivered from starvation, "and this for God's sake." [73] Still others had already been laid off, and petitioned to be given work of any sort. The petition was accompanied by a letter from the local justices, who were nervous about the projected ban.[74]

The privy council apparently extended the time-limit of the proclamation. During the summer the question was referred to a committee, and in December the whole matter was argued before the board, in the presence of the men concerned with the manufacture and sale of Stroudwater reds. Specimens of the cloth were compared with specimens from Suffolk, and an official trial of the mozing mill was ordered. Meanwhile the ban was relaxed to the extent of prohibiting only new mills. The locations and owners of existing mills were to be recorded, but at least for the time they were allowed to continue operation.[75] If the attempt to suppress them was later renewed, it was unsuccessful. Mozing mills were common on Stroudwater seven years later, and were still being used at the beginning of the nineteenth century.[76]

73. The petition was sent to the assize judges; they forwarded it to the privy council, with a covering letter suggesting that the peace of the county was at stake. S.P. 16/244/1 (I).

74. "Our county depends much upon clothing, above twenty thousand poor people being maintained thereby." (*Ibid.,* IV.) The danger of unemployment was of course an equally good weapon for the other side, which employed the stock argument against machinery. "The gigmill, being managed by one man and a boy, will do the work of eight men that labor by hand, whereby many thousand able men . . . will want employment, and be forced to beg, starve, or steal." S.P. 16/243/73.

75. MS. A.P.C., XLIII, 199, 373; S.P. 16/250/53.

76. The commissioners for trade, in 1640, reported that one of the reasons why the sale of cloth was declining was the prevalence of gigmills in the Stroudwater district. They were peculiar to that region, and were called mozing mills to avoid the penalties of the Edwardian statute. "They daily more and more increase, to the great disgrace, prejudice, and danger of the ruining of the manufacturers there, if not in time prevented." The commissioners recommended their suppression after a year's warning, "to the end the clothiers there may have time sufficient to provide themselves of workmen to supply what these en-

At the same time that the council was hearing arguments about the gigmills, it was also wrestling with the problem of the market spinners. These were poor folk who bought and spun their yarn, and sold it in the open market to clothiers who could not afford to employ spinners of their own.[77] The Merchant Adventurers asked to have these humble yarn-makers suppressed, because their yarn was so bad that it injured the trade. The privy council ordered the Gloucestershire justices to investigate and report.

The J. P.'s held a large meeting at Tetbury, to which they called the clothiers and the spinners. The former supported the latter, apparently to a man. "There are divers clothiers," the justices reported, "whose marts are in good request, that keep many looms on work; and yet they buy little or no wool, but deal altogether in yarn bought in the markets. . . . The clothiers do confess that the spinners that now spin to them do abuse them in sophisticating their yarn. . . . [But] in case they were freed from the market spinners, they would not undertake

gines performed." From a transcript of the MS. report at Welbeck Abbey, lent me by the courtesy of Mr. G. D. Ramsay; the MS. is summarized in *H.M.C., Portland MSS.,* VIII, 2–3.

A writer in 1803 commented on the prevalence of mozing mills in Gloucestershire, and added that there was still doubt whether they were the same as the gigmills prohibited by statute two and a half centuries before. See E. Lipson, *The History of the Woollen and Worsted Industries* (London, 1921), p. 188.

77. A writer in 1615 asserted that more than half the cloth of the three counties of Wilts, Gloucester, and Somerset was made from the yarn of such spinners as these. (S.P. 14/80/13, printed in George Unwin, *Industrial Organization in the 16th and 17th Centuries* [Oxford, 1904], pp. 234–36.) Lipson, in quoting this statement, distinguishes between such men and the market spinners, who he says were a group of capitalistic employers. (*Woollen and Worsted Industries,* pp. 39, 41 note, 64; see also Barford, "West of England Cloth Industry," pp. 532–33, and S.P. 16/243/23.) While this distinction was undoubtedly valid for Wiltshire, it does not seem to have been so for Gloucestershire. The market spinners at Tetbury, as the justices pictured them, were quite too poor to be employers. "Some of them, with a small stock of money, do maintain their own families and all their children, dispersed into several families, that otherwise would perish." S.P. 16/248/1.

to make cloth according as the statutes enjoin them, though they might thereby make it the better.[78] And all the clothiers say that notwithstanding the false yarn, cloth hath been truer and better made for these twenty years than ever heretofore." The justices concluded that the spinners should be left alone. Suppressing them would not only impoverish hundreds of families, but would injure the whole trade. The clothier of small means would be driven out of business, and the industry would be monopolized by a few great capitalists.[79] The privy council apparently agreed with the justices, for we hear no more of the matter.

So much for the ways in which government sought to regulate the industry. How successful were they? Did the ulnager and the searcher and the privy council and the justices succeed in maintaining prosperity? The answer is patently no: the period is punctuated by industrial depressions. The reasons were partly internal and partly external, and the authorities were incapable of dealing effectively with either. This incapacity can best be understood by a brief survey of the doldrums between 1590 and 1640.

At the beginning of the period, the wars in the Low Countries were disrupting the foreign market and bringing privation to the county.[80] Southern and eastern England was compensated by the influx of foreign weavers, with their improved techniques, and the spread of new

78. The meaning is presumably that better yarn might be had from hired spinners, but that hiring them would disrupt the clothiers' economy.

79. A letter from the justices to the council; S.P. 16/248/1. According to Wither, these justices were "with much partiality inciting and encouraging market spinners, affronting and controlling the clothiers in all their speeches, so that . . . market spinners are encouraged to proceed to increase their falseness." Quoted by Barford, "West of England Cloth Industry," p. 540; see also pp. 532–33 for a discussion of the rivalry between the clothiers and the market spinners.

80. "During this time work was very scant for poor people, very small utterance of cloth by reason of the wars in Flanders; so as the poor were miserably distressed in the countries near Wales and in Wales." 1587; Glouc. Corp. Rec. 1450, fo. 60v.

draperies in Gloucestershire would suggest that they came to the west as well.[81] Whether or not this is true, the local industry seems to have recovered by 1600. If absence of complaint is an index of prosperity, all was well with the wool trade until the middle of King James's reign. Then came the bombshell.

In the summer of 1614, a royal proclamation forbad the export of unfinished cloth, and within a year the Cockayne experiment was under way. Alderman Cockayne's company was given a monopoly of buying unfinished cloth from the country clothiers, finishing and dyeing it, and selling it abroad. But the foreigners refused to buy finished cloth, and the market almost ceased to exist. The results were serious in all parts of England, and Gloucestershire suffered with the rest.

In July of 1616, the justices complained to the privy council that Cockayne's company was discriminating against Gloucestershire cloth, and implied that such discrimination menaced public order. The council asked the merchants "the reasons of their slackness in buying of the cloth of that county more than of other places where there is made a greater bulk of cloth, and from whence there cometh no complaint." The merchants answered that it was because Gloucestershire cloth was so faulty that the Dutch would have none of it. The council thereupon answered the justices by giving them stale advice: they should see to it that the clothiers made true cloth.[82]

81. Proof of the presence of foreigners is practically nonexistent; it is limited to a few French terms used in the wool trade, and to a very few French and Flemish family names. See *V.C.H.*, II, 158; W. H. Marling, "The Woollen Industry of Gloucestershire: a Retrospect," *Trans.*, XXXVI (1913), 316.

82. S.P. 14/88/41. The government was confident that the situation was well in hand, and that business would soon mend; "therefore if any clothier there shall discharge his workmen without any just cause, you shall let them know that we will take an account of them for the same." (*A.P.C., 1616–17,* p. 1.) In September, the justices of Wiltshire and Gloucestershire were instructed to inquire into local conditions, and ascertain the number of idle looms and men. The inquiry was to be "not too public, to make a noise among the people, or to give more encouragement to complaints." *Ibid.,* pp. 21–22.

At the same time, some local clothiers appeared before the council to air their grievances. They were offering their cloth at 5 per cent less than they had received three years before, when wool had been much cheaper. The merchants refused to buy unless they cut their prices by 10 per cent, which would ruin them. There were many thousands of poor in the county who were dependent on them, "and unless some present remedy were taken, the trade of clothing could not long continue in that country." But nothing could be done with the merchants. "As the clothier complained of £5,000 or £6,000 worth of cloth lying on his hands here in London, so might they complain of £400,000 worth lying on their hands unsold." [83]

The council tried to carry things with a high hand. Cockayne was told that he must arrange to purchase all the Gloucestershire cloth in London "without further complaint." He did not complain, but merely disobeyed. The council stigmatized his conduct as "a scorn of so high a nature as will not be endured," and then proceeded to endure it. For it was impossible, as Cockayne pointed out, "to lay all upon the poor merchant, so many ways already engaged, toiled, entangled." [84] No more could be accomplished until the whole experiment was abandoned. This was done the next year, but not before the industry had been disrupted almost beyond repair.

The years which followed were lean ones. The Merchant Adventurers were reinstated, to win back the market which Cockayne had lost. They could not do it, and by 1622 the country was approaching the depths of depression. In February of that year the council sent a circular letter to the justices of ten clothing counties. It began with the philosophical remark that "so great a business as the mystery of clothing, having relation to so many per-

83. *Ibid.*, pp. 2–3; see also Gardiner, *History of England*, II, 389.

84. S.P. 14/88/51; *A.P.C., 1616–17*, pp. 9, 18. For further details, see Astrid Friis, *Alderman Cockayne's Project and the Cloth Trade*, pp. 306–11, 320–21.

sons, trades, and circumstances, cannot be expected to proceed at all times after one and the same manner, with like benefit to each party interested therein." The council was doing all in its power to increase the market for cloth, and the justices, in return, must do everything in their power to keep the clothiers from discharging their employees, who would be likely "to disturb the quiet and government of those parts wherein they live." If there was not enough work to go around, the clothiers must be subsidized to take on extra hands. Prices must be cut all along the line, in order to set business on its feet again. "Whosoever had a part of the gain in profitable times since his Majesty's happy reign, must now in the decay of trade (till that may be remedied) bear a part of the public loss, as may best conduce to the good of the public and the maintenance of the general trade." [85]

The Gloucestershire justices had been alarmed by "mutinous assemblies" of malcontents, and therefore acted on the council's letter with unusual thoroughness. They summoned before them the clothiers who were employing the largest numbers of poor, and urged them to keep their workers for another month. The clothiers refused to do so for more than a fortnight. They drew up a long memorandum of their reasons, which the justices forwarded to the council with the comment that "we observe the clothiers are generally grieved as well as the poor workman, and that they cannot continue their trade without vent of cloths and return of their stocks." [86]

85. *A.P.C., 1621–23,* pp. 131–33.

86. A large part of the clothiers' memorandum consisted of complaints against the Merchant Adventurers and their handling of the foreign market. The inadequacy of this market had brought trade to a standstill. The clothiers had cut their prices, and bought their wool so cheaply as to impoverish the growers; still they could sell their cloth only at a ruinous loss. Their entire capital was tied up in unsold stocks, which they were having to pawn in order to keep their men at work. The men's wages had fallen to little more than a shilling a week, "being much too little." But the clothiers could do nothing about it, since the county had fifteen hundred looms to be kept busy. S.P. 14/128/49

Conditions grew worse as the spring went on. In May the council sent another circular letter. There had been riots in the west, and as the emergency became more acute, the authorities changed their tone. It was no longer the clothiers who were to be admonished, but the poor who were to be suppressed. Work was to be provided for them by the constables and overseers in their parishes, and more than the usual amounts of relief were to be collected from the wealthy. All this was temporary, according to the council; returning prosperity was just around the corner. "His Majesty, in his princely commiseration of his people's wants, hath directed a course for restoring the trade of clothing to as good and flourishing an estate as these times will any way admit." [87]

This hope must have been cold comfort for the justices. They answered the council in two letters; these are worth quoting at some length, as illustrations of what happened to the whole economic life of the county when the market for wool declined. In the first, the justices began by commenting on the parlous state of the clothier. "All trade besides this is much decayed, money grown scarce, the yearly profits of livings much fallen, and our whole county greatly impoverished and stored with other poor than those that have their dependency upon clothing. . . . There is an inability to maintain the great number of poor of that sort by raising of public stocks for their employment in work, or by any other means but by their trades wherein they have been bred and exercised." [88]

The second letter was sent on the first of June, when conditions were going from bad to worse. "The complaint of the weavers and other poor people depending on the trade of clothing (in this dead time thereof) do daily in-

and (I), printed by Clutterbuck, "State Papers Relating to the Cloth Trade, 1622," *Trans.*, V, 156–58.

87. *A.P.C., 1621–23,* pp. 224–25.

88. If the clothiers failed, as they must do unless relief were forthcoming within the fortnight, "the misery of our county will be very great." S.P. 14/128/50.

crease, in that their work and means of relief do more and more decay, and in that their masters for the most part do still allege that their trade grows worse and worse. Our county is thereby, and through want of money and means, in these late times grown poor, and unable to relieve the infinite number of poor people residing within the same (drawn hither by means of clothing) but by that trade wherein they have been brought up and exercised. And thereby very many of them do wander, beg, and steal, and are in case to starve, as their faces (to our great griefs) do manifest. And they do so far oppress these parts . . . that our abler sort of people there are not able much longer to contain the same. . . . We much fear that the peace thereof will be very shortly endangered, notwithstanding all the vigilance we use or can use to the contrary."[89]

The justices apparently succeeded in keeping the peace, although by a narrow margin.[90] But neither they nor the council could cure the depression, which continued for at least a decade. It was aggravated by an epidemic of plague, which swept the county in 1624-25. In the next year the authorities of Gloucester reported that they had only two or three clothiers in the city, "and those men of mean ability, whereas we have heretofore had near twenty men of good estates, who had kept great numbers of poor on work."[91] Things were no better in the outshire. In 1628, the deputy lieutenants wrote the privy council that unless business picked up, "the numbers of spinners, weavers, and others depending upon the manufacture of cloth are like to be cast on our country's charge to maintain."[92] Business did not pick up, but such wholesale unemployment was prevented by extending credit to the

89. S.P. 14/131/4, printed by Clutterbuck, "State Papers Relating to the Cloth Trade, 1622," *Trans.*, V, 159–60.

90. See above, p. 135 note 1.

91. Quoted from Glouc. Corp. Rec. 1540, in *H.M.C., Twelfth Report*, IX, 476.

92. S.P. 16/90/35.

clothiers. By 1633 the only thing which was keeping them in business was credit, given them presumably by both wool-growers and local merchants.[93] How the creditors kept going we do not know, but in some way the industry staggered on.

From this survey it will be apparent that government regulation failed of its ostensible purpose. The prosperity of the wool trade was not assured, and could not be assured by laws and letters. Gloucestershire cloth might have been worse, and the market for it even scantier, if there had not been legal standards of quality, and searchers to enforce them. Be that as it may, the fact remains that statutes and searchers did not keep the looms at work.

The concern of the government with keeping the peace is quite another matter. The men of the border counties were an unruly lot. Violence was in their blood, and privation was likely to bring it out. The fact that order was preserved, even through the worst depression, is therefore a tribute to the men who composed the governmental machine. The food supply was protected, so that poverty did not lead to famine; the clothiers were encouraged to

93. "By reason of the deadness of the times for sale of cloth, . . . their estates are decayed. And also . . . ready money for their cloths is hardly to be had for the most part, so as generally the said clothiers are so disabled to hold up their trade that had not large credit been given them, as well for their commodities whereof they make their cloth as for money also, many of them could not have subsisted in their trades, but had been enforced to have put off their workfolk long since." (S.P. 16/244/1 [V].) There must have been considerable unemployment as it was, and there was certainly unrest: the old castle at Beverstone was garrisoned, in order to overawe the nearby clothing district. Baddeley, *A Cotteswold Manor,* p. 183.

The only subsequent records of the industry, before the Civil Wars, indicate a continued depression. In the city of Gloucester, in 1635, "the trade of clothing and weaving has been so far decayed . . . that whereas there were heretofore above an hundred looms going, now there are not above six or seven looms constantly wrought in all the city." (E. 134/11 Chas. I/M/45.) Four years later, a clothier in the city was given a £20 loan by the corporation, "in regard there are no more clothiers in the town to employ the same in the trade of clothing." Glouc. Corp. Rec. 1543, fo. 12v.

keep their workers; the poor were cared for in their parishes. Some of this was not done without opposition. But it was done without evoking violence. Against the inefficient paternalism of government must be balanced the fact that the king's peace was preserved.

VII

THE FOREST OF DEAN

WITHIN the framework of county government were a number of quasi-independent units. The largest of these was the Forest of Dean. It was not exempt from the jurisdiction of the sheriff and lord lieutenant; it had its deputy lieutenants and its trained bands, its J. P.'s, hundred bailiffs, high and petty constables, charged with the ordinary work of government. But the forest also had an officialdom of its own, which was concerned only incidentally with such work. The land was crown property, and as such was under the direct authority of the king in all which concerned his interests. The forest officials, and the forest courts, dealt with offenses involving the king's game, the king's timber, the king's iron and coal. Both the officials and the courts were relatively unimportant, and may be briefly described. The same is not true of the county government; its action in the forest was revealing, and merits a fuller description.

The king's representative in Dean was theoretically the constable of the Castle of St. Briavels. The office seems to have been purely honorary, often held *in absentia* by the lord president of the Council of Wales.[1] The highest active official was the deputy constable. Sometimes there was one, and sometimes two; he was appointed by royal patent, usually from among the resident gentry of the forest. His duties fell under three general heads. He endeavored to protect the king's property from the inroads of the inhabitants. He supervised the lower officers, to make sure that they also were protecting instead of despoiling it. He

1. The chief officer of a royal forest was usually the warden; the term *constable* seems to have been peculiar to Dean. (G. F. Turner, *Select Pleas of the Forest,* p. xxiii.) The only perquisite of office which I have found was the right to an oak and a beech every year as "fee trees." E. 134/14 Jas. I/H/8.

summoned various forest courts, and at times presided over them.[2]

The protection of crown property involved him also in the preservation of public order, because "lawless and disordered persons" were as much of a menace to the king's timber and game as to the king's peace. The breeding places of disorder, according to the government, were the numerous alehouses in and about the forest. Since much of the land was not in any parish, there were no parochial officers to suppress such houses. Suppression was therefore assigned to the deputy constable, and he was told to repeat the process from time to time.

Various groups in the forest were regarded as chronic thieves, and these he was empowered to deal with in summary fashion. Any makers of wooden articles, "who do apparently supply themselves with timber for their several uses by stealth," were to be expelled. All cabins in the forest, except those of workmen in the king's ironworks, were to be pulled down; the occupants were to be punished, and forced to give security that they would leave and never return. The same applied to all charcoal-burners and their employers, unless they were licensed by the crown. Those who claimed common of estover were to be allowed to take only such dead and dry wood as had lately been granted them in the exchequer; stealers of cordwood were either to be bound over to appear at the exchequer, or given such bodily punishment as the deputy constable thought fit.[3]

In all these activities he was presumably intended to have the help of the lower officers. There were a number of these men; each in theory was assigned a separate phase

2. See H. G. Nicholls, *The Forest of Dean; an Historical and Descriptive Account,* p. 260; and below, p. 186.

3. From instructions in 1634 to "the lieutenants and deputy constables" at St. Briavels; C. 99/31. The difficulties involved in "the quiet exercising this unquiet office" are suggested by a quarrel between a chief constable and his deputy in 1596–97, for which see *H.M.C., Salisbury MSS.,* VI, 47–48; see also *A.P.C., 1597–98,* p. 73.

of a common task, the protection of the king's wood and the king's game. In practice their functions must often have overlapped, and are not easy to differentiate.

The highest officers under the deputy constable were the four verderers. They were "esquires, gentlemen of good account, ability, and living, which are wise and discreet men and well learned in the laws of the forest." [4] They were elected by the freeholders in the county court, and thus occupied a mediate position between the crown and the people.[5] Their duties were both administrative and judicial. They were government inspectors, charged with examining damage to the covert and to the wild beasts which it sheltered; they were coroners, to view the bodies of the king's game; they were judicial officers of the court of attachments, "to take true sayings and presentments of all the foresters." [6]

Below the verderers were the two regarders. They were usually elected by the jury of the justice seat, and the election was a solemn matter. The jury was told that "it is a business of a high nature, and such as the king's eye and care is fixed on, and they are to be mediate officers of a king. . . . His Majesty might have chosen them, and my lord chief justice in eyre might also appoint them for this journey[7] only. But because they are freely chosen by writ, they are to enjoy it with privilege during life." [8] They took their oath "to range through the whole forest and

4. Quoted by R. J. Kerr, "The Customs of the Forest of Dean," *Trans.*, XLIII (1921), 66–67.

5. *Ibid.*, p. 66.

6. Stowe MS. 164, fo. 138; see also John C. Cox, *The Royal Forests of England* (London, 1905), pp. 17–18; John Manwood, *A Treatise of the Lawes of the Forest* (third edition, 1615), fos. 189–91. The verderers also served on occasion as technical advisers to the crown: we once see them testing, by careful experiment, the worth of an improved process for making iron. S.P. 16/347/32.

7. *jorney.* Probably used either in the sense of a day, or of a day's business.

8. Stowe MS. 164, fo. 140. The regarders might also be chosen, like the verderers, in the county court, or might be appointed by letters patent; Manwood, *Lawes of the Forest,* fos. 191v, 192v.

through every bailiwick of the same, as the foresters there shall lead you, to view the same forest." [9] But even more, to view the same foresters: to inquire into misconduct of officers and inhabitants, and to present offenders at one of the forest courts.[10]

Below the regarders were the rangers, sworn "to make their range over the forest, and go up and down to present the king's wild beasts." They were to pursue any beast which escaped from the forest, and drive it back with their hounds. They were to present in court any case of illegal hunting.[11] For these services they received a yearly salary of £9 2*s.* 6*d.*[12] To judge by one case, the government was wasting its money. A ranger was haled before star chamber in 1632: he had "entertained one called Skinnington, and let him hunt and kill a deer, and he threatened and used some violence to the agents there for the king, [saying] that he would serve them as he did others that entrenched upon his liberties in the Forest of Dean." [13]

Below the rangers were the lowest officers, the "fosters in fee" or foresters, and the keepers and underkeepers. They were charged with protecting the game, and with presenting anything in the forest which was forfeit to the king. It is a commentary on the nature of the forester that

9. Stowe MS. 164, fo. 139. The writer uses *foresters* indiscriminately, now for the inhabitants of the forest, now for the officers of that name. In this case it apparently refers to the officers; I shall use it in that sense except where the other is clearly indicated by the context.

10. The regarder was supposed to make his regard, or rounds of inspection, either every three years or before each justice seat. Since there was only one justice seat during this period, his duties could not have been onerous; for a fuller description of them, see Manwood, *Lawes of the Forest,* fos. 195–96v.

11. Stowe MS. 164, fos. 138–39.

12. This salary was the same as that received by the constable of the Castle of St. Briavels. (Bodl. MS. Eng. Hist. E. 30, fo. 35.) According to Manwood, the ranger's salary was usually between £20 and £30; *Lawes of the Forest,* fo. 186.

13. S. R. Gardiner, *Reports of Cases in the Courts of Star Chamber and High Commission* [1631–32], p. 95. The ranger's guest was presumably the Skynnington who was a ringleader in the riots of 1631–32; see below, pp. 198–99, 200, 201.

he had to swear to "be of good behavior yourself towards his Majesty's wild beasts." [14] Most of these minor offices were attached to certain lands in the forest. The owners assigned their duties to deputies, who were notoriously lax; they "follow their masters' business and neglect the king's." The result was that the verderers had few or no presentments to act upon. An attempt to remedy this situation was made at the end of James's reign. The government did not try to make the forest administration efficient, which would have been a herculean task. It sought instead to override local officials by appointing an "overseer" who was directly responsible to London, and who was empowered to bring offenders before the privy council. There is no indication that the experiment was successful, although it continued for some years.[15] One officer, single-handed, could not effect radical changes, or rejuvenate a system in decay.

These various officers were the survival of an earlier age, and had changed far less than those in the rest of the county. The same may be said of the people as a whole. In the world of the seventeenth century, Dean was a small island of the middle ages. The tide of change was gradually washing it away: the game was dying out, the woods were giving place to farms, and the mines were ruining what timber was left. The change was extremely slow, however, and affected the physical aspect of the forest

14. Stowe MS. 164, fo. 139. The inhabitants of all the towns in the forest, except Newnham and Ruddle, paid a yearly rent to the crown for their "herbage, pawnage, and other liberties within the same forest." (E. 134/34 Eliz./H/23.) The officer who gathered this money was the agister, about whom I have no information; for a description of his duties, see Manwood, *Lawes of the Forest,* chapter xi, and for a description of the other minor officers see *ibid.,* fos. 184–86v, 200v.

15. The only account of this overseer is in a MS. of later date. His duties were to supervise the allocation and cutting of wood for the ironworks, and to present all offenses against vert and venison to the lord treasurer or the privy council. As soon as his presentments were made, messengers were sent from the council to bring the offenders to London, "which more deterred them from meddling in the forest than the forest law, being not likely to be put in execution." G.P.L. MS. LX 10.3, fo. 3.

more quickly than it did the people. In their character and their customs, the men of the forest were still centuries behind the rest of the county.[16]

Their principal occupation, since the time of Edward the Confessor, had been the mining of coal and iron. In the course of centuries the miners had acquired a number of prescriptive rights, and these they were trying to maintain against the king and other outsiders.[17] The first was their status as a close corporation: no one was supposed to mine, or even come near the mines, who was not a native and resident of the forest.[18] The miners might dig where they pleased, cut timber where they pleased, and sell their ore to whom they pleased.[19] Each pit was worked by four

16. Mention must be made of the other royal forest in Gloucestershire, although it was negligible by comparison with Dean. Kingswood Forest, near Bristol, was noted principally for the coal which it supplied to that city. There were keepers and rangers, but little or no game; the chief occupation of the officers seems to have been to impound interloping pigs. The crown had almost completely lost its authority and its property rights. The lords of adjacent manors, and the inhabitants themselves, "do swallow up the whole forest, not allowing his Majesty the breadth of a foot, the timber, wood, bushes, soil, coal mines, and all other profits altogether carried from his Majesty by unknown rights." S.P. 14/84/46; for further references to the state of the forest, see E. 138/8 Jas. I/E/33a; C. 2/Jas. I/D/6 (I); Harl. MS. 368, fo. 110; *H.M.C., Twelfth Report,* I, 129; *V.C.H.,* II, 266–67; J. U. Nef, *The Rise of the British Coal Industry,* I, 72–73, 315 note 2.

17. The best discussion of the free miners and their rights is in *ibid.,* I, 277–81; for further references, see [T. F. Dibdin,] *The History of Cheltenham . . . and a Concise View of the County of Gloucester,* pp. 303–04; Rhys Jenkins, "Iron-Making in the Forest of Dean," *Transactions* of the Newcomen Society for the Study of Engineering and Technology, VI (1925–26), 44; Nicholls, *The Forest of Dean,* pp. 13–15. I have summarized these references in a paragraph of generalization, qualified in footnotes by whatever MS. material Nef has not already used.

18. The close corporation was breaking down by the end of the period; see Nef, *British Coal Industry,* I, 279. In 1638, the farmers of the ironworks "caused a restraint to be made . . . of digging of mines," and thereby impoverished many of the miners. These farmers, it may be mentioned, were in the habit of paying the miners in the form of provisions, at a profit to themselves of twopence in the shilling. E. 134/14 Chas. I/M/42.

19. The government tried to abolish this privilege in 1634, by instructing the deputy constables "that no man be suffered to carry any mine

miners; the king was a ghostly fifth, and his proxy might be added to the group.[20] The officer who was in charge of adding these proxies was the "galer," or gaveler. He also took a penny for the king from each miner in the pit, when it was opened, and a penny for each week in which the miner's profit exceeded 9*d*.[21] In selling this ore, the miners might not underbid each other, any more than a Gloucester butcher might underbid his fellow guildsman; there was a "bargainer" to ensure fair play. The miners controlled themselves, and did not gladly suffer outside interference.[22]

or cinders out of the forest or precincts thereof, to any other works than the king's own." (C. 99/31.) At various times during the period, individuals attempted to do away with other privileges by appealing to the courts; for examples, see Fosbrooke, *Abstracts Formed into a History,* I, 111–12; Nicholls, *The Forest of Dean,* p. 26; Rudder, *History,* appendix, p. iii.

20. As early as 1624, an attempt was being made to establish the king's right to take ore from freehold land. According to one witness, "it is more than ever he knew" that the king's officers or farmers might take such ore for the king's use; taking it was the privilege of the free miners, who commonly sold it to the farmers at an agreed price. The freeholder might not prevent their doing as they pleased with it, any more than he might prevent their digging on his property. His only right, like the king's, was that of placing a proxy in the pit. E. 134/22 Jas. I/E/8.

21. As soon as a pit was opened and judged to be worth working, "the said miner or miners repair to the galer and acquaint him therewith, and name their pit, and give him one penny for the recording of the same pit and name thereof." The record was presumably entered in the book of the minelaw court; this was a pure formality, which in no way limited the right of the miner to dig where he pleased. "It is not the office of the king's galer . . . to assign and appoint the places where any ore shall be gotten or digged within the said forest." *Ibid.*

22. One of their curious customs was that concerned with debt. A miner might take a debtor's horse "if he be saddled with a work saddle and with no other saddle; and be it that the horse be half within the door of the smith[y], so that the miner may take the tail of the horse, the debtor shall deliver the horse to the miner. And if he so do not, the miner shall make and levy hue and cry upon the said horse, and then the said horse shall be forfeit to the king for the hue and cry made and levied. And yet the miner shall present the debtor in the minelaw, which is the court for the mine." Add. MS. 6683, fos. 147v–48. This MS. was written shortly after the Restoration, and Dibdin, Nicholls, and Nef agree that there is no proof of the existence of the

Their court was the minelaw, which was peculiar to itself. It was held "not in any certain place or house, but as occasion is offered: sometimes under a tree or under a hedge, or if there be a house upon the said mine, then in the said house." The court was attended by the chief constable or his deputy, the gaveler, the steward, and the free miners.[23] It had a variety of functions. It was the parliament of the miners, where they made such laws for themselves as occasion demanded.[24] It was a probate court, with an eminently simple procedure: the legatee produced either a written will or two witnesses to an oral one, "and then, as right is, he shall be delivered without any cost made or asked." [25] Above all, it was a trial court. If a case was brought against a miner in any other court, it was transferred by the constable to the minelaw.[26] "The matters triable in this court are first, to try the right betwixt the king and the miners, and also between miners and miners, and also between the miners and other folk." [27] Judgment was given by a jury of twelve or more miners.[28]

minelaw before that time. There is. In 1624, the court had been in operation for at least forty years. E. 134/22 Jas. I/E/8.

23. The court was called by the gaveler "when there be three actions to be tried, and as need shall require." (*Ibid.*) There were two gavelers, and I have been unable to determine whether one or both had the right to summon the court. There is also doubt about who the presiding officer was; some witnesses claimed that he was the deputy constable, and others that he was the gaveler. (E. 134/13 Chas. I/M/42.) The reason may be merely that the deputy constable did not always trouble to attend. The steward of the minelaw was the clerk of the Castle of St. Briavels; he also attended the swanimote and the hundred court of St. Briavels, and received a salary of £1 13*s.* 4*d.* a year. E. 134/22 Jas. I/E/8.

24. Didbin, *History of Cheltenham,* pp. 302–03; Nef, *British Coal Industry,* I, 290.

25. A miner's share in his pit was a chattel which he could will to whomever he pleased. Add. MS. 6683, fo. 150.

26. H. G. Nicholls, *Iron Making in the Olden Times: as Instanced in the Ancient Mines, Forges, and Furnaces of the Forest of Dean,* p. 78 and note.

27. The "other folk" were mostly the owners of ground which was being mined, and the men who carried the ore from the mines. E. 134/22 Jas. I/E/8.

28. "Sometimes there have been thirteen, sometimes more, and sometimes sixteen as I remember." E. 134/13 Chas. I/M/42.

From their verdict there was an appeal to a jury of twenty-four, and from it to another of forty-eight; the verdict of the forty-eight "shall be affirmed firm, and shall be without calling again forevermore." [29]

Aside from the minelaw, there were in theory three other forest courts.[30] The court of attachments was held every six weeks by the verderers, to examine (but supposedly not to try) offenses against the king's timber and game. The foresters made presentments to the verderers, and the accused were "attached," or compelled to furnish pledges for their appearance at the next justice seat. The court of swanimote, according to the lawyers of the time, met at the Speech House three times a year, and dealt with similar offenses. It was composed of the freeholders of the forest, and there was a jury which received presentments from the foresters. The jury might convict, but might not sentence; its conviction amounted to an indictment, and trial was held at the next justice seat. Thus both these courts were intended to be subsidiary to the justice seat, "as it were but two hands to deliver matters unto it." [31]

So much for theory, with which practice had little relation. To judge by the silence of the records, the court of swanimote had either become of negligible importance, or had never existed at all.[32] The court of attachments, on

29. Add. MS. 6683, fos. 149v–50; see also Nicholls, *Iron Making in the Olden Times,* 78 and note; *V.C.H.,* II, 222.

30. A fifth also met in the forest, at the Castle of St. Briavels. This was a combination of the courts leet and baron of the manor of St. Briavels, and also the court of the coterminous hundred. I shall discuss it later as a manorial court; see below, pp. 289 note 63, 291 note 67.

31. Manwood, *Lawes of the Forest,* fo. 188; see also chapters xxii and xxiii for the fullest contemporary description of these courts as they were supposed to be. For modern references, see Dibdin, *History of Cheltenham,* pp. 300–01; Kerr, "The Customs of the Forest of Dean," *Trans.,* XLIII, 67.

32. One authority denies that the swanimote was a court during the middle ages, or that the word was more than a term for a forest assembly. (Turner, *Pleas of the Forest,* pp. xxviii–xxx, xxxvi–xxxviii, xliii–l.) If this was true in the seventeenth century, we have the phenomenon of a court which existed only in the minds of the lawyers. That it did exist there is unquestionable, quite aside from Manwood's description of it. One of the standard charges to the jury of the jus-

the other hand, had a somewhat larger scope in practice than in theory. It had taken on itself the right to try cases arising from damage to the woods, and to levy fines on offenders.[33] It was also concerned with granting timber for the repair of houses, and with making sure that the grant was not abused.[34] It neither was nor could be an important court, but it played its part in forest government.

The highest court of the forest was the justice seat. It was the only court which was not always held in the forest; it supposedly met every three years at some town in the county. It was presided over by the chief justice in eyre south of Trent, and dealt with all important offenses

tice seat, for example, was to present whether the swanimote had been held three times a year (Harl. MS. 4850, fos. 24 ff.); two of the cases at the justice seat for Dean, in 1634, were initiated by presentments of the swanimote (G.P.L. MS. LF 6.2, fos. 3, 5). The first fact may be explained by the assumption that the legal mind was tenacious of an *idée fixe*. To explain away the two presentments requires a further assumption, that *swanimote* was a synonym in the Forest of Dean for the court of attachments, as it is said to have been at this time in other forest. (J. C. Cox, *Royal Forests,* pp. 13–14.) If these assumptions are correct, the reason why I have found no court records of the swanimote is that no such court existed.

33. A commission inquiring into such damage, in 1617, reported to the exchequer that there was a "speech court" held in the forest every six weeks, before the constable and verderers, for the purpose of protecting the forest and the deer; this is unquestionably the court of attachments. "The offenders have been . . . presented and amerced at the same court, and the amercements have been estreated into his Majesty's exchequer and collected to his Majesty's use." (E. 178/3837.) I have found two lists of such amercements, one among the sheriff's estreats; the most common offenses were the commoning of unauthorized cattle, and the cutting of trees, parts of trees, and holly. E. 137/13/4; E. 146/1/34.

34. If a man's tenement was in decay, he applied to the court for timber. The court was then supposed to appoint agents, to establish first that it was "an ancient tenement and ought of right to be repaired with the king's timber; next that it is truly in decay; lastly that no more timber be granted, nor more taken, nor of better quality . . . than the necessary use of that tenement requires." After the repairs had been made, the same agents were to certify to the court that all the lumber had been used for that purpose and no other. From the instructions of 1634; C. 99/31.

against the king's property in Dean. There was a grand jury to make presentments, and a larger jury to judge cases.

The matters presentable by the grand jury were various. It was charged to say whether the forest officers had been duly chosen, and the forest courts held; whether the officers had done their work, and prevented illegal hunting in the forest, or the carrying of "bows bent or guns charged"; whether dogs in the forest had been lamed;[35] "which of the foresters are stout, strong, and of courage to take offenders in the forest, and who be not, or have not done it when they might." [36] The jury was also to act like that of a court leet: to inquire into the sowing of corn, the condition of woods, wastes, hedges and fences, the location of eagles' and hawks' nests; to present any ports "newly" created (since the time of Henry I); to ascertain whether there was any honey in the forest, and who ought to have it; to present any one who had made a hedge or ditch large enough to hinder the passage of a doe and her fawn, any one getting profit of turbary, illegally enclosing or building, obstructing or changing a right of way to church or market, or even introducing a new custom injurious to king or country.[37]

The only meeting of the justice seat since the thirteenth century was held in Gloucester Castle in July of 1634.[38] The major business of the session was the trial of cases, and for this purpose the grand jury of fifteen was enlarged by the addition of twelve recorders, and four men

35. The laming of dogs, to protect the game, had been required since King Canute's charter in 1016. Manwood, *Lawes of the Forest,* fo. 4; see also chapter xvi, especially fos. 110v, 114v.

36. Harl MS. 4850, fos. 24–27; for a fuller but different version of the charge to the jury, see Manwood, *Lawes of the Forest,* fos. 241–48v.

37. Stowe MS. 164, fos. 140–44.

38. The Stowe MS. gives the location as Painswick, but this is at variance with the other MS. accounts. Lord Holland, chief justice in eyre south of Trent, was assisted by a justice of the king's bench, and the chief justice of the palatine county of Chester. C. 99/31.

and the constable of each township in the forest.[39] The cases tried by this jury throw light on the court and the forest, and are worth description.

The first was the most important. The government, in its effort to assert all forms of the royal prerogative, was anxious to reëstablish the borders of the forest as they had been in the early middle ages. Seventeen townships claimed that they had since been disafforested, and hence exempted from forest law. They were included in an early perambulation, but omitted from a later one of 28 Edward I. Their counsel further claimed that they had been disafforested by prescriptive usage, to which the crown lawyers "answered that no justices in eyre had been there since the tenth of Edward I, and so no man could say what was the usage." After a great deal of argument and evidence, the matter was submitted to the jury. Its verdict was anything but definite: the townships lost their case; but since their evidence was too good to ignore, and they had been immune from forest law for more than three centuries, the jury referred it to the court whether they should not be disafforested. The judges assured them that their scruples were bad law, and the king's counsel then urged them to omit the latter part of their verdict. They did so. "By this the king hath much enlarged the forest, and all within those several seventeen townships were fearful they should have been questioned for many things done contrary to the forest law. But the king's counsel, in regard of their being but new brought in, and long usage, thought it not fit to proceed with any of them at that justice seat." [40]

39. G.P.L. MS. LF 6.2, fo. 2. The author speaks of four men and the *reeve,* who was presumably the constable; *recorder* is probably used in the sense of a witness, rather than a town official.

40. *Ibid.,* fos. 2–3; see also Gardiner, *History of England,* VII, 362–64. This decision was a grievance to the inhabitants for the next seven years, principally because it restricted their available common. Shortly before 1640, some of the gentry and freeholders offered the crown the half of a year's value of their land, if they could be freed from forest law or disafforested, and have a third of the forest waste for their

The other cases may be more briefly mentioned. The first was the trial of a presentment by the swanimote against Mr. Gibbons, the secretary of the Earl of Portland, for spoiling the king's timber and cutting trees marked by the royal officers. He was tried, convicted on both counts, and fined nearly £9,000.[41]

Next it was the turn of Sir Basil Brooke and Mr. Mynne, assigns for the Earl of Portland. They also had been presented at the swanimote for stealing timber, and convicted in their absence; the case was then carried to the justice seat. It rested for the most part on "but a probable argument," which was more complex than convincing.[42] A number of other charges were therefore brought to support it. Among them was that of threatening the forest officers with ejection from office if they were too diligent, "whence it came that the officers were for the most part combines and confederates with them." The defense witnesses, when questioned closely, "took occasion to desert the defense, and proceeded no further, but left themselves *in misericordia regis*." The judges directed a verdict, which the jury brought in: the two defendants were guilty to the tune of almost £58,000. It must have been a relief to them that "the lord chief justice set the fine only proportionably to the value found by the jury, and not according to the forest laws by twelve times the value." [43]

The last case was that of Sir John Winter, accused of

common. (E. 134/16 Chas. I/M/36.) Other freeholders claimed that this allotment would be wholly inadequate, and petitioned the house of commons. (E. 134/16–17 Chas. I/H/1.) The matter was finally settled by statute: the decision of the justice seat was reversed by 16 Charles I, c. 16, and the forest limits were restored as of 1623; the principle was established that seventy-five years of freedom from forest courts and officers should henceforth constitute prescriptive disafforestation.

41. G.P.L. MS. LF 6.2, fos. 3–4v.

42. They had a known number of forges, which must have produced a given amount of iron; the manufacture of the iron would have taken a given amount of charcoal; this in turn would have been made from a given amount of cordwood. The result of this arithmetic was an amount of wood in excess of their allowance. *Ibid.,* fo. 5v.

43. *Ibid.,* fos. 5–7v.

stealing 45,700 cords in six years. He changed his plea in court from innocent to guilty, and was fined £20,230. The crown may well have been satisfied, for the justice seat brought in a paper profit of some £87,000.[44]

In such ways as these the government tried to curb the misconduct of the powerful. Gibbons and Brooke and Winter were the sort of men who troubled the crown, and made life difficult for the verderers and regarders. But they were not the men who troubled the forest, and kept the sheriff up all night. While the crown officials had to protect the king's interests, the county officials had the far more arduous task of preserving public order; in doing so they were involved with numberless little men, to whom violence was second nature. It was these who troubled the peace of the forest.

Disorder was intermittent throughout the whole period. As early as 1591, there are two significant entries in the Gloucester accounts. The first is a payment to two men for riding into the forest to examine some trees which

44. *Ibid.*, fos. 7v–8; see also Gardiner, *History of England,* VII, 364; Dietz, *English Public Finance,* p. 273. Both books give larger figures for the amount of wood stolen and for the resultant fines; I have followed the MS. because it appears to be an eye-witness account of the proceedings.

Winter soon petitioned, denying all the charges to which he had pleaded guilty, and begging to have his fine remitted. Brooke also petitioned, enumerating his troubles and expenses (among them the usual burden of children and grandchildren), and throwing himself on the royal clemency. (S.P. 16/289/105; S.P. 16/293/69.) Brooke and Mynne were pardoned two years later, on paying £12,000 and surrendering the ironworks. (Gardiner, *History of England,* VII, 364.) It is doubtful whether a significant fraction of the other fines was ever collected. Like those in star chamber, they were probably intended more as a measure of disgrace than as a sum to be actually paid.

It is the accepted view that these trials of individuals were unfair, and were prompted partly by the crown's need of money, partly by Lord Holland's spite against Lord Portland and his agents. (*Ibid.;* Dietz, *English Public Finance,* p. 273; *V.C.H.,* II, 272–73.) The account from which I have quoted, if it is trustworthy, establishes a strong presumption that the defendants were guilty as charged. If so, their prosecution by the crown may be justified as self-protection: the forests had been plundered for years, and action against individual despoilers was the only effective means of maintaining the king's property rights.

had been given to the city. The second follows it closely: "Paid Roger Lowe . . . which he spent when he rode to help the workmen out of trouble that felled the trees." [45]

These entries are explained by a letter from the mayor to Cecil. The trees had been granted by the queen for the repair of Over Bridge; they were duly marked, and the magistrates tried to get them cut. None of the carpenters in the forest would be hired, and workmen had to be sent out from Gloucester. The trees were felled, squared, and sawed, but the foresters did not welcome the intrusion. Fifteen tons of the lumber were destroyed in the night, and what remained was likely to receive the same treatment. "Divers of the forest, perceiving that those trees were marked, and some felled and some to be felled, murmured and grew discontented, giving forth words to this or the like effect, that the same trees were never like to be had forth of the forest." The result was a sudden scarcity of transport. Waggoners could not be hired, even for exorbitant prices, because they were scared by threats from their neighbors.

"Go to, see how you carry any more timber, for ye shall have an arrow shot into your ox, and know not from whence it came."

This hostility was not confined to the common folk. The royal officers impeded the work (and enriched themselves) as much as they were able; they asked for tips, charged for using axes and saws, and levied a tax on each sawpit. What was even more significant, two gentlemen arrived one day at the head of forty men; they threatened the workmen, and temporarily confiscated their tools.[46] When it came to resisting foreigners from Gloucester, all classes were united.

The Earl of Pembroke, in 1612, had a similar experience. His men tried to avoid trouble by cutting and cording his wood while the people were at church. But it did them little good. "Some fifteen desperate knaves set it on

45. Glouc. Corp. Rec. 1500, fo. 279v.
46. Lansd. MS. 76, no. 47, fo. 105–05v.

fire, . . . and dancing about the fire cried, 'God save the king!' They still walk the woods with weapons, and as I hear with shot; they call their neighbors cowards for not assisting them. . . . The justice hath given order for their apprehension, but the country favor them." The privy council called upon the sheriff, the J. P.'s, the lord and deputy lieutenants, to aid in suppressing and apprehending the "seditious rogues," but there is no record that they did so.[47]

As time went on, the grievance of the people changed. By the reign of King Charles it was no longer the gathering of wood by strangers, but the larger matter of enclosures. About these there had been mild and sporadic trouble for years. Whenever the government tried to preserve its timber by enclosing it, the inhabitants were likely to throw down the fences and restore their commons. The crown had patiently pointed out, as early as 1615, that this was bad economy. The people were requested not to spoil the woods, and not to throw down fences built to protect the trees from cattle "for the breeding of wood in time to come." [48] But the government was desultory in its attempts to breed wood, and apparently did not make enough enclosures to provoke serious disorder. The crisis was delayed until 1631. By that time the crown, pressed for money, had farmed out large parts of the forest. The farmers were business men, and intended to profit from their lands; their profit might come from mining or from lumbering, and in either case the first step was to enclose. As soon as they tried to do so, the fat was in the fire.

Sir Giles Mompesson, as agent for Lady Villiers, began enclosing some land in Mailscot Wood, between Staunton and English Bicknor. For once his schemes miscarried.

47. "Had the matter been put into the hand of the gentlemen who could have tempered the wild humors of those Robin Hoods, things had been carried in a better fashion. But the earl is extremely odious, and with attributes that concern himself will put other matters in distemper." The Earl of Northampton to the Earl of Rochester; S.P. 14/70/49.

48. Warrants, James I; S.P. 39/5.

"The foresters [being] grieved with this attempt of his, some twenty persons threw part of the enclosure in again, not without opprobrious words uttered by them against the said Mompesson, whom they termed to be an odious projector. All this did not qualify him, for he notwithstanding put men eftsoons on work there to dig for coals. This did stir up and exasperate their giddy brains, and [they] seconded their first attempt by sound of drum and ensigns, in most rebellious manner, carrying a picture or statue appareled like Mompesson, and with great noise and clamor threw it into the coalpits which the said Sir Giles had digged." [49]

A few weeks after this scene, the men of the forest were on a worse rampage. On 5 April, a crowd of some five hundred assembled, with the usual drums and fifes, and also guns and other weapons. After filling in some new ditches, they turned their attention to a man who was apparently Mompesson's agent. They came to his house in Mailscot, according to him, and fired several volleys at it; he was told that if he opened his mouth, his house would be pulled down about his ears. The mob then went to the coalpits, attacked the colliers and filled in three pits, and then amused itself by throwing a large quantity of oak lumber into the River Wye. When this work was done, the men returned to the agent's house. They told him that if he did "the like work against May Day next, they would be ready to do him the like service; and dared him to come out of his house, which he feared to do." They threatened further destruction, including that of the Speech House, and assured him "that they had on this side the said River of Wye seven or eight score Welshmen to aid them; and that if they at any time wanted help, they could have five hundred persons out of Monmouthshire to aid and back them." [50]

49. *H.M.C., Twelfth Report,* I, 430.

50. S.P. 16/188/20. The crowd was also estimated at three thousand, which seems less probable than the figure which I have accepted; see *H.M.C., Twelfth Report,* I, 430.

These riots were like a flood. They swept into their current not only Welshmen, but household servants and even vicars. One householder, Thomas Yarwood, was experienced with riots, and had "always locked up his people within his doors, because he would not suffer them to go out at such time as the rioters met." But this time a servant was caught outside the house; "one of the said company stood over him with a club, and said that if he did not work, he would strike him dead." So work he did, to his master's great disgust; Yarwood professed to be a snob, who would have no traffic with the rioters. "All the persons that ever he could hear of that were in the said action were very beggarly and naughty people, and such as he never saw or took notice of." [51]

The presence of the curate of Newland was more surprising to the authorities. After the tumult was over, they not unnaturally asked him to explain himself. He did so by expatiating on his pastorate. "At his coming thither he did find the people there very rude and untaught, and hopeth that God hath so blessed his ministry . . . that they have more sense of their duties to God and religion than formerly they had." As for his accompanying the rioters, it was "but in the present affliction, by exhortation to them and prayers with them, to bring them to patience and the acknowledgement of their offense." In further exoneration, he offered to produce his notes of his catechism on the fifth commandment.[52]

The rioting continued into the early summer, and spread to other parts of the forest. The privy council was thoroughly alarmed, and the county authorities were bombarded by letters. Slowly, creakingly, the administrative machine was set in motion. Every agency was used: the sheriff, the J. P.'s, the military officials, even the trained bands. During the spring and summer of 1631, we have our clearest view of county government functioning as a whole.

51. S.P. 16/195/5.
52. S.P. 16/190/45.

On 5 April, the deputy lieutenants were told to get ready the trained bands. Hitherto they had done nothing; the council found it strange "that so foul a riot should be committed, and we never received any advertisement thereof from them; or so much as hear of any endeavors of theirs to repress the same." [53] Three days later, the order was repeated with greater urgency. Another riot had broken out elsewhere in the forest, involving a thousand men; the lord lieutenant was ordered there in person.[54]

In June, the riots were increasing. By the middle of July, the council was baffled to know why its orders for suppressing them had had such slight effect, "as though it were in the power of a loose number of lazy and unruly persons to affront his Majesty's government and the public justice." [55] A special messenger was sent from London, with a warrant from the council, to arrest those who had escaped into other counties. When they were caught, they were to be arraigned at the assizes; special care was to be taken that the witnesses against them "be not withdrawn either by terror or other practice." [56] Some of these witnesses had already been terrified into fleeing the county; to apprehend and bring them back, the Council of Wales was instructed to issue warrants to the sheriffs of adjacent shires.[57] An American police official would have found these problems familiar: frightened witnesses who disappear, criminals who escape over state borders, the hunt for them by federal authorities, the calling out of the militia, even the special agent from the capital. *Plus ça change. . . .*

The task of the officers was in one way harder then than

53. MS. A.P.C., XL, 436.

54. *Ibid.*, fo. 445. The lord lieutenant's first intimation of trouble had been from the privy council. He was told to find out which of his deputy lieutenants lived nearest to the forest, and why he had had no word from them. *Ibid.*, fo. 452.

55. *Ibid.*, XLI, 105; see also fo. 45.

56. *Ibid.*, fo. 158. "I assure you, the great fault in these cases is that none will appear to complain, be the fault never so foul and apparent, and so the offenders escape unpunished." S.P. 16/195/9.

57. MS. A.P.C., XLI, 159.

now, for the criminals were supported by a large and violent section of public opinion. In July, the lord lieutenant was instructed to appoint "the best and fittest householders" in the forest as watchmen, to arrest and bring before the J. P.'s any rioters whom they could catch.[58] But if these amateur detectives were ever enrolled, there is no sign that they accomplished anything.

Even the professionals had a difficult time. A privy-council messenger, one John Wragg, was sent from London to arrest William Vertue, "a known animator and styled captain of the rioters in the said forest." Vertue led him a merry chase. Wragg finally caught him in Bristol, and was about to bring him to trial at Painswick when the tables were suddenly turned: Vertue had Wragg arrested on a writ out of the Bristol piepowder court, on an action for false imprisonment. In spite of his privy-council warrant, Wragg was imprisoned and badly used. But Vertue's ruse failed; he was eventually fined £100, imprisoned for a year, and bound to good behavior for life.[59] Another man was tried with him, and given a similar sentence. But by November, these two convictions seem to have been the sole result of the efforts of officialdom. Eighty-six other rioters had been indicted, and the sheriff had promised to look for them.[60] There is no record that he found them.

In April of the next year, two officers did succeed in arresting Skynnington, "the most principal offender and ringleader." But they paid dearly for it. "They were of late, on the sixth of this month, assaulted in the parish church of Newland by a multitude of insolent and rebellious people, armed with stones and staves, to the great

58. *Ibid.,* fo. 158.

59. This punishment "implied he was a delinquent, not fit to be countenanced in an action to defeat his Majesty's service." Wragg therefore petitioned to have action taken against those who had been responsible for his mistreatment at Bristol. S.P. 16/203/104; see also Latimer, *Annals of Bristol,* pp. 120–21.

60. S.P. 16/203/7.

endangering of the lives of the said Cowse and Boles and their servants." The J. P.'s were instructed to furnish them on request with a strong and sufficient guard.[61]

These lesser men were not the only ones who ran foul of the inhabitants. The official who was in principal charge of the man-hunt had to cope with physical danger as well as with political. He was defied from below and harried from above, between the devils of Dean and the deep sea of Whitehall, and in his predicament we see him as a human being. The most interesting aspect of the riots is the light they throw on the sheriff.

In August of 1631, the council was informed that he had gone to arrest the principal offenders. After he had arrested two men, he was confronted by "such multitudes of people armed to withstand him" that he did not dare go on, but left the forest with his two prisoners. The deputy lieutenants were ordered to assist him with the trained bands.[62] At the same time he was sternly rebuked by the council. "We do much marvel that you, being high sheriff, should be so soon and easily repulsed by such base disorderly people; and did not according to your authority take your power of the county for the better execution of the commissioners' warrants." He was told to be more diligent in future, and to use the soldiers if necessary.[63]

61. MS. A.P.C., XLI, 521. This Skynnington seems to have been a professional rioter, who made a business of destroying enclosures. He and five confederates came to Frampton on Severn in 1631, to examine an enclosure there, because they had heard that "the country thereabouts would allow victuals and other content to Skynnington and his company if they would come thither and throw it open." Instead they were arrested, but Skynnington apparently escaped. S.P. 16/194/60 (I).

62. MS. A.P.C., XLI, 157.

63. *Ibid.,* fos. 160–61. The sheriff's "power of the county," or *posse comitatus,* was composed of every able-bodied man in the shire, whether or not he was a trained soldier; see Lambard, *Eirenarcha,* p. 315. Such a body would have been impossible to use for suppressing a forest riot, and the attempt to use it would probably have brought out a conflict of authority between the sheriff and the lord lieutenant. There are indications of such a conflict in the analogous case of the Northamptonshire insurrection in 1607, for which see Wake, *Montagu Musters Book,* pp. xlvi–xlix.

In November, he answered the council with a long justification of his conduct:

I had first a warrant, whereupon my undersheriff, with 120 men by me provided, passed over the River of Severn late in the night with an intent to take the said offenders; and for that purpose watching all night, repaired before the break of the day towards the house of one John Williams, called by the name of Skynnington, thinking to have caught him in his bed. But being discovered by some of the inhabitants of that place, they only apprehended two of the offenders, and so retired for that time; which, with a woman brought in at the next sessions, was all the service could be done upon that warrant. But may it please your lordships, neither myself, undersheriff, servants, nor assistants were at any time repulsed, as your honors seem by your letters to conceive.

The second time I received a writ, by virtue whereof I made warrants to the high constable of the hundred where the delinquents dwell, and to the petty constables of every parish, commanding them to apprehend them. And also . . . my undersheriff and bailiffs laid wait for them at the fairs and markets of those parts, during the continuance of that writ; by all which means two of the rioters, together with William Vertue (fetched upon your honors' warrant from Bristol), were brought in at the last sessions. . . .

I forthwith took course for the calling together of the trained bands of the forest division, . . . hoping to have apprehended some of the offenders at that meeting, divers of them being trained soldiers. But only one of them appeared, whom I apprehended. From that meeting I went myself with a great force from place to place that day, part of that night, and the next day, where the rioters dwell, and searched their houses for them; but found not any of them at home, they being . . . fled into Herefordshire and Monmouthshire, notwithstanding I gave notice by my letters unto the sheriffs of both those counties of the day of my coming, wishing them to be near at hand within their own limits; but I heard not of them.

I have also sithence apprehended one of the drummers in the said riots. . . . And I have likewise dealt with some parties for the taking of Skynnington which are very likely for that purpose, and for their encouragement I have given them some ready money, and promised them a large reward. And this is as much as I have done, or could by any means do. . . .

I have done my endeavors, and have been and still am seriously willing and desirous to do such service in this business, as no ensuing sheriff should do more. But may it please your honors, in regard of Severn on the one side and the River of Wye and the other two shires on the other side, and the hills, woods, minepits and coalpits where they dwell, the apprehending of them becomes very difficult, and must be effected only by policy, never by strength.[64]

Not enough of them were apprehended to discourage the rest. There were riots at Mailscot again in 1633; the king was informed "that those evil disposed servants have received private encouragement from some gentlemen of quality in those parts, which we are sensible of as a dangerous consequence, and will by no means endure." [65] There was an attempt the next year to overawe the foresters with the authority of the Council of Wales, but its effect was only temporary.[66] In 1637, the miners asserted

64. S.P. 16/203/36. At the end of November, when a new sheriff had been chosen for "that county in which the public peace hath been so much disturbed," the privy council wrote to remind him of the duties of his office, and that neglect of them would not be tolerated. MS. A.P.C., XLI, 277.

65. S.P. 16/243/25.

66. The deputy constables of the forest got a commission from the Council of Wales, "by virtue of which we call in all offenders, of what quality or degree soever, binding some to the council board, some to the council of the marches, and others the constable sendeth to the Castle of St. Briavels. Already this service worketh wonderful effects with all people of the forest, and especially with the officers." Broughton to Sir John Coke; *H.M.C., Twelfth Report,* II, 51.

their prescriptive rights by rioting against the farmer of the coal and grindstone mines. His servants were "outrageously beaten and drawn out thence for dead, their works smothered and fired, and the whole business with much violence hindered and perturbed, by certain people of base and mean condition, intruding and taking unto themselves a power and right to dig coal and grindstone in the said mines and quarries, though without color of reason to justify their actions." [67] In 1638, enclosures at Flaxley Abbey were destroyed with such thoroughness that enclosing was not attempted there again until 1672.[68] The farmers of the king were slow to learn what the Gloucester burgesses could have told them forty years before—that the people of Dean were as friendly with strangers as a swarm of wasps.

These people were the tribulation of the county government. The forest officers were useless. They were of the forest themselves, and there is no sign that their interests differed from those of their neighbors. Their duty was to preserve the king's game, not public order; if Sir Giles or Sir John was encroaching on the commons, the result was no concern of the verderers and regarders. The gentry of the forest were equally useless. Their interests were local, and they were as apt to egg on the rioters as to restrain them. The whole burden of keeping the peace fell on the county authorities. Their attempts to keep it, as the sheriff pointed out, were seriously handicapped by geography, and even more seriously by public opinion. In the rest of the county they preserved order with moderate success, because their power to do so was

67. The J. P.'s were ordered to suppress the rioters; MS. A.P.C., XLVII, 303–04.

68. The owner had attempted to enclose these lands in 1630, but the people "did beat down the enclosures; and though the wood was cut afterward, yet they made no enclosures thereof." In the second attempt, in 1638, some of the land was left for common; "but the inhabitants near adjoining, not satisfied therewith, did again throw down the said enclosures." G.P.L. MS. LF 1.1, fos. 17, 28.

not seriously questioned. In the forest it was flouted, and was thereby revealed as an authority of uncoördinated parts, with no reserves of force against an unwilling people. In the crisis of 1631, the sheriff was as helpless as the commissioners of the loan in 1627. "The power of the county" was merely a sonorous phrase.

VIII

THE TOWNS

THE seventeenth-century town is an artificial category, and town government is a phrase without distinctive meaning. At one extreme was the city of Gloucester, with its large degree of autonomy guaranteed by royal charter. At the other was such a town as Chipping Sodbury, governed in conjunction by the inhabitants, the lord of the manor, and county officials. Examples can be found for almost every stage between; it is impossible to say where municipal ends and manorial begins. A line must therefore be drawn at some point. For the present it will be between towns which did and did not have officials who were justices of the peace *ex officio;* the towns which did not will be postponed for consideration as part of the manorial system.[1] The present chapter will deal first with the officers of two specific towns, and then with the functioning of town government in general.

There was only one city in Gloucestershire, and hence its administration was unique in the county. The officials of Gloucester were numerous, ranging from the mayor to

1. I am adopting the arbitrary line used by the Webbs, who define municipalities as towns "which, whether by prescription or charter, actually enjoyed the privilege of clothing one or more of their members or officers, within the limits of the borough, without personal appointment by the crown, with the well-known powers elsewhere given by the commission of the peace." *The Manor and the Borough,* I, 266–67; see also pp. 262–67, for the difficulty of defining a municipal borough or corporation.

No town in Gloucestershire, so far as I can discover, had established a prescriptive right to J. P.'s *ex officio.* The first part of this chapter is therefore confined by definition to Gloucester and Tewkesbury, the two towns which had such a right by charter. Each in its way was typical, Gloucester of the rural city, and Tewkesbury of the manorial town which had outgrown even nominal dependence on its lord. For a discussion of the manorial towns as such, see below, pp. 297–304.

the bellman and water bailiff.[2] Its privileges were equally numerous. Some have already been mentioned: the exemptions from outside control which were part of its independence as a county.[3] Others affected its internal government. The mayor and burgesses elected the principal officers, and taxed the inhabitants for the welfare of the city. The mayor, recorder, and aldermen were justices *ex officio;* any three, with the recorder, might hold quarter sessions, and any five, with the mayor and recorder, might make jail deliveries for everything but treason.[4]

The aldermen were an inner group of the common council. There were only twelve of them, whereas by 1627 there were forty or more common councilors.[5] The distinction seems to have been important only at the election of the mayor. The electoral body was composed of the twelve aldermen, of whom the retiring mayor was one, and twelve more "of the most ancient burgesses" on the council. If a mayor died in office, his successor was chosen by the aldermen alone, without the "ancients." [6]

The mayor was a personage. Going through the streets in his scarlet gown, with the sword of state, the cap of maintenance, and the four sergeants-at-mace, his pomp must have stood out even against the costumes of the day. He was the king's representative, the administrator of justice, the head of the corporation, "set above others not to insult over them, as if he was above the laws, but to take care of them by watching for their good; to dis-

2. For lists of these officials, and details about them, see Rudder, *History,* pp. 112–13; Dorney, *Certain Speeches Made upon the Day of the Yearly Election of Officers in the City of Gloucester,* pp. 16–18.

3. Such as its independence of the Council of Wales, the sheriff of the outshire, and the lord lieutenant; see above, pp. 26 note 16, 41, 74–75.

4. Rudder, *History,* p. 122; Fosbrooke, *History of the City of Gloucester,* p. 402. The privilege of making jail deliveries does not seem to have been exercised during the period. This privilege was a rarity: the Webbs mention only three instances, of which Gloucester is not one, out of more than two hundred corporations which they discuss; *Manor and Borough,* I, 282 and note.

5. Rudder, *History,* p. 122; Fosbrooke, *History,* p. 402.

6. St. Ch. 8/188/12.

cover dangers, and prevent them; abuses, and reform them; advantages, and procure them."[7] His salary, in a period of rising prices, was inadequate for maintaining his "hospitality"; it was raised in 1596 to £40, and in 1620 to £60.[8] Even this stipend does not seem excessive, and it may be presumed that the office was coveted more for its prestige than for its income.[9]

The mayor was also clerk of the market, in charge of supervising weights and measure, administering the assizes of bread and ale, and insuring the quality of flesh and fish. For this purpose he was supposed to meet the sheriffs and stewards of the city, every Friday in the year, and to go with them to inspect one or another of the city's markets.[10] These markets sometimes needed inspection, and the mayor was not always the man to do it. At the beginning of the period, the privy council complained that the mayor and his predecessors, who were the local bureau of standards, were in the habit of giving the citizens measures which were too large by two or three quarts in the bushel. With these the inhabitants bought their corn at market, and cheated the countrymen accordingly.[11]

7. Dorney, *Certain Speeches,* p. 16.

8. Glouc. Corp. Rec. 1451, fos. 162v, 473v.

9. Perhaps also for its opportunities of graft. Thomas Rich, according to his enemies, bought a vote for himself as mayor by offering an alderman the office of bellman, worth some £20 a year. When elected, Rich put his trade of mercer to good use: he sold the city a large number of shrouds for victims of the plague; many of the shrouds were too short, but all of them were expensive. (St. Ch. 8/4/9.) "To discover . . . advantages, and procure them"!

10. He was supposed to have a similar meeting every Saturday morning, "for the weighing of bread and other like service." (From a city ordinance of 1601; Glouc. Corp. Rec. 1451, fo. 188v.) The court of king's bench, in 1588, had decided that Gloucester had the same market privileges as Winchester and London: every day was an open market for freemen, and livestock might be sold in any part of the city. *Ibid.,* fo. 124.

11. *A.P.C., 1590,* p. 200; see pp. 300–01 for the complete text of an apparently identical letter to the mayor of Sarum. The council ordered the false measures destroyed, but failed to impose a standard bushel. When the Gloucester authorities bought grain from London in 1597,

The recorder of the city was originally a magistrate, with criminal and civil jurisdiction, and the responsibility of keeping in mind the laws and customs of the city. By this time, however, the office seems to have been little more than a sinecure. In May of 1603, King James wrote to the mayor to command the election of his candidate, "whereof fail you not as you expect our gracious favor." [12] The corporation ignored the new king's attempted dictation, and elected another man: Nicholas Overbury, a lawyer of the Middle Temple. He had already agreed to live in the city, but the corporation pointed out "that they mind not to tie him to continual residence, in such sort as may tend directly prejudicial to his health, and other his necessary occasions." He continued as recorder until 1626, and on his retirement was rewarded with an annual stipend of £40 for life.[13]

The other sinecure was the office of lord high steward. It did not involve residence in Gloucester, and could therefore be used for purely political purposes. In 1604, for example, it was given to Robert Cecil, together with an annuity and £20 in plate, in order to procure "his honorable friendship and favorable countenance." [14] This

they discovered that there were two London measures, of which the larger was that used at the waterside in Billingsgate. The standard finally agreed upon was the measure used by the surveyor of the Gloucester wheat market. Glouc. Corp. Rec. 1451, fo. 165v.

12. S.P. 15/35/21.

13. Quoted in *N. & Q.*, VII, 111. The information about the recorder of Gloucester is so scanty that it is impossible to say how close his relationship was with the city. That it was sometimes close, even intimate, is shown by the example of Leicester; see Bateson and Stocks, *Leicester*, III, 276, 278–81, 345–46.

14. A similar gift was made to Sir. Edward Coke, lord high steward in 1615. (Glouc. Corp. Rec. 1451, fos. 200v, 267v.) The city also made minor presents to other dignitaries, such as the recorder and the bishop, and frequently to the lord keeper and the Archbishop of Canterbury. When Queen Elizabeth came to Sudeley Castle, the city helped to defray Lord Chandos's expenses, and gave £7 to the lord treasurer "for gratification of his lordship's coming in the progress into this country." Tewkesbury, on the same occasion, contributed a £6 hogshead of wine, bought from voluntary contributions. *Ibid.*, 1500, fo. 279 and *passim;* Tewkes. Corp. Rec. 1, fo. 19.

friendship was put to the test in the following year, when King James ordered the city to give a valuable lease to one of his friends. The corporation petitioned against the order, which would deplete its income. It also wrote urgently to Cecil, asking him to support the petition. The order was rescinded, and a few months later Cecil received a further gratuity "in remembrance of the honorable favors his honor doth bear towards this city." [15]

The work of the steward's office was performed by a number of local officials. The four stewards were in charge of payments and receipts, and the chamberlains of keeping the accounts; "they are the city purse-bearers, whose burthens are most heavy when the common purse is most light." The treasurers were entrusted with the seals, and with the preservation of the city records.[16] The functions of the other officers are either apparent from their names, or must be left in obscurity.

The governing body of the city was the common council. It was self-perpetuating; new members were elected by the councilors from among the more important burgesses. The requirement for being a burgess was the same as it had been in the middle ages: the payment of scot and lot in the city.[17] The privileges were numerous: rights in the city common, the freedom to carry on trade, the opportunity of being elected to the council. Once a

Tewkesbury also had a high steward, to whom I have found only one reference: he presented the town, in 1624, with £150 to relieve it from debt. Giles Geast Rent Book, *anno* 1624.

15. Glouc. Corp. Rec. 1451, fo. 212v; see also fos. 211–12.

16. Dorney, *Certain Speeches,* p. 18. The chamberlains were also responsible for preventing encroachments on the streets. It was charged against Alderman Taylor, in 1615, that he "had called the chamberlains of this city knaves and dogbolts, and had threatened them to be even with them, for that they by appointment of the mayor and aldermen of this city did view Mr. Taylor's new buildings now in hand, whereby he hath without license encroached into the streets three or four foot." Glouc. Corp. Rec. 1451, fo. 266v.

17. A man was admitted a burgess by the council, on payment of a fine. The council might attach further conditions, as in 1593, when a servant was admitted on payment of a £5 fine and "upon condition that he will marry the late wife of Mr. Morris ap Powell." *Ibid.,* fo. 142v.

man was admitted a burgess, it by no means followed that he would remain one; the council's favorite punishment was to disfranchise an offender, partially or wholly. Sometimes he was deprived of his common, sometimes of his trade, sometimes of his office as councilor, sometimes of all three together. No one might keep his common if he moved outside the city liberties, and ceased to pay scot and lot. If he was away for a year, and refused to bear office or pay taxes in the city, he might be either disfranchised or fined. Disfranchisement might result from a number of other offenses—perjury, disobedience, contempt, misdemeanors. One of the most common causes was the charge that a burgess had taken into his shop a man who was not a freeman, and had allowed him to work under cover of his employer's franchise.

The common council was patient with offenders, and often failed to enforce a sentence. But if its patience was tried too long, the result might be disastrous for the burgess. When Samuel Drinkwater lost his franchise, he ignored the matter entirely. "In contempt of the governors of this city [he] doth keep an inn, and doth entertain guests and take the benefit of the liberties of this city, as though he still remained a perfect burgess and had good right so to do; wherefore it is now ordered that the present sheriffs of this city shall pull down the sign of the said Drinkwater, and suppress him in using other course as a burgess of this city." [18]

Such sternness was rare. When a sentence was not enforced, the council was inclined to forget about it. Its forgetfulness sometimes caused difficulties. In one case a disfranchised burgess acted like Drinkwater, but more successfully: he went on with his trade, the fine was forgotten, and after a time men again considered him a burgess. He was then nominated and elected a member of the council—a legal *impasse*, solved by his submission

18. Quoted from Glouc. Corp. Rec. 1451 in [G. S. Blakeway,] *City of Gloucester. Printed Extracts from Charters, Grants, &c., Relating to the Hams and Common Meadows, 681–1885,* p. 31.

and reinstatement.[19] In another case a worse tangle arose over Alderman Taylor. He had been four times disfranchised for "misdemeanors and miscarriages," and several times imprisoned.[20] Each time he had promised to amend his ways, had paid a fine, and had been restored to his place. He was displaced a fifth time, for corruption and drunkenness, and another alderman was elected in his stead. Taylor then got a writ from the court of king's bench, commanding his restoration. The city fathers were sorely puzzled: there were already twelve aldermen, the maximum allowed by the charter, and the writ was "so short and peremptory that we could not have time to send to London to our counsel to be advised in that behalf." The situation was saved by the resignation of an old alderman; the council thankfully accepted it, and rewarded him with a £10 annuity.[21]

The council had also a paternal aspect, illustrated by its wardship of orphans. Gloucester in this adhered to the custom of London: if a burgess's child was orphaned under the age of twenty-one, and inherited money from any burgess, the corporation took the legacy and brought up the orphan. The money was repaid to a boy at twenty-one, to a girl either at twenty-one or at her marriage; for the use of the money, the city added a yearly interest of 5 per cent. If the girl married a burgess before she was twenty-one, without the consent of the corporation, she forfeited 5 per cent of the original legacy; if she married a "foreigner" without consent, she forfeited 15 per cent of the legacy, and all the accrued interest. Unless she

19. Blakeway, *City of Gloucester,* pp. 30–31.

20. Glouc. Corp. Rec. 1451, fo. 266v. Imprisonment was unusual, particularly for an ex-alderman. The prisons rarely received a person of importance, and perhaps for this reason the information about them is slight. The Tewkesbury jail, after 1612, was in the lower part of the belfry, a detached building on the site of the present school. There were two jails in Gloucester: the city prison, which was the scene of occasional riots, and Ailesgate, a house adjacent to but distinct from the bridewell. Tewkes. Corp. Rec. 1, fo. 30v; Glouc. Corp. Rec. 1500, fo. 280v; 1452, p. 112; 1451, fo. 246v.

21. *Ibid.,* fo. 439v.

wished to lose a good part of her fortune, the consent of the council was vitally important. The city fathers, during her most marriageable years, stood *in loco parentis*.[22]

The common council of Tewkesbury was little different from that of Gloucester. It was composed of twenty-four principal burgesses, and a number of assistant burgesses; the latter had all the rights of the principals, except that of voting. The council was to assemble on demand, and apply itself "orderly and comely" to all matters brought before it by the bailiffs. There were two bailiffs, a high and a low. They supervised the markets, and the shipment of goods at the quays; they administered the assizes of bread and ale; they were responsible for the presentation of the town accounts, and the holding of the town court. This court was presided over by them, assisted by four principal burgesses; the six, by the charter of 1609, were J. P.'s *ex officio*, and independent of the county justices. The jurisdiction of the court was limited to civil cases involving £50 or less, and such cases between townsmen must be initiated there before being taken to an outside court. "By which is only meant and intended to avoid quarreling and chargeable suits among neighbors." [23]

22. One such orphan was left £100 by her father. Before she came of age, she married a yeoman of whom the council disapproved, "a man of no trade, nor having any goods nor lands, nor being a competent match for her, nor being a freeman or burgess of the said city of Gloucester." The council accordingly refused its consent, and paid her only £85; she and her husband brought suit for the residue and the interest. (C. 3/247/126.) Gloucester derived this authority over orphans from letters patent, granted by the crown in 1560; Req. 2/117/11.

The use of orphans' legacies was not the only way in which the corporation approximated a modern bank. Lending money to the city was a common form of investment, akin to the purchase of municipal bonds today. A typical entry in the minute books is one in 1609: a yeoman "hath lent and committed unto the chamber of this city the sum of £250 until one year next after his decease, at the rate of £6 in the hundred for the use thereof." Glouc. Corp. Rec. 1451, fo. 224v.

23. This provision was common in manorial courts, and Tewkesbury had retained it after its incorporation. Half of the fines levied in the court went to the bailiffs, and half to the town. (Tewkes. Corp. Rec. 2, *circa* 1608; see also Bennett, *History of Tewkesbury,* pp. 378–83.) There is only one indication that the Tewkesbury J. P.'s held their own

The bailiffs were chosen in rotation from among the principal burgesses, and the election was usually a quiet affair.[24] If any one wished exemption from office, it could be arranged through a gift to the town. When a man gave £5 toward the repair of the Long Bridge, the council promised that his son should never be elected bailiff against his will. Another benefactor obtained the same privilege for his son-in-law, and a third bought his own exemption by a present of £20.[25]

The same procedure worked with lesser offices. A man was chosen as both sergeant-at-mace and constable; he was released from both, "upon entreaty and submission and mediation of friends," and on payment of a £5 fine.[26] His duties as sergeant-at-mace would scarcely have been worth the trouble: a sergeant merely accompanied the bailiffs and constables. The constables had a busier life. They served processes from the J. P.'s, supervised watch and ward, made "night walks" through the town, searched alehouses, and every Sunday looked for drunkards and idle persons who were absent from church. They also controlled vagrants, at the beginning of the period, and made

sessions of the peace: the town gave a patent to a Londoner in 1640, appointing him "town clerk, clerk of the peace for and concerning all sessions of the peace, and steward of the court leets and court barons to be holden within the said town." (G.P.L. MS. R 302.17.) I have no reason to think that such sessions were ever held.

24. The one exception, apparently, was at the end of 1607, when the bailiffs naïvely plotted to renew their term. Since it was necessary for the bailiffs elect to take oath before the incumbents, the latter hoped that their absence on inauguration day would keep them in office. They stayed away, and "the common council were of necessity enforced to displace them, and to elect . . . bailiffs for the day, who being sworn, the bailiffs elected for the next year were sworn before them." Giles Geast Rent Book, *anno* 1607.

25. Tewkes. Corp. Rec. 2, *anno* 1641 and *passim*. The bailiff's office was not always an easy one. When the bailiffs for 1597 were summoned to London before the lord chief justice, they asked for their expenses. The council refused unanimously, on the ground that it was the bailiffs' private case, "although they were apparently wronged by false surmises charged upon them." *Ibid.*, 1, fo. 22.

26. Giles Geast Rent Book, *anno* 1617; for similar fines in Bristol, see Latimer, *Annals of Bristol*, pp. 33, 35–36.

sure that no strangers—especially such as might become chargeable—were allowed to settle in the town; every quarter they made a search for such suspicious characters, and presented their names to the bailiffs.[27]

Tewkesbury officialdom had its lighter side. A favorite occupation was dining, and the banquets, even in an age of good trenchermen, were a subject of steady comment. Before 1609, while the town was still a royal manor, the manorial steward was supposed to give the bailiffs dinner on court days. He frequently did not: there would be two dinners, at separate inns, as a sign of a rift in the governmental lute.[28]

The bailiffs also gave dinners of their own on special occasions. The meals were a financial burden, which they often tried to evade.[29] The same was true of the burgesses. A week after his election, every principal burgess was expected to give a banquet for the principal and assistant burgesses and their wives; an assistant burgess had the

27. The constables were supposedly freemen, but a man who was not was in one case forced into the office. (Giles Geast Rent Book, *anno* 1638.) The other town officials were the chamberlain, and such parochial officers as the churchwardens and the surveyors of the highways. Tewkes. Corp. Rec. 2, *circa* 1608.

28. In 1599, the steward announced that he would make no allowance to the bailiffs; instead he dined himself and his friends at the Bull. The bailiffs and their company thereupon dined at the Ram, "and paid every man for himself, saving some liberality over from the bailiffs." The bailiffs had an equally unsatisfactory meal the next year at the Swan, because the deputy steward "would contend and dine by himself, with such of the jury as him liked best, at the Bull." Tewkes. Corp. Rec. 1, fo. 24–24v.

After a bitter quarrel over the common at Chipping Sodbury, in 1585, an arbitrator ordered that the bailiff should henceforth give an annual meal "for the increase and continuance of neighborly love, continual amity, and friendship." By this means the inhabitants were to "become faithful lovers and friends, according to the order of Christianity." Chipping Sodbury MSS.

29. They did so in 1601, on payment of £5 apiece for the Long Bridge, and again in 1606 without having to pay. In 1608, the town clerk noted with asperity that "the bailiffs kept no general feasts at Christmas, but as pleased them for their friends." Tewkes. Corp. Rec. 1, fos. 24v, 27v, 28v; for similar difficulties with the sheriffs of Nottingham, see Stevenson, *Nottingham,* IV, 320, 328–29.

same responsibility, except that two hosts might join together for one feast. The cost was fixed at £6 13*s*. 4*d*.; the burgess gave the money to two of the common council, who acted as his stewards. Omitting the dinner involved a heavy fine, proportioned to the rank of the delinquent host. When he paid under threat of the fine, it must have been small comfort to him to know that he was acting "for the better increase of amity and society in the said corporation whereof he is a member." [30]

There is no indication that such amity was increased by heavy drinking. The Tewkesbury burgesses seem to have been abstemious, but in this they were exceptional. Drunkenness was widespread in the county, and even the town authorities were not always sober. We find a mayor of Wickwar spending the afternoon in "carousing of wine" in his own tavern, and the evening in abusing a luckless townsman.[31] A mayor of Gloucester was a notorious drunkard, who had to be helped home at night from the wine tavern.[32] When such men were "set above others,

30. The fines ranged from £1 13*s*. 6*d*. for an assistant burgess to £13 6*s*. 8*d*. (twice the cost of the dinner) for a low bailiff; there is no record of what the high bailiff had to pay. (Tewkes. Corp. Rec. 2, *anno* 1638.) Similar fines were used at Oxford when the city was in particular need of funds; see H. E. Salter and M. G. Hobson, *Oxford Council Acts, 1626–1655,* p. 20. The persistence of burgesses' feasts is illustrated by Arundel, where by the nineteenth century the corporation seems to have become merely an expensive eating club; see Webb, *Manor and Borough,* I, 177.

31. The mayor and his boon companions were accused of dragging the man by the legs, "letting his head fall and beat and knock upon the stones." They pulled off most of his clothes, and put him in the stocks for the night. (St. Ch. 8/206/18.) For an example of the effect of drunkenness in disrupting the work of a common council, see Salter, *Oxford Council Acts, 1583–1626,* p. 316.

32. "Mr. Taylor was charged not only to be a common drunkard and a man very scandalous, and that he hath not long since been drunk in the city of Bristol many times, where some were fain to carry him to bed (having foully berayed himself), to the great discredit of the magistrates of this city; but also that he was divers times drunk in this city the last year (he being the mayor thereof), as is well known to many of this council, insomuch that some have been fain to lead him home (being not able to go by himself); and that he broke his face and had a black eye with a fall in the wine tavern that year. And that this present year,

. . . to take care of them by watching for their good," town government was in a parlous state.

Drunkenness was widespread among the people, particularly in the towns, and was likely to breed violence and confusion.[33] The authorities tried to meet the difficulty by curfew and licensing laws, but these depended for their enforcement on local opinion and on the police. The matter of drunkenness, therefore, is only a detail in the larger subject of preserving public morals and public peace. The means of preserving them are worth attention, because the means of the town were not in all respects the same as those of the county.

The great agency of molding public opinion has not yet been discussed. The church in Gloucestershire had little relation to county government, as distinct from parochial, and county officials made little attempt to interfere with it. The church in the city of Gloucester, on the other hand, was far more closely connected with government. The common council encouraged preachers of whom it approved, and at times was willing to support them even against the king.

There was a city lectureship in divinity, which was used to help young men of promise. This is best illustrated by the case of William Groves, a young schoolmaster who took holy orders in 1597. The council believed that he

1615, he hath been divers times drunk, especially at two public meetings of the mayor and aldermen . . . , whom he then so much abused, he being then overheated with drink as was conceived." Glouc. Corp. Rec. 1451, fo. 267.

33. A case in point is that of a soldier, in 1628, who uttered strange threats in the streets of Gloucester. "Ere it be long, you shall have wild fireballs enow flying about your ears!" He explained, when questioned, that he had overheard a captain planning with his friends to burn the city with fireballs. The magistrates clamored to the privy council; the council applauded their diligence, but pointed out that both the soldier and the plotters had obviously been in their cups. S.P. 16/107/4; MS. A.P.C., XXXVIII, 216.

Wine was consumed in large quantities, but spirits were almost unknown. The most popular drinks, then as now, were beer and ale. "It is likely that here is good ale, for here is a great noise!" St. Ch. 8/230/23, fo. 20.

had "a good guise of grace," and was likely to go far in his new profession. Private citizens had contributed to a stipend for him; £20 a year had been pledged by 1598, and more was expected. In return he was to give a weekly lecture at St. Michael's, and was apparently expected to spend the week in preparing it: the council decided that he could not continue his teaching without endangering his health and neglecting his students. In order that "he should be comforted in that gift of preaching," the city guaranteed him a further stipend of £20 a year, until it was revoked or he obtained a benefice of greater value.[34] Mr. Groves may well have been comforted by £40 a year for a weekly lecture.

The lectureship was reëstablished in 1611, at the same salary.[35] The incumbent had apparently left by 1619, and another was appointed at £20 a year. His name was John Workman, and he was destined to become a *cause célèbre.* The election was unanimous, since he was "well approved by all the members of this house."[36] Workman held his position for fourteen years; he seems to have kept the approval of the council, even though his views became increasingly radical. By 1633, he was inveighing against images and dancing, and was preaching that the election of ministers should be in the people.[37] The bishop questioned him about his dangerous doctrines "and refractory carriage to the canons and established government of this church," but without improving his views or conduct.[38]

At this point the central government intervened. In the opinion of Archbishop Laud, Workman "had done so

34. Glouc. Corp. Rec. 1451, fos. 176v–177. The wording is obscure, and it is possible that the city was underwriting the £20 subscription instead of doubling it. The salary of the mayor at this time was £40 a year; see above, p. 206.

35. Glouc. Corp. Rec. 1451, fo. 235v.

36. *Ibid.,* fo. 467; see also fo. 468.

37. William Prynne, *Canterburies Doome. Or the First Part of a Compleat History of the Commitment, Charge, Tryall, Condemnation, Execution of William Laud Late Archbishop of Canterbury* (London, 1646), pp. 103, 491; Gardiner, *History of England,* VIII, 112.

38. MS. A.P.C., XLIII, 405.

much harm, and made such a faction in Gloucester, as that the high commission thought it not fit to continue him there."[39] The court made sure that he did not continue, by sentencing him to suspension, excommunication, submission and public recantation, payment of costs, and imprisonment.[40] The city countered with a gesture of defiance: in September of 1633, Workman's £20 stipend was confirmed to him "so long as he shall be pleased to inhabit and live in this city, whether he preach or not."[41] In December, the government struck back by summoning several aldermen before the privy council. Two of them were fined £10 apiece, and all were put to considerable expense.[42] The common council repealed the grant, and tried to justify its conduct in a petition to Archbishop Laud.[43]

39. "And he was not willing to go from thence, where he had made his party." William Scott and James Bliss, eds., *The Works of the Most Reverend Father in God, William Laud* (7 vols. in 9; Oxford, 1846–60), IV, 234.

40. Prynne, *Canterburies Doome,* p. 107; see also the concise account of the case in *V.C.H.,* II, 34.

41. Glouc. Corp. Rec. 1452, p. 18. Laud's actions in this case were later the basis of an article in his impeachment. His accusers claimed that the grant from the city was made *before* Workman's trial in high commission; although the justification of Laud's later conduct in the case hinged on this question of fact, it was one of the many never settled during the trial. The peculiar wording of the grant strongly suggests that it was made after Workman's trial; it was certainly made after he had been questioned by the Bishop of Gloucester. See MS. A.P.C., XLIII, 405; Prynne, *Canterburies Doome,* pp. 107, 491, 495–96.

42. *V.C.H.,* II, 34. It seems that only the town clerk and another alderman appeared before the council; they and four others were turned over to Laud, to be proceeded against in high commission. (MS. A.P.C., XLIII, 405.) Laud claimed that the grant of 1633 had been taken out of city funds allocated to poor relief; he defended the treatment of the aldermen, and justified the punishment of a few on the ground that "the noise would be too great to call all." He also asserted that the fines were later remitted. (*Works of William Laud,* IV, 235; Prynne, *Canterburies Doome,* p. 491.) This last assertion was probably right. The accused aldermen, six years later, petitioned the common council to be reimbursed for their expenses in London, since they had been summoned for what had been "thought to be a good and charitable act"; they made no mention of having paid a fine. In the next year, 1640, the common council dared to grant Workman £20 "in regard of his long weakness and sickness." Glouc. Corp. Rec. 1452, pp. 121–22, 167.

43. *Ibid.,* pp. 22–23.

The city had scarcely made its peace with the government before it was again in difficulty. The source of trouble the second time was a schoolmaster instead of a preacher, but the religious issue was substantially the same. There were two grammar schools in the city: Christ School, which was privately endowed, and the College School, which belonged to the dean and chapter of the cathedral.[44] The common council subsidized both, and exercised a measure of control over the schoolmasters. This control brought it into conflict with the crown. In 1628, the master of the College School was John Langley.[45] In 1639, the council shifted him to Christ School, where the curriculum was in a parlous state. The incumbent master, John Bird, had been so negligent in his teaching "that very few able scholars have been sent thence to the universities, in comparison of other free schools. . . . The Greek tongue and other learning are at this day taught in many free schools, for the better instructing and fitting of youth for the university, whereof Mr. John Langley hath given good testimony in teaching and instructing many of the burgesses' sons of this city and others, and enabling them for the universities." Langley was therefore designated as Bird's assistant.[46]

44. The name of the College School implies a connection with the cathedral, and I assume that it was what a royal letter referred to as "the school in Gloucester belonging to the dean and chapter." *Ibid.,* p. 148; see also p. 132; 1451, fo. 521v.

45. He was offered a position at Dorchester at £60 a year. The common council wished to keep him, "in regard of his good demeanor in his place, and his careful teaching and educating the youth of this city and the sons of divers noblemen and gentlemen, to the great grace and credit of this city." His salary was accordingly increased by £10 a year. There is no record of the total, but it was enough to make him decline the Dorchester offer. The master of Christ School, after 1620, was paid £26 13*s*. 6*d*. a year, half from the endowment and half from the city; the school usher received £13 6*s*. 8*d*. By the standards of the day, these salaries were surprisingly high. *Ibid.,* 1451, fo. 521v; see also fo. 474v; 1452, pp. 143–44.

46. *Ibid.,* p. 132. Langley's salary was the same as Bird's, £26 13*s*. 6*d*.; this expensive addition to the staff doubtless gave the council a financial incentive for getting rid of Bird. *Ibid.,* p. 134.

Cirencester was involved in a simultaneous, but apparently uncon-

The experiment was not a success. Bird's negligence continued, and the council had numerous complaints from parents "that they shall be enforced to withdraw their sons from thence and to place them elsewhere, which will turn to their great charge and the disgrace of this city." The council therefore ordered that Bird's salary should be cut in half, "and that care be taken for the speedy removing of the said Mr. Bird, and the placing of a more diligent man in that place." [47] The diligent man was without doubt Langley.

At this point the educational reformers on the council were checked by the interference of no less a person than the king. Bird obtained a letter from him, in which Langley was stigmatized as "a man factiously set against the government of the Church of England," and Bird was lauded as "a very sober man of conversation, and learned in that way, and [one who] hath deserved very well of you and that city, in the instruction and education of the children there." The letter went on to command that Bird should be kept, that his old salary should be restored, and that Langley should never be appointed to the place without express license from Canterbury.[48] The council gave

nected, quarrel with its schoolmaster. In 1639, the vestry expressed dissatisfaction with the teaching of Mr. Topp at the Free Grammar School. He was warned to be more diligent, and to obtain an usher, apparently at his own expense; otherwise the churchwardens were to give him notice. He ignored the warning, despite all admonitions; a year later, twenty-nine parishioners certified that there had been continuing complaints of his slackness in conducting himself and the school. He was then expelled, and the twenty-nine agreed to share the cost of whatever legal proceedings he might institute. He stayed for another year, and left only on receipt of an £80 settlement in cash. Cirencester Vestry Book, fos. 56v, 58v, 60.

47. Glouc. Corp. Rec. 1452, pp. 143–44.

48. Langley was accused of making a scene during Archbishop Laud's visitation in 1635. "He publicly, in court before the vicars general, obstinately refused to conform himself to those things which were required of him according to law." (*Ibid.*, p. 148.) This is presumably the same John Langley who in 1616 had denounced Laud, then Dean of Gloucester, for moving the communion table in the cathedral; see Prynne, *Canterburies Doome*, p. 75.

way, and Bird kept his position as long as King Charles kept his power.[49]

So much for the city's concern with preaching and teaching. The rise of Puritanism, in church and council, increased the problems of municipal government by creating friction with the crown.[50] But this friction appeared only sporadically, and only in the last decade of the period. In general, neither the churches nor the schools can be ranked among the difficulties which beset the corporation. While it was interested in public morals, and in the proper education of the young, it was more interested in protecting the public from immediate dangers, such as murder and plague and fire. These were the perennial, never-ending problems of town government, and to them we may now turn.

The enforcement of the statutes and town ordinances, and the preservation of peace, depended on the constables and watchmen. The constable has already been discussed; there is no reason to suppose that the urban constable was different from the rural, either in his nature or his capacity. The watchmen were pressed into service by him, and were as variable as his other amateur helpers; one of

49. When Gloucester sent a lobbyist to the Long Parliament, in 1640, one of his tasks was to defend the liberties and privileges of the city against Mr. Bird and others. In March of 1641, Bird's stipend was reduced to £9; in May, after the city had obtained leave from the harassed king, he was formally evicted. Langley was not appointed in his place, which was given to another at £30 a year. Glouc. Corp. Rec. 1452, pp. 172, 174, 176–78, 180.

50. There is no sign of such difficulties in Tewkesbury, although the town had its quota of Puritan preachers in the 1630's. (See S.P. 16/421/92; Gardiner, *Reports of Cases,* p. 244.) I have found only one instance in which heterodoxy affected town government: three men were removed as burgesses because they refused to "acknowledge the fourth commandment to be a perpetual moral law of God, and the Christian Sabbath or Lord's Day to be God's holy ordinance, and that it is not in man's power to alter the number of one day in seven for a Sabbath to any other proportion of time." The Council of Wales bound over the recalcitrants to appear before high commission; they later made public recantation, and were restored as burgesses. Tewkes. Corp. Rec. 2, *anno* 1620.

them in Gloucester turned out to be a petty criminal.[51] When they had no cause to do otherwise, they might enforce curfew or licensing laws with moderate success. Their major function was another matter. They were the sole guardians of public safety in the towns, and guardians who were wholly unreliable. The inadequacy of the police system is well illustrated by the story of the Vicaries murder.

There had been a long feud between the Vicaries family and some men in Tewkesbury. John Vicaries came to town alone one Saturday, to buy provisions at the market, and afterward went to a tavern to drink with friends. Some of his enemies saw him, hurried home to arm themselves, and returned to pick a quarrel. They failed, though not from lack of trying; they did succeed in stealing his weapons, and went outside to wait for him. Vicaries was now thoroughly alarmed, and tried "to go privily away." His enemies caught him in the street, and stabbed him.

At this point the watch arrived, and the attackers retired. But Vicaries, "having a mortal wound and yet hoping of life, fearing the watchmen were not able to defend him from further assaults of the other murderers, did then, bleeding freshly, arise up from the ground, and in a great maze ran away about six score yards, and hid himself in the market house." His fear of the watchmen was well grounded: they ran up the street, away from danger. One of the attackers followed Vicaries into the market house, "and searched for him until he had found him, and when he had found him cried out,

" 'Here he is!'

"Another straightway answered him, 'Kill him, kill him! Knock him down!'

"And then he that so came in weaponless, ran away from them down the street, and he in the white doublet

51. He was arrested for neglecting the watch, "being thereunto warned by the constables," and also "for his misdemeanors and night-walking." Glouc. Corp. Rec. 1566, Trinity, 1633.

with others followed him. And presently this deponent saw a light in the street, by which he discerned the said party that came away from the others to be about the pavement. . . . He there lay and was knocked down, albeit the people suddenly gathering to the place hid the sight thereof from him." Vicaries was dead, and the gang feud had run its course under the noses of the police.[52]

The year after this affair, in 1608, the Tewkesbury common council tried to encourage the watchmen by having the streets lighted. It was ordered that between the eve of All Saints and the morrow of Candlemas, every member of the common council, and every taverner, innkeeper, chandler, and victualer, and one additional man in each section of the town, should hang a lantern on his street door from nightfall till 8:00 P.M., except at such times as the moon was shining. The system was primitive to a degree, and was limited to the early evening. But it was a step in the right direction, and one which might have prevented murder the year before.[53]

Lighting the streets was a matter of much less interest to the authorities than keeping them clean. In Gloucester the water supply for that purpose, and for the general use of the inhabitants, was drawn in conduits from Robinswood Hill. These conduits were presumably numerous, since by 1622 a man was being paid £10 a year for their upkeep. From 1600, official street-cleaners were appointed by the common council.[54] But the major responsibility for

52. St. Ch. 8/18/7.

53. Tewkes. Corp. Rec. 2, *circa* 1608. This regulation was unusually progressive for the period, and may well have been inspired by the fact that the Vicaries affair had become a star-chamber matter. For a similar ordinance at Oxford, in 1614, see Salter, *Oxford Council Acts, 1583–1626,* pp. 240–41, 246. Gloucester seems to have done nothing for safety in the streets, beyond ordering that only an officer might carry a sword or dagger. (Glouc. Corp. Rec. 1450, fo. 236v.) In Bristol, there was almost no provision for lighting the streets until 1660; see Latimer, *Annals of Bristol,* pp. 31, 263, 301.

54. Glouc. Corp. Rec. 1451, fos. 488, 185. Robinswood Hill is an isolated spur of the Cotswolds to the south of the city. Such community conduits were no rarity. Manchester had one, for example, and was extremely proud of it; the order in which citizens were served was an

the streets fell on the inhabitants. At the end of the period, each householder was charged with cleaning the pavement in front of his door. Every Saturday afternoon, he was to sweep up the dirt and take it to the common miskin, on pain of a 1*s.* fine; four sanitary inspectors went the rounds on Monday, to make sure that the job had been done.[55]

Substantially the same regulations were in force in Tewkesbury. Householders were responsible for repairing the pavement and cleaning it; they must not sweep dirt into the gutter, or allow "any dead dog or other carrion or noisome thing" to lie in the street before their doors. As in Gloucester, swine and ducks were not allowed in the streets. Sewage must not be left near a watercourse; if complaint was made to the bailiffs "by the neighbors annoyed," the offender was to take his dunghill to the town miskin.[56] Householders at Cirencester had the same responsibility for removing "muck lying before their houses," and punishment was supposed to be visited on "such as in a rude and brutish manner do foul and defile the streets."[57] In Gloucester, at least by the end of the period, this problem was simplified by the existence of municipal privies.[58]

In the interest of cleanliness and public health, the towns enforced a number of restrictions on butchers and

hereditary privilege. J. P. Earwaker, *The Court Leet Records of the Manor of Manchester,* II, 150, 187, etc.; III, 164, 229, 247, 251–56; see also Salter, *Oxford Council Acts, 1583–1626,* pp. 245, 253.

55. 1641; Glouc. Corp. Rec. 1452, pp. 201–02. The householder's responsibility for the pavement in front of his house had been enforced on Londoners, living in Holborn and the Strand, since before 1540; see 32 Henry VIII, c. 17.

56. It was further provided that mastiffs must not be allowed out of the house unmuzzled. (Tewkes. Corp. Rec. 2, *circa* 1608; see also Glouc. Corp. Rec. 1450, fo. 236–36v.) Manchester at this time had the same problems; among the common offenses were failing to dispose of sewage, and allowing swine and dogs in the streets. See Earwaker, *Leet Records of Manchester,* II–III, *passim.*

57. Cirencester Vestry Book, fos. 45v–46. The officer in charge of enforcing these provisions was the beadle of the beggars, for whose other duties see below, pp. 250–51.

58. Glouc. Corp. Rec. 1501, *passim.*

fishmongers. They were forbidden to throw offal into the gutters, or into the Severn at any but specified places. The fishmongers of Gloucester might not sell fish at the Cross, or keep their "filthy vessels" there; those of Tewkesbury might not sell rotten fish, "neither they nor any butcher to empty or caste down any their stinking waters, blood, or filth into the common streets or gutters." [59] The prohibition on selling bad meat seems to have been universal, and to have been occasionally enforced: in Northleach, in 1597, the authorities confiscated some mutton and veal from a foreign butcher, because inspection had shown that it was "not man's meat." The rest of the sentence has been crossed out: "which meat was given to the poor." [60]

These various measures of public health assumed vital importance on occasions when they became "a great means under God to prevent the infection of the plague." [61] The infection struck four times during this period. The first was in 1592–93, and the second in 1605. The third was in 1624–25, just after the death of King James; "princes die not alone, but being the heart of the commonwealth, other members suffer with them." [62] The fourth was in 1636–37. At these times the sanitary regulations were tightened. At Gloucester, in 1593, each inhabitant was fined 20*s*. if a pig of his died, and he failed to bury it at least four feet deep.[63] At Tewkesbury, in 1625, every householder was ordered to wash his pavement and gutter

59. *Ibid.,* 1450, fo. 236; Tewkes. Corp. Rec. 2, *circa* 1608. At Bibury, there is an order of the manorial court "that none do henceforth caste any filth or dip any foul pail or hang any foul clothes in or over the well called Fairwell." Court roll of Bibury, 9 October, 14 Charles I; no. 79 in case 6 of Sherborne MSS.

60. Northleach Court Book, p. 309.

61. Tewkes. Corp. Rec. 2, *anno* 1625.

62. There had also been an outbreak after Queen Elizabeth's death, during which 30,578 were said to have died in London alone; the death rate there in 1624 was reported as 41,313. Giles Geast Rent Book, *anno* 1624.

63. Glouc. Corp. Rec. 1451, fo. 143.

twice daily.[64] Cleanliness was difficult to achieve, but its importance was realized.

It is difficult to imagine the horror of one of these epidemics; it is comparable with the modern horror of an air raid. The plague came slowly, unlike the bombers, but it was more inexorable and more deadly. Although the government did what it could, precautions were of little use. Even the dry records of a common council show the terror growing. There is plague in Abergavenny; then there is plague in Hereford, and the fair is canceled; next there is plague in Worcester—the county is encircled by death, and the tide is rising. Tewkesbury is infected: money and food are contributed for the sick, and the county is taxed for their relief; the well either flee the town, or wait helplessly.[65] The plague moves south to Gloucester. The council tries to recall the citizens who have fled, "to the scandal and discredit of the city," by imposing a fine for each day's absence.[66] The bishop is among the refugees; he shuts himself in his country house, and bars the doors against any who come from the town.[67]

64. He was instructed to keep his children indoors, "other than such as go to school, without suffering them to lie playing in troops in the streets, in such manner as they have heretofore used." Tewkes. Corp. Rec. 2, *anno* 1625.

65. The contributions in 1592 were to the value of £12. The J. P.'s assessed the county at the rate of £30 a month for the relief of the town, but only £22 was paid in all. "Many of the inhabitants forsook the town because of the sickness, and the townsmen were very straightly barred to frequent any market town, and were forced to carry certificates with them of their sound dwelling." *Ibid.*, 1, fo. 19v.

66. This was probably a financial measure. The plague, in 1593, was costing the city £10 a week, and even special taxes were not bringing in sufficient money. Glouc. Corp. Rec. 1451, fos. 143v–144.

67. This isolation was imputed to the fears of the bishop's wife, "having the only guide of his lordship's house." Its result was to throw diocesan affairs into chaos. (Req. 2/163/90.) The effect of the plague on civil government might be equally disruptive. At Chipping Campden, for example, a riot broke out during a time of plague. The constable called on a J. P. to stop it, but the justice (who had just come out of hiding in Worcestershire) declined to stir out of his house for fear of the sickness. He ordered the constable "to do his office in that behalf as appertained," but the constable refused. St. Ch. 7/10/55.

The plague of 1636–37 was particularly severe in Gloucester. The first sign of trouble was in October of 1636: the council ordered that the watch at the gates should be continued after Michaelmas, when it usually ended.[68] By the following March there was plague in Monmouthshire, and travelers from the west "may prove dangerous to these parts"; two men were therefore appointed to watch the west gate by day, and to admit no "wandering and suspicious persons" without the consent of the mayor or a justice. As the plague spread through the country to the north and east, the watch was strengthened at one gate after another; two men were posted at the quayside, and a common councilor was given charge of each gate.[69] There were also watchmen outside the walls, but they seem to have done little good. "One came from Worcester the last night, and the watchmen at Newland . . . went and drank with him . . . , whereby great danger may accrue to this city."[70] The fear was well grounded, and the danger soon accrued.

Townsmen in time of plague were a menace to the countryside. Take for example a letter from a village on the edge of Worcestershire. "The sickness is very dangerously dispersed in Gloucester, and therefore I wish you not to send anybody thither upon any occasion. We cannot keep the people of Gloucester from coming hither upon holidays, which makes us the more fearful and haste away the sooner." (Bodl. MS. Rawl. D 859, fo. 36.) A similar situation arose at Rudford during the epidemic of 1592: the constable called on a woman, with an order from a J. P. "to require her to abstain from the company of her neighbors for a season, for that she had received her son from Gloucester, who came from amongst them . . . that were visited with sickness." Gloucester Diocesan Records, LXXIX, 106v.

68. The watchmen were to make sure "that the wickets be kept fast, as that no passengers may come in." This presumably applied only at night. Glouc. Corp. Rec. 1543, fo. 8.

69. Gloucester canceled its two fairs, and notified neighboring towns that it had done so. *Ibid.,* fos. 9v–10.

70. Two of the delinquent watchmen, and the victualer who had supplied them with drink, were quarantined by order of the council. (*Ibid.,* 10v.) The use of watchmen to keep out plague-carriers was not peculiar to Gloucester, although information about them elsewhere is scanty. In July of 1625, a J. P. warned the constable of Bibury, together with a neighboring tithingman, to be on the lookout for travelers from London, and to take order "for the keeping out and putting by of all such

Once the enemy was inside the gates, the authorities took further precautions. Dogs were thought to be carriers, and were exterminated as thoroughly as possible.[71] Pesthouses were erected, where the sick might die in isolation.[72] Lastly, post-mortems were held at the expense of the city. These need a word of explanation. The disease, while it was running its course, was not always obvious to the doctors; if the patient died, it was important to determine whether or not he had been a victim of plague. There were two ways to do this: goodwives might be sent to view the body, or an autopsy might be held. The corporation, in 1636, sent two women to the house of a dead man (after fortifying them with a pint of sack), and shut them in the house until they had made their diagnosis.[73] In another case, in 1605, the women decided that a man by the name of Parker had died of worms. The city apparently distrusted their verdict, and the house was quarantined for plague. Parker's child died two months later,

travelers as aforesaid, vagrants or other suspicious, wandering, and idle persons; and them to punish which you shall find disorderly and dangerous." (Bibury MS. 130 in Sherborne MSS.) More ineffective orders for quarantine would be hard to imagine.

71. "Paid . . . for a horseshoe to kill dogs in time of infection, 3*d.*" (Glouc. Corp. Rec. 1501, fo. 73; for similar entries at Leicester, see Bateson and Stocks, *Leicester,* IV, 235, 260.) The plague at Chipping Campden, in 1636, was supposedly caused by "an infected dead dog, which was thrown amongst growing hemp, and infected those which gathered the hemp a month after." S.P. 16/333/34.

72. A laborer was reimbursed in 1637, by order of the J. P.'s, "for his loss in suffering pesthouses to be erected in the vineyard garden." (Glouc. Corp. Rec. 1452, p. 80.) The MS. accounts of St. Michael's contain an item in the following year for links to light a goodwife to the pesthouse; these are the only references I have found to such houses in Gloucester. At Tewkesbury, in the plague of 1624, houses were built in Oldbury Field, and people were removed to them as soon as they became infected; the death toll was thereby reduced to twenty. Giles Geast Rent Book, *anno* 1624.

73. The women's diet and wages, the diet of a family shut up with them, and the wages of a woman who took them their provisions, cost the city a total of £2 12*s.* Glouc. Corp. Rec. 1501, fo. 10–10v; for examples of the same procedure elsewhere, see Bateson and Stocks, *Leicester,* IV, 71; Guilding, *Reading,* II, 241, 244; Salter, *Oxford Council Acts, 1583–1626,* pp. 153–54, 173–74, 186, 331–32.

and the mayor ordered a municipal surgeon to perform an autopsy. The surgeon, an old apothecary, decided that the child also had died of worms, "which said child being so boweled as aforesaid, the citizens of Gloucester were well persuaded that it was not from the beginning the plague which was in the house of the said John Parker." [74]

But the authorities were not persuaded. Parker had been a servant of Alderman Taylor; the mayor and council were convinced that both Parker and another servant had died of the plague, and that Taylor had wilfully concealed the fact. Immediately after the first servant had died, Taylor had spent three or four hours with the mayor and councilors. He had ignored his neighbors' warnings that there was plague in his house, and had tried to keep the matter secret. Parker by then had a sore under his armpit, and his master "did procure one Goodwife Clarke, a woman experienced therein, to look to him and search him. She therefore . . . did employ medicines wherewith she broke the same sore, which did run upon him the most part of a whole week." During that week Taylor had brought Parker with him into the presence of the mayor and aldermen, and had entertained at his house. As a result, "divers persons and other houses are already infected with that sickness, and many more to be feared are like to be infected, to the great danger and hurt of the state of the whole city, and hazard of many lives."

The authorities finally got wind of the danger. They were probably scared, and certainly angry. The mayor ordered the house closed and guarded, thereby invoking the heavy penalties of the statute against any one who left it.[75] Taylor's son, however, "did in great scorn and contempt of the said order not only break up the doors of the said house, and offer to discharge pieces against such

74. St. Ch. 8/4/9.

75. If a man left a house which he had been forbidden to leave, he was to be punished as a vagabond and bound to good behavior for a year; if he had on him a plague-sore, he was to be punished by death. See 1 James I, c. 31; Lambard, *Eirenarcha,* pp. 227–28.

as were appointed to keep them in, but also delivered and pronounced most railing and rude terms against the said Mr. Mayor."[76] The council retaliated promptly. The father was deprived of his commonage and fined £100; the son was also discommoned, fined £66 13*s.* 4*d.*, and sentenced to spend three market days in the stocks.[77] Quarantine was the only effective weapon in the hands of the councilors, and they could not afford to have one of their own members ignore it.

The plague was only one danger which worried the city fathers. It came every decade or two; it gave warning of its approach, remained for a few months or years, and then disappeared. A second menace was always present; it never gave warning, and might obliterate the town overnight. When the churchbells gave the alarm, the mayor and citizens turned out to save their homes from fire. They fought with primitive weapons: firehooks, ladders, and bucket-lines. With such equipment, and with houses which might as well have been tinder, the dread of fire is not surprising. The wonder is that there was not even a near disaster during the period.

Disaster did strike in the surrounding counties. The authorities must have been kept alert and fearful by the news that Stratford had been ravaged by fire, that Banbury had been practically destroyed.[78] To reduce the danger, the common council of Tewkesbury passed a series of ordinances in 1608. No one might thatch any part of his house or barn if there was a chimney nearby,

76. The quotations in this and the preceding paragraph are from Glouc. Corp. Rec. 1451, fo. 203.

77. The son's punishment was later remitted *in toto,* and the father's fine reduced to £80. (*Ibid.,* fos. 203v, 206, 211; see also St. Ch. 8/280/16.) Remission of sentence was a common practice. There are few instances of effective retribution for breach of town laws; it was more usual to levy a fine, and then either to rescind it or forget it. Other punishments were almost never employed, and even the threat of the stocks is unusual for a man of Taylor's position.

78. The effect of a fire on increasing precautions in nearby towns is illustrated by the conflagration in Dorchester in 1615, and a resultant presentment of the Southampton leet; see Hearnshaw, *Leet Records,* II, 483.

or if it was otherwise dangerous to himself or his neighbors. No one might build a chimney in any building among stables, barns, or storehouses for hay or straw. No one might keep hay or straw in the front of his house, toward the street, when there was a chimney near. "No manner of person shall wilfully set on fire any chimney within his house, to th' intent to make clean the same thereby, nor else negligently to suffer his chimney to take fire, to be seen out at the top, to the terror and danger of his neighbors." [79] Small cottages near the town were an equal menace at this time. One had been converted into "three poor dwellings of idle people," and four more had been built beside it. They were thatched, and their chimneys were made of wood and mortar, "the which are very dangerous to be suffered, for fear of firing that part of the said town." [80] An opinion which savors of understatement.

Fire prevention was an integral part of town government. The fire chief was the mayor, the firemen were the citizens, and the fire station was the church. The fire-fighting equipment was listed year after year by the churchwardens, and great care was spent on keeping it in condition. In Gloucester the buckets were the property of the city, and elsewhere of the parish; they were made of leather, and frequently needed repair.[81] Their number varied, doubtless with the zeal of the officers and the finances of the parish. In Gloucester, for example, there were 183 in 1633, distributed among the various

79. Tewkes. Corp. Rec. 2, *circa* 1608. Manchester and Liverpool had similar regulations against fire, but they were less strict. See Earwaker, *Leet Records of Manchester,* II, 83, 95, 288; III, 7–8, 25, 101, etc.; J. A. Twemlow, *Liverpool Town Books. Proceedings of Assemblies, Common Councils, Portmoot Courts, &c., 1550–1862,* II, 575–76, 607, 611, 808. For further references, see Horrocks, *Assembly Books of Southampton,* I, 92; J. G. de T. Mandley, *The Portmote Records of Salford,* Chetham Society, new series, XLVI, 114; XLVII, 23; Salter, *Oxford Council Acts, 1583–1626,* I, 85.

80. St. Ch. 8/276/14.

81. One parish would sometimes repair the buckets of its neighbor, as when the churchwardens of Tetbury received the large sum of £4 8*s.* for mending the Beverstone buckets. Tetbury churchwardens' accounts, p. 57.

churches.[82] By 1639 the number had decreased, and the city stewards were told "to inquire where the buckets are, and what number in every church, and to take course for the more safe keeping and repairing of them." [83]

A fire was a menace, but in Gloucester it was also a social occasion. The mayor attended, and in at least one instance the firemen were provided with a barrel of beer.[84] No great imagination is needed to reconstruct the scene: the crowd milling in the street, and jostling the bucket-line from the nearest conduit; the buckets passing from hand to hand, up the ladder and into the house; the mayor as fire chief, bellowing directions to men stamping out sparks on adjacent roofs and tearing at thatch with their firehooks; the tankards of beer going from hand to hand; the smoke and glare and noise, with the bells of St. Michael's still clanging to rouse the town.

The authorities in Gloucester permitted or provided other entertainment for the citizens. There were plays, music, and municipal celebrations. Traveling players frequently came to town. They were given gifts by the corporation, and occasionally entertained.[85] Men who brought "sights and shows with dancing on the rope"

82. There were also eighteen firehooks; St. Michael's had twenty buckets and two long ladders. Glouc. Corp. Rec. 1501, fos. 32–34v; churchwardens' accounts in St. Michael's MSS.

83. Glouc. Corp. Rec. 1452, p. 141. The stewards seem to have reported that there were only 170 buckets. (*Ibid.,* 1501, fo. 122.) The equipment of Cirencester, by 1633, included only eighteen buckets, two firehooks, and two ladders. Cirencester Vestry Book, fo. 51.

84. There is an entry in the city accounts, 1636–37, for links to light the mayor home from a fire, and in 1593 for a barrel of beer used during a fire. (Glouc. Corp. Rec. 1501, fo. 41v; 1500, fo. 298v.) If the beer was drunk before the fire was out, the results may well have been unfortunate. Gloucester beer was strong (or Gloucester heads inordinately weak), and firemen as drunk as Mayor Taylor would have been a menace.

85. A troop of players was given breakfast by the city in 1591. (*Ibid.,* fo. 278v.) The same accounts contain numerous gifts to players, even though it had been ordered in 1589 that none should be given "without good occasion." It had been ordered at the same time that no plays should be given on Sunday, and the order presumably remained in force throughout the period. *Ibid.,* 1451, fo. 130.

met as liberal a reception. Amusements were welcomed by the magistrates, except in time of plague; even then the jugglers and players had little to complain of, since they received as much from the city for not performing as they would have had for performing.[86]

The authorities also provided modest entertainment of their own. There were four public musicians, later increased to six. They played in the chief streets of the city at four in the morning, presumably so that the burgesses, like Montaigne, might wake in a pleasant humor; they also played at "the solemn usual assemblies," such as the installation of a mayor.[87] These assemblies were amusement for the populace as well as the officials; sometimes there were refreshments, and sometimes fireworks.[88] Seventeenth-century Gloucester must have offered almost as much entertainment as it does today. The cinema has replaced the players and jugglers, and the alarm clock serves instead of musicians; the pageantry is more solemn, the fireworks more expensive, and only the pub and the fair remain as changeless diversions.

The amusements of that day stand out from a background which to the modern eye is dour. Town government could not exorcise the dangers of violence or plague

86. In 1640, a juggler received £1 6*s.* 8*d.* for his performance, and a player soon after received the same amount for not performing. The juggler returned, and was paid to cancel his show because "the time of contagious sickness might prove dangerous." (*Ibid.,* 1501, fo. 40.) I have found no other reference to plague in this year.

87. They received £2 a year, for their services and liveries. When their number was increased, the allowance for each was doubled. (*Ibid.,* 1451, fo. 157v; 1567, p. 3.) For information about town waits elsewhere, see Bateson and Stocks, *Leicester,* III, 439, 451; IV, 53, 236; Earwaker, *Leet Records of Manchester,* II, 29, 163; Horrocks, *Assembly Books of Southampton,* III, 57–58; Latimer, *Annals of Bristol,* pp. 35, 70; Mandley, *Portmote Records of Salford,* Chetham Society, new series, XLVI, 21; Salter, *Oxford Council Acts, 1583–1626,* p. 151; Salter and Hobson, *Oxford Council Acts, 1626–1665,* pp. 48, 55, 79.

88. "In cates [?] when Mr. Hands was sworn coroner," £1 2*s.;* "for the charge of the fireworks on the election day," 11*s.* 6*d.;* "for a waggon in the pageant for the Turk," 10*s.* (Glouc. Corp. Rec. 1500, fos. 271v, 305; 1501, fo. 138v.) A municipal bowling green was planned in 1628, but perhaps not built. *Ibid.,* 1451, fo. 522v.

or fire. The constables and watchmen were inefficient, and violence was frequently beyond their control. The plague was an act of God, to be endured as such. Cleanliness was desirable, and quarantine was important; but neither could be fully enforced, and public health went no further. If the menace from fire never materialized, it was apparently because of good fortune rather than good management. The dangers were beyond the scope of the authorities, and disaster was always in the offing.

Yet in spite of uncertainties, town life for the most part was quiet enough, and town government functioned with moderate success. The reason is not that it was any more effective than county government, but that it was never seriously tested. Ship money aroused less opposition in the towns than in the country, and there were no urban riots like those in the Forest of Dean. The townsmen went their ways, and fought and drank and watched the players, and left the problems of government in the hands of their common councilors. Those councilors were not expert. But since they were never called upon to be more than adequate, they were able to muddle through their task without great crises or open failure.

IX

THE PARISH AND POOR RELIEF

THE parish is as difficult to delimit as the town. The connection between parochial and ecclesiastical government is for the most part irrelevant to a discussion of civil administration. But the chief concern of the parish was with poor relief, and this is a subject which surpasses parochial boundaries; it was as important to the quarter sessions, and the trustees of private charities, as it was to the parish officers. The present chapter, therefore, deals with a variety of subjects. The focus of the first half is the churchwardens: their care for the church, the sources of their income, their disbursements for the community, their rôle in helping the poor. The focus of the second half is the poor themselves, and the means for their relief afforded by overseers, quarter sessions, common councils, and various private endowments.

In most towns there were two prominent buildings: the booth hall, or guild hall, and the church. The two symbolized two aspects of community life. The booth hall was the seat of government, whether a common council or a court leet; the church was the fire station, the rostrum for public and private business, and in a sense the library and news agency. The assessors of the subsidy met at times in the church; the vestry met there, to conduct parish business; there bequests were distributed to the poor, and debtors were ordered to pay their creditors.[1] Whenever a

1. I omit the vestry as an organ of parochial government, because it rarely appears as a distinctive institution. The exception is at Cirencester, where it was active as a recording and legislative body; it met in the church, "the ordinary place for the assembling of the said town for such occasions." (C. 91/1/10.) Elsewhere there are only sporadic glimpses of the parish meeting, engaged in business such as the sanction of special assessments, and the approval (or occasionally the rejection) of the churchwardens' accounts.

financial transaction required especial solemnity, the church was likely to be the setting.

In all but the largest towns, the church was also the only library. There was a Bible, which was read so much that from time to time it had to be replaced.[2] There were three devotional works required by the government, and numerous books of prayers for special occasions.[3] These volumes were sometimes bought by the parish, and sometimes given by private donors; they were a cherished part of the contents of the church, and were itemized year after year by successive churchwardens.[4]

One other possession of the church had a secular use. No parish expense was more regular than that for the bells. They were always getting out of repair, because they were used for a variety of purposes: they not only gave the fire alarm, and rang to service; they also proclaimed great national events, and celebrated their anni-

For the use of the church by assessors, see above, pp. 114–15. A bequest at Tewkesbury was distributed in the church: "the number of the poor did exceed nine hundred, and yet country poor were excluded." (Tewkes. Corp. Rec. 1, fo. 17.) A man was ordered by the Council of Wales to pay a £5 debt on a certain day, "in the parish church of Peter Ampney." St. Ch. 5/B/97/31.

2. It was an expensive book. A copy for St. Michael's, in 1612, cost £2 *6s. 8d.*, while "carriage for him" and "a register for him" cost *6s. 4d.* more. (A thing was commonly *he*, as it is in Gloucestershire today.) My description of the parish is based largely on the churchwardens' accounts described in the bibliography; citing each one would be repetitious and unnecessary. Hence when a statement contains a place and a date, but no source, it is derived from the accounts of that parish for that year. The price of the Bible, for example, is taken from the accounts of St. Michael for 1612, in the St. Michael's MSS.

3. The works were Erasmus's *Paraphrases*, Foxe's *Book of Martyrs*, and Jewel's *Apology;* they had been required since early in Elizabeth's reign, and the requirement was intermittently enforced. (J. C. Cox, *Churchwardens' Accounts from the Fourteenth Century to the Close of the Seventeenth Century* [London, 1890], pp. 118–19.) The special prayers were for such things as relief from plague and earthquake, for the birth of a prince, and for the fleet at sea.

4. A London grocer left £5 to the parish of Cheltenham, "where I went to school for some years," to buy a three-volume set of Foxe's *Martyrs*, on a revolving stand, "to the end that the same may be free and in common for all to read at convenient times." Cheltenham Vestry Book; for a similar gift, see Cirencester Vestry Book, fo. 13v.

versaries. There was a peal in 1586 "for joy of taking of the traitors of England," and two years later "for the victory God gave us against the Spaniards"; other occasions were the proclamation[5] and coronation of King James, "the discovery of the treason" in November of 1605, "the prince his coming home" from the Spanish escapade of 1623, his accession as king two years later, the birth of Prince Charles, and the news in 1640 that "the king's majesty did condescend to the parliament." [6] The payments to the bell-ringers are a homely index of the exciting moments in the period.

The machinery for operating the bells was crude, and was constantly in need of repair or renewal.[7] The bell-metal, also, must have been extremely soft, because at frequent intervals a bell had to be recast. This happened at North Nibley in 1640, when the churchwardens contracted for "five good, sufficient, musical bells, as deep in note as Slimbridge or Dursley bells . . . or half a note deeper, whereof two only to be of new cast, and the three bells already in the steeple at Nibley to be in such wise chipped as they be not thereby hurt or impaired, but to be all five bells thereby brought to be musical and tunable." [8]

5. The proclamation of the new sovereign ended a dangerous interregnum, during which the authority of local officials might be challenged on the ground that there was no law. This does not seem to have happened in Gloucestershire, but there were instances elsewhere in 1603 and 1625. (Tait, *Lancashire,* pp. 165, 167; Atkinson, [North Riding] *Sessions Records,* III, 234.) The interregnum of 1603 was shorter in the west than in the north: Queen Elizabeth died on Thursday, and on the following Sunday the bailiffs of Tewkesbury proclaimed King James, "upon the certain report made of the like in some other places [the] day before done." Tewkes. Corp. Rec. 1, fo. 25v.

6. From the treasurer's accounts, Gloucester Cathedral, and the accounts of Tewkesbury and St. Michael's; for similar entries elsewhere, see J. C. Cox, *Churchwardens' Accounts,* pp. 219–21. News was also disseminated in church by the vicar, who was required by law to make certain announcements; see Sedley L. Ware, *The Elizabethan Parish in Its Ecclesiastical and Financial Aspects,* pp. 12–13. For the vicar's other statutory duties, see Lambard, *Duties of Constables,* pp. 67–69.

7. The most common expenses were for the baldrics which attached the clappers to the bells, and for "liquor for the indggine," or oil for the machinery.

8. When the work was finished, two local critics were to determine

The importance of the bells is illustrated by the scandalous affair at Withington. The parson, Mr. Knollis, had a number of enemies in the village. Some of them went to an alehouse, where they "did then and there drink, bowse, and debowse, until they were all very near drunk and cupshot." In this state they broke into the church, and rang the bells. The parishioners, supposing that there was either a fire or momentous news, assembled at the church. When they had all collected, one of the drunkards made a proclamation. "Know all men that [we] rang the bells for Knollis's calf, and we rang them backward because it was a bull calf." The incident was not taken lightly, but became a star-chamber matter.[9]

The bells were only a part of the churchwardens' concern with the building. There were holes in the walls to be repaired; the windows had to be reglazed; the stonework was overgrown with weeds; the roof needed new leads, or the tower new battlements.[10] Painters were employed to decorate the interior; it was sometimes dressed with green boughs at Christmas, or perfumed with incense to ward off the plague.[11] There were charges for

whether the bells were tunable; if not, the bellfounder was to make them so at his expense. The churchwardens provided him with "good bell-metal by them bought and brought down from London." He was to pay for any metal left over, and to be paid for what he cast and what he cut from the old bells. (G.P.L. MS. RZ 216.1, fo. 2.) The recasting had apparently been ordered by the ecclesiastical authorities; it cost the parish the staggering sum of £101 15*s.* 8*d.* North Nibley accounts for 1639–40, in Gloucester County Council MSS.

The parishioners' love for "their sweet ring of bells" appears at Olveston in 1606, when lightning ignited and destroyed the belfry. They complained of the disaster "as if the spheres of heaven were the wheels of fortune, and the clouds, hail, lightning, thunder, and all the terrors of God else, were but a cast at hazard." G.P.L. MS. RX 224.1.

9. St. Ch. 8/190/34; for further reference to this case, see my article, "Lawyers and Litigants in Stuart England: a County Sample," *Cornell Law Quarterly,* XXIV (1938–39), 554. For a similar case in Yorkshire, which came before the quarter sessions, see Atkinson, *Sessions Records,* I, 244.

10. In spite of such repairs, it is not unusual to find entries for cleaning snow out of the church.

11. For examples, see Bodl. MS. Tanner 147, fos. 204 ff.; St. Michael's accounts for 1623, 1634; Tewkesbury accounts, 1637–40. Incense first

keeping dogs out of the church, for pruning the trees in the churchyard, even for catching a swarm of bees there. There were gifts of money, wine, and beer to visiting preachers and officials, of beer to facilitate bargains with contractors, and of more beer for the workmen.[12]

The churchwardens had other minor expenses. If there were houses or lands belonging to the parish, they were responsible for this property.[13] They paid bounties, according to the statute, to parishioners who destroyed "noisome fowl and varments." [14] They had various traveling expenses on secular business: to buy bell-metal, or fetch the bells home from the foundry; to take the leads of the roof to a neighboring town for repairs; to place parish apprentices; to appear before the justices at petty or quarter sessions.

Most of their traveling, however, was on ecclesiastical business. From the viewpoint of the churchwardens, the church courts and officials must have been an unmitigated nuisance. The parish was constantly paying clerical fees,

appears at Chipping Campden in 1636, when it was used "to burn in the church in the time of the visitation of sickness." The notion that it warded off the plague apparently spread to Tewkesbury and to St. Michael's, Gloucester, where it was in use within the year.

12. "To the singing men, to drink with a stranger that sang with them in the choir"; "for a pottle of buttered beer, bestowed upon the archdeacon at the visitation." (Accounts, Gloucester Cathedral, 1624–25; Chipping Campden, 1638.) The Minchinhampton accounts contain two entries (pp. 96, 113) for removing poor folk who had taken to living in the church porch; see also Ratcliff and Johnson, *Warwick,* I, 190–91.

13. The houses or lands were usually leased. But at Minchinhampton, where the parish owned a tavern, a number of butchers' shops, and some land, the churchwardens paid for repairing the houses and harvesting the land. The same was true at Northleach; see Royce, "Northleach Court-Book," *Trans.,* VII, 108.

14. The churchwardens were empowered to make a parochial collection for these bounties, and the rate for each animal was fixed; see 8 Elizabeth, c. 15, and Lambard, *Duties of Constables,* pp. 78–80, 91–94. In some Gloucestershire parishes, the statute seems to have been a dead letter. In others it was not: North Nibley, in 1616, paid a total of £2 3*s.* 10*d.* in bounties, and the Minchinhampton churchwardens were paying far more than the legal rate for certain kinds of "vermin." North Nibley and Eastington also employed a professional sparrowcatcher, and paid him by the dozen.

and fines for one or another small oversight. The churchwardens were summoned to a nearby town, for a visitation from the bishop or archdeacon; they were summoned to Gloucester, to deliver a transcript of the church register to the registrar's office, or a certificate of the outside ministers who had preached in their parish; they were haled before the archdeacon's or chancellor's court, to explain why they had failed to provide a book of homilies or a pulpit cushion, or new machinery for their chimes, or even to be excommunicated "for our not appearing when we were not warned to appear." [15] Each trip involved expense, whether in fines or fees or bribery of court officers.[16]

Another and more important burden on the parish was the upkeep of the roads. This was only in small part a

15. Minchinhampton, 1605–06. Chipping Campden, in 1637, paid 16*s.* 6*d.* at the archdeacon's court, "our bills being refused and [we] put to great trouble." These church courts are for the most part irrelevant to a discussion of civil government. But it may be noted that their jurisdiction was often as ill defined as that of other county agencies. The courts of the archdeacon and chancellor, which considered similar petty offenses, were sometimes at loggerheads with each other. When the churchwardens of Mickleton, for example, were haled before the archdeacon's court to deliver a presentment, they were sternly forbidden to do so by the chancellor. The summons encroached on his sphere, "which innovation is not only a main wrong unto you, but unto my jurisdiction also, which I must be careful to preserve." (A letter from the chancellor, 14 September, 1632, in the Mickleton MSS.) The chancellor's court was also in occasional conflict with civil authorities; for local examples, see Skeel, *Council of Wales,* pp. 124–25; *H.M.C., Fourth Report,* p. 31. This court is described in F. S. Hockaday, "The Consistory Court of the Diocese of Gloucester," *Trans.,* XLVI (1924), 195–288, and its records are preserved in the Gloucester Diocesan Records.

16. For the prevalence of bribery, see Ware, *The Elizabethan Parish,* p. 53 and note. The accounts rarely mention it as such, but there are some suggestive entries: a payment of £1 16*s.* to be freed from an amercement, a gift to the archdeacon's servant to win his master's goodwill, presents to the apparitor "for respite," "at his earnest request," and "to see whether we could keep our sidesmen at home, being summoned to Gloucester." (St. Michael's, 1621, 1623; North Nibley, 1622; Tewkesbury, 1639.) The apparitor often acted as a delivery man for the churchwardens: he carried their presentments or certificates to the ecclesiastical courts, and even documents or money to the justices at the sessions.

financial matter: the old obligation of the king's subjects to repair the king's highway was one of the few which had not yet been commuted to a money payment. There were surveyors in each parish, to enforce the parishioners' duty of working on the roads. Because it was an onerous duty, a dishonest surveyor might make it into an instrument of graft. One such case came before star chamber. A surveyor had deputed his job to "a man of very busy and light carriage and behavior." The deputy tried to seize the tools of poor men who refused to work, and took money from the wealthier parishioners "to discharge them from danger of any labor or service in the mending of the said ways." He claimed, no doubt with truth, that the money would hire more efficient labor. But a J. P. smelled bribery, and summoned him to answer for his conduct at the sessions. He countered by charging the justice with neglecting his share of the work, a charge which was indignantly denied: every year "this defendant hath caused his plough and servants to carry and place in the highways leading from this defendant's house directly to the city of Gloucester as many stones as three of the best ploughs besides in all that parish have yearly carried." [17]

In Gloucester, the burden of road repair was occasionally lightened by individual gifts. One example, in 1640, illustrates the methods of construction. An alderman left a £100 bequest for repairing and paving a part of the Cirencester road, from Birdlip Hill to the outskirts of Gloucester. The sessions ordered that each parish on the way should provide the usual materials, gravel and pitch, and that the executrix should "pay for the said stone and the pitching thereof into a causeway of four feet broad as the work shall require, so far as the said £100 shall go." [18]

17. St. Ch. 8/4/8. For a description of the statutory powers of the surveyor, and the duties of the parishioners, see Lambard, *Duties of Constables,* pp. 82–90; Webb, *The Story of the King's Highway,* pp. 14–19.

18. Glouc. Corp. Rec. 1567, July, 1640. For a more detailed description of a similar road, also four feet wide, see Bateson and Stocks,

There were certain roads which belonged to the city of Gloucester, and the magistrates were continually concerned with their repair. The task was sometimes assigned to an individual contractor, as when a man was given a yearly grant of 10*s.* and a load of "stone of pimple," to maintain the road from the Cross to a southern suburb.[19] But more often the authorities relied on getting labor from the inhabitants of the inshire. Individuals and parishes were continually presented at the quarter sessions for not carrying stones to repair the roads. The magistrates were usually lenient, and merely ordered the work to be done by a given time. In one case they commanded a man, three days behind in his work, to do six days more in recompense.[20] In another case, when the Tewkesbury road was in such decay "that the king's liege people and their cattle cannot pass without danger," four parishes on the road were summoned to repair it before the next court, on pain of a £20 fine.[21]

Such a fine would have been paid by the parish as a whole, probably as a special assessment. Extraordinary taxation of this sort was a common method of meeting a parochial emergency. In Tewkesbury, for example, the churchwardens took most of the covering off the abbey

Leicester, IV, 294–95. The narrowness of these roads is striking proof that wheeled vehicles were a rarity, and that most transportation was by packhorse; see Webb, *King's Highway,* chapter v.

19. Glouc. Corp. Rec. 1451, fo. 491.

20. *Ibid.,* 1566, Epiphany, 1632/33. A man was indicted, soon after, for enclosing part of a path from Gloucester to Tewkesbury, an offense which should have cost him a shilling for each day that the right of way was blocked. (Lambard, *Eirenarcha,* p. 477.) He was merely ordered "to lay open the said ancient footway," and thereupon discharged. Glouc. Corp. Rec. 1566, Trinity, 1633.

21. Since this was a summer of floods, the delinquents at Michaelmas were given another year of grace. (*Ibid.,* 1567, Easter and Michaelmas, 1640.) Such delinquency was brought before the sessions by presentments, either from individuals or the grand jury; for a discussion of this cumbersome process, see Webb, *King's Highway,* chapter iv. The procedure for maintaining an important road is well illustrated by 1 Mary 3, c. 6, which empowers the sessions to assess the various hundreds on the road from Bristol to Gloucester, and to appoint collectors and overseers for the work.

roof in 1594, and then found that they had not the money to recover it. After the roof had been open for almost a year, they made a £30 assessment on the town. Only a fraction was collected, with the result that the bailiffs discharged the churchwardens and took over the task of reparation.[22] The churchwardens seem to have learned their lesson. When they wished to build a battlement on the tower, in 1600, they decided to raise the money by giving plays in the abbey. Some of the parishioners contributed wheat and malt, which were sold at the time of the plays. The performances brought a meager profit, but the grain fetched almost twice its value; the whole affair netted the churchwardens just over £6, or a tenth of the cost of the battlement. While the experiment was scarcely a financial success, it seems to have given great pleasure to the town.[23]

The usual expenses of the parish were paid from the income of the churchwardens, which came from a variety of sources. The most important was the church rate; this and the poor rate were the foundations of parochial finance. A "church pay," or assessment for the maintenance of the fabric, was levied on every parishioner of substance, according to a rate which seems to have been

22. Tewkes. Corp. Rec. 1, fos. 20–21. Church repairs at Westerley were handled in equally haphazard fashion: one of the churchwardens spent between £4 and £5 of his own money on them; the parish approved his repairs and his accounts, but he had to sue the later churchwardens to get his money back. (Req. 2/390/573.) A similar expense at North Nibley was borne more equitably, by rating contributors to the church at their usual rate, and contributors to the poor at double their usual poor rate. G.P.L. MS. 16,526, fo. 99 (2).

23. An assumption based on the amount of comment provoked. The plays made a profit of only 14*s.* 6*d.*, and the grain a profit of £5 12*s.*; the final cost of the battlement was £66. (Tewkes. Corp. Rec. 1, fo. 24; Tewkesbury churchwardens' accounts, pp. 130–31; Bennett, *History of Tewkesbury,* pp. 308–09.) The same churchwardens wished to hold a church-ale, but were forbidden to do so because they would not eliminate the accustomed abuses. (Tewkes. Corp. Rec. 1, fo. 24.) This is the only reference I have found to a church-ale, aside from some contemporary stories quoted in *N. & Q.*, I, 448–49. For a discussion of this pious excuse for carousing, see Ware, *The Elizabethan Parish,* pp. 70–75.

determined, as with most taxes, by the land which he held.[24] Payment was usually in cash, although it might be wholly or partly in kind.[25] For special occasions, such as buying a new Bible, procuring a deed, or repairing damage from lightning, the amount levied on each man would be a multiple of his regular rate. The churchwardens, with or without the advice of other parishioners, would estimate the needed sum and assess accordingly; if they were left with a surplus, there were other good uses for it.[26]

A secondary source of income was the rent of parish property. This property might be in the form of houses, lands, or even an aisle of the church leased to a neighboring parish.[27] Its most common and important form, how-

24. At Hampnett, in 1611 and 1613, the unit for parochial assessments was the yardland. The same was true at Welford; fields which were not yardlands were rated in a parish meeting "after the same proportion, considering the quantity and quality and according to the value of the rents." (Gloucester Diocesan Records, CXXVII, 17 May, 1622.) A similar system prevailed at Mickleton in 1637.

25. The rate at Minchinhampton was paid in cash or kind, and in one case "in money and malt and the commodity made thereof." Accounts, p. 138.

26. Large assessments were usually sanctioned by the parishioners, and small ones made by the churchwardens alone. The Cirencester vestry, in 1637, ordered that all levies by churchwardens, constables, or overseers of the poor should be announced in advance, so that any one unfairly assessed might complain before the rate was confirmed by the justices. (Cirencester Vestry Book, fo. 55.) The churchwardens, like the commissioners of the subsidy, paid "as far forth as any other inhabitants." (North Nibley accounts, 1633.) I have found only one instance of their being partial to themselves; see the Gloucester Diocesan Records, XCV, 27 November, 1604.

A deficit in a collection might be met by a further levy, in which the distinction between "church pays" and "poor pays" was likely to be forgotten. Another method was for the churchwardens, as at Westerley, to advance the money themselves. A third was to borrow at interest; the Dursley and Mickleton accounts are full of payments for "use," at 8 to 10 per cent. Churchwardens were also lending money at interest; a bequest was sometimes more than doubled by such "long keeping and improving." Dursley, 1622; see also 1603; North Nibley, 1617.

27. The Minchinhampton tavern brought £2 a year. An aisle of the church was leased to the parish of Rodborough at £1 a year, and Minchinhampton occasionally had to sue for the rent.

ever, was the church seats, which were made to yield a considerable revenue.

A seat was a valued possession, and its size and location reflected the consequence of the owner. There was constant rivalry for position, which was carefully regulated for the profit of the parish. At Minchinhampton, a parishioner might build a seat on payment of a fee; it was then to belong permanently to him and his posterity, or occasionally to the occupant of his house.[28] At Tewkesbury, the traffic was controlled in minute detail by the common council.[29] Even the churchwardens might not evade its rules, as they found to their cost in 1628: their accounts were rejected because they had changed the seating arrangements, "such the ancient letting of seats being the only or chief maintenance of the reparations of the church, which being large and spacious, requireth yearly great charge and expense, the beauty and state of the church being a great ornament to the town." [30]

When there was a dispute about a pew, the churchwardens were not unnaturally tempted to favor the highest bidder. The result, as the period wore on, was more and more stately pews, and more and more irascible occupants. At Slimbridge, by 1639, there was "a large double pew or seat, at least six foot high, being very

28. At Dursley, where there was no fee, the builder had only a life interest in his seat. For a discussion of such fees and rents, see Ware, *The Elizabethan Parish,* pp. 80–82.

29. The custom provided that a year's absence from the town ended all claim to a seat. If a man's wife died, he might have another woman put in her place by the churchwardens and bailiffs; she might stay until he remarried, and meanwhile he must not complain. (From a decree of the common council, 1595, quoted in the accounts, p. 107.) There are frequent entries of fees for changing to better seats, and occasional payments to holders of seats which were torn down.

30. From a decree of the common council, 1628, quoted in the accounts, p. 254. The churchwardens had been leasing seats for long terms, such as life, and ignoring the rule that a year's absence voided the lease. When a seat was vacated at Cirencester, no one might have it until a committee had pronounced the candidate "fit to be ranked with the other that were in the seat before." Cirencester Vestry Book, fo. 43.

indecent and inconformable to the other seats in the said church." [31] At Tetbury, a man's quarrel with the churchwardens about his pew was settled in 1624, by allowing him to retain it at the exorbitant rent of 10*s.* a year.[32] The same church, fourteen years later, was the scene of a violent altercation between two families claiming a single pew; the churchwardens were unable to settle the dispute, and it was carried to the court of the arches.[33] If the seats had been free, the churchwardens would have had less money but fewer cares.

One of the most important uses for their money has not yet been mentioned. The accounts are full of payments to the migrant army of the poor—men and women from all over Great Britain and Ireland, who came begging through the county with briefs from the authorities. If a man's house had been burned, or he had suffered some other great loss, he petitioned the local justices for a brief.[34] As soon as it was granted, he went on a tour of

31. The court of the arches ordered it destroyed. "This abuse hath crept into many churches, both in the diocese of Gloucester and elsewhere." (S.P. 16/424/52.) At Chipping Campden, in 1638, the churchwardens obtained an order "for pulling down the seats that did trespass upon the alley."

32. But with the thrifty proviso that this rent should not excuse him or his successors "in case the said parish church or steeple do require any extraordinary reparations." Accounts, p. 38.

33. The court decided in favor of one claimant, but the other ignored the order when it was shown to him in church. There followed "unseemly words" and a scuffle. "I required him, by virtue of the seal and inhibition, he would give place and go into his father's seat, and he said he would not. Nor he did not." (S.P. 16/386/5.) Such disputes frequently came before the consistory court; see Gloucester Diocesan Records, LXV, 14 December, 1591; LXXIX, 28 October, 1595; XCV, 27 March, 1604. I have found no such Gloucestershire cases before the civil courts, but elsewhere they were heard in quarter sessions and even star chamber; see Bates Harbin, *Somerset,* I, 31, 55; II, 140; Bateson and Stocks, *Leicester,* IV, 124; Gardiner, *Reports of Cases,* pp. 139–44.

34. By 1 Edward VI, c. 3, a sufferer from fire might obtain a brief from the lord keeper or the lord chancellor, if his application was approved by the local sessions; for an example of such a recommendation, see Glouc. Corp. Rec. 1566, Easter, 1638. This sort of brief allowed begging in a wide area, whereas a brief for the county alone might be granted by the quarter sessions; see Gretton, *Oxfordshire*

the country, gathering contributions where he could. Every sort and condition of person came through Gloucestershire: a gentleman who had been imprisoned in Turkey; a Scottish woman whose house had been burned; poor travelers, poor scholars, poor soldiers and sailors; a woman with five children going from Hereford to London; a lame man traveling to the baths; a minister's wife out of the West Indies.[35] It is not until the time of King Charles that two large groups appear in this miscellany of vagrants. One is Irishmen (and women), who arrived in droves at the beginning of the reign; the other is soldiers, returning from the king's ill-fated expeditions or from the Thirty Years' War. These two groups were a drain on parochial finance throughout the rest of the period, and only at the end is there any sign of efforts to control their exactions.[36]

Problems nearer home were of more immediate concern. The primary interest of the parish was in its own paupers, and in the relief given them by the churchwardens and other officers. These others were subsidy men or substan-

Justices, pp. xl–xliii. I have found no record of county-wide collections for the benefit of individuals, although they were common enough in Somerset to merit explicit regulation; see Bates Harbin, *Somerset*, II, 386–87.

35. Gloucestershire paupers, conversely, caused occasional trouble in neighboring counties, and licensed beggars got at least as far as Devon. See Willis Bund, *Worcestershire*, pp. 267–68, 396; Ratcliff and Johnson, *Warwick*, I, 100; *H.M.C., Fifth Report*, p. 573.

Local churchwardens contributed to a number of general charities: a poor hospital in Middlesex, a college in Chelsea, the Huguenots in the Isle of Rhé, "the soldiers in Turkey." These last were probably captives to be ransomed, for whom similar contributions were solicited in Devon. (Hamilton, *Quarter Sessions*, pp. 62–65.) They may have been victims of the Barbary pirates; individuals who had been imprisoned by these "Turks," or who were trying to ransom relatives from them, appeared in a number of parishes between 1616 and 1629.

36. It was decided at North Nibley (5 December, 1640) that payments to men with passes should in future be made only by the constable or tithingman; such payments by the churchwardens would be disallowed. Chipping Campden, in 1641, ordered "that no money shall be given to any soldier or traveler out of the church stock."

tial householders, nominated by the vestry and appointed by the J. P.'s, to act with the churchwardens as overseers of the poor and collectors of the poor rate.[37] This rate was levied on every one who could afford it, and was reduced with a decrease in the rate-payer's fortunes. At Gloucester, the quarter sessions were continually occupied with petitions for abatement. A surprisingly large number were effective; the rate was often reduced, and sometimes abolished entirely.[38] If such leniency was the rule, it is questionable how much the poor rate brought in.

The rate was commonly collected once a week at the church, after service was ended. The one glimpse of a collector at work is revealing enough to deserve mention. He was making his collection in Thornbury churchyard when he saw Philip Harris, the collector for the year before. He asked Harris to give an account of the £5 which he had collected during his term, and of which no more had been heard. Harris not only refused, but gave him the lie and challenged him. When he declined the challenge, Harris

37. The position of the overseer was defined by 39 Elizabeth, c. 3, which stipulated that there should be four in each parish. According to the 1614 edition of Lambard, however, two J. P.'s might appoint from two to four in each. (*Eirenarcha,* p. 360.) For a full description of the work of these overseers, see Eleanor Trotter, *Seventeenth Century Life in the Country Parish with Special Reference to Local Government,* pp. 51–80.

38. In a typical instance, a man confessed that he had not paid his rate for a year, and the court gave him another year in which to make up the arrears. (Glouc. Corp. Rec. 1566, Easter, 1632.) The reason for this leniency may have been the discretionary power of the court to impose special assessments for poor relief; see 39 Elizabeth, c. 3; 43 Elizabeth, c. 2; Lambard, *Eirenarcha,* p. 611. For examples of the use of this power, see below, p. 258.

A vicar of Rodmarton was taxed for the poor rate, although his predecessors had been exempt. He offered a tenth of the total amount, and also a rate on his glebe; the assessors refused, and taxed him on the whole value of his benefice. The quarrel apparently dragged on for six years, until he carried it to the sessions. The justices decided that his offer should stand, and that he should pay on the glebe as the parishioners paid on each yardland *(virgata).* Entries in the Rodmarton Register Book for 1635, 1641.

proclaimed him coward and base fellow—and presumably kept the £5.[39]

The only material about overseers is concerned with their work at North Nibley. Among their normal expenses were such items as a shroud for a poor man, the charges of a foster-mother for keeping a bastard child (and the cost of the child's funeral), the price of houseroom for an old almsman, a substantial payment to a woman and her daughter "so that she come no more nor her child to Nibley." "Thomas Phelps keepeth his sister, and for her is allowed what upon him is assessed."[40] Such matters were relatively simple, especially in a small village. At times, however, the overseers were troubled by more thorny problems.

An example in point is the case of Mary Heath, which shows the brutal side of poor relief. She had been born at Stinchcombe, but had lived for some time with her mother at North Nibley. She became pregnant, at the age of twenty or so, and left town either "of her own accord or by the means of Nibley men." After seven weeks she was back with her mother, although the old woman had been "forewarned by Nibley men before and since her coming again not to receive her any more; where she was with her mother guestwise for some short time." Then she left once more, for a village in the parish of Alkington, "where she

39. The collector, who was also high constable of the hundred, had been appointed by a single justice instead of two. St. Ch. 8/133/6.

40. G.P.L. MS. 16,526, fos. 96–97. A sheet of similar accounts, of the "masters of the poor" for 1609, is preserved in the Chipping Sodbury MSS.; with it is an undated sheet, presumably of the Civil War period, which mentions the purchase of thirty pikes for the town's use, and the hiring of a night-watchman against fire. Items of poor relief at Chipping Campden include £10 for a winter's coal for the poor, the expenses of sending a woman to London to be cured of the king's evil, money to "a woman ready to die" (a condition in which she remained for years) and to "a poor man making moan," gifts to women at their confinement, to a husband nursing his wife, to a bonesetter of Broadway and the men who held his patient, to three boys "that were appointed to go to the Isle of Providence." From the treasurer's accounts of the Chipping Campden trust for 1630, 1637–39.

was whipped for begging and was sent from thence by warrant to her place of birth, being Stinchcombe." There her child was born a few weeks later.

Stinchcombe, Nibley, and Alkington were at once in dispute over which should support the mother and child. The fact that Mary had lived at Nibley during her pregnancy—in spite of the best efforts of Nibley men—seems to have created a possible obligation on that parish. Alkington would have had none, except for two facts: the warrant deporting her to Stinchcombe was of dubious legality, because it had not been signed by the minister, and there was some question "whether a woman within a month of her delivery may be sent to her place of birth as a rogue." If Nibley and Alkington were legally rid of the pair, Stinchcombe was perforce responsible. It agreed to take them, but only if there was no way to shift the burden elsewhere.[41] The question was referred by petition to the quarter sessions, and three justices were ordered to investigate.[42]

A single justice occasionally intervened to obtain relief for a pauper. In 1636, for example, the churchwardens and overseers of Bibury turned a man out of "a small and unfitting room in the church house, wherein he formerly with great inconvenience made hard shift to dwell in, and so thereby with his wife and children [he] is enforced to lie in the streets." A neighboring J. P. commanded the parish authorities to give the family decent lodging. When they ignored his warrant, he ordered the

41. G.P.L. MS. 16,526, fo. 109. The Alkington warrant says that the expectant mother was put in the stocks, rather than whipped. (*Ibid.*, fo. 110.) In either case her treatment was mild by comparison with the brutality which this aspect of the poor law could evoke; for extreme examples, see Bates Harbin, *Somerset,* II, 116; Saunders, *Official Papers of Sir Nathaniel Bacon,* p. 63.

42. G.P.L. MS. 16,526, fo. 111. A dispute between two parishes, one in Gloucestershire and one in a neighboring county, might be expected to raise the question of which quarter sessions should assume jurisdiction. But there is no sign of this difficulty in two such cases which came before the Somerset court; see Bates Harbin, *Somerset,* II, 263–64, 296.

constable and tithingmen to fine them £1, and to devote the proceeds to poor relief.[43] The churchwardens and overseers were apparently out of pocket, but there is no telling whether the family in question ever received either money or lodging.

More difficult problems, like that of Mary Heath, were handled collectively by the justices in quarter sessions.[44] The inshire sessions also appointed an officer for controlling the poor. The grand jury, when so instructed by the privy council through the lord lieutenant, named a provost marshal "for the apprehending and punishing of such vagrants and idle persons as live not in any lawful vocation, and in times of suspicion and trouble may by tales and false rumors distract the people's minds, or otherwise in fact commit insolences and outrages." The grand jury also assessed the wages of the provost marshal, which in 1639 were the handsome sum of £20 a year; the magistrates confirmed his appointment, and instructed all constables and tithingmen to assist him in the performance of his duty.[45]

A similar official was sometimes appointed by the parish itself. Cirencester, for example, had in the latter half of the period a "beadle of the beggars" for the control of vagabonds. His first duty was to keep all strange beggars

43. Bibury MS. 150, A and B, in Sherborne MSS.; for similar interference by the same justice, see *ibid.*, 144 A, 155 B, and for an example at North Nibley (where the warrant was obeyed) see the Nibley accounts for 1629.

44. Such a case might be brought before them by a petition either from a parish or an individual. An example of the latter is an appeal for relief from a Gloucester woman, who was keeping her daughter and grandchildren because her son-in-law was too poor to support them. The court ordered the responsibility divided between her and the paternal grandmother, either by dividing the family or by a money payment. Glouc. Corp. Rec. 1566, Michaelmas, 1637.

45. *Ibid.*, 1567, pp. 2–3. The city had a marshal of its own as early as 1631; he was appointed by the justices, and received only £5 a year. (*Ibid.*, 1451, fo. 496v; 1566, Michaelmas, 1631.) This officer seems to have been originally an agent for enforcing martial law on wandering soldiers; for an example in 1627, see Gardiner, *History of England*, VI, 156. By the end of the period, however, he had lost the traces of his military origin.

out of town. His second was to supervise the conduct of the local paupers: to make sure that no alms were given to "such wicked poor as are able by their own labor and travail to earn their own living," and that they were brought to the house of correction; to discover any deserving poor who were sick or needy, and report them either to the overseers or to charitable townsmen; to see to it that those who were allowed to beg were respectful in their behavior, "that with their noise of chiding and striving amongst themselves they give no offense to such as relieve them, assuring them that they shall receive punishment for it, and be shut out from their part in the orderly and weekly alms that are given."[46]

While the justices might deal with difficult cases, and the provost marshal or the beadle with vagabonds, the general operation of the poor law was left to the churchwardens and overseers. The law did not always operate smoothly, and there were marginal cases which required interpretation. If a poor man had residence in the parish, and took to begging, might he be deported to the parish of his birth? If a family was to be deported, how should the members be divided among their natal parishes? Of the poor who could not be deported, which should be given alms and which should be put to work? The answers to such questions, in their aggregate, determined the local

46. He also had the ticklish task of preventing parents from bringing to church "such of their children as either by crying or other noise shall be any disturbance in divine service," and of correcting the obstreperous. (Cirencester Vestry Book, fo. 45v; see also fo. 60.) The office was created about 1618; Tewkesbury appointed a similar beadle four years earlier, but his duties are not described in detail. Tewkes. Corp. Rec. 2, *anno* 1614.

The popular fear of "vagrants and idle persons" approximated a phobia. Even a preacher, when praising the poor above the rich, excepted those persons "going under the name and title of the poor, who by reason of their lewd and wicked course of life deserve no jot of these good speeches, but rather the whip and correction and all manner of disgrace." Philip Jones, *Certaine Sermons Preached at Ciceter . . . Wherein the Two Several States, of the Riche and Poore Man Are Compared and Examined,* sig. E vi; for similar quotations, see R. H. Tawney, *The Agrarian Problem in the Sixteenth Century,* pp. 268–72.

policy of poor relief. In some cases answers were given by the courts, and wise overseers took note of the decisions.[47] In others, each parish was left to work out its own salvation.

One of the most important parochial problems was to provide work for the poor; idle hands were both dangerous and expensive. Gifts of money for employing them was a favorite form of private charity, and the residue was provided from parochial funds. The method of employment took two forms, which may be considered in turn: the apprenticing of children, and the use of adults in subsidized industry.

If there was an outside market for apprentices, in neighboring towns or even in London, the churchwardens would pay the parents to send their children away.[48] The domestic market was equally important, and more susceptible to control by the parish. At North Nibley, for example, the vestry took a census of the children who "are fit to be bound apprentice to other men, and that now live pilfering and stealing in every corner."[49] When the intended employers proved recalcitrant, some years later, the parish invoked the authority of the sessions to force apprentices on them. The justices were requested to place apprentices with seven specified men, who were "of the best sort amongst us for means and ability, and much better fitted for such servants than many others who have conformed themselves to his Majesty's direction and your authorities; men whom we have often prayed to be like their neighbors, and not out of a stiff and settled willfulness to affront both his Majesty's directions, yourselves

47. The particular questions in the text were settled by judicial decision in London; see Lambard, *Eirenarcha,* pp. 207–11. This decision was carefully noted in North Nibley, and paraphrased under the title of "Resolutions and Advices." G.P.L. MS. 16,530, fo. 46.

48. For examples, see *ibid.,* 16,526, fos. 96–97; 16,527, fo. 4; St. Aldgate's accounts in St. Michael's MSS.

49. G.P.L. MS. 16,526, fo. 99. A task of the Cirencester beadle was to see to it that no children over seven were allowed to wander the streets, but that all were set to "knitting, spinning, or some other labor, according to their age and ability." Cirencester Vestry Book, fo. 45v.

his worthy magistrates, and the body of us their neighbors. Wherein for that we prevail not, we appeal to your wisdoms therein."[50]

A parish occasionally succeeded in apprenticing children without cost. Usually, however, it was an expensive matter, which in a large parish might come to as much as £10 a year; the charges were either for clothes, or for lump payments to the masters.[51] The money came from regular parochial funds, from a special assessment, or from charitable bequests.[52] The expense justified itself; apprenticeship was one of the few ways in which the burden of the poor could be shifted from public to private shoulders.[53]

Apprenticing children to a trade was integrally connected with the use of the poor in industry. The employment of adults was merely an extension of the idea behind the employment of children. The procedure was the same in both cases: the parish gave the employer a subsidy, assigned the poor to him, and then usually left him a free hand. At Gloucester, for example, a lady left a bequest for setting the poor to work, which was used to encourage the making of flax. A man was given £6 a year from the city for his house, "now employed by the flaxmen, . . .

50. The parish was burdened with fifty-three poor children, of whom less than half had been apprenticed. G.P.L. MS. 16,527, fo. 4.

51. St. Michael's, in 1633, paid more than £11 for clothing and indenturing parish children bound apprentice by the mayor and J. P.'s; Eastington had similar charges in 1632. Chipping Campden, at the same time, was clothing children to be sent to Oxford and London, and paying masters there to take them at £2 or £5 apiece; see the treasurer's accounts of the Chipping Campden trust for 1629–34.

52. When funds were collected at Chipping Sodbury for an act to define manorial customs, part of the money was to be spent for the act, "part for putting forth apprentices borough-born children," and part for poor relief. G.P.L. MS. 16,528, fo. 58.

53. Some entries suggest that apprenticeship, like the pressgang, was used by local authorities to rid themselves of the most troublesome elements among the poor. A girl was apprenticed for five years, and her master promised "that she shall not go abroad idly to trouble and burden the town any more during the said term." Another girl was sent into domestic service, because she was "now suspected for an incontinent life." Northleach Court Book, p. 321; G.P.L. MS. RV 216.15.

and likewise the stewards to pay the spinners and work-folk for their labor to the sum of £40, being the Lady Fettiplace money." A month later, two men were given £200 from the city to provide stock "to put the poor of this city on work in spinning, according to the propositions made by the committee now read, and a convenient house for the term of six years." In one case the city paid the wages, in the other it paid for the raw material, and in both it paid for the factory.[54]

There is record of only one instance in which employers were even mildly supervised, and it was presumably exceptional. This was in Gloucester, in 1631, when the common council created a system of industrial control. A group of aldermen was appointed, in each ward of the city, to set the poor on work. They were charged with hearing complaints from employers if the work was neglected, and complaints from the poor if their wages were withheld; offenders were to be punished by the justices. The poor apparently had no redress for any grievance except not being paid, but even this modicum of protection was a novelty.[55]

The most interesting example of an industry employing the poor is the manufacture of pins. This trade is supposed to have been introduced into Gloucester in 1626, by one John Tilsley of Bristol.[56] It is doubtful that he was the originator, but there is no question that he was the most important of the early pin-makers.[57] He was in

54. Glouc. Corp. Rec. 1452, pp. 107, 109.

55. *Ibid.,* 1451, fo. 550. The poor were also put to work in the city bridewell, or house of correction; the master, in 1613, was ordered to remove looms from the adjacent prison, which he had been using like part of the bridewell. *Ibid.,* fo. 246v; see also S. and B. Webb, *English Local Government: English Poor Law History: Part I. The Old Poor Law,* pp. 78 note 1, 84–85, 249–52.

56. Fosbrooke, *Abstracts Formed into a History,* I, 160; *V.C.H.,* II, 207.

57. Either John Tilsley or his brother was at Bristol in 1623; the corporation lent him £100, but he became insolvent. (Latimer, *Annals of Bristol,* p. 85.) He did not introduce the trade into Gloucester in 1626: the common council, in 1625, gave £1 to "Evans, the pinner," to

Gloucester in the spring of 1627, although not yet firmly ensconced. A man in Berkeley wrote to John Smyth, to explain that Tilsley and his pins were about to settle the problem of the Berkeley poor:

> Being at Gloucester assizes, it was my fortune to meet with an honest tradesman, one well known in these parts, whose business there was to set up a work for . . . poor children and lame people to get their living by. [*In the margin:* He is a maker of pins, his name Tilsley.] I prevailed with him, and brought him off from there to Berkeley, where now it is concluded between the parish and him to go forthwith forwards with it here. From eight years upward, men, boys, women, or girls he will receive, and from the number of thirty to as many as they will provide him. All shall have weekly pay in a reasonable manner, to find them meat and drink, and as they grow experienced (which he doubts not will be quickly), with many he will mend their ways. Five he will take 'prentices, to teach them his trade and maintain them at his own present charge. Twenty pounds he is to have of the parish when the work is set up, and the children somewhat profited in their trade.[58]

The Berkeley experiment was apparently not a success. Tilsley was soon back at Gloucester, where he flourished as the green bay tree. "Tilsley of Gloucester keepeth above eighty boys and wenches at work to make pins. Had begun about six years since; the town lent him £100, and gave him another hundred to set up the trade and take children. He was then nothing worth, and is now worth above £2,000." [59]

take on an apprentice who had been chargeable to the city. Glouc. Corp. Rec. 1451, fo. 505v.

58. "Only a house for this purpose is wanting. . . . They will repair the house, and leave it at any time upon reasonable warning, and provide another." The writer requests Smyth's intercession with Lord Berkeley for the use of a house. 1627; G.P.L. MS. 16,532, fo. 21.

59. "His brother hath done the like at Bristol. They buy wire at the brass works at Taynton, within five miles of Gloucester by Huntley."

Such employment of the poor was arranged with the authorities, who subsidized and encouraged a man like Tilsley. But small employers were strictly forbidden to take on the poor without license, and a householder might not even receive a poor man to live with him. The parish might well have been only too glad of work or houseroom for its poor—since there was rarely enough of either to go around—if it had not been for the universal fear of vagabonds. To permit individual charity would be to permit the settlement of strangers from outside, who might at any time become chargeable. The obvious way to exclude them was to keep a watch on householders, and to punish those who evaded the law. "Richard Gibbs, pewterer, appeared to an indictment proffered against him for receiving inmates into his house. He making it appear it were his children, was discharged and ordered to remove them."[60] The incident was typical. "Inmates," or indigent guests, had to be licensed by some authority—the justices, the mayor, the lord of the manor. If they were not, the householder was subject to indictment and fine.[61]

The same pressure might be exerted on a landlord who had poor tenants. One such landlord at Gloucester, in 1635, was ordered to make a weekly payment for the relief of the poor, as a form of insurance against his tenants' becoming chargeable to the parish.[62] At Tewkesbury, in

A note on the back of a sheet, in the hand of Secretary Coke; S.P. 16/205/11, tentatively catalogued as 1631, but probably several years later. For details of the establishment of the pin trade at Reading in 1633, see Guilding, *Reading,* III, 202.

A man proposed to introduce the manufacture of kersey at Gloucester in 1639. After a committee of the common council had studied his proposition, the council awarded him £75 with which to set up his trade. Glouc. Corp. Rec. 1452, pp. 125–26.

60. *Ibid.,* 1566, Easter, 1637.

61. 31 Elizabeth, c. 7. Inmates were specifically forbidden at Wotton in 1599, except with the consent of the lord and the town authorities, on pain of a 10*s.* fine. At North Nibley, in 1604, a census of unauthorized inmates was taken in a parish meeting. G.P.L. MSS. 16,529, fo. 25; 16,526, fo. 99.

62. He had taken into his house a man and his wife; the latter "is now brought to bed, whereby great charge is like to grow [to] the said parish." Papers of St. Aldgate in St. Michael's MSS.

1623, the town was overcrowded with poor. Many landlords had erected small cottages in remote places, and had converted stables and pigsties into habitations; the tenants paid their rents out of what they made from pilfering. Such conversion was forbidden in future, without a certificate that the building was fit for habitation, and it was ordered that no one might lease to an outsider any property worth less than £2 unless both he and his tenant would give £10 bonds to keep the parish harmless.[63] The very frequency of such injunctions suggests that they were ineffective.

These inmates exposed the parish to the further danger of having to support their bastards. We have seen how the quarter sessions dealt with the matter.[64] The parochial authorities were equally concerned, because they had to support a child whose parents were penniless. At North Nibley, the vestry inquired about "what bastards are in the parish that either receive relief from the parish or from their reputed fathers, and who such reputed fathers are."[65] At Gloucester, if the parish was lucky enough to find a putative father with means, he was forced to give bond to keep the parish safe from all charges about the child.[66]

63. Tewkes. Corp. Rec. 2, *anno* 1623.

64. See above, pp. 67–69.

65. From the parochial investigation of 1604, parts of which I have already cited. Other matters for inquiry were the number of almsfolk, deserving poor, and able-bodied idlers, the principal wood-stealers in the parish, and the principal disorderly houses. G.P.L. MS. 16,526, fo. 99.

The discovery of a putative father often taxed the ingenuity of justices and overseers, who were at best amateur detectives. A guilty man might cover his trail with great ingenuity. (For examples, see Gloucester Diocesan Records, XCV, 3 and 11 June, 1605; 19 October, 1605.) I surmise that the authorities often selected a well-to-do suspect, regardless of proof, and that he paid to avoid expense and scandal.

66. Such a father was a windfall to the parish. He not only took the child off its hands, but might be fined by the ecclesiastical court for the benefit of the parochial poor. (See *ibid.*, LXV, 2 November, 1590.) If no father was found, on the other hand, supporting the child might force the parish to complicated expedients. In an instance at Dursley, in 1603, £3 for the support of a bastard came in part from the overseers, in part from an old debt owed to the parish, in part from money collected from communicants.

To the churchwardens and overseers, even more than to the justices, bastardy was a purely financial problem.

The money for relief of the poor came from a variety of sources. If the poor rate was inadequate for an emergency, the magistrates levied a special taxation. In time of plague, for example, a weekly tax was levied at Gloucester for the poor who were sick; it was collected in accordance with a fixed rate in the city, and in the country by the yardland.[67] At the same time, the parish of St. Aldgate petitioned that it was unable to maintain its own poor, and needed relief from other parishes. The justices referred the petition to a tax committee of the common council, which levied a general assessment for relief.[68]

There were various other ways of supporting the Gloucester poor. A lottery was held from time to time, and the proceeds went to buy fuel for them.[69] During a food shortage in 1623, "the poor of this city are grown into great want and misery"; a grant was therefore made from the city treasury to "such as are very poor, old, and not able to stir abroad to seek relief."[70] One of the aldermen had collected money for fire buckets at the same time; he was left with a surplus, which was used for supplies with which to set the poor on work.[71] In such ways as these the city supplemented the inadequate receipts from the poor rate.

Another supplementary agency remains to be discussed. The indifference of the rich to the poor was the subject of philippics from the pulpit.[72] But the evidence outweighs

67. Glouc. Corp. Rec. 1566, Epiphany, 1637/38.

68. *Ibid.,* Easter, 1637, and ff. Such assessment was a common procedure, just as it was common for one parish, with more money or fewer poor, to contribute to the relief of poor in a neighboring parish.

69. *Ibid.,* 1451, fo. 448v; 1452, p. 3. At Cirencester, in 1620, "the lottery men . . . gave in money £40 to be put forth to interest, the use thereof yearly to come to the poor forever." Cirencester Vestry Book, fo. 12v.

70. Glouc. Corp. Rec. 1451, fo. 496v.

71. *Ibid.,* fo. 511v.

72. Such philippics as this, at Stroud in 1609: "Where is there one man or one woman so won by the word that layeth apart one link of

the oratory, and indicates that the rich were often far from indifferent. There was a great deal of private charity throughout the county, in the form of sporadic gifts or permanent endowments, and this charity was by no means a negligible part of poor relief.

The city of Gloucester administered a number of bequests. Sir Thomas White left funds for the relief of poor clothiers, from which the common council from time to time made individual grants of £25. Another man left money for loans to the deserving poor; the council doled it out, in units of £3 6*s.* 8*d.*, and brought suit when the loans were not repaid. The council also made charitable gifts on its own account: a weekly allowance to an impoverished ex-sheriff, a yearly allowance of £10 to the family of a minister, who had ruined himself in his lifetime by gifts to the poor.[73]

There were various charitable foundations throughout the county. The manor of Longney, near Stroud, was owned by a Londoner as part of his nationwide charity.[74] Chipping Campden received a number of benefactions from its patron, Sir Baptist Hickes.[75] Sir Thomas Roe

his golden chain, one lace of her velvet sleeve, or abateth one breadth of their broad ruffs, or setteth apart one dish of their dainty superfluities at every feast, towards the relief of so many poor lazars as abound round about us at this day? Yea, what have I seen to the contrary? Namely thus: that where there hath been a motion made on the Sabbath day in the church by the minister to the whole congregation assembled, in behalf of two poor, sick, naked, hungry, and impotent persons for some relief, there hath been gathered in the same day, in the afternoon, four times as much for a bearward and his bear, as hath been given and collected towards those two poor Christian persons." Woodwall, *A Sermon Wherein Are Shewed the Causes of This Dearth Now, 1608 and 1609,* pp. 28–29.

73. Sir Thomas White's funds were granted only to clothiers who could provide security for the proper use of the money; loans to the deserving poor were similarly secured. Glouc. Corp. Rec. 1451, fos. 217, 232; 1452, p. 5.

74. The Londoner was Henry Smith, who left his large estate in trust for charitable purposes in stipulated parishes. According to Rudder, in 1773, Longney itself did not benefit; in 1884, however, the parish was receiving substantial sums from the income of the manor. Rudder, *History,* p. 535 and note n; *N. & Q.,* IV, 627.

75. See below, p. 262.

presented his old constituency of Cirencester with £25 a year in rentals, most of which was to be used for apprenticing poor children.[76] A Gloucester alderman left funds for the same purpose.[77] The receipts of the market at Tetbury, worth some £120 a year, were left to the town for the use of the poor.[78] At Dursley, lands to the value of £50 a year were left in trust for the poor, although the churchwardens had great trouble in getting their hands on the money.[79]

The private charity of Tewkesbury is of especial interest. It was founded by one Giles Geast in the middle of the sixteenth century, and derived its income from the rents of tenements in the town. The collection of the rents was in the hands of the town bailiffs and others, who received each year a stipulated sum for their work. The receipts varied from year to year, but in general showed a steady increase; they were slightly over £7 in 1585, and slightly over £19 in 1640.[80] The distribution of the money seems to have been extremely slipshod until 1638, when reforms were introduced. "The bailiff and feoffees this year found great inconvenience (thorough increase of the poor) in

76. W. R. Williams, *Parliamentary History of the County of Gloucester,* p. 155. For details of this and other gifts to the Cirencester poor, see Cirencester Vestry Book, fos. 1–23.

77. The money was given as grants of £7 10*s.* to each master, in return for which he bound himself to maintain and instruct his apprentice, and at the end of his term to return him part of the sum as his stock in trade. Glouc. Corp. Rec. 1451, fo. 518v.

78. Of this £120, £13 went to poor relief, £13 to maintaining a schoolmaster, £6 to a lecturer, and the remaining £88 to the bailiff for his hospitality, "to credit and countenance his place for the well governing of the said town." The arrangement broke down, and the funds eventually came into the hands of several inhabitants who refused to account for them; they were consequently sued. C. 3/326/101.

79. The donor had conveyed the land to three or four feoffees to the use of the poor. By the end of King James's reign, the one surviving feoffee had made the land his own, sold it for £60, and given bond for the purchaser's quiet possession. He then told the churchwardens that if they would pay him £20 and discharge him from the bond, "he would bring them to the light of it, how and in what manner he had sold the premises." Instead they brought suit. C. 21/D/12/4.

80. Giles Geast Rent Book, dates cited.

distributing the money from house to house, whereby strangers sped as well as town poor, and by that means some two or three several times by deceipt got alms. Therefore agreed that the said money shall be given by a note of names to be presented to the said bailiff and feoffees, and they to tot it, . . . and they, or at least two of them, to see the same distributed accordingly, and divide the town as they in discretion shall think fit."[81]

A favorite object of charity was free schools. That at Chipping Campden had been endowed at the end of the fifteenth century by the gift of a manor, but by 1640 the income had been stolen through private fraud.[82] At Tewkesbury, in 1600, the ambitious churchwardens not only built a battlement on the church, but made a collection from "the best disposed" with which they finished the school.[83] A generous endowment for it was subsequently provided by Sir Dudley Digges, and by relatives of the town's high steward.[84] At St. Aldgate's, Gloucester, there were gifts to the parish to buy books for poor boys in the school.[85] The educational level of such schools was probably low, but it is apparent that they were an object of attention from the rich.

Another form of charity was the endowment of almshouses and hospitals. The difference between the two seems to have been one of age and size, rather than of function: the hospitals were usually older and larger, and were confined to the towns; almshouses might be anywhere, in rural or urban parishes. A typical country almshouse was that at North Nibley. It was built in 1601–02, at the charge of the parish. Various parishioners contributed what they

81. *Ibid., anno* 1638.

82. The inhabitants petitioned the house of lords for redress. *H.M.C., Fourth Report,* p. 50.

83. Tewkes. Corp. Rec. 1, fo. 24.

84. At the same time there were a number of other gifts: £30 for the poor, the church, and the highways, £5 a year for the poor, etc. Giles Geast Rent Book, *anno* 1624.

85. Other typical gifts were for relief of poor tradesmen, repair of the highways, etc. St. Aldgate's accounts in St. Michael's MSS.

had: timber, thatch, stone, waggons to carry them. The house when completed had "six distinct habitations, with chimnies in them," and each with a door of its own.[86] The house stood on land belonging to the church, but paid nothing to the church rate; the question later arose of whether the land was being properly used. The matter was referred to a jury, which decided not to present "in regard of the great numbers of poor people there, destitute of habitations, living for the most part from relief and alms of the inhabitants."[87]

The city of Gloucester had a number of almshouses in its various parishes, each with a small quota of almsfolk.[88] Cirencester had two; both were smaller than that at Nibley, but were called hospitals because of their great age.[89] Chipping Campden was given an almshouse by Sir Baptist Hickes, who endowed it lavishly.[90] Thornbury received a similar house from Sir John Stafford, with a £10 yearly income. "A long time he lived (as himself on his deathbed confessed) in the frail and slippery course of a soldier and a courtier, from the time of his manhood near unto the time of his death." But by his endowment he apparently redeemed himself in the eyes of the parish.[91]

An almshouse was not always an unmixed blessing; it

86. G.P.L. MS. 16,526, fos. 96–97.

87. The inquisition was held about 1625, by which time "the great numbers of poor people" seem to have risen from six to thirteen. *Ibid.*, fo. 112.

88. Glouc. Corp. Rec. 1567, Michaelmas, 1640.

89. One supported a clergyman, three almsmen, and three almswomen, the other only two poor women "commonly called new sisters." C. 91/1/11.

90. The house supported six men and six women. It cost Sir Baptist £1,300 during his lifetime; he bequeathed it an annual endowment of £140, plus a weekly allowance of 3*s.* 4*d.* to each inmate, and a yearly provision for each of a hat, a gown, and a ton of coals. (Bodl. MS. Rawl. B 323, fo. 9.) He also left £500 for setting the poor on work, and more than £500 for the church; *N. & Q.*, IV, 408.

91. From Sir John's epitaph, 1624, in Thornbury church. An epitaph at Cirencester records a similar bequest, of "six habitations for six poor widows with six shillings weekly forever." At about the same time, the town was given six more such houses in Dollar Street; Cirencester Vestry Book, fo. 13.

might be almost as repugnant as a pesthouse to those who lived near it. A good illustration of this feeling was at Haresfield in 1635. One of the villagers, who was undoubtedly a snob, testified that the house "doth stand in an inconvenient and unfit place for the habitation of poor people, considering the neighborhood thereabouts, there being of divers of the best houses in the said parish of Haresfield near thereunto adjoining. Besides, there is no convenient place fit for the said poor persons to ease themselves, but they must upon such occasions needs be discovered to the public view of the neighbors and passengers there."[92]

It is a far cry from these country almshouses, each with its handful of inmates, to the hospitals in the city of Gloucester. The latter were the largest and most important poorhouses in the county; one of them held as many as fifty inmates, who were maintained in a style which Haresfield or Nibley would have considered extravagant. These were the élite among Gloucestershire poor. Their lives were set in a narrow pattern, hedged about with official restrictions; but it was a more tolerable pattern that that of most of their fellows, and is worth examining as one extreme in the scale of poor relief.

Gloucester had three hospitals, all under the control of the common council. St. Margaret's and King James's were little larger than almshouses, but St. Bartholomew's had twenty men and thirty women. A minute set of regulations for the government of the three institutions was adopted by the common council in 1635, and from these regulations we can reconstruct the life of the inmates.[93]

The management was vested in a board of governors, but the actual work was done by a host of subordinate officials. One group of these officials was in charge of

92. The almshouse, which contained four inmates, was said to be the private charity of the owner. If so, it is the only such instance which I have found. E. 134/11 Chas. 1/M/49.

93. The regulations are contained in an anonymous pamphlet, *Civitas Glouc.;* on this my description of the hospitals is based.

finances: the maintenance of hospital lands, and the collection of rents from them; the recording of gifts and legacies; the payment of weekly allowances to the inmates. Two almoners, like the regarders in the Forest of Dean, were concerned with supervising the officers of the separate hospitals. These officers were a governor, a resident minister, physician, and surgeon, and a rent-gatherer or "overseer of the manners of the poor."[94]

The overseer is the only member of this bureaucracy who is worth more than passing mention. At St. Bartholomew's, at least, he combined his hospital duties with a general care for the city poor. He received gifts from private citizens and guilds, and used them for a number of purposes: individual relief, burials during the plague, the support of fatherless children (to the tune of more than £12), and subsidies of as much as £30 a year to various parishes.[95] His duties at the hospital were those of an inspector of morals and sanitation: he was to attend public prayers, and observe who were absent; to see that the inmates were in their own rooms at night, and to inspect whatever rooms he might think were not "fit and sweet lodging"; to take note of any inmates who had lodgers with them, and of any suspicious outsiders who frequented their rooms, "the reformation whereof he shall endeavor by admonition." If admonition failed, he had recourse to the board of governors.[96]

The inmates were chosen by the board. Preference was

94. The officials in charge of finance were closely connected with the common council: the president of the board of governors and the treasurer of hospital funds were both aldermen; of the two surveyors of hospital lands, one was an alderman and the other an ex-sheriff; the almoners were both ex-sheriffs, and the two scrutiners, in charge of gifts and legacies, were ex-stewards. The officers of the separate hospitals were chosen directly by the mayor and council. St. Bartholomew's had a governor, who received the generous salary of £38 a year, and a surgeon, who received £1 *5s. 8d.* (Glouc. Corp. Rec. 1378; 1451, fo. 264.) The surgeon and the physician were forbidden to be absent without leave for more than twenty days a year, "that the city and country also may know where to have him in time of need." *Civitas Glouc.*, p. 17.

95. Treasurer's accounts, St. Bartholomew's; Glouc. Corp. Rec. 1402.

96. *Civitas Glouc.*, pp. 19–20.

regulated by a careful scale, which was designed to favor the families of burgesses, and particularly such as "once lived well, and did themselves help to relieve those that were poor."[97] Once an inmate was admitted, life was by no means luxurious. The weekly allowance varied in the different hospitals, but was never large.[98] Every one, within a week of admission, had to furnish his or her own room "with all things of necessity for the comfort of their lives."[99] The furniture was as meager as the comfort, and the fittings of the building were equally scanty. Even St. Bartholomew's must have been a dreary place, of cold and bare rooms. There were trestle tables and benches in the great hall, covered at mealtimes by hempen tablecloths; there were tables in the parlor, covered by old bits of carpet. The only room with a ray of cheerfulness was the buttery, where there was a settle for drinking beer. Even the chapel had nothing to recommend it, except "a fine lining cloth for the communion table."[100]

Attending communion and daily prayers seems to have been the only duty of the inmates. The rest of the time was their own; they had to be in at night, but apparently could wander as they pleased during the day. Their conduct was supervised by "fathermen" and "motherwomen," chosen from their own number by the board of governors. If they misbehaved in minor ways, such as being absent from chapel or smashing a window, they were fined from their weekly allowance. More serious misbehavior entailed

97. The order of preference was burgesses of seven years' standing or their widows, then their children, then inhabitants of the suburbs, then country folk of the inshire. All those admitted had to be without gainful occupation, and either over fifty-two or afflicted with some "unrecoverable infirmity." Expulsion was the penalty for marriage, or for admission by bribery or false pretenses. *Ibid.*, pp. 25–27.

98. The range was from 1*s.* 6*d.* to 2*s.* 6*d.* a week for each inmate. (*Ibid.*, p. 25.) A comparison of these rates with those at Leicester makes the Gloucester institutions seem almost luxurious; see Bateson and Stocks, *Leicester,* IV, 111–14.

99. *Civitas Glouc.*, p. 29.

100. From an inventory of hospital furniture in 1636, on a loose and uncatalogued paper in the Glouc. Corp. Rec.

expulsion, if they were convicted by the board of governors. The charges on which the board might act were various, ranging from incest or fornication to drunkenness, scolding, or otherwise being "a common troubler of the company of almsfolk there."[101]

These almsfolk were the privileged poor. They were recruited by preference from the better classes in the city, and they were paid a relatively substantial allowance. While it is apparent from the regulations that their life was a meager one, it was unquestionably superior to that of most of the poor—such people as those who took shelter in the church porch at Minchinhampton, or who roused the compassion of the minister at Stroud, or who lived by thieving at Tewkesbury. The poor were an inarticulate class, and their betters were seldom sufficiently interested to describe their condition; it is therefore impossible to reconstruct it now. But if St. Bartholomew's was comparative luxury, we may conjecture that the almsfolk of North Nibley lived on the thin edge of existence. The villagers would not have understood how it could be otherwise. So long as the poor were not unruly or too expensive, their neighbors bothered with little more than the perfunctory attempt to keep them alive.

Are there not many good laws and orders made for the relieving and keeping of the poor in every parish, and every parish hath overseers to provide them harbor and sustenance? Yes, it is so, I grant; and yet for all this, the poor lie still and complain in vain, without both houseroom and food. Though the king make his statute, and the justice send his precept, yet saith Christ, the poor ye shall have always with you, and so ye have, as poor as ever were, and as I suppose never more.[102]

101. Expulsion was also the penalty for more than eight days' absence during the year. *Civitas Glouc.*, pp. 34–35.

102. Woodwall, *A Sermon Wherein Are Shewed the Causes of This Dearth Now, 1608 and 1609,* pp. 61–62.

X

THE MANOR

A MODERN authority has said that the manor may be largely disregarded by the close of the sixteenth century, because the manor and the manorial court were rapidly becoming a forgotten institution.[1] This is not true of Gloucestershire. The manor was by no means forgotten, and its court was so active that it cannot be disregarded.

The lord and his agents had their part in governing the people. The part was marked out by custom rather than statute, and was less apparent than that of sheriffs and constables, lieutenants and J. P.'s; but it was no less important because it was less obvious. The same is true of the court leet. While it operated in a humbler sphere than the county courts, and by a law of its own, it was both a focus of community life and an active agency of government. The principle of authority was personified for the countryman in the manorial steward as much as in the village constable, and the law which affected him most nearly was the custom of the manor, as administered in its court, rather than the king's law of sessions and assizes. To him and his fellows, the manorial system was the government of daily life.

The bases of this system were as much economic as social. Manorial administration was rooted in the land, and was integrally connected with the tenures by which the land was held. Tenure is a subject for the economist. But it must be mentioned here, as a prerequisite to a survey of the customary law by which the manor was governed. With this background it will be possible to discuss

1. Cheyney, *History of England,* II, 397, 399.

the government as such: the relation of the lord to his tenantry, the nature and procedure of the manorial court, and lastly, the rôle of the court as the governing body of a town.

The nature of land tenure in this period was infinitely complex, but the complexities are for the most part irrelevant. The line between various types was still distinct for the lawyer, and the legal form of the tenure normally determined the services which the tenant owed to the lord. It was these services, rather than the forms of tenure, which were of practical importance in the administration of the manor, because they usually provided the lord with his financial support. It follows that the tenants in whom he was most interested were those whose services were not fixed by their tenures, but might be increased at his will. His other tenants, whose services were fixed and unalterable, were outside the focus of his interest, and played at most a minor part in manorial economy.

From this standpoint freehold, in its various forms, was of negligible importance. Tenants by knight service had a military obligation, which had either been commuted or had lapsed with the passing of feudalism; when a man held by knight service alone, he approximated an outright owner, and had little concern with the manorial system.[2] Tenants by free socage, on the other hand, were an integral part of this system, as evidenced by their service in the manorial court. But their other services, like those of all freeholders, were fixed and unalterable, and they were protected by the royal courts from any attempt of the lord to exploit them. They were in consequence a rela-

2. I have found only one case in which this obligation was enforced. When King Charles called on his tenants-in-chief for an army, in 1638, Lord Berkeley summoned his vassals in feudal style. "Taking notice that you, by the tenure of your land which you hold of me by knight's service, are to serve me . . . at your own charges, I do hereby require that you send me one able horse arrayed for war, and yourself or some other sufficient man with it, to attend me at York." Quoted from a MS. in private hands by J. H. Cooke, "Wanswell Court, and Its Occupants for Seven Centuries," *Trans.*, VI (1881-82), 316.

tively static element, which was seldom troubled by the manorial authorities and seldom gave them trouble.[3]

Below the freeholders, in the legal if not the social scale, were the copyholders, leaseholders, and tenants at will. These folk were not strictly the rural proletariat; men of wealth and birth held copyholds and leases, just as humble men held land by knight service or socage. But it is probably true, at least in Gloucestershire, that there was a rough approximation between the inferior tenures and the lower classes of countrymen. It is unquestionably true that such tenures provided a less favorable legal position than freehold. That in itself was one reason why they were of importance to the lord; the other was that they often provided the bulk of his income.[4]

The copyholders were the core of the manor, and the primary concern of its government. The security of their tenure varied widely. At best it approximated that of freehold; at worst it depended on the sufferance of the lord or his agents. The degree of protection was determined

3. These tenures were subject to feudal law, which occasionally affected the relations between lord and tenant. Wardship was incident to knight service, but a mesne lord might lose it if his tenant acquired any land held directly from the crown; Smyth describes bitterly how one such transaction deprived Lord Berkeley of a number of wardships. (*Description,* pp. 314–15.) Escheat was still operative, and at times affected the course of justice. (See S.P. 16/231/79–80.) Lord Berkeley levied a feudal aid on his freeholders in 1610, for the knighting of his son and heir; in this he presumably took his cue from the king, who had levied an aid in the previous year for the knighting of Prince Henry. (Dietz, *English Public Finance,* pp. 122–23.) Some of Lord Berkeley's tenants paid 1¼ per cent of the value of their land, but most paid twice that rate; the assessors excused a number of men, and readily reduced the valuations of others—in one case from £140 to £6. G.P.L. MS. 16,059.

4. Figures on the value of different tenures are rare, and the following are worth mention. The rentals on nine manors, in 1613, were listed under freehold, leasehold, and copyhold. On three of the nine, almost the entire income was from leasehold, and on two from copyhold; on the other four, copyhold predominated in greater or less degree, and on all nine freehold was insignificant. (G.P.L. MSS. 16,060, fos. 33–55; 16,526, fo. 29.) The rentals on seventeen manors, in 1614, were grouped under freehold, leasehold plus tenure at will, and copyhold; the ratio of yield was approximately 2:8:7. *Ibid.,* 16,062; 16,063.

by the custom of the manor, as expressed in the decision of the manorial court. This custom was complicated by local variations: the law of one manor differed from that of its neighbors, and the differences are not conducive to generalizations.[5] But behind the differences were certain fundamentals, which can best be brought out by a discussion of the legal relationship between the lord and his copyholders.[6]

This relationship began with the surrender and regrant of the copy. There was great variation in the length of time for which it was granted. Sometimes it was for a term of years, or for a tenant's life and his widow's, so long as she remained sole and chaste. Sometimes it was for one life in possession and anything up to four in reversion, depending on the custom, on the lord's discretion, or on his agreement with the individual tenant. Sometimes it was an estate of inheritance, the best form of copyhold. Ownership always remained with the lord, and the land

5. "There is no general law of copyhold because its essence is to be local and peculiar." R. H. Tawney, *The Agrarian Problem in the Sixteenth Century,* p. 293; see also pp. 287–310 for a discussion of the degree to which the copyholder was protected by common law and equity. My evidence agrees with Tawney's conclusion, that the courts supported the tenant only where he could base his claim on the custom of the manor.

6. My description of manorial custom is based on a survey of all the local manors on which material is available. To avoid redundant citation, I append an alphabetical list of these manors, with the principal sources of information about them; hereafter I shall in general omit citations, except for additional material.

Ashton-under-Hill (G.P.L. MS. R 24.1); Awre (G.P.L. MSS. RF 30.4, RF 30.5); Barnwood (E. 134/37 Eliz./H/3); Bullens (G.P.L. MS. RF 321.4); Cheltenham (C. 89/12/1, quoted in John Goding, *Norman's History of Cheltenham,* pp. 52–54); Churchdown (Req. 2/387/70); Didbrook (E. 134/41 Eliz./T/5); Dymock (Bigland, *Historical Collections,* I, 526 note); Haresfield (E. 134/18 Chas. I/E/7); Hill (Smyth, *Description,* p. 226); Kemble (copy of the custom, 1613, in Gloucester County Council MSS.); Oxenton (Additional Charter 18,545); Painswick (Anonymous, *An Exemplification of the Inrollment of a Decree, Made in the High Court of Chancery* [12 James I], pp. 10–21, 30–40); Prestbury (E. 134/6 Jas. I/E/12); Sapperton (G.P.L. MS. RV 260.2); Thornbury (Bodl. MS. Top. Glouc. E. 3); Upton St. Leonards (E. 134/37 Eliz./H/3).

might be forfeited to him on a number of grounds, such as commission of waste by the tenant, failure to reside on the land or perform court service, demising without license for more than a certain time.[7] The duration of this unlicensed demise was an index to the customary law of the manor. If the custom was unfavorable to the copyholder, leasing without license for more than a year cost him his land; if the custom was favorable, such a lease might run for as long as twelve years after his death.[8] It was in any case a temporary expedient. But it was advantageous to the tenant, because the alternative of surrendering his copyhold and having it regranted involved a substantial fine to the lord.

In some cases the amount of this fine was not fixed by the custom, and there was then opportunity for endless friction. At Thornbury, for example, the lord was allowed to increase the fine when giving a new copy, although only with the consent of three or four copyholders. This compromise apparently broke down, and in 1618 there was a suit in chancery. The court fixed the fine as one and a half years' rent for land which was not heriotable, and one year's rent for land which was.[9] At Chelten-

7. At Haresfield, such demising on the part of a tenant in reversion ended his reversionary interest. For a fuller list of offenses involving automatic forfeiture, see Charles Calthrope, *The Relation betweene the Lord of a Mannor and the Coppy-Holder His Tenant,* pp. 50–51.

8. Examples are respectively Hill and Cheltenham. The length of such leases at Cheltenham was a matter of dispute until the custom was defined in 1624; see E. 134/5 Jas. I/E/10–11. The same question was disputed at Painswick until 1615, when it was determined in chancery that a lease might be made without license or fine, but ended in the year of the lessor's death.

9. The tenants were dissatisfied with the decree, and sought a more favorable decision by act of parliament. (Notestein, *Commons Debates, 1621,* V, 178–80; VII, 184–85.) The fine of one to one and a half years' rent was less than that on a number of manors at this time. At Painswick, for example, transfer to any but the heir normally involved a fine of seven years' rent. John Smyth observes, in one of his undated papers, that when the fine is arbitrable, "it is an usual experience in the chancery . . . that the lord is enforced to take five or at most seven years' old rent for his fine." (G.P.L. MS. 16,526, fo. 34.) The Thorn-

ham, the fine was fixed when the land was surrendered and regranted to the tenant's heir, but uncertain when it passed to any one else. It was therefore advantageous to the lord to have a copy come into the hands of an outsider, and even more advantageous to have the tenement divided among several: each new tenant would then have to pay an uncertain fine and a heriot.[10]

Heriot was the typical obligation of the copyholder.[11] It was normally paid to the lord whenever a copyhold changed hands, either by death or surrender; it took the form of the best beast, the best piece of household stuff, or a money payment. The choice between these might be left to the lord (occasionally with a maximum value fixed by the custom), or to agreement between the lord and the individual tenant, or even to a jury of the tenants.[12] Whatever the medium, the heriot was likely to be expensive: it often came to more than a year's rent of the copyhold.[13] The tenant was fortunate if the custom set a limit to the lord's exaction.

bury decision, however, anticipated the general policy of the courts by the reign of Charles I, for which see Tawney, *The Agrarian Problem,* p. 296 and note 3.

10. E. 134/15 Jas. I/H/6; see also E. 134/15 Jas. I/M/10. Under a favorable custom, as at Cheltenham and Painswick, a copyhold might be transferred outside the manorial court, subject to formal ratification in court. A copyholder at Prestbury, likewise, might surrender his tenement to two other tenants, to the use of any one who wished to take it; the transfer was presented at the next court, and the new tenant formally admitted by the lord.

11. It was, however, not peculiar to copyhold, but was sometimes due from tenants by knight service or free socage. For examples, see Smyth, *Description,* p. 47; E. 134/16 Chas. I/M/33; G.P.L. MS. RV 260.2.

12. Such a jury existed at Thornbury, and assessed the heriot in kind; if the lord refused it, the tenant had the option of buying it back. An instance of agreement, in which the tenant bound himself to pay £5 6*s.* 8*d.* in lieu of two heriots, will be found in St. Ch. 5/N/13/38. The reason for such a double heriot is explained in a legal treatise of the time. "If the tenant by heriot alienate parcel of his tenancy, then two heriots shall be paid; and if he purchase the same again, yet he shall pay them both." [N. J. Hone, ed.,] *"A Mannor and Court Baron"* (*Harleian MS. 6714*), pp. 41–42.

13. The largest heriot which I have found was £9 10*s.* Lady Berkeley received in one year £68 15*s.* 4*d.* from fourteen heriots, or almost £5

When it came to other aspects of inheritance, the customary law was more complicated. Its underlying purpose was to protect the tenant's family against eviction by a stranger, even one to whom the tenant himself had demised his holding. The member of the family who received particular consideration was the widow. Her rights were everywhere safeguarded, in greater or less degree, by securing her a portion of her husband's land as compensation for the dowry which she had brought him. This estate was terminated only by her remarriage, incontinence, or death, and was known as her freebench.

Freebench varied in size and privilege, according to the custom of the manor and the wording of the copy. In most cases it was heriotable, although in some it was not.[14] It often consisted of a third of the land which the husband had held during his married life.[15] Sometimes it consisted of his entire holding: he was not allowed to demise any of it without his wife's consent; she held the land until she remarried or died, and "neither can the tenant in reversion . . . nor the lord of whom the land is holden enter the possession, but must tarry till that time be come."[16] She normally lost her freebench on remarriage, but not always; at Painswick, for example, she retained it even if she acquired "sundry husbands at sundry times."[17] In

apiece. (G.P.L. MSS. 16,532, fo. 14; 16,525, fo. 25.) At Awre, on the other hand, a maximum value of £3 6*s*. 8*d*. was fixed by the custom, and at Cheltenham, after 1624, heriot was commuted to a fixed fine of £1 10*s*.; these figures indicate the favorable position of tenants who were protected by the custom.

14. One of the exceptional cases is Awre, where she owed nothing on admission to her freebench, and no heriot was due at her remarriage or death.

15. As at Cheltenham, after 1624, where she held a third unless she had consented to a surrender by her husband.

16. Ashton-under-Hill; G.P.L. MS. R 24.1, fos. 3v–4. The same was true at Thornbury. (Req. 2/189/40; C. 3/277/5.) At Sapperton, she might be debarred if her husband had surrendered his land in court, but otherwise received it all at his death.

17. This question often hinged on the wording of the copy. In the hundred of Berkeley, the widow had an estate for life if her name appeared before her husband's; if it appeared after his, she lost her estate on remarriage. (Smyth, *Description,* p. 18.) At Kemble, the

general, even under an unfavorable custom, she was assured of some land of her own so long as she remained unmarried and chaste.[18]

The other important member of the tenant's family was of course the heir. He was not always the eldest son; the old custom of borough English still survived in parts of the county.[19] Whether he was the eldest son or the youngest, his rights were protected by the custom, sometimes to the extent of forbidding the copyholder to alienate his land to any except his heir.[20] But it was not always easy

crux of the matter was whether she was mentioned by her Christian name: if so, she held all her husband's lands for life, apparently even if she remarried, and certainly if she was merely incontinent; see the next note.

18. Incontinence almost always involved forfeiture of the freebench. This fact exposed the lord to obvious temptation, and I am surprised to have found only one reference to it: a rumor that a lord tried to have a widow seduced, in order to acquire her estate. (C. 21/T/2/2.) I know of only one manor in the county where such a plot could not have succeeded. At Kemble, "where a widow doth live incontinently or unchaste, that appertaineth unto an ecclesiastical correction; our custom hath not to do with it, but for her living she shall enjoy it by our custom."

19. As at Awre, where copyholds of inheritance went to the youngest son, and failing a son to the youngest daughter, and failing either to the next of kin. At Cheltenham, the youngest son was heir to an estate outside the borough, and the eldest to one inside it. (Add. MS. 6,027, fo. 24v.) Gavelkind does not appear in this period, but at Thornbury, as late as 1558, there were "gavelkind land, whose nature was to be partible among brethren, and very much other free lands at the common law, whose nature was to be partible among sisters." G.P.L. MS. RQ 303.2.

20. At Kemble, a copyholder might debar his children by a surrender unless they had helped to purchase the copy, and had had their help attested in court. At Cheltenham, there was a dispute about the right of the next of kin. In 1607–08, it was said that no one else might have the conveyance of a copyhold of inheritance, even with the consent of the lord; in this view the steward concurred. Ten years later, this opinion was contested; those who upheld it cited the example of a son who had brought a successful action of ejectment, at the Gloucester assizes, against a stranger to whom his father had demised his copyhold. (E. 134/5 Jas. I/E/10–11; E. 134/15 Jas. I/H/6.) The custom of Didbrook was remarkable. The reversion of a copyhold, even if not an estate of inheritance, might be granted to a stranger only with the consent of the tenant or his children. When a man wished to buy such a

to determine who the heir was. If a tenant left no children, and there were several claimants to the estate, the dispute could usually be settled by a jury of the neighbors.[21] But if a tenant married twice, and there were children by each marriage, the problem became more complicated. Assume, for example, that a widow remarried. She might hold all her first husband's estate by her freebench, and might have it regranted to her and her second husband and their children. What then became of the first husband's heir? If he was specifically designated in the copy, he might be able to gain possession on the widow's remarriage.[22] Otherwise, he had at best a remote claim. If there were children by the second marriage, they would inherit before him; if not, the second husband might hold the land after his wife's death, either for a period of years or for as long as he remained unmarried and chaste.[23] In either case, the original heir was barred from his inheritance for at least a considerable period. This aspect of manorial custom must have played its part in swelling the ranks of the vagabonds.

The copyholder's admission to his tenement was the legal beginning of his relations with the lord. Those relations varied, and were not always demarcated by the custom. But one obligation was almost universal; this was the payment of rent, the most common attribute of all

reversion, he was told that he must agree with the tenant's son, although the latter had no estate in the tenement by copy. He eventually paid the son's fine, and received in return a reversion for two lives.

21. As at Thornbury, where a jury of eighteen tenants was provided for the purpose. I presume, without specific evidence, that such questions elsewhere were settled in the manorial court.

22. For an example, in which the new husband made claim in court for his stepson, see Additional Charter 18,548.

23. At Cheltenham, for example, the youngest son of the second marriage was heir, in preference to any child of the first marriage. If the second marriage was childless, and the second husband survived the wife, he held her land for twelve years; it then reverted to the heirs of the first husband. Add. MS. 6027, fo. 24v; see also E. 134/5 Jas. I/E/11; C. 3/276/1; and for a slight revision of the custom in 1624, Goding, *History of Cheltenham,* p. 53.

types of tenure.[24] While it was often paid in money, it was equally often paid partly in kind. Hens and capons were the most popular medium; a certain number were reserved each year to the lord, and the payments were painstakingly listed in one rent roll after another. Whatever was not needed for the lord's household could be sold back to the tenants, so that a payment in capons became in effect a payment in money.[25]

The other obligations of the copyholder to the lord had for the most part either been commuted or fallen into disuse. There is one remarkable instance, in 1612, of a lord who demanded manual service on the demesne, even from his freeholders.[26] But this is exceptional. By and large, the old obligations had disappeared; they were rarely made the subject of a court presentment, or even mentioned in the custom.[27]

24. An example of the commutation of services into a single rent is that of a woman who held "by the yearly rent of 4*s.* halfpenny, and 20*d.* yearly for and in the name of work silver, and 4*d.* yearly for tithing silver, and 1*d.* yearly in the name of Peter penny." Cheltenham, 1607; E. 134/5 Jas. I/H/3.

25. Lady Berkeley received rents in money, wheat, beans, eggs, and fowl. (G.P.L. MS. 16,060, fos. 37–55, 59–61.) "Now for our rent capons at this day due," a new agent wrote to Smyth, "I desire to know how I shall dispose of them. To sell them to the owners I hold it best; 3*s.* a couple was our rate from whence I came." *Ibid.*, 16,532, fo. 21.

Rents in kind provided food for the lord who had rented his demesne, as most of them had by 1550. (Tawney, *The Agrarian Problem,* p. 202.) In this respect the Berkeleys were behind the times. Lord Henry gave instructions for such renting, on condition that his son might resume possession on a year's notice; but by the time of Lord Henry's grandson, in spite of Smyth's disapproval, much of the demesne was still in the hands of the family. G.P.L. MS. 16,524, fo. 29; Smyth, *Lives of the Berkeleys,* II, 6.

26. At Nether Barton, near Tewkesbury, the lord claimed service from all tenants, whether copyholders or freeholders, for a number of days at the hay and grain harvests. The tenants precipitated a suit by refusing these services; one of them claimed that he had worked for the lord "as one neighbor usually doth for another, in good will and neighborhood, but never upon duty, custom, or service at all." (C. 2/Jas. I/C/1/68.) Such service from freeholders was a rarity by the sixteenth century; see Tawney, *The Agrarian Problem,* p. 29.

27. The long records of the Sherborne court contain only one such entry, when fourteen tenants were presented for refusing to grind their

What survived were the prohibitions on the copyholder. He might not let his tenement decay, on pain of forfeiture. He usually might not fell timber on his land, or take branches or underbrush without license from the lord.[28] If his buildings needed repair, he might get the timber either from his own land or from the lord's wood.[29] But to be seen cutting it for any other purpose was on most manors a sure way to forfeit his copyhold.[30] The lord, on the other hand, "may at his pleasure fell and carry away and sell and give and convert to his pleasure all the timber trees, at any time when it shall be his will and pleasure."[31]

The burden of heriot and the danger of forfeiture were disadvantages of copyhold tenure at its best. The copyholder was relatively well off, however, if these were his only worries, as they were likely to be if he held an estate

grain at the lord's mills; some of them had been refusing for six years. (Uncatalogued book of the court baron of Sherborne, 3 November, 17 James I, in the Sherborne MSS.) The custom of Sapperton contained a provision that the copyholders owed the lord a day's work on the demesne during the grain harvest. Neither of these examples indicates that the obligations were fulfilled.

28. The exceptions are Kemble, where copyholders were entitled to "lops and shreds and underwoods," and Painswick, where timber on estates of inheritance might be used for any purpose without license.

29. If a copyhold at Sapperton did not have enough timber for repairs, the lord must either supply it or waive his claim to forfeiture in case of decay. At Kemble, he was responsible for all such timber.

30. This provision was sometimes a means of intentional forfeiture. When a man at Standish wished to break a bargain which he had made for some of his land, and to benefit the holder of the reversion, he merely cut down two trees. But the plot was foiled; the homage refrained from presenting, because the lord was bribed to say that the trees had been cut with his license. Otherwise he would have been debarred by the custom from dispensing with the forfeiture. E. 134/5 Jas. I/E/3.

31. Ashton-under-Hill; G.P.L. MS. R 24.1, fo. 4. When the vicar of Slimbridge needed wood for his barn, Lord Berkeley gave him permission to buy the necessary number of trees. Those marked were all on one copyhold, and written authorization was necessary to allay the copyholder's fear of forfeiting his estate. (G.P.L. MSS. 16,525, fo. 67; 16,533, fos. 63, 65.) The manorial official who should have supervised such lumbering was the woodward. I have no information about him, beyond brief references to his existence in the Forest of Dean: E. 134/34 Eliz./H/23; E. 134/21 Jas. I/M/36.

of inheritance under a favorable custom. Below him were the great majority of tenants, most of whom held their copies for one or more lives, and some for a term of years.[32] On many manors these were the forgotten men: the custom gave them at most a nebulous protection, which might be withdrawn if the royal courts or the manorial jury decided against them. It is small wonder that such tenants, "holding their said lands and tenements by an uncertain, base, and bond tenure, fineable at the lord's pleasure, subject to sundry charges and forfeitures, did (as they could get the lord's consent) alter and change their estates from copy or bond tenure to estates by indenture, for good consideration given to the lord . . . and for the freeing themselves from divers burdens which so base and bond tenure laid upon them, knowing their estate to rest at the lord's will, and being loath to yield such services and duties as formerly by court rolls have been answered."[33] Leasehold, in other words, was replacing the lower forms of copyhold and tenure at will.

This change was undoubtedly beneficial to the lord. It removed the leaseholder from the protection of the court

32. Even below such copyholders were the tenants at will, who held by no copy at all. They were rare by the sixteenth century (Tawney, *The Agrarian Problem,* pp. 282–83), and I have found only one disputed case of such tenure in Gloucestershire. This was at Winchcomb, where the question of tenure was aired in an exchequer suit. Lands there changed hands freely, without the lord's intervention; the buyer paid cash, and received the key of the house, with no formalities other than a small payment to the steward. Some of the tenants considered themselves, except for the payment of rent, as "absolute owners and freeholders . . . and no tenants at will." But the majority seem to have felt that they were tenants at will. "They did wonder that the complainant would let his title sleep so long, and not take fines of them, saying further that they knew it was only his . . . right." E. 134/14 Chas. I/M/31.

33. A description of the tenants of Churchdown in 1605. A copyhold of inheritance here was created only by a grant *sibi et heredibus suis;* grants *sibi et sequele, sibi et assignatis suis,* or *sibi et suis* created only tenure at the sufferance of the lord, according to a presentment of the homage, although this could not have been outright tenure at will. The leases which replaced such copyholds were commonly for eighty years, determinable on three lives. Req. 2/387/70.

and custom of the manor. It enabled the lord to rent his land on short-term leases, and thereby to raise the rent, as the leases fell due, to whatever level the market would bear.[34] Most important of all, it expedited the process of enclosure, which was the surest means of improving his rents.

Much of the land in the county was already enclosed by the beginning of the period. "In all that vale under Cotswold hills, from Bristol to Gloucester, and so in effect to Evesham, the course is shorter in our days: for all along that tract of ground we enclose, convert, and keep in several to ourselves our grounds which before lay open with the common fields."[35] But enclosure was by no means a closed issue. It was going on throughout the period, and was arousing "a rural reluctation" in the tenantry of numerous manors.[36] It entailed a revolution in manorial economy, and a revolution which was usually precipitated from above. The process is therefore worth attention, if only for the light which it throws on the relations between the lord and his tenants.

The men of the Forest of Dean expressed their disapproval of enclosures by the forthright method of rioting.[37] This seems to have been less popular in other parts of the county, presumably because much of the enclosing was

34. It was apparently exceptional to allow leaseholders to alter their land. One man paid £600 for a six-year lease; "the reason why he paid so great a fine was for that he had power by his lease to break up the pasture, and this deponent supposeth he had power to break up the meadows also and to convert it into tillage." C. 21/R/2/8.

35. Smyth, *Lives of the Berkeleys,* I, 114; see also p. 161. The purpose of enclosing seems to have been for the most part to create pasture, as at Berkeley and Cowley. (Smyth, *Description,* pp. 89, 152.) At Haresfield, in the decade between 1616 and 1626, the common fields were converted from tillage to pasture and orchard. (G.P.L. MS. RZ 152.1, fo. 25.) In the Cotswolds around Cirencester, "the country inclineth daily more and more to enclosure," presumably also for pasture. *Ibid.,* 16,526, fo. 34.

36. Smyth's phrase about the enclosure of a park at Nympsfield. The inhabitants ascribed to this act the sudden death of the lord soon after, and the subsequent sale of his lands to a Londoner. *Description,* p. 303.

37. See above, pp. 194–202.

done by agreement, and was beneficial to the tenantry as well as to the lord. Wherever it benefited only the lord, as it did in the Forest of Dean, there was likely to be trouble. Even Lord Berkeley's tenants, who were for the most part a docile lot, were not above recourse to violence when they felt that their rights were infringed.

At Slimbridge and Frampton, on the edge of the Severn, some new land had been created by a shift in the river. The tenants of both manors claimed right of common in this land, and when it was enclosed by Smyth, as steward for the manor of Slimbridge, the fat was in the fire. "On Wednesday were the workmen beat from their work. . . . On Thursday, the morrow after, . . . came from Frampton over the bridge near one hundred persons, whereof some threatened death and bade kill, others struck the workmen, others filled up the ditches, others chased the justices' horses up and down the grounds, others wrested the horses from Mr. Thorpe's man which he held, others offered violence to others in the company, . . . and laid violent hands upon Mr. Thorpe and Mr. Huntley [the justices?], to their exceeding danger and amazement."[38] There followed a spate of litigation, in which one of the justices apparently played a part.[39] The result was victory for the Berkeley interests, a victory "which so cooled the great heat of Frampton inhabitants, that they have permitted those our enclosures to stand quiet to this day."[40]

The best example of enclosing by agreement is at Mick-

38. 1610; G.P.L. MS. 16,073, fo. 1.

39. In 1611–12, a Mr. Thorpe and his cousin were suing about the new grounds. Since victory would give Lord Berkeley "a very great benefit by the large expense of our money, without his lordship's charge at all," they asked him to use his influence in London to procure a favorable decision. *Ibid.,* 16,530, fo. 98; for a similar petition to Sir Edward Coke, see Tawney, *The Agrarian Problem,* pp. 412–13.

40. Smyth, *Description,* pp. 330–31. Smyth had no patience with the opposition of the tenantry. At Slimbridge, for example, enclosing the waste would yield more than £1,500 a year; unenclosed, Slimbridge proved the rule "that the more large the waste grounds of a manor are, the poorer are the inhabitants." *Ibid.,* p. 328.

leton in 1616–18. The prime mover was the lord, but at first he had the full coöperation of the tenants. He held a number of meetings with them to agree on a general basis for redistributing the land. When this was settled, arbiters were appointed to determine the specific land which each tenant should receive. At once, however, it was apparent that there were difficulties.

The first was the vicar, who threatened to make trouble on the two issues of tithes and glebe. His tithes would be drastically reduced by enclosing, which would convert large areas of arable to pasture and meadow. The arbiters disposed of this problem by compensating him with eight acres of arable, twenty of meadow, and the right to the hay of twelve specified plots of land; the lord promised him in addition a cash compensation of some £10 a year. The glebe was a more serious difficulty. It was so thoroughly intermingled with the lands of the lord and tenants, in the open fields, that the vicar's consent was prerequisite to enclosing. Even when he had given it, the tenants remained distrustful. They feared that after they had received their new land in severalty, he still might claim some of it as glebe, and it was not until the lord had guaranteed each of them against such a claim that they were willing to proceed.[41]

The other difficulty was the poor. The cottagers and tenants at will had certain privileges in the unenclosed manor: their hogs might wander "in the opentide" after harvest was in; their cattle might be pastured in the common, on payment of 6*s.* 8*d.* a year; they were allowed to gather underbrush for fuel. These benefits would be lost by enclosure, and they not unnaturally opposed it. Their opposition was apparently ignored at the beginning, and only later made itself felt.

The original plan had been to allot forty-seven acres for each yardland[42] of freehold, and smaller proportions

41. For similar trouble in another enclosure, see C. 21/S/12/16.

42. The yardland seems to have been an uncertain unit. In the hundred of Berkeley, if I interpret correctly an involved definition of

for the different types of copyhold. When the actual allotments were measured, however, it was found that one of them was much better land than the rest. This allotment was consequently reduced to only thirty acres, and the remaining seventeen were at first distributed among the other tenants. At this point the lord intervened in the cause of the poor. He persuaded the tenants to give up the seventeen-acre windfall, and prevailed on most of them to decrease their allotments by an acre apiece. In this way thirty-three acres were reserved from the enclosure, and set aside for the use of the poor. The lord augmented this gift by individual charity: he gave copyholds or leases to numerous tenants at will, for low fines or none at all, and was lavish in his presents of money, food, and clothes. By the time that the process of enclosing was finished, every one seems to have been satisfied—the poor with their charity, the larger tenants with their allotments, and the lord with a handsome profit on his improved demesne.[43]

This example of enclosure indicates how much power the lord still exercised in the manorial community. It was the power of a constitutional ruler, circumscribed on the one hand by custom and on the other by the royal courts, but it was no less real because it was limited. He exercised it in two ways. One was by direct personal interference

Smyth's, it contained forty acres. (*Lives of the Berkeleys,* II, 13; see also Tawney, *The Agrarian Problem,* p. 67 and note 5.) At Mickleton, no one could say how large it had been before the enclosure; afterward it contained forty-six acres "or thereabouts." (E. 134/14 Jas. I/E/17.) It will be seen from the text that this result was largely accidental.

43. The exception was the vicar, who went to law on the ground that the poor had been defrauded. The consensus of almost all the witnesses was that the position of the tenantry had been improved by enclosure; some even claimed that the tenants had gained more than the lord. Numerous copyholds were converted from estates for life or lives into estates of inheritance; one such conversion trebled the value of the tenement, although the enclosure had halved its size. My description is based on testimony in four suits: E. 134/14 Jas. I/E/17; E. 134/15 Jas. I/T/4; E. 134/15 Jas. I/M/16; St. Ch. 8/145/22. Copies of further depositions, apparently from the same suits, are preserved with the Mickleton MSS.

in the affairs of the manor; the other was by the legal authority deputed to his steward in the manorial court. These two will be considered in turn.

The lord, by the nature of his position, had great influence over his tenantry. We have seen how it appeared at Mickleton, and there is reason to suppose that it was equally apparent wherever there was enclosure by agreement.[44] But it was not confined to such periods of revolution. Even in the routine functioning of manorial life, the lord had considerable leeway. He might waive his claim to heriot if the new copyholder was poor.[45] He might remit the fines which were levied in his manorial court.[46] He might reduce the rent when land was damaged by flood, or when the times were hard. "Many have will, but few the money that we require. They all wish they had my lord at home to deal with."[47] When the tenants were in financial straits, the lord was the final arbiter.

He also had considerable latitude in determining who

44. A more striking example is an enclosure by agreement at Ampney Crucis. One copyholder stood out for a time against the agreement, and refused to give up his land. Later, however, he "did accept of land in another place in lieu of the said eight acres, after the mounds were made, because he needs must, and in regard he could not conveniently come to it without trespassing of . . . his landlord, and this deponent being fearful to contend with his said landlord." E. 134/16 Chas. I/E/17.

45. "As for the heriot, I trust you will not look [for] one of me. . . . My wife left me five poor fatherless [*sic*] children, and nothing to maintain them. Good Mr. Smyth, do me what favors you may." (G.P.L. MS. 16,533, fo. 10.) The lord also had latitude in disposing of heriots collected. "There is a ox and a bullock for a heriot; the price of them is £9 10*s*. There was a better ox at the house, but Thomas Hourne sayeth that it [is] his ox. . . . If you have them not, neither Thomas Hourne buy them (because I would not have his evil will), I would desire you that I might have them for my money." (*Ibid.,* 16,532, fo. 14.) For a similar case of confusion between a heriot beast and the new tenant's own beast, see *ibid.,* RF 354.23, fo. 29.

46. "Received for amercements in your halimote courts this year nothing, because your ladyship pardoned all wherever you came in your person." (*Ibid.,* 16,071, fo. 37v.) A tenant of Sir Thomas Sackville was with his dying father when he should have been in court, and prevailed on Sir Richard Berkeley to intercede for the remission of his fine. Bibury MS. 87 in Sherborne MSS.

47. G.P.L. MS. 16,532, fo. 32. For an example of a drastic reduction in rents after a flood, see *ibid.,* 16,527, fo. 107.

his tenants should be. "Mr Huntley said . . . that the said Creeds were harlotry fellows, and that they should hold no living of his."[48] There was a natural inclination toward old tenants in preference to new, although the inclination was unlikely to be proof against a chance of profit. On this subject Lord Berkeley gave explicit instructions: as long as his incumbent tenants offered as high rents and fines as any one else, they were to be continued in preference to all outsiders.[49]

But they had to behave themselves. The Berkeleys were quick to resent any trifling with their manorial authority, and to lay down the law to a tenant who crossed them. When Smyth interceded for a widow who was in Lord Henry's bad graces, the old man replied with some asperity. "I am content to follow your desire almost in every part, though the widow's obstinacy, leaning to others more than to me, she being my tenant, deserveth it not." He went on to say exactly what she was to do, where her son was to stay during his minority, how his marriage was to be arranged, and what the fine should be. "But I will talk with her myself first at my next coming into the country, to understand who hath so set on my tenant so long against me."[50]

Lady Elizabeth, his daughter-in-law, was a spicy and forceful woman. If a man wished to obtain a copyhold from her, he had to meet with her approval. Smyth, as her steward, once sent her a would-be tenant whose eagerness was his undoing. She was an old lady at the time, and her temper had not improved with age. "Good Mr. Smyth,

48. E. 134/41 Eliz./E/17. Another lord told his wife that he had sold a man the reversion of a copyhold. "Mr. Wynter," she replied, "I have heard you swear an oath that neither Smalcome . . . nor any of his should ever have the said tenement." He then tried to get out of his promise by offering Smalcome money, and assuring him "that he should have any bargain that was to be sold within his manor of Dyrham £10 better cheap than any other man." C. 21/S/12/16.

49. G.P.L. MS. 16,524, fo. 29. For an instance of a servant's obtaining a reversion from his master for a quarter of what a stranger was offering, see C. 3/237/21.

50. G.P.L. MS. 16,525, fo. 42.

you have sent me such an importunate suitor for this change that I could heartily chide thee. I pray send me no more."[51] When her tenants slighted her authority, she was in a towering rage. At one time there was trouble about cattle, which had apparently strayed onto her demesne. She wrote Smyth to impound the beasts and prosecute the owners. If the trouble continued, "it shall, I vow, make me take such an order in those parts where they hold anything under me as they never yet dreamt of, that all after widows shall wish there had never been such an abuse offered in so worthy and noble a custom.

"Let there be no hour lost for the speedy bringing of it to a trial, that I may the better resolve how to d[eal] with others; and let James Atwood know from me that I hold him to be, as I understand, a great dealer in this business. . . . If he continue it, I will make him as famous in Gloucestershire as Markwick is in Sussex, upon whom they now thunder all their curses."[52]

Such rousing threats were apparently considered an effective means of dealing with a tenant. Smyth was himself lord of a manor, as well as the Berkeley's steward. When one of his tenants refused to liberate an apprentice whom he wished to have educated, his authority as lord was invoked with complete success. The procedure is explained in an illuminating letter to him from his agent.

"Worthy Sir

I . . . thought it fit, having fit opportunity, to give some overture to Thomas Dorney of your displeasure conceived

51. *Ibid.,* fo. 83.

52. *Ibid.,* fo. 65. Her reference was to a dispute with the tenants of Bosham, Sussex. She called a court when her son inherited his estates, to review the copies and determine the heriots. One man asserted that the tenants were freeholders, that they did not owe service to the court, and that she had no right to hold it. (Smyth, *Lives of the Berkeleys,* II, 432–34.) She then sued them in chancery, and John Markwick was one of the defendants. The court decided that the tenants were copyholders, and that their fines were arbitrary at the will of the lord. John Ritchie, *Reports of Cases Decided by Francis Bacon . . . in the High Court of Chancery (1617–1621)* (London, 1932), pp. 14–16.

against him, and to set it forth in the most truculent and terrible forms as I could; hoping thereby that (his mind being prepossessed with some perturbation) when your unexpected writ should be served upon him, his fear would be the more fatal and himself the more flexible, which is fallen out accordingly. . . . He saith that . . . he hopeth you will be propitious to an yielding adversary. His apprentice he promiseth to manumize, and that not on his own but your conditions. . . . Now, Sir, my request unto you is that [you] . . . prosecute your cause no farther against a submitting man, who defieth the very thought of opposing his weakness against your strength, and being your tenant desireth rather to flourish under your favor, than any way to displease you or oppose you. . . . It is a policy in war to undermine those walls that cannot be scaled, and I hope our dealing in the case can be thought no other than a pious policy, seeing the *ultimus finis* is a public good, *viz.*, the education of those whom God and nature have made dear unto us." [53]

The converse of such intimidation by the lord was his protection of the tenants against outsiders. He was often harsh when they crossed him, but equally often he rallied to their defense. Lord Chandos, for example, was appealed to by some of his tenants, who were defendants in a tithe suit in the diocesan court. He requested Sir Julius Caesar to stay process for three months, in order to give his lawyers time to collect their evidence. The plaintiff "thinks to fear my tenants, but . . . he shall find that threats shall not prevail him."[54]

A similar situation arose in a quarrel between Slimbridge and Frampton. Both villages were on Berkeley land, but only the Slimbridge tenants held directly.[55] They petitioned Lord Berkeley that their neighbors of

53. G.P.L. MS. RX 354.27.
54. Add. MS. 12,506, fo. 311.
55. Frampton was held by a single man in freehold. G.P.L. MS. 16,063.

Frampton had been troubling them for several years by commoning cattle, geese, and swine on some land in Slimbridge which was "the free common of your petitioners and no others." They asked for Lord Berkeley's evidence, the help of his solicitor, and money for a lawsuit to vindicate "your lordship's right and our own." Lord Berkeley thereupon summoned a meeting of all the principal freeholders, copyholders, and leaseholders of Slimbridge, to discuss what steps should be taken.[56] The upshot was that the tenants bound themselves to prosecute jointly all suits against the men of Frampton over waste grounds in Slimbridge, and to pay whatever costs might be assessed upon them, according to the acreage of their holdings, by specified agents of Lord Berkeley.[57] The initiative had apparently been transferred to the lord, and he and his tenants were coöperating for the welfare of the manor.

The Berkeleys seem to have been unusually successful in such coöperation. Many lords had disputes with their tenantry, and sometimes went to law against them.[58] But there is no record of such litigation on any Berkeley manor

56. The men of Frampton were said to have four thousand sheep on the contested common. (G.P.L. MS. 16,527, fo. 81.) If the Frampton common was as large then as it is today, the additional flocks in Slimbridge indicate that sheep-raising was a profitable activity.

There is a note at the bottom of the MS., in Smyth's hand, that a man sent him word "that he would lay his life that our ditch would be thrown in. *Q[uaere]* how he knoweth it?" This suggests that the Slimbridge-Frampton quarrel was connected with the enclosure of the new grounds mentioned above, p. 280. What seems to have been the same land was in dispute in 1600, when it was said to be "not in any parish certain, nor within any lordship or manor." St. Ch. 7/11/2.

57. G.P.L. MS. 16,527, fo. 68.

58. The bailiffs of Stow on the Wold were at law for thirty years with the lord of the manor, to prevent his interfering in the affairs of the town; he finally petitioned the house of lords to have his rights settled by act of parliament. (*H.M.C., Fourth Report,* p. 65; below, pp. 301–02.) Similar disputes at Cheltenham and Painswick were settled by decrees in chancery, whereby the lords received respectively £1,200 and £1,450 from their copyholders; both decrees were subsequently confirmed by act of parliament. See above, p. 271 note 8; Anon., *An Exemplification,* pp. 38, 67–72; Baddeley, *A Cotteswold Manor,* pp. 177–78; Notestein, *Commons Debates, 1621,* VII, 20–23; 1 Charles I, c. 7, sect. 3.

in Gloucestershire. This may have been due in part to the tact and shrewdness of the Berkeley steward, and in part to the character of his successive masters and mistresses. It was probably due in larger part to the Berkeley habit of defining systematically tenures and customs. Such definition occurred on other manors, either in or out of the manorial court, but it was usually the result of a disagreement between the lord and tenants.[59] On Berkeley manors it occurred in time of peace, as a means of forestalling such disagreement.

The usual method was either to summon a special meeting of the tenants, or to refer the matter to the manorial court. When part of a manor was changing hands, for example, Lord Berkeley instructed Smyth to assemble all the tenants, to examine their tenures, and to threaten suit against any who might be recalcitrant about the change of lords. "Let them all expressly know and understand from me that if any of them shall refuse to become my tenants, and to pay to me their rents, that to such a one I will refuse to become their landlord. And thereto let them trust."[60]

Another Lord Berkeley, some years later, wished to define the customs of his three boroughs of Berkeley, Wotton, and Tetbury, and the copyhold customs of his manors. He therefore instructed Smyth to refer the question to the next meetings of the borough and manorial courts. At each court, Smyth and the tenants between them were

59. Definition by parliamentary act, as at Cheltenham and Painswick, was rare. When the lord and tenants disagreed, they commonly appealed to the courts; an example is at Prestbury, where the copyholders obtained and paid for a commission from the court of exchequer, and in the rôle of jurors presented their custom to the commissioners. (E. 134/6 Jas. I/E/12.) When the lord and tenants were agreed, the common method was to present the custom in the manorial court.

60. G.P.L. MS. 16,527, fo. 62. A change of lords was a matter of concern to the tenants, and they occasionally had the boldness to urge their candidate. "It is the earnest desire of all us, your worship's tenants and friends, that we be put into the power and hands of a neighbor and a good friend whom we know, and not of a stranger, especially him who is a stranger to our church, and little less to our king and laws if he be a very Papist indeed." Bibury MS. 81 in Sherborne MSS.

to put into writing all the customs and privileges, "or as many of them as you can call to mind and agree upon, used at this day." The writings were to be sent to Lord Berkeley and entered in his rent book, for the avoidance of all future argument.[61]

So much for the place of the lord in manorial government. He always could, and often did, play an important part in the affairs of the community. But the nucleus of the manor was the manorial court, and to this the remainder of the chapter will be devoted. The two subjects are interrelated, because the character of government in any given manor was largely determined by the extent to which the lord controlled the court. He sometimes dominated it, either directly or through his agents. It was sometimes the center of resistance to his authority, and an effective curb upon it. Occasionally it had escaped entirely from his control, and become an independent governing body. These differences in its position mark the gamut of manorial administration.

The court was a many-sided institution. In one guise it was the court leet, a royal court in private hands, which was charged with presenting any offense under the degree of high treason, but not with passing judgment. In another guise it was the court baron and customary, the private court of the lord, charged with trying petty civil actions, with preserving the customs of the manor, and with presenting matters prejudicial to the lord. It sometimes had a third side as well, the old hundred court in private hands.[62] These three aspects were distinct in the minds of the lawyers, and they are occasionally distinguishable in the procedure of a specific court. For the most part, however, the distinction of theory was lost in practice, and is largely irrelevant to a discussion of practice.[63]

61. G.P.L. MS. 16,525, fo. 54.

62. See above, p. 47 note 25; below, p. 291 note 69.

63. Even that meticulous lawyer, John Smyth, did not always keep clear the distinction between the courts leet and baron; for an example

The functions of the court were as varied as its origins. It was a trial court, to settle actions between tenants. It was both a presenting and an administrative agency, to report offenses against the crown, the lord, or the community, and to exercise a general surveillance of manorial welfare. It was a recording body, to witness the grant or surrender of copyhold, and at times to declare and register the custom of the manor. Finally, as an outgrowth of this last function, it was the instrument by which the tenants could resist the lord. Its recording capacity has already been discussed; the others will be dealt with in turn.

The custom usually provided that any suit between copyholders must first be brought in the manorial court, on pain of forfeiture. "This is daily broken."[64] The court was incompetent to consider any suits which involved more than £2, but this restriction seems also to have been broken on occasion.[65] The greatest practical difficulty was in insuring the presence of the defendant. He was usually permitted to ignore several successive meetings, with a mounting fine; sometimes his goods were attached, to discourage his escaping from the manorial jurisdiction.[66]

of confusion, see *Description,* p. 197. At St. Briavels, similarly, the jury in a view of frankpledge was presenting heriots due to the crown. (E. 134/16 Chas. I/M/33.) For further discussion of the lack of practical distinction, see F. J. C. Hearnshaw, *Leet Jurisdiction in England, Especially as Illustrated by the Records of the Court Leet of Southampton,* pp. 90, 110–11, 156; W. S. Holdsworth, *A History of English Law,* IV (first edition, 1924), 128–30; Webb, *The Manor and the Borough,* I, 12–13, 31–32.

64. Cheltenham, 1617. Any one obtaining a warrant from a justice outside the manor, to arrest any one within the manor, forfeited his copyhold unless he compounded with the lord. Add. MS. 6027, fo. 24v.

65. An action for property valued at £5 was brought in the Berkeley court in 1606. (G.P.L. MS. 16,530, fo. 72.) The Cheltenham court was said to be able to settle "actions of debt and other personal actions to any sum or value whatsoever." E. 112/16/198.

66. At Newnham, an absentee defendant did not lose his case until the fifth default, whereas at Northleach he lost at the third. At Berkeley, his goods might be attached as surety even if he lived outside the hundred; if he and the plaintiff did not appear at two successive courts, it was assumed that the case had been settled by agreement. St. Ch. 8/230/23, fo. 7; Northleach Court Book, pp. 215–16; Smyth, *Description,* pp. 12–14.

Once he and the plaintiff were both in court, their suit might be settled in several ways. In many cases compurgation was still an acceptable defense.[67] If judgment was necessary, in cases not involving copyholds, the judging power was in a bench of freeholders.[68] The evidence on procedure is meager, but it suggests that a trial consisted of nothing more than the statements of the principals and witnesses, followed by the decision of the bench.[69]

The criminal jurisdiction of the court was supposedly negligible. In practice, however, it seems to have had some importance. Serious offenses were of course excluded, but these were comparatively rare. It was the minor breaches of the peace which disturbed the everyday life of the com-

67. In an action of trespass at St. Briavels, the defendant might wage his law for any part of the damages claimed. He came into court with five compurgators, and swore to the truth of his case; the compurgators then swore to their belief in his oath. If they did so without error, or withdrawing their hands from the book, judgment was given to the defendant. Add. MS. 6683, fos. 153v–54; for a similar procedure in the Berkeley court, see Smyth, *Description,* p. 12.

68. There were various methods of selecting the benchers. At Dymock, the steward and tenants chose a bench of twelve, of whom three constituted a quorum. At St. Briavels, the free suitors were the hereditary judges. (Add. MS. 6683, fos. 155–58.) The same was true at Berkeley, where the free suitors seem to have been synonymous with the freeholders; there were more than four hundred of them, and the bench was rarely less than twenty. (Smyth, *Description,* pp. 12–13, 16.) Cases involving copyholds came before the court as a court customary, of which the steward was the judge; see Holdsworth, *History of English Law,* I (third edition, 1922), pp. 181–82.

69. At Northleach, the plaintiff told his name and the defendant's, the sum for which he was suing, and the reasons why it was due him; he then asked for judgment. The defendant went through a similar procedure, and at the end either confessed or asked for "good costs and consideration for wrongful trouble." (Northleach Court Book, p. 217.) At Berkeley, the plaintiff tried to prove his case by calling witnesses. Smyth, *Description,* p. 12.

Smyth describes the great leet held twice a year at Berkeley, attended by the constables and tithingmen of twenty-eight townships. (*Ibid.,* p. 103.) This was a fuller meeting of the ordinary three-weeks' court, and was a survival of the hundred court in private hands; see Hearnshaw, *Leet Jurisdiction in England,* pp. 253-54; Webb, *The Manor and the Borough,* I, 34–36. The Webbs go on to describe (pp. 38–40) the procedure in the borough courts of the hundred of Berkeley, on the basis of material which is no longer accessible.

munity, and these could be brought into court by jury presentments and punished by fines.[70] The bench was likely to know the details of the offense and its background, and the court was the natural place to settle the matter. If its verdict was unfair, the victim might appeal to the lord.[71] Even then the dispute remained in the manor, and was not exposed to the uncertain judgment of strangers. The assizes were far away, and presided over by foreigners from London; even the J. P.'s at the sessions had a less intimate knowledge of local affairs than the tenants at the manorial court. The satisfactory way to deal with offenders was at home.

> "I was at Gloucester assizes, where there was neither Sir Maurice Berkeley nor his father; so that nothing is yet done to our Peter Ganners [and others]. If we punish them not in our own courts, I think it were best to deliver them over to the mercy of the sessions. There is one will do it and put me to no further pains. And justice you know is far from us." [72]

The most homely aspect of the court was the jury presentments. These were more than a catalogue of offenses against the crown, the lord, or the neighbors. They included opinions of the jury on what was wrong with the manor, and sometimes orders for setting matters to rights. Their abominable writing testifies that they were made by tenants who were barely literate. For that very reason they are valuable, as almost the only surviving records of an important and inarticulate class; through them we have a glimpse of the small concerns of the copyholder.

Widow Drill's chimney is cracked and dangerous, and

70. The usual fine for private fights *ad effusionem sanguinis*, or to the disturbance of the neighbors, seems to have been 3*s*. 4*d*. (Additional Charter 26,507; G.P.L. MS. R 229.45.) The court occasionally punished common scolds. In one case a woman was presented on a certificate of her neighbors; witnesses were called, the jury convicted her, and she was ducked. Gloucester Diocesan Records, LXXIX, 61v.

71. When arbitrators decided against a man, in 1631, they ordered him to admit that he had lied in petitioning Lord Berkeley against the steward and grand jury of the lawday. G.P.L. MS. 16,532, fo. 108.

72. *Ibid.*, fo. 20v.

her house needs thatch. Jeoffrey Jenkins is commanded to remove three tenants from his cottage, or to obtain license from the lord. Thomas Powell is told to scour his ditch. No one is to trespass on Richard Webb's meadow, on pain of a fine.[73] John Bowers has died on his farm; the jury surveys the property, and finds it "ruinous down and out of reparation." [74] Tenants have been cutting too much wood, and the jurors comment on each case: sometimes there has been great destruction, and the land is no longer worth the rent; sometimes the lumbering has "left it very well"; sometimes there is "great store left, and this is not to the destruction thereof." [75] One tenant has usurped the common, and another has pastured a mangey horse upon it; a third has allowed his tenant's son to become "a common hedge-breaker," a fourth has kept "ill rule in his house in the night time," and a fifth has diverted a stream into another parish.[76] In dealing with such offenses as these, the court was both dispensing justice and governing the manor.

Its governmental function is more clearly apparent in its regulation of the tenantry as a whole. Take for example the Sherborne court, of which unusually full records have survived.[77] The pasturing of horses, cattle, and sheep in the common fields was carefully regulated, to prevent damage to the crops, and the leasing of pasture rights to outsiders was forbidden. The entire homage was periodically ordered to make a perambulation of the

73. *Ibid.,* RX 354.13.

74. In the opinion of the jury, more than £66 would be needed to "set it in reparations as it ought to be." *Ibid.,* 16,532, fo. 118.

75. *Ibid.,* 16,533, fo. 105.

76. *Ibid.,* R 229.45. Several of these presentments resemble those made by the petty constable; see above, p. 51. The deliberations of the manorial jury were sometimes secret, as at Oxenton, where "if any man of the twelve doth disclose anything that we have done, the pain is 10*s*." Add. MS. 28,211, fo. 107; see also Mandley, *Portmote Records of Salford,* Chetham Society, new series, LXVI, 208; Stevenson, *Nottingham,* V, 189.

77. My description is based on the uncatalogued book of the court baron of Sherborne, 25 Elizabeth to 20 James I, in the Sherborne MSS.

manor, in order to determine the boundaries of each man's land (the subject of frequent disputes), and to see that they were marked by balks of the proper width.[78] At times it was necessary to dig a ditch which would benefit every one, or to fill a swamp in the common; the labor of all the tenants was then conscripted by the court.[79] For the rest, the task of surveillance was deputed to such officers as the hayward, the herder, and "the supervisor of the fields," whose wages were paid by a fixed contribution from each tenant; for work which was outside their competence, the court appointed special agents to act for the manor. The common concerns of the tenants, in short, were all under the direct or indirect supervision of the court, which from their standpoint performed a vital function.

Whether the court was equally useful to the lord is another question. It was certainly expensive for him, because the steward and jurors had to be fed. His returns in the form of fines were speculative, and we have the word of an expert that they "do seldom defray the stewards' and juries' charges and diet in holding the said court." [80] But no matter how much it cost him, the lord had no alternative. When his steward ceased to preside at the court, he ceased to be lord of the manor.

The holding of the court, as court baron, was in itself a proof of title to the manor. If the court was held in the name of some one other than the rightful lord, the usurper acquired thereby a strong presumptive claim to lordship;

78. The balks were supposed to be one foot wide, a provision reiterated often enough to suggest that they were regularly encroached upon. Boundary disputes were often settled by arbitrators appointed in court, by whose award the disputants bound themselves to abide; in one case the lord himself was arbitrator. These are humble examples of a practice widespread in the litigation of the period; see my article, "Lawyers and Litigants in Stuart England," *Cornell Law Quarterly,* XXIV, 542–43.

79. On 28 April, 38 Elizabeth, all the inhabitants with carts were ordered to carry stones for four days "for mending of the sloughs in the beasts' pasture"; those who did not have carts were to spend the same time in digging stones, "with all the help they have."

80. John Smyth; G.P.L. MS. 16,526, fo. 34. In 1613, the cost of meals at Lord Berkeley's courts came to £8 18*s.* 6*d.; ibid.,* 16,525, fo. 17.

conversely, if the court was not held at all, the manor ceased to exist.[81] These two aspects of the court as title can be illustrated by two examples.

In the first, at Rodley, a man resorted to violence in order to assert his claim. While the incumbent's deputy steward was holding court according to form, two gentlemen invaded the room with an armed mob at their heels. They expelled the steward, broke up the meeting, impaneled a jury from among their followers, and proceeded to transact the business of a court.[82] In the second instance, at Stow on the Wold, the bailiffs and burgesses were trying to make good their claim that no manor existed. When the lord's steward attempted "to call a court baron, at the time when the leet of the said town of Stow was holden, . . . the suitors there did refuse to be sworn at the said court baron. But the steward then calling the leet, being holden for the late queen, he (this deponent) and the rest did answer, and the same court proceeded." [83] In both cases the court was important not in itself, but as a proof of title.

Few tenants dared to go as far as the burgesses of Stow. But many opposed the lord in lesser ways, and the center of this opposition was likely to be the court. The battle might be carried to the exchequer, to chancery, even to parliament, but the first engagement was usually between the steward and the homage. The courtroom was the natural scene for such a struggle. The steward spoke there with the full measure of his authority; the tenants

81. Copyhold could not exist apart from the court. If a copy was given in the court of a *de facto* lord, it was in many cases good at law; if a rightful lord, on the other hand, did not grant a copy and enter it in open court, the grant was invalid. (Calthrope, *The Relation betweene the Lord of a Mannor and the Coppy-Holder His Tenant,* pp. 36–37.) A manor on which there were no freeholders could not have a court baron, but was not a manor in the strict sense; Holdsworth, *History of English Law,* I, 182–83.

82. St. Ch. 8/94/10. John Smyth was accused of keeping an equally illegal court baron at Wotton under Edge "in his own name, as lord and owner of all the school lands." G.P.L. MS. RX 354.20, sig. A iii.

83. E. 134/5 Jas. I/T/1; see also below, pp. 301–02.

opposed him with an authority of their own, compounded of their corporate anger and their interpretation of the custom.

Victory often went to the lord, if only because he had the advantage of the initiative. "The steward continued the court eighteen days by divers adjournments, whereby the tenants were driven to continual attendance so long, by reason of conference to be had about questions captiously moved by him. . . . They were also abused in the court, as namely Edward ap Price threatened to be put in [the] stocks for speaking his conscience in defense of their custom, and to be fined of perjury, to the great terror of the rest of the poor tenants." [84] Such tactics as these would wear down all but the most hardy opposition.

Such opposition, however, was sometimes forthcoming. Take for example the case of Didbrook, where the tenants were far from being terrified. The jury, in a presentment, interpreted the custom unfavorably to the lord; the steward "angrily refused the same, telling them that their livings were all gone and in danger within the breadth of his thumb." He advised them to reconsider, and to spend a shilling apiece to get a lawyer's advice, "whereunto the homage answered they could say no more than they had said, if they should ask never so much counsel." They refused to amend their verdict, and he refused to accept it.

The result was a scene in open court. According to the steward's servant, some of the tenants acted so outrageously that "the manner of their savage and irreverent behavior in speeches will . . . never out of his memory." Richard Croswell, who seems to have been their ringleader, left the court and said that he would never serve there again. The steward called him back, and admonished him to be better advised, but "Croswell so raged and

84. The steward tried to have Price's tenement declared forfeit, but this the homage refused to do. (Weston [Subedge?], 1590; Lansd. MS. 65, fo. 1.) In a milder instance at Standish, in 1607, the steward refused to swear a copyholder's witnesses, or admit her evidence, because the lord had ordered him to leave the case for trial at the common law. E. 134/5 Jas. I/E/3.

brawled that he seemed not only careless of that her Majesty's said court, and of her said officers there, but also utterly to contemn all authority, seeming by his outward gesture and behavior that he came thither prepared rather to quarrel than to do her Majesty any service that day. Insomuch as the steward, not being able to pacify or overrule him, was sundry times abouts to depart the court and leave the service unperformed, praying the people there to remember and bear witness of the abuses and outrages offered." Many of the bystanders were shocked by his patience; if they had been in his place, they would have clapped Croswell into the stocks. But the steward contented himself with fining him, whereupon Croswell dared him to collect.

"'For,' said he, 'let Townsend (meaning the queen's bailiff of the said manor) come upon any ground of mine to distrain for that, or touch or meddle with any cattle or thing of mine, and I will make him that he shall never go home again!'"[85]

So much for the court as battle-ground between the lord and the tenantry. The fortunes of war varied with the nature of the combatants, and of the causes for which they fought; the result was usually to establish a new balance of power, with somewhat more weight on one side of the scales. In some manors, over a long period of time, the scales had been tipped more and more in favor of the tenantry, until the lord had become only a figurehead in a community which was to all intents self-governing. These manors seem to have been entirely in the smaller towns of the county. Almost every town had acquired a degree of independence, and some were wholly autonomous. This discussion of the court, therefore, has for its conclusion the government of the manorial town, which at times was synonymous with the operation of its court.

A convenient measure of the lord's authority in a town is the method by which the bailiff or mayor was chosen. At Cirencester, for example, the bailiff was the lord's ap-

85. E. 134/41 Eliz./T/5.

pointee, and governed under the nominal direction of the steward. He was removable, presumably by the steward, but there is no indication that this was ever done. He held a piepowder court at the fairs, and a manorial court through which he and his subordinates "did govern and rule the town in good sort and civil manner." [86] Much the same was true of the mayor of Wotton under Edge, except that he was chosen in conjunction by the steward and the court. The jury presented the names of three candidates, the old mayor among them, and from these the steward selected one. The new mayor then chose one of the other two for his sergeant-at-mace, who was charged with gathering the lord's rents and profits from the borough for the ensuing year.[87]

The position of the Tetbury court, at the beginning of the period, was much like that of Wotton. The bailiff was selected in the same way as the mayor of Wotton, and the lesser officers were also chosen in court. The lord's privileges were restricted to his steward's rôle in naming the bailiff, to pasture rights in the fallow field,[88] and to the profits of the market. Lord Berkeley leased the market to a Londoner, who in 1610 bequeathed the remainder of his lease to a body of trustees for the town.[89] From this seed, in the space of thirty years, grew an autonomous borough.

86. The bailiff executed warrants and precepts directed to him by the sheriff or justices, and was assisted by two constables, two sergeants-at-mace, and other officers. (E. 178/959; see also E. A. Fuller, "Cirencester—Its Manor and Town," *Trans.*, IX [1884–85], 342.) The only indication that the lord's rights might still be asserted is a complicated case, in 1637, of his right to treasure-trove, which he had apparently acquired by royal franchise. E. 134/14–15 Chas. I/H/9.

87. If both new nominees for mayor refused to serve, the steward might fine them as much as £10 apiece; the old mayor then served again. This seems to have been the extent of the steward's power; he himself says that it is the court "wherein consisteth the government." (Smyth, *Description,* pp. 399–401.) The method of choosing the mayor remained in force till 1835; see Hearnshaw, *Leet Jurisdiction in England,* p. 320.

88. He might pasture in fallow fields throughout the year, and in other fields when not sown. C. 2/Jas. I/B/17/19.

89. See above, p. 260 and note 78.

The process of growth was not a tranquil one, because Lord Berkeley (or his dominating steward) did not submit tamely to a decline in his power. The bailiff, in 1629, took it upon himself to alter the market day in time of plague. As one of the trustees for the market, he doubtless thought that he was within his rights. The steward thought otherwise; he promptly ousted the bailiff, fined him and the other officers, and demanded a written acknowledgment that they had wronged Lord Berkeley. Until he got it, he refused to choose a new bailiff from the court's three nominees, and said "that he would leave the town as it was not for many years left, that was without a bailiff." The acknowledgment was not forthcoming, and the town remained for a time without a head.[90] Three years later, perhaps as a result of this *impasse*, the trustees and other tenants bought the manor from Lord Berkeley, and completed the process in 1640 by buying the reversion of the lease of the market. The town thereafter was entirely self-governing, and the court was held by seven feoffees as joint lords of the manor.[91]

The bailiff of Chipping Sodbury was appointed by the lord or his steward, but seems to have had a large degree of independence. He received the income of the town lands, and employed it in any litigation which might arise over them, in relieving the poor, and in repairing the highways; if he was left with a surplus, he invested it in buying more land for the town. He also received the income of the church lands and employed it about the church, which suggests that he was a combination of bailiff and churchwarden. He was not independent of the court: his actions were subject to "the consent or approbation of all or the greatest part of the burgesses and inhabitants," and he

90. C. 91/1/8.

91. The governmental evolution of Tetbury is described at length in Webb, *The Manor and the Borough,* I, 151–55; see also T. W. Walker, "Some Notes on Tetbury, Its Church and Court Leet," *Trans.,* XXXVII (1914), 61–67. I have confined myself to an outline of the Webbs' description, amplified by new material.

rendered his accounts yearly at a meeting of all the townsfolk.[92]

The constitution of Cheltenham, like that of Tetbury, was in process of development during the period. The town was part of a royal manor and hundred, which was to a certain extent independent of county officials.[93] The chief officer was the manorial and hundred bailiff, who was supposed to preside over the court either in person or through his steward. This court seems to have been a fusion of two bodies, the piepowder court of the town and the court of the manor. It was held at the bailiff's pleasure, and he summoned to it the bailiff and burgesses of the town, who owed service there as part of their burgage tenure. There were thus two bailiffs in court, one of the manor and hundred, and the other of the town. The two were in disagreement by 1600, when the burgesses were endeavoring "to deface, disgrace, and overthrow the said court of piepowders"—to replace it, in other words, by an independent court of their own. The town bailiff claimed that he was the presiding officer, and that the court belonged to the burgesses. He tried to sit above the hundred bailiff, and "offered with force and violence to pull up the said steward forth of his place." When this failed, he marched out of the room with the burgesses at his heels.[94]

How this quarrel ended we do not know, but in the long

92. C. 91/3/12. Detailed information about the bailiff's and burgesses' regulation of the town pasture, and other lands, may be found in E. 134/10 Jas. I/M/16, and in copies of depositions in this or a simultaneous case, preserved in the Chipping Sodbury MSS.

93. "A hundred exempted from the ordinary power of the officers of the county of Gloucester." (E. 112/16/198.) A contemporary MS., which I have been unable to locate, asserts that the court elected justices of assize and of the peace, sheriffs, stewards, bailiffs, escheator, and coroner, and that no county officer might interfere within the liberty without license from the lord. (Quoted by Goding, *History of Cheltenham,* p. 65.) If this were so, the manor would have had a phenomenal degree of independence. But some of the statements, such as that an assize justice was elected in the manorial court, are patently incredible, and I have found no substantiation of most of the others.

94. At the next court he forcibly presided himself. E. 112/16/198.

run the burgesses had their way. By 1617, the hundred bailiff was debarred from entering the borough to serve a warrant, and seems to have lost all power of interfering with town government.[95] The executive authority was the town bailiff. He was in charge of policing the town, of taking precautions against fire and safeguarding the water supply, of keeping the highways passable, of forcing strangers to give security for themselves, and preventing an influx of poor.[96] The office was important enough for the burgesses to make sure that it remained in their own hands.[97] They had shaken off the authority of the lord, and were apparently on the way to making Cheltenham a close corporation.

The conflict at Stow on the Wold has already been mentioned. It seems to have been won by the town more quickly and more completely than at Cheltenham, for by 1607 the inhabitants were entirely self-governing. They elected two bailiffs in court, along with other officers. The bailiffs collected the tolls of the markets, the profits of two fairs held in the town each year, and various amercements; for these they rendered no account to the lord of the manor. They held the courts, regulated the affairs of the markets, purchased land, and in general conducted themselves as free agents for the common welfare. The lord, according to universal testimony, had nothing to do with their selection, and had no share in the profits of the

95. Add. MS. 6027, fos. 24–25. Parts of the Cheltenham custom could not have existed if there had been no lord; how then can the independence of the town be reconciled with the survival of the custom? The solution may lie in the distinction between the borough and the "foreign," or part of the manor outside the borough: it is conceivable that copyhold tenure was restricted to this foreign, and that it had a court of its own. If so, it is surprising that I have found no mention of such a court. The more probable explanation is that the crown retained its titular lordship, and that the manorial and hundred bailiff, or the town bailiff as his deputy, transacted copyhold business in the borough court. Whatever the solution, the problem does not seem to have existed for the people concerned.

96. Goding, *History of Cheltenham,* p. 58.

97. The bailiff might depute his office to another burgess, but not to an undertenant. Add. MS. 6027, fo. 25.

market. The only vestige of his authority was the steward who presided over the court, and even this vestige was questionable. One of the bailiffs himself did not know whom the steward represented, and some thought that he was the agent of the bailiffs rather than the lord. The manor, in short, had practically ceased to exist. Each witness deposed that "he knoweth not that the said town of Stow is a distinct thing from the said manor, because he knoweth not the said manor." [98] The burgesses would have liked to complete the process, by legalizing their prescriptive claim to the status of a corporation.[99] In this they failed, but their practical autonomy seems to have been almost as great as that of Gloucester.

One manorial town had succeeded in obtaining corporate status. This was Chipping Campden, whose prescriptive privileges were confirmed and defined in 1605 by a royal charter.[100] The manorial court continued, as a court of record to try small civil actions. The presiding officers, as at Stow, were the two bailiffs and a steward, but in this case the steward's position was unequivocal: he was elected by the common council, and held office during its pleasure. The other provisions of the constitution were similar to those at Tewkesbury, and need not detain us.[101]

One of the most interesting manorial towns was North-

98. E. 134/5 Jas. I/T/1; for subsequent litigation about the tolls of the markets and fairs, see E. 134/6 Jas. I/E/36; E. 134/7 Jas. I/E/18.

99. In two cases at the Gloucester assizes, shortly before 1620, the bailiffs claimed that they were a corporation. One of the judges gave it as his opinion that they were merely "bailiffs of government," but left it to the jury to determine whether they were "an ancient corporation by prescription." The jury apparently decided that they were not. E. 134/18 Jas. I/H/8.

100. John Savage, who had long resided in the town, lent the burgesses £100 with which to obtain the charter. He had difficulty in getting back his money, and went to law in 1623. C. 3/342/87.

101. The council was composed of fourteen capital burgesses, of whom two served as bailiffs, and twelve inferior burgesses. A contemporary copy of the charter is in the Gloucester County Council MSS.; for further details, see S. E. Bartlett, "The Manor and Borough of Chipping Campden," *Trans.*, IX (1884–85), 180–81; Rudder, *History,* pp. xxxix–xliii; Webb, *The Manor and the Borough,* I, 180 note 2.

leach. It was scarcely more than a village, but before the beginning of the period it had acquired complete autonomy.[102] The court was composed of every one who practiced specified trades, and presumably included almost all the substantial townsmen. The bailiff was elected in court, and was assisted in conducting court business by a bench of six principal burgesses, or "arbitrators." This committee of seven might have been expected to assume executive functions, like the common councils of other towns; but there is no indication that it did so. The administration remained in the court, which was both legislature and executive. It had a wide range of activities, and was omnicompetent in local affairs.

Each newly elected bailiff, at his first court, summoned at least one inhabitant of each house, and read them the town ordinances. These ordinances were added to, amended, and enforced by the court. Tradesmen were admitted to their trades, on payment of fines which varied with the person and the occupation.[103] But this was only a small part of court business. A steady stream of people and problems required attention, from a woman who failed to pay her servant's wages to a baker whose bread was under weight. There were apprentices to be bound to their masters, and tradesmen to lease stalls in the market. Some Winchcomb butchers refused to pay for their stalls, and the bailiff was authorized to distrain on their beef. A man who had lost a horse in Tewkesbury was given license to cry his loss in Northleach, and at another time a horse trade was solemnly witnessed by the bailiff and burgesses. "Roger Russell hath given his word unto Mr. Bailiff and

102. Its constitution has all the earmarks of manorial origin. But even John Smyth, in 1608, could not find a lord of the town. (*Men and Armour,* p. 265.) I have had no better success; there was not even an ambiguous steward, as at Stow, and I conclude that the manor had ceased to exist.

103. The usual fine for such humble folk as card-makers and hucksters was 6*d.,* for most others 12*d.,* and for brewers, clothiers, and bakers between 2*s.* and 4*s.* While the rate varied with individuals, the highest payments seem to have been from bakers. Northleach Court Book, p. 303 and *passim.*

the bench that he will bring in for his tenant, the tailor, some pledge to be bound for his honest behavior by the next court, or else to depart out of the town."[104] No aspect of community life was too trivial for the attention of the court, and little escaped its notice.

It is apparent that such a court was equivalent to the council in a chartered borough. The two had the same sort of administrative functions, and were in the same relation to the titular executive. The manorial court had also its judicial aspect, in which it resembled that part of a common council which sat as quarter sessions. The cases before the two differed widely in nature and importance, as well as in the procedure by which they were tried; the resemblance is not in externals, but in essential purpose. Both courts dealt with the daily problems of the people; both were conducted by men who knew the offenders or litigants, and could temper due process of law by the use of neighborly discretion.

Such a comparison does not imply that the manorial courts were as important governmentally as the common councils, or judicially as the quarter sessions. They obviously were not. The manor was a decaying institution, and its court was decaying with it. As leasehold became more common, suit of court ceased to be the accepted rule; as the dangers of travel decreased, as the roads improved and the country grew more peaceful, there was less and less need for self-sufficient communities under the aegis of their lords. Change had undermined the economic and social bases of the manorial structure, and the structure itself was cracking. But it had not yet fallen, and the reason is apparent.

The old cannot give place to the new before the new appears. Enough has already been said about the government of Gloucestershire to indicate its cumbrous inefficiency. In spite of the exhortations of the privy council, it never functioned with speed or with precision; in normal

104. *Ibid.*, p. 323; see also pp. 211–14, 219–20, 314, 340–42; Royce, "The Northleach Court-Book," *Trans.*, VII, 90–103.

times it was barely adequate, and in an emergency it was almost helpless. Its agents were for the most part amateurs, who had to attend to their own affairs as well as to those of government: they were either country gentlemen with farms to cultivate, or burgesses with shops to manage. It was natural that some sought to profit from misusing their authority, and that many more neglected it for the sake of their private concerns. On such a basis it was impossible to build an effective administration for a county addicted to lawlessness.

But the people had to be governed, and their lawlessness only increased their need. They clung to the manorial court because they had no alternative which worked so well. They allowed their lord to bully them, up to a point, because he was still the most effective power in the community. They wished that they had him at home to deal with, because they had no other way to adjust their rents. The vitality of the manor, with all its archaisms, was the converse of an attenuated central authority. Manorial jurisdiction could not collapse until there was something to replace it—royal courts which made justice a reality for poor men, and royal officials who had strength behind them. Until that time came, the lord and his tenants had to govern themselves in the old ways, through the old courts. "Justice you know is far from us."

BIBLIOGRAPHICAL NOTE

MANUSCRIPTS

THE manuscript material on the county falls into two general categories, of approximately equal importance: the records of the central government preserved in London, and the private and official papers preserved in Gloucestershire. Of the London records, the most voluminous, the most rewarding, and the most difficult of access are the archives of the courts; the registers of the privy council and the files of the state papers are of comparatively secondary importance. In Gloucestershire, the richest material is the collection in the Gloucester Public Library; equally valuable, although smaller in scope, are the muniments of the corporation of Gloucester. The other records in the county, both private and public, are in their aggregate less numerous and less varied than either of these collections.

The most useful London courts, for a study of local government, are star chamber, exchequer, chancery, and requests. Their usefulness is in the order named, and is determined by two factors: the nature of the business before the court, and the accident of how its archives are now indexed in the Public Record Office. An index of subjects is unreliable, because the subject is often unrelated to the incidental information contained in the testimony, but an index of places is necessary for isolating local material in any quantity. The formal bills and answers are for the most part unrewarding; it is the depositions, in their entirety, which always yield something of value.

By far the most important depositions are those in star chamber (St. Ch.). The cases have been indexed by county and subject from 1602 to 1625; cases after 1625 are almost nonexistent, and cases before 1602 are indexed merely by plaintiff, so that those from one county can seldom be segregated without a prohibitive waste of time. But within the period which is fully indexed, the testimony has a variety and a vividness which give it unique value. The equivalent material in the court of exchequer (E.) is well indexed and hence accessible; much of it is singularly dull, but the rest throws a great deal of light on such subjects as commercial regulation and manorial custom. The administrative records of the exchequer, as distinct from the records of the court, are with some exceptions too formal for the purposes of this study. The same is true of the few administrative documents in the chancery archives (C.). The depositions in chancery are difficult to isolate for a county, because most of them are indexed only by plaintiff; much of the material which I have been able to find, however, is of the greatest interest. Just the opposite is true of the court of requests (Req.): the depositions are excellently indexed for the reign of James I, but are far less rewarding than those in the other courts.

The strictly administrative records of the central government, in its relation to local authorities, are of two sorts. The *Acts of the Privy Council* are in print until 1627; thereafter they are in manuscript (MS. A.P.C.). Since the council was interfering less frequently in local affairs after 1627 than before, the later minutes are of only occasional value. The domestic series of the state papers (S.P.) contains a far wider variety of material than the classification indicates; much of it has little relation to affairs of state. The nature of the material is apparent from the printed *Calendar*, but this résumé cannot do justice to the sidelights and highlights in the original documents. I have cited these manuscripts, as well as all others in the Public Record Office, by the system now used in that office: a citation, for example, of State Paper Domestic, Charles I, vol. CCCCXLVIII, no. 4, becomes S.P. 16/448/4. S.P. 12 is Elizabeth; S.P. 14 is James I, 15 is James I addenda, and 38 is James I dockets; S.P. 16 is Charles I.

The manuscript collection in the Gloucester Public Library (G.P.L. MSS.) has for its nucleus the papers of the two John Smyths of Nibley, father and son. These papers relate almost entirely to the hundred of Berkeley, but their geographical limitation is outweighed by their variety: there are stewards' accounts, agents' accounts, personal accounts, presentments by manorial juries, records of parochial business, and a mass of private correspondence. The rest of the collection consists of miscellaneous documents, such as rent rolls and private accounts, relating to various parts of the county. The whole of the manuscript and printed material has been excellently arranged and catalogued by the ex-librarian: Roland Austin,

Catalogue of the Gloucestershire Collection; Books, Pamphlets and Documents in the Gloucester Public Library Relating to the County, Cities, Towns, and Villages of Gloucestershire (Gloucester, 1928).

There are in existence two other groups of papers connected with the elder John Smyth. One is a volume of documents relating to the Virginia Company, which is now in the New York Public Library; these are of negligible value for the history of Gloucestershire. The other is the papers of John Smyth, as steward of the Berkeleys, preserved among the muniments in Berkeley Castle. These muniments are perhaps the most important private collection in the county, but one which for years has been firmly closed to scholars.

The records of the corporation of Gloucester (Glouc. Corp. Rec.) are preserved in the Guildhall. They include minute books of the acts of the common council, records of the city quarter sessions after 1631, chamberlains' accounts for the beginning and end of the period, and letter books of the corporation. There are also account books of a few minor officers, and a mass of miscellaneous deeds and papers. The collection was catalogued by the Historical Manuscripts Commission (*Twelfth Report*, IX, 400–529); the catalogue was later amplified by its author and published separately: W. H. Stevenson, *Calendar of the Records of the Corporation of Gloucester . . . Issued under the Authority of the Corporation* (Gloucester, 1893). One letter book, containing important information about military affairs, seems to have escaped notice both times; I therefore cite it as uncatalogued.

The remaining material on town government is somewhat fragmentary. The only other town which has what might be called muniments is Tewkesbury. The corporation records are in the Town Hall, and consist principally of two books. The first (Tewkes. Corp. Rec. 1) is in two divisions, numbered from each end of the volume; one is minutes of the common council and a register of apprentices, and the other is town ordinances, copies of letters, etc. The second (Tewkes. Corp. Rec. 2) is a freemen's roll, unpaginated; the first part contains a series of ordinances, beginning about 1608, and various other acts of the council. A third volume of town records is now in the custody of Moore & Sons, Auctioneers; this is the rent book of the Giles Geast charity (Giles Geast Rent Book), also known as the Feoffees' Book. It contains the rent roll of the lands with which the charity was endowed, the expenses of distributing money to the poor, and miscellaneous entries about local and national events throughout the period.

A volume similar to this rent book is at Chipping Campden. This is the accounts of the treasurer of the trust for the free school and the poor, now in the custody of Mr. C. J. Lucas (New & Saunders, Solicitors). The accounts begin in 1629, and contain a potpourri of information about the school and poor relief. At Chipping Sodbury, documents relating to the town trust are in the custody of Mr. L. M. Harris (Old Bank House, Broad Street); few of them are in the period, and there is little to be gleaned from most of those which are.

One of the most interesting manuscripts in the county is a volume at Northleach, in the custody of the bailiff of the manor. This is the "Court Book of the Town of Northleach in Gloucestershire, 1583–1701." The book contains for the most part the acts of the manorial court, and reveals both the functioning of the court and the nature of village life. The series of ordinances for regulating the two (pp. 211–20) is strikingly similar to that at the beginning of Tewkes. Corp. Rec. 2.

A volume of almost equal interest is the Cirencester Vestry Book, 1586–1886. It describes the working of the vestry, and throws considerable light on the government of the town. The only other vestry book in the county is that of St. Mary's, Cheltenham, 1636–1724; the portion in the period is of negligible value. The same is true of all local register books, with one exception: the Rodmarton Register contains comments of a vicar, in obscure Latin, on his share in parochial assessments between 1631 and 1641.

Ecclesiastical records, as distinct from parochial, are of little use. There are voluminous muniments of the consistory court (Gloucester Diocesan Records), which are now on deposit in the Gloucester Public Library. The only relevant material is in the depositions, of which there are some thirty volumes in the period. I could do no more than sample these, but it is apparent that they contain little which bears on local government; for the social historian they would be a mine of information. The cathedral archives contain two volumes in the period, but both are unrewarding; one is the Act Book of the chapter, beginning in 1616, and the other is the accounts of the cathedral treasurers, beginning in 1623.

Among parochial records are two collections of miscellaneous papers, one for two urban parishes and one for a country parish. The first is at St. Michael's, Gloucester (St. Michael's MSS.); it contains the churchwardens' accounts of St. Michael's, a few of St. Aldgate's, Gloucester, and a number of documents relating to the affairs of the two. The other is at Mickleton, where the amount of material is larger, but its value is less; the churchwardens' accounts, on loose sheets, do not begin until 1639, and most of the other papers are on routine matters.

With these two exceptions, the only surviving parochial records are churchwardens' accounts, which are few and far between. They vary widely in their interest, depending on how informative the entries are. The best among the urban accounts are unquestionably those at Tewkesbury, which were kept in minute detail throughout the period, and even include some excerpts from the acts of the common council. The best of the rural accounts, as such, are those at Minchinhampton. The reader can reconstruct from them much of the business of a country parish, although the first volume (1555–1693) does not, like later ones, mention the overseers and the vestry; see John Bruce, "Extracts from the Accounts of the Churchwardens of Minchinhampton . . . with Observations Thereon," in *Archaeologia*, XXXV (1853), 409–52; Webb, *The Parish and the County*, pp. 54–55. The best material on the parish meeting, except for Cirencester, is in memoranda sandwiched among the accounts of North Nibley; one volume of these accounts (1615–68) is preserved among the Gloucester County Council MSS. The other extant accounts are at Chipping Campden (from 1626), Dursley (from 1566, lacking some years), Eastington (from 1616, lacking 1623–26), Hampnett (a leaf for 1611 in the register), and Tetbury (from 1589). None of these is particularly interesting, but all of them illustrate the routine aspects of parochial government.

The final group of manuscripts is thoroughly miscellaneous in character. There are one or two relevant volumes in each of a number of collections at the British Museum (Add. MSS., Lansd. MSS., etc.); few have any great value, and what they have is for specific points rather than the general subject. The same is true at the Bodleian Library, Oxford (Bodl. MSS.), where the material is even more meager. At the Shire Hall, Gloucester, Mr. Roland Austin has begun a collection of local records for the county council (Gloucester County Council MSS.); aside from the North Nibley accounts, and a copy of the manorial custom of Kemble, this collection does not yet contain anything of significance for the period.

There are few private papers extant in the county. Those at Berkeley Castle have already been mentioned; those of Sir Anselm Guise, at Elmore Court, have nothing in this period, although a great deal in earlier centuries. The only other noteworthy collection is at Sherborne House. These muniments were catalogued, and the result privately printed in 1900 without place or author: *A Calendar of the Charters, Rolls and Other Documents (Dating from A.D. 1182), as Contained in the Muniment Room at Sherborne House, in Gloucestershire, Belonging to the Rt. Hon. the Lord Sherborne, Baron of Sherborne.* As the records are arranged at present, they bear little resemblance to this book; I have therefore cited them by their location rather than their catalogue number. There are numerous manorial rolls in the period, and one exceptionally interesting volume of the court baron of Sherborne. The latter is the only manuscript of its kind which I have found in the county; it is in the muniment room, and seems to have escaped the cataloguer. The other volume of especial interest is in Lord Sherborne's library: the Bibury Manuscripts, containing private correspondence in the period, and official papers of Sir Thomas Sackville, J. P., from 1625 to 1636.

PRINTED SOURCES

General Sources

The most important records of the relationship between central and local authorities are in manuscript, with one obvious exception. This is the *Acts of the Privy Council of England* from 1542 to 1627 (except the missing years, 1604–13), edited by John Roche Dasent, 42 vols. (London, 1890–1938). A certain amount of material on local affairs, as they were aired in one parliament, may be found in the *Commons Debates, 1621*, edited by Wallace Notestein, Frances H. Relf, and Hartley Simpson, 7 vols. (New Haven, 1935); a few disputes about parliamentary elections in the county are described in John Glanville, *Reports of Certain Cases, Determined and Adjudged by the Commons in Parliament, in the Twenty-First and Twenty-Second Years of the Reign of King James the First* (London, 1775). Some local cases before the court of star chamber are contained in Samuel Rawson Gardiner, *Reports of Cases in the Courts of Star Chamber and High Commission*, 1631–32, Camden Society publications, second series, XXXIX (London, 1886), and in John Hawarde, *Les Reportes del Cases in Camera Stellata, 1593–1609*, edited by William P. Baildon (London, 1894); Hawarde is particularly valuable because he gives decisions of the court, which are not extant in manuscript. The only other source of significant value is a digest of royal proclamations: Robert Steele, *Tudor and Stuart Proclamations, 1485–1714*, 2 vols. (Oxford, 1910).

There are several contemporary descriptions of the county, imbedded in the guidebooks of the period. The information to be had from them is gossipy and not always reliable, but it is the only substantial basis for understanding what the county was like. The principal guidebook in prose is William Camden, *Britain, or a Chorographical Description of the Most Flourishing Kingdomes, England, Scotland, and Ireland, and the Ilands Adioyning, Out of the Depth of Antiquitie* (London, 1610); this work was amplified in the eighteenth century by the Rev. Thomas Cox, *Magna Britannia et Hibernia, Antiqua & Nova, or a New Survey of Great Britain, Wherein to the Topographical Account Given by Mr. Camden, and the Late Editions of His Britannia, Is Added a More Large History, Not Only of the Cities, Boroughs, Towns and Parishes Mentioned by Them, but Also of Many Other Places of Note, and Antiquities Since Discovered*, 6 vols. (London, 1720); Gloucestershire is II, 753–844. A useful guidebook in verse is Michael Drayton, *Poly-Olbion: a Chorographicall Description of All the Tracts, Rivers, Mountains, Forests, and Other Parts of This Renowned Isle of Great Britain* (London, 1622). The only other poet of the period whose verse and prose are at times of descriptive value for the county is John Taylor: *The Works of John Taylor, the Water Poet, Not Included in the Folio Volume of 1630*, 5 vols., Spenser Society publications, VII, XIV, XIX, XXI, XXV (Manchester, 1870–78). Some material may also be found in his garrulous contemporary, Thomas Fuller, *The History of the Worthies of England*, edited by P. A. Nuttall, 3 vols. (London, 1840). A spirited account of a journey into western England, by an anonymous traveler from Norfolk, is contained in vol. XVI of *The Camden Miscellany: Relation of a Short Survey of the Western Counties*, edited by L. G. Wickham Legg, Camden Society publications, third series, LII (London, 1936).

The other general sources are the legal manuals of the time.

The most important of these is William Lambard, *Eirenarcha, or of the Office of Iustices of Peace, in Foure Bookes* (London, 1614); of somewhat less value is the same author's *The Duties of Constables, Borsholders, Tythingmen, and Such Other Lowe and Lay Ministers of the Peace. Whereunto Be Adioyned, the Severall Offices of . . . Churchwardens* [etc.] (London, 1614), which is commonly bound with the *Eirenarcha.* The other major handbook for justices is Michael Dalton, *The Countrey Justice, Containing the Practice of the Justices of the Peace Out of Their Sessions* (London, 1655). This book is useful principally to supplement Lambard; the two together give an excellent theoretical picture of the work of the justices. The classic treatise on the law of the forest, and the forest courts and officers as they should have been, is John Manwood, *A Treatise of the Lawes of the Forest: Wherein Is Declared Not Onely Those Lawes, as They Are Now in Force, but Also the Originall and Beginning of Forests. . . . Also a Treatise of the Pourallee . . . Whereunto Are Added the Statutes of the Forest, a Treatise of the Several Offices of Verderers, Regardors, and Foresters, & the Courts of Attachments, Swanimote, & Iustice Seat of the Forest,* third edition (London, 1615). Three contemporary treatises on manorial courts and custom have been printed by the Manorial Society; they are complementary in treatment, and provide in conjunction a theoretical background for the study of the manor: Anonymous, *A Fac-Simile Reproduction of the Order of Keeping a Court Leet & Court Baron,* reprinted from the 1650 edition (London, 1914); Sir Charles Calthrope, *The Relation betweene the Lord of a Mannor and the Coppy-Holder His Tenant,* reprinted from the 1635 edition (London, 1917); "*A Mannor and Court Baron*" (*Harleian MS. 6714*), edited by Nathaniel J. Hone (London, 1909).

Local Sources

The most obvious source of printed local records is the *Reports* of the Historical Manuscripts Commission (*H.M.C.*). With the exception of the Gloucester city archives, however, the local material in these reports is meager to a degree, and such as there is yields only minor details. Other printed records are important only for specific subjects. The most imposing is John Smyth, *Men and Armour for Gloucestershire in 1608. The Names and Surnames of All the Able and Sufficient Men in Body Fit for His Majesty's Service in the Wars, within the County of Gloucester,*

Viewed by the Right Hon. Henry Lord Berkeley, Lord Lieutenant of the Said County, . . . in the Month of August, 1608 (London, 1902). This volume gives reliable data on the size of the trained bands and the amount of armor in the county; its value for local government is otherwise negligible. A small but interesting collection of the state papers, domestic series, has been published by the Rev. R. H. Clutterbuck, "State Papers Relating to the Cloth Trade, 1622," in *Transactions* of the Bristol and Gloucestershire Archaeological Society, V (1880–81), 154–62; the collection is confined to Gloucestershire, but does not include all the relevant state papers even for 1622. Two pamphlets contain extracts from the Gloucester archives. One of them gives a mass of detailed information, no longer available in manuscript, about the government of the city hospitals: Anonymous, *Civitas, Glouc. Ordinances . . . Ordained by the Mayor, Aldermen and Common Council, . . . Anno Domini 1635, for the Good Government of the Several Hospitals of St. Bartholomew, King James's Hospital, and the Hospital of St. Margaret;* the pamphlet was presumably printed at Gloucester and before 1830, when the rules were revised. The other was edited by G. Sheffield Blakeway, also without date or place of printing: *City of Gloucester. Printed Extracts from Charters, Grants, &c., Relating to the Hams and Common Meadows, 681–1885;* these are selections from the extant archives. Another anonymous pamphlet, giving interesting details of Sandys's project for navigation, is *River Avon. Orders in Council, His Majesty's Commission and Certificate of the Commissioners, in the Year 1636, Relative to the Navigation of the River Avon* (Tewkesbury, 1826). The only other record worth mention is the anonymous publication of a chancery decree (C. 89/12/1) defining the manorial custom of Painswick, one of the most interesting in the county: *An Exemplification of the Inrollment of a Decree, Made in the High Court of Chancery betweene Henry Jernygan, Esquire, Lord of the Mannor of Painswicke, in the Countie of Glouc, and the Customary Tenn[an]ts of the Said Mannor.* With the decree, which is dated 1 February, 12 James I, is printed an act of parliament confirming it (21 James I, c. 50); the pamphlet bears no place or date, but was probably printed at Stroud shortly after 1800.

These miscellaneous printed records are supplemented by the equally miscellaneous compositions of local authors. Among these men John Smyth is outstanding; his great work is *The Berkeley Manuscripts. The Lives of the Berkeleys, Lords of the*

Honour, Castle, and Manor of Berkeley . . . from 1066 to 1618. With a Description of the Hundred of Berkeley and Its Inhabitants, edited by Sir John Maclean, 3 vols. (Gloucester, 1883–85). These volumes are as valuable among printed sources as are the author's papers among manuscript sources. The first two volumes, which I cite as *Lives of the Berkeleys,* are for the most part concerned with an earlier period, and are of only incidental use; but the third, which I cite as *Description,* is packed with detailed information about land tenure in the hundred, and with local lore and proverbs; the whole work is flavored with the salt of Smyth's personality.

The remaining material in this category is largely pamphlets. One of the most delightful, but least valuable, is *Speeches Delivered to Queen Elizabeth on Her Visit to Giles Brydges, Lord Chandos, at Sudeley Castle,* edited by Sir Egerton Brydges (Lee Priory, 1815); although the style sometimes approximates the unreality of a masque, the best parts of the speeches are instinct with the character of the Cotswolds. Further material on country life, but not on local government, may be found in *Annalia Dubrensia, or Celebration of Captain Dover's Cotswold Games,* edited by the Rev. Alexander B. Grosart (Manchester, 1877), and in the Guise memoirs, edited by G. Davies: *Autobiography of Thomas Raymon and Memoirs of the Family of Guise of Elmore, Gloucestershire,* Camden Society publications, third series, XXVIII (London, 1917). Two contemporary sermons throw a more sober light on the social conditions of the time, and on the problems of poor relief. These are Philip Jones, *Certaine Sermons Preached at Ciceter . . . Wherein the Two Several States, of the Riche and Poore Man Are Compared and Examined* (London, 1588), and William Woodwall, *A Sermon . . . Wherein Are Chiefly Shewed Both the Originall & Accidentall Causes of Euerie Dearth and Famine, and Especially of This Dearth in England Now, 1608 and 1609, with the Effects and Fruites of the Same, as Also the Helpes & Remedies Thereof, if They May Be Speedily and Effectually Practised* (London, 1609); the latter sermon was preached at Stroud, and has considerable local color. Two other books contain some slight information about the government of the city of Gloucester, in its military and civil aspects respectively. The first is John Corbet, *An Historicall Relation of the Military Government of Gloucester: from the Beginning of the Civill Warre . . . to the Removall of Colonell Massie from That Government* (London, probably 1645); the only valuable part is the beginning, where the author describes the condition of the trained bands at the opening of the wars. The second is John Dorney, *Certain Speeches Made upon the Day of the Yearly Election of Officers in the City of Gloucester* (London, 1653); the speeches were made between 1643 and 1652, but some of them clarify the general nature of the offices. The remaining pamphlets are of negligible importance. One is an anonymous polemic against the Council of Wales, written just before its abolition by the Long Parliament: *Arguments Proving, the Iurisdiction Used by the President and Counsell in the Marches of Wales, over the Counties of Gloucester, Worcester, Hereford, and Salop to Be Illegal* (London, 1641). The other is a petition to parliament by Benjamin Crokey, dated 1625, which throws some light on conditions at Wotton: *To His Sacred Maiestie, the Lords Spiritual, and Temporal, and the House of Commons in This Present Parliament Assembled* (no placc or date of printing); only two copies are extant, of which one is catalogued and cited as G.P.L. MS. RX 354.20.

Comparative Sources

In order to set the government of Gloucestershire against the background of local government in England as a whole, I have used the printed records of other parts of the country for purposes of comparison. The following list of such records does not purport to be complete. It includes only those which yield enough information about the work of local authorities to justify close study.

The most interesting category of comparative sources is the records of quarter sessions. In this group five works are outstanding, because of the light which they throw on the varied activities of the court, both administrative and judicial. These are the Rev. J. C. Atkinson, editor, North Riding *Quarter Sessions Records*, North Riding Record Society publications, 4 vols. (London, 1884–86); the Rev. E. H. Bates Harbin, editor, *Quarter Sessions Records for the County of Somerset*, 1607–60, Somerset Record Society publications, 3 vols. (London, 1907–12); J. W. Willis Bund, editor, *Worcester County Records. Division I. Documents Relating to Quarter Sessions. Calendar of the Quarter Sessions Papers*, 1591–1643, Worcestershire Historical Society publications (Worcester, 1900); vols. II, III, and IV of *The Staffordshire Quarter Sessions Rolls*, edited by S. A. H. Burne, William Salt Archaeological Society publications, 4 vols. (Kendal, 1931–36); W. J. and W. Le Hardy, editors, *Hertford County Records*, 7 vols. (Hertford, 1905–31), of which the relevant volumes are I: *Notes and Extracts from the Sessions Rolls, 1581 to 1698* (1905), and V: *Calendar to the Sessions Books and the Sessions Minute Books* (1928). Similar records, which are less valuable because more stereotyped, are two volumes in the series of the Record Society for the Publication of Original Documents Relating to Lancashire and Cheshire: Ernest Axon, editor, *Manchester Sessions*, XLII (London, 1901), and J. H. E. Bennett and J. C. Dewhurst, editors, *Quarter Sessions Records with Other Records of the Justices of the Peace for the County Palatine of Chester, 1559–1760, Together with a Few Earlier Miscellaneous Records Deposited with the Cheshire County Council*, XCIV (Chester, 1940). In the same group belong H. Hampton Copnall, editor, *Nottinghamshire County Records. Notes and Extracts from the Nottinghamshire County Records of the 17th Century* (Nottingham, 1915); the Rev. John Charles Cox, editor, *Three Centuries of Derbyshire Annals, as Illustrated by the Records of the Quarter Sessions of the County of Derby, from Queen Elizabeth to Queen Victoria*, 2 vols. (London, 1890); A. H. A. Hamilton, *Quarter Sessions from Queen Elizabeth to Queen Anne; Illustrations of Local Government and History Drawn from Original Records (Chiefly of the County of Devon)*, (London, 1878); John Lister, editor, *West Riding Sessions Rolls, 1597/8–1602*, the Yorkshire Archaeological and Topographical Association, record series, III (Worksop, 1888); vols. I and II (1625–50) of Sidney C. Ratcliff and H. C. Johnson, editors, Warwickshire *Quarter Sessions Order Book, Easter, 1625, to Epiphany, 1665*, 4 vols. (Warwick, 1935–38); James Tait, editor, *Lancashire Quarter Sessions Records. . . . Vol. I. Quarter Sessions Rolls, 1590–1606*, Chetham Society publications, LXXVII (Manchester, 1917). Among the most important records in the period are those of Middlesex: John C. Jeaffreson, editor, *Middlesex County Records*, 4 vols. (London, 1886–92); this work must be used with caution, for purposes of comparison, because of the peculiar nature of the Middlesex court. Some further material may be found in Mary S. Gretton, *Oxfordshire Justices of the Peace in the Seventeenth Century*, Oxfordshire Record Society publications, XVI (Oxford, 1934), and in the *Quarter Sessions Records of the County of Northampton* for 1630 and 1657–58, edited by Miss Joan Wake, Northamptonshire Record Society publications, I (for 1921–22, Hereford, 1924). The introductions to both these volumes are especially valuable; Miss Wake's introduction, written by Mr. J. E. Morris, contains an account of the duties imposed by statute on the justices of the peace, the best work which I know on the subject since Lambard.

The records of town corporations have been printed in considerable number. Two works are distinctly superior to the rest, because of the remarkable insight which they give into the problems of urban communities during the period, and the way in which these problems were met. The first is edited by Miss Mary Bateson and Miss Helen Stocks: *Records of the Borough of Leicester, Being a Series of Extracts from the Archives of the Corporation of Leicester*, 4 vols. (London and Cambridge, 1899–1923); the relevant volumes are III (1905) and IV (1923), edited by Miss Bateson and Miss Stocks respectively. The second work is edited by the Rev. J. M. Guilding: *Reading Records. Diary of the Corporation*, 1431–1640, 4 vols. (London, 1892–96), vols. II and III. Similar but less rewarding material may be found in the Rev. William Hudson and John C. Tingey, editors, *The Records of the City of Norwich*, 2 vols. (London and Norwich, 1906–10); in two volumes of the Oxford Historical Society publications, edited respectively by the Rev. H. E. Salter and by him and M. G. Hobson: *Oxford Council Acts, 1583–1626*, LXXXVII (Oxford, 1928), and *Oxford Council Acts, 1626–1665*, XCV (Oxford, 1933); and in W. Henry Stevenson and others, editors, *Records of the Borough of Nottingham, Being a Series of Extracts from the Archives of the Corporation*, 6 vols. (London and Nottingham, 1882–1914), of which I have cited only vols. IV (1889) and V (1900), edited by W. H. Stevenson and W. T. Baker respectively. A valuable work based upon city archives, although not a compilation of them, is John Latimer, *The Annals of Bristol in the Seventeenth Century* (Bristol, 1900).

Records of the smaller towns in this period are often the records of the manorial court by which the town was governed. One of the most interesting volumes of this sort is edited by J. G. de T. Mandley, in the *Remains Historical and Literary Connected with the Palatine Counties of Lancaster and Chester: The Portmote or Court Leet Records of the Borough or Town and Royal Manor of Salford from the Year 1597 to the Year 1669 Inclusive*, 2 vols., Chetham Society publications, new series, XLVI, XLVII (Manchester, 1902). A similar work, although unfortunately for only a small fraction of the period, is vol. II (1571–1603) of the *Liverpool Town Books. Proceedings of As-*

semblies, Common Councils, Portmoot Courts, &c., 1550–1862, edited by J. A. Twemlow, 2 vols. (Liverpool, 1918, 1936). Equally interesting are the relevant Manchester records, edited by J. P. Earwaker: vols. I and II of *The Constables' Accounts of the Manor of Manchester from the Year 1612 to the Year 1647, and from the Year 1743 to the Year 1776*, 3 vols. (Manchester, 1891–92), and vols. II and III of *The Court Leet Records of the Manor of Manchester from the Year 1552 to the Year 1686, and from the Year 1731 to the Year 1846*, 4 vols. (Manchester, 1884–89). The material on Southampton is even more abundant, thanks to four publications of the Southampton Record Society: J. W. Horrocks, editor, *The Assembly Books of Southampton*, 1602–16, 4 vols. (Southampton, 1917–25); D. M. and F. J. C. Hearnshaw, editors, *Court Leet Records* [of Southampton], . . . *A.D. 1550–1624*, 3 parts in 2 vols. (Southampton, 1905–08); F. J. C. Hearnshaw, *Leet Jurisdiction in England, Especially as Illustrated by the Records of the Court Leet of Southampton* (Southampton, 1908). The last of these works is exceptionally good; it is written with charm and distinction, and is of the greatest value for understanding the governmental function of the leet.

The other comparative sources which I have used are miscellaneous. One of the most valuable is edited by H. W. Saunders, *The Official Papers of Sir Nathaniel Bacon of Stiffkey, Norfolk, as Justice of the Peace, 1580–1620*, Camden Society publications, third series, XXVI (London, 1915); this has been continued under the editorship of F. R. Brooks in vol. XVI of *The Camden Miscellany: Supplementary Stiffkey Papers (1578–1620)*, Camden Society publications, third series, LII (London, 1936). These papers show the varied work of a country justice, and are particularly useful for his work out of quarter sessions; the only comparable material with which I am familiar is the "Note Book of a Surrey Justice," edited by Granville Levenson-Gower in the *Surrey Archaeological Collections*, IX (London, 1888), 161–232. A different sort of notebook, which has occasional sidelights on local government, is Henry Best, *Rural Economy in Yorkshire in 1641, Being the Farming and Account Books of Henry Best*, Surtees Society publications, XXXIII (Durham, 1857).

A number of works on the military organization in other counties are composed in whole or in part of original records. The most valuable of these are two publications of the Northamptonshire Record Society, edited by Miss Joan Wake: vol. III (for

1925), *A Copy of Papers Relating to Musters, Beacons, Subsidies, etc., in the County of Northampton, A.D. 1586–1623* (Kettering, 1926), and vol. VII (for 1933), *The Montagu Musters Book, A.D. 1602–1623* (Peterborough, 1935). Two other works are somewhat less useful, because less rich in the details of military administration; these are vol. III of the Surrey Record Society publications: *Surrey Musters (Taken from the Losely MSS.)*, (London, 1919), and John Harland, *The Lancashire Lieutenancy under the Tudors and Stuarts*, 2 vols., Chetham Society publications, XLIX, L (Manchester, 1859). Some documentary information about conditions in Essex may be had from two articles by the Rev. Andrew Clark in *The Essex Review:* "The Essex Territorial Force in 1608," XVII (1908), 98–115, and "The Essex Territorial Force, 1625–38," XVIII (1909), 65–74.

SECONDARY WORKS

General Works

By far the best survey of English local government in this period is in vol. II of Edward P. Cheyney, *A History of England, from the Defeat of the Armada to the Death of Elizabeth; with an Account of English Institutions during the Later Sixteenth and Early Seventeenth Centuries*, 2 vols. (New York, 1926). Professor Cheyney's account is in general terms, based on the statutes and manuals of the period, and he is therefore concerned with the nature of institutions rather than their actual operation. He also deals with a large subject in a small compass, which forces him to oversimplify, and to give the impression of a more systematic and orderly machine than ever existed in fact. But it is impossible to take issue with any of his major conclusions (except that manorial government was unimportant), and his account remains the standard treatment of the subject.

The other outstanding work in the field is that of Sidney and Beatrice Webb (Lord and Lady Passfield) on *English Local Government from the Revolution to the Municipal Corporations Act*, 1689–1835, of which I have used the following volumes: *The Parish and the County* (London, New York, etc., 1906); *The Manor and the Borough*, 2 vols. (London, New York, etc., 1908); *The Story of the King's Highway* (London, New York, etc., 1913); *English Poor Law History: Part I. The Old Poor Law* (London, New York, etc., 1927). The bulk of this monumental survey is of course in a later period, but the authors lay a solid groundwork in the early seventeenth century. They confine themselves to the rôle of local institutions in organizing public services, as distinct from their rôle in administering national justice. (See *The Parish and the County*, pp. 280–82.) This distinction may well be perceptible after 1689, but before 1640 it has little or no reality.

For the political events of the period, the classic history is still the best: Samuel Rawson Gardiner, *History of England from the Accession of James I to the Outbreak of the Civil War, 1603–1642*, 10 vols. (London, 1883–84). Two classics of legal history are equally indispensable for reference, particularly on the legal background of manorial government: Sir Frederick Pollock and Frederic W. Maitland, *The History of English Law before the Time of Edward I*, 2 vols., second edition reprinted (Cambridge and Boston, 1911), and Sir William S. Holdsworth, *A History of English Law*, 10 vols., various editions (London, 1923–35). The best survey of the immediate economic and social background of the manor is R. H. Tawney, *The Agrarian Problem in the Sixteenth Century* (London, New York, etc., 1912).

On all questions relating to the revenues of the crown in this period, the authoritative work is Frederick C. Dietz, *English Public Finance, 1558–1641* (London and New York, 1932). On the most momentous financial experiment, ship money, there is surprisingly little else in print. The precedents for it are traced in Ada H. Lewis, *A Study of Elizabethan Ship Money, 1588–1603* (Philadelphia, 1928), and the yield from King Charles's tax is discussed by M. D. Gordon, "The Collection of Ship-Money in the Reign of Charles I," in *Transactions* of the Royal Historical Society, third series, IV (London, 1910), 141–62. The financial aspect of the military establishment is discussed in Gladys Scott Thomson, *Lords Lieutenants in the Sixteenth Century. A Study in Tudor Local Administration* (London, New York, etc., 1923); this is an excellent book, which embraces, as the subtitle implies, far more than the merely military functions of the lord lieutenant. A comparable work in a field which is equally broad, but which has a more specific relation to Gloucestershire, is Caroline A. J. Skeel, *The Council in the Marches of Wales: a Study in Local Government during the Sixteenth and Seventeenth Centuries*, Girton College Studies (London, 1904).

The other general works are of value for specific subjects. The medieval background of forest law, for example, is discussed at length in G. F. Turner's introduction to his *Select Pleas of the Forest,* Selden Society publications, XIII (for 1899, London, 1901); there is an excellent description of the miners and mine-law of the Forest of Dean during this period in vol. I of John U. Nef, *The Rise of the British Coal Industry,* 2 vols. (London, 1932). The structure of the seventeenth-century wool trade is described in Herbert Heaton, *The Yorkshire Woollen and Worsted Industries,* Oxford Historical and Literary Studies, X (Oxford, 1920); more specific material on the trade in Gloucestershire during part of the period is contained in Astrid Friis, *Alderman Cockayne's Project and the Cloth Trade. The Commercial Policy of England in Its Main Aspects, 1603–1625* (Copenhagen and London, 1927). Two books which are helpful for understanding the background of parochial government are Eleanor Trotter, *Seventeenth Century Life in the Country Parish with Special Reference to Local Government* (Cambridge, 1919), and Sedley L. Ware, *The Elizabethan Parish in Its Ecclesiastical and Financial Aspects,* Johns Hopkins University Studies in Historical and Political Science, series XXVI, nos. 7–8 (Baltimore, 1908). The legal background and status of the petty constable are discussed in an article by H. B. Simpson, "The Office of Constable," in *The English Historical Review,* X (1895), 624–41.

Local Works

Gloucestershire, like the rest of England, witnessed an outburst of local histories in the late eighteenth and early nineteenth centuries. The principal histories of the county, in the order of their appearance, are Sir Robert Atkyns, *The Ancient and Present State of Glocestershire . . . Printed in the Year MDCCXII,* second edition (London, 1768); Samuel Rudder, *A New History of Gloucestershire, Comprising the Topography, Antiquities, Curiosities, Produce, Trade, and Manufactures of That County. . . . In the Course of This Work Is Given the History of Every Parish, Tithing, and Extraparochial Place in the County, Also the Ecclesiastical, Civil, and Military History of the City of Gloucester, from Its First Foundation to the Present Time* (Cirencester, 1779); Ralph Bigland, *Historical, Monumental and Genealogical Collections, Relative to the County of Gloucester; Printed from the Original Papers of the Late Ralph Bigland,* 2 vols. (London, 1791); Thomas D. Fosbrooke, *Abstracts of Records and Manuscripts Respecting the County of Gloucester; Formed into a*

History, Correcting the Very Erroneous Accounts, and Supplying Numerous Deficiencies in Sir Robt. Atkins, and Subsequent Writers, 2 vols. (Gloucester, 1807). None of these tomes is of more than incidental use for my purpose. Atkyns and Rudder are almost wholly worthless; Bigland is valuable only for a footnote in the first volume, describing the manorial custom of Dymock, and Fosbrooke has not even a profitable footnote. The four authors either record the events of the period, which were trifling, or model themselves on the fifth chapter of Genesis. "Common occurrences," as Rudder remarks on p. 402, "are improper for history, because uninteresting; and the marvelous and wonderful are to be admitted with caution."

The early town histories are of the same calibre. There is little or nothing to be derived from the other work of Thomas D. Fosbrooke, *An Original History of the City of Gloucester, Almost Wholly Compiled from New Materials; Supplying the Numerous Deficiencies, and Correcting the Errors, of Preceding Accounts; Including Also the Original Papers of the Late Ralph Bigland, Esq.* (London, 1819); from James Bennett, *The History of Tewkesbury* (Tewkesbury, 1830); or from Samuel Y. Griffith, *Griffith's History of Cheltenham and Its Vicinity*, third edition (Oxford, 1838). Another book on Cheltenham has a good discussion of the custom of the manor during the period; this is John Goding, *Norman's History of Cheltenham* (London and Cheltenham, 1863). A third, in spite of its title, is useful solely for its material on the Forest of Dean: Thomas F. Dibdin, *The History of Cheltenham and Its Environs: . . . and a Concise View of the County of Gloucester* (Cheltenham, 1803). Two other works on the Forest of Dean, by H. G. Nicholls, contain interesting but undocumented information about the miners and their customs: *The Forest of Dean; an Historical and Descriptive Account* (London, 1858), and *Iron Making in the Olden Times: as Instanced in the Ancient Mines, Forges, and Furnaces of the Forest of Dean* (London and Coleford, 1866).

Among modern histories, the most obvious is the Victoria (*V.C.H.*); this was edited by William Page, and only vol. II has been published: *The Victoria History of the County of Gloucester* (London, 1907). This work is more serviceable than that of Atkyns or Rudder, but it is unimportant for much the same reason: the period was one of common occurrences, upon which no county historian can be expected to dwell. The other general work is William Retlaw Williams, *The Parliamentary History of the County of Gloucester . . . from the Earliest Times to the Present Day, 1213–1898, with Biographies and Genealogical Notices of the Members* (Hereford, 1898); this is principally useful as a reference book, and for generalizations about the town and county members during the period.

There are two compendia of the work of Gloucestershire antiquaries, in both of which it is possible to find relevant material. One is the *Transactions* of the Bristol and Gloucestershire Archaeological Society (*Trans.*), 60 vols. (Gloucester, 1876–1939); these volumes contain papers on the widest possible range of local subjects. The other is *Gloucestershire Notes and Queries* (*N. & Q.*), edited by the Rev. Beaver H. Blacker, 10 vols. (London, 1881–1914); these notes are much more brief than the papers in the *Transactions*, are equally miscellaneous, and aside from a few printed documents are of negligible importance. Books by local antiquaries are also unrewarding, with the exception of two histories by Welbore St. C. Baddeley: *A History of Cirencester* (Cirencester, 1924), and *A Cotteswold Manor, Being the History of Painswick*, second edition (London, etc., 1929). Both volumes, and particularly the latter, contain interesting information, although its usefulness is decreased by the fact that Mr. Baddeley rarely gives his sources.

This discussion of printed material leads to two conclusions. One is that there are no printed sources for Gloucestershire of more than incidental value, apart from *The Acts of the Privy Council* and *The Berkeley Manuscripts*. The other is that while the secondary works are important for the general background or for some aspect of county administration, none of them covers any such aspect in detail. The printed material on the county, in other words, is for the most part far less illuminating than the manuscripts, and it is on them that the major part of this study is based.

INDEX

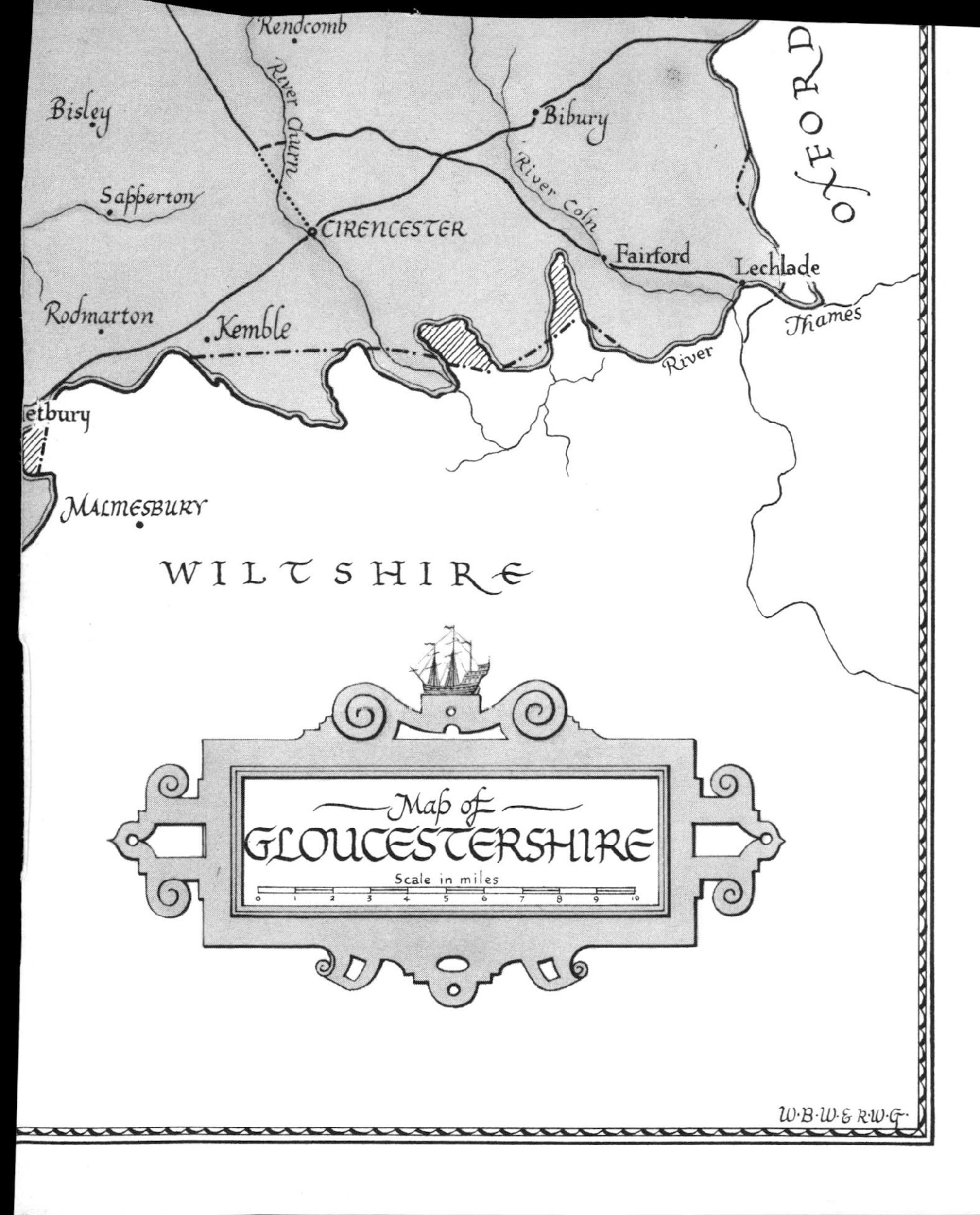
Rendcomb
River Churn
Bisley
Bibury
Sapperton
River Coln
CIRENCESTER
Fairford
Lechlade
OXFORD
Rodmarton
Kemble
Thames
River
etbury
MALMESBURY
WILTSHIRE
Map of
GLOUCESTERSHIRE
Scale in miles
0 1 2 3 4 5 6 7 8 9 10
W·B·W·& R·W·G·

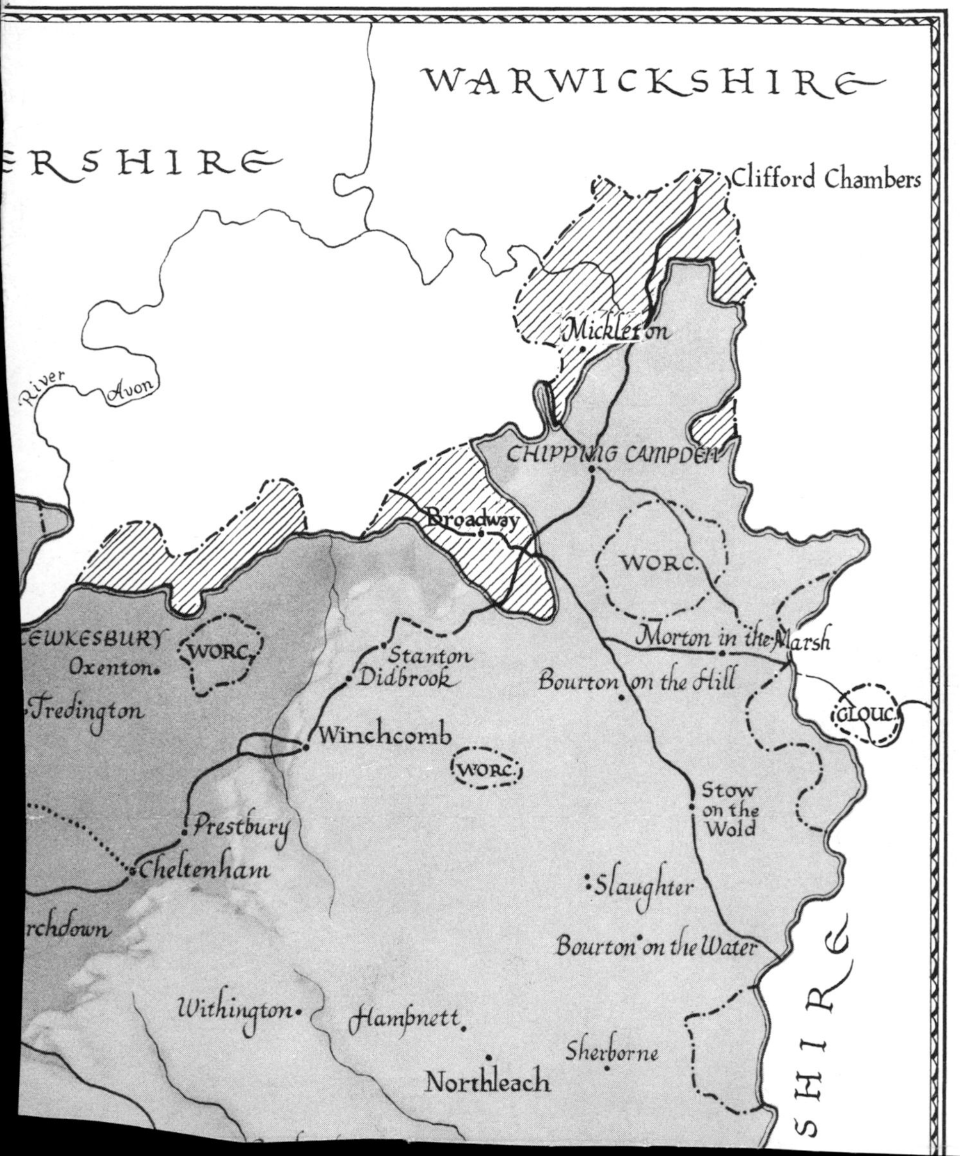

WARWICKSHIRE

ERSHIRE

Clifford Chambers

Mickleton

River Avon

CHIPPING CAMPDEN

Broadway

WORC.

TEWKESBURY

WORC.

Oxenton

Stanton

Didbrook

Morton in the Marsh

Bourton on the Hill

Tredington

GLOUC.

Winchcomb

WORC.

Stow on the Wold

Prestbury

Cheltenham

Slaughter

rchdown

Bourton on the Water

SHIRE

Withington

Hampnett

Sherborne

Northleach

LEGEND

- ——— Principal old roads – certain
- - - - Principal old roads – conjectural
- .... Minor roads
- ═══ Present county boundries
- —.—.— Old county boundries

WORCESTE

HEREFORDSHIRE

River Severn

Dymcock

River Leadon

Hasfield

Norton

Newent

Taynton

Huntley

Mitcheldean

GLOUCESTER

Barnwood

Ruardean

Minsterworth

Robinswood Hill

English Bickner

Upton St. Leonards

Cinderford

MONMOUTH

Longney

Newnham

Speech House

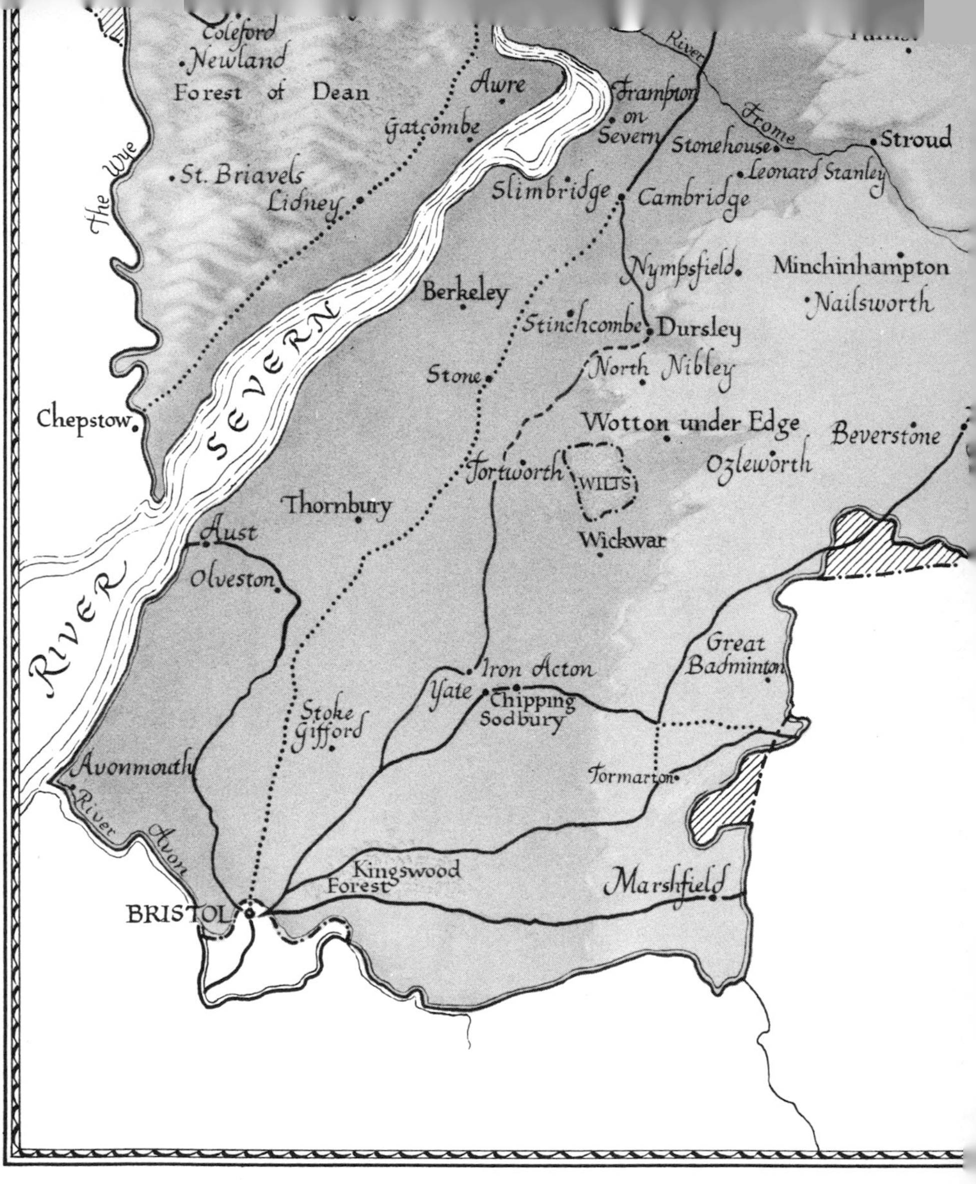

Coleford
Newland
Forest of Dean
Awre
Gatcombe
Frampton on Severn
River Frome
Stonehouse
Stroud
The Wye
St. Briavels
Lidney
Slimbridge
Cambridge
Leonard Stanley
Nympsfield
Minchinhampton
Nailsworth
Berkeley
Stinchcombe
Dursley
North Nibley
Stone
Chepstow
RIVER SEVERN
Wotton under Edge
Beverstone
Ozleworth
Tortworth
WILTS
Thornbury
Aust
Wickwar
Olveston
Great Badminton
Iron Acton
Yate
Chipping Sodbury
Stoke Gifford
Avonmouth
River Avon
Tormarton
Kingswood Forest
Marshfield
BRISTOL